# Migration, Memory, and Diversity

**Studies in Contemporary European History**

Editors:

**Konrad Jarausch**, Lurcy Professor of European Civilization, University of North Carolina, Chapel Hill, and a Director of the Zentrum für Zeithistorische Studien, Potsdam, Germany

**Henry Rousso,** Senior Research Fellow at the Institut d'histoire du temps présent (Centre national de la recherche scientifique, Paris)

*For a full volume listing, please see back matter*

# MIGRATION, MEMORY, AND DIVERSITY

## Germany from 1945 to the Present

Edited by

## Cornelia Wilhelm

berghahn
NEW YORK · OXFORD
www.berghahnbooks.com

Published in 2017 by
Berghahn Books
www.berghahnbooks.com

© 2017, 2018 Cornelia Wilhelm

**Library of Congress Cataloging-in-Publication Data**
A C.I.P. cataloging record is available from the Library of Congress

**British Library Cataloguing in Publication Data**
A catalogue record for this book is available from the British Library

ISBN 978-1-78533-327-9 (hardback)
ISBN 978-1-78533-838-0 (paperback)
ISBN 978-1-78533-328-6 (ebook)

# CONTENTS

# ACKNOWLEDGEMENTS

This volume was first conceived in 2013, during my tenure as DAAD Visiting Professor in the Department of History and the Jewish Studies Program at Emory University, when I and a number of other scholars met to share research related to "Migration, Memory, and Diversity in Germany." I want to thank both the German Academic Exchange Service (DAAD) as well as Emory University for their generous financial support of this project. Much of its success was based on the strong interdisciplinary tradition, commitment, and framework at Emory University, which was evident from the cooperation with its faculty, departments, programs, and institutes to organize, host, and engage in this event. Therefore, I would like to extend my special thanks to the Department of History, the German Studies Department, and especially to the Halle Institute for Global Learning and the Tam Institute for Jewish Studies of Emory University for their lasting support of the conference and publication project.

It is particularly the Tam Institute for Jewish Studies to which I owe thanks for its dedication to this publication. The completion of this volume was unexpectedly in jeopardy in April 2015, when Marcia Rothschild, the copyeditor who had helped—not only, but especially—our German authors to find an English voice, tragically died in a car accident and left a void that could not be filled. Nevertheless, with the assistance of the Tam Institute, I was able to continue the project with Ruth Einstein, who heroically embarked on completing it. I want to thank her for her unreserved collaboration, professionalism, and dedication to completing this work without major delay. Based on the tragic circumstances, I would like to dedicate this volume to the memory of Marcia Rothschild as a friend and colleague.

Special thanks go to Konrad Jarausch, who participated in the conference, provided valuable guidance in the design of the publication concept, shared his expertise as editor with me in the manuscript preparation, and invited me to submit this manuscript for publication in his Contemporary European History series with Berghahn Books. I am especially grateful that he has contributed his thoughts on the relevance of a discourse on immigration for Germany and Europe in a special preface at the beginning of this volume. Last, but not least I want to express my deep appreciation to Marion Berghahn and her husband Volker Berghahn. Marion has not only rendered special care to this volume as publisher, but has provided active guidance and practical assistance during the completion of this manuscript and actively encouraged the inclusion of Holger Kolb's summary and outlook on the recent structural changes in Germany's migration and integration policies, highlighting Germany's gradual transformation to a modern country of immigration, which is increasingly acting in an *European*, rather than an exclusively *national* framework. We owe it to the collegial generosity of Volker Berghahn, who was willing to share his scholarly and linguistic expertise and time and volunteered to translate this part of the volume in the last minute of the production process, that we can conclude with this very current outlook as "afterword."

# PREFACE

*Konrad H. Jarausch*

Historians have played only a minor role in the immigration debate, since they have largely failed to inform the public about the important impact of migration on the German past. Under Klaus Bade's leadership, the IMIS Institute in Osnabrück has attempted to draw attention to the issue, but in the German master narrative of contested rise, dictatorial hubris, and democratic redemption the topic is almost entirely absent, as if the country had fixed borders and a stable population—although exactly the opposite was the case during the last two centuries. This lack of attention is unfortunate, because a rich and varied *Migrationsforschung* (research on migration) has developed which is contradicting traditional clichés by throwing light on the complexity of migration processes and exploring the difficulties of acculturation. In order to explain Berlin's surprising welcoming reaction to the current wave of Near Eastern refugees, which contradicts the stereotype of xenophobic Germany this volume places it in the context of earlier discussions by introducing some of the recent results of migration research.

This new scholarship has succeeded in dismantling the popular cliché that Germany was merely a source of emigration by pointing to the streams of immigrants who have come into the country during the past centuries. No doubt, the deep memory of earlier emigration to eastern Europe or North and South America is accurate, since religious sectarians, landless farmers, unemployed industrial workers, and so on, left to pursue opportunities elsewhere. Many folksongs, such as "Ade, Du mein lieb Heimatland,"[1] as well as countless emigrant letters preserve this heritage. But at the same time, Germany has long attracted groups such as French Huguenots, Polish miners, eastern European Jews, Balkan

Notes for this chapter begin on page xiii.

migrants, and Russian refugees. Since the end of World War II, the balance has swung decisively in the direction of immigration, because the outflow eventually dried up while millions of migrants thronged into the FRG, and to a lesser degree the GDR.

Migration research has also begun to break down the political distinction between privileged ethnic newcomers and problematic foreigners by pointing out that both groups were the product of large-scale population movements. As part of the responsibility for Nazi atrocities, the country accepted close to twelve million Germans who had been expelled from Eastern Europe, and integrated the approximately three million refugees from the GDR as citizens while continuing to welcome later ethnic remigrants from Poland, Romania, and Russia. In contrast, the so-called "guest workers" from Mediterranean countries, the Balkans, and Turkey were considered temporary laborers; but to everyone's surprise many of them decided to stay and to bring their families. While the limited numbers of political asylum seekers during the Cold War were usually accepted, the much larger influx of economic migrants was merely tolerated in exceptional cases and usually not allowed to work until their appeals were decided. In spite of differences in legal status, all these groups were migrants who encountered similar problems of displacement and adjustment.

New scholarship also increasingly reflects the voices of the immigrants themselves, no longer treating them as bureaucratic objects, but exploring their own agency. This inside perspective sheds new light on the complicated process of acculturation through the formation of ethnic ghettos, which serve both to provide transitional protection and to conserve cultural difference. Similarly, recent studies have started to analyze the issues of language acquisition and the school performance of immigrant children, which are crucial for personal identity formation and potential job success. This migrant viewpoint also reveals the complex mixture of German prejudice and immigrant defensiveness that tends to inhibit integration even in the second or third generation. But at the same time it also shows encouraging signs of an emergent cultural hybridity, such as in the exciting films of Fatih Akin, the poetic prose of Zafer Şenocak, and the green activism of Cem Özdemir.

Finally, recent work also embeds migration discussions more in transnational processes, which helps reduce the perception of German peculiarity. The increasing influx of young professionals from depressed Mediterranean countries is hardly noticed, because it is taking place within the European Union, and fears of being overwhelmed by Polish laborers have proven illusory due to the improving chance for a better life in that country. More problematic has been the continuous migration into the Federal Republic that stemmed from regional pressures such as the wars during the breakup of Yugoslavia and the lack of opportunity in other Balkan countries. Most challenging is the recent wave of hundreds of thousands of desperate African and Asian migrants who appeal to humanitarian sympathy while at the same time raise fears of being overrun by foreigners. Since a single country, however well-intentioned, cannot deal with this "human tsunami" alone, much of the discussion on border policing, migrant distribution, and immigration policy has already shifted to the European level, forcing the creation of a joint European agency of border policing, called FRONTEX.[2] Ironically, Germany is now at the forefront of advocating a Europe-wide solution to the migration problem that both accepts genuine refugees escaping from human rights violations and reaffirms control over external borders in order to maintain free travel within.

These brief comments on current research suggest that Germany has gradually become a major immigration country in spite of itself. Clearly the reality on the ground has advanced further towards pluralizing conceptions of Germanness than political statements or foreign commentaries indicate. For instance, group photos of the World Cup winning soccer team shows different skin colors and cultural styles as representing Germany. Prompted by Pegida resentment,[3] the current integration debate has moved a step forward, because the Berlin Republic is trying to decide which commonalities of the Basic Law in regard to gender equality are essential and which cultural differences—such as wearing headscarves—ought to be permitted. The incipient decline of the population due to the low birth rate makes an increase in immigration inescapable in the future, since industry is already unable to fill many jobs. The chapters in this volume therefore explore some of the political developments which have led Chancellor Merkel to argue for openness in accepting the newest wave of refugees with the vow: "We can get it done." It can only be hoped that the recent wave of terrorist attacks will not derail the federal government from its liberal course.

*January 6, 2016*

## Notes

1. "Ade, Du mein lieb Heimatland" is a line of a popular German folk song. Translated into English, it means "farewell, my dear home country."
2. FRONTEX is the abbreviation for European Agency for the Management of Operational Cooperation at the External Borders of the Member States of the European Union, FRONTEX, accessed 15 May 2015, http://frontex.europa.eu/.

3. Pegida is the abbreviation for "Patriotic Europeans against the Islamization of the Occident," a highly xenophobic populist movement that emerged as a grassroots protest movement in Germany in the fall of 2014, has its center in Dresden, and surfaced with weekly public demonstrations in the winter and spring of 2014/15.

**Konrad H. Jarausch** is Lurcy Professor of European Civilization at the University of North Carolina in Chapel Hill and senior fellow of the Zentrum für Zeithistorische Forschung in Potsdam, Germany. He has written or edited approximately forty books on modern German and European history. His latest title, *Out of Ashes: A New History of Europe in the Twentieth Century* (2015), is a comprehensive synthesis.

# MIGRATION, MEMORY, AND DIVERSITY IN GERMANY AFTER 1945

*Cornelia Wilhelm*

Ever since the founding of the modern German nation state, labeling immigrants as "other" and "foreign" to Germany's cultural—and at times, even racial—identity has been a central element of German identity building. The challenge of defining the nation was inherent to the construction of the German nation state and has often been met by branding others as "alien" and as a "threat."[1] As a result, Germans have long failed to understand diversity and cultural difference as positive features of their society, even though migration has been a central element of Germany's social and economic reality.[2] Yet, Germany has managed to depart from older patterns of understanding immigration and diversity, and proudly demonstrated this change of attitude recently in displaying a formerly unknown "welcome culture" for Syrian refugees in the fall of 2015. In fact, since 2012, Germany has received the largest number of immigrants in the European Union and ranks second only to the United States as a "country of immigration" worldwide.[3] Such changes are due to a number of reasons, such as demographic and political challenges, but have also resulted from changing concepts of "history," "memory," and "the nation," which have allowed the Germans to reinvent themselves in a postnational age—a topic that this volume seeks to explore.

The view of immigrants as alien and threatening persisted during and after World War II and the defeat of Nazism. In fact, many post–World War II migrations arose directly from the Nazi expansion across Europe, German atrocities in occupied territories, and the Holocaust, or else resulted from reactions of local populations to the Nazi presence. After 1945, West Germany embarked on a steady, though not perfect, process of democratization and developed an increasingly pluralistic society in an

---

Notes for this chapter begin on page 8.

effort to depart from its Nazi past; however, encounters with large-scale migrations and their cultural memory in the postwar era continued to be difficult.[4] The Allies' reconstruction of the western zones, democratization, and westernization offered opportunities for radical change and a departure from older—and at times racist, exclusive, and ethnocultural—definitions of German citizenship and identity.[5] However, it was not only the persistence of racism from the Nazi period but also the emerging Cold War that limited the potential for exchanges about the Nazi past, changing memory, and the passing of legislation, which might have helped West Germans understand why so many expellees, displaced persons, and other migrants lived in their midst.[6]

In the ideologically charged climate of the Cold War, West Germany struggled to address its historic responsibilities with respect to the expulsion and dislocation of millions of German expellees, or the displacement of millions of so-called displaced persons; rather, as the only democratically legitimized Germany, it claimed sole lawful representation of all Germans, rejected East Germany's right to exist, and upheld the constitutional mandate for reunification. Moreover, it was preoccupied with its own national postwar legacies and the challenge of constructing West Germany as a "center of the German nation." Its Cold War political claims enforced the traditional ethnocultural definition of Germanness, as well as a commitment to a "single German nationhood," which facilitated the legal inclusion of expellees, ethnic Germans, and refugees from the GDR in the postwar era.[7] Such a self-image prevented Germany from confronting its social reality as a rising economic power that depended on foreign labor. While economic success played a large role in solidifying a West German identity, the growing labor force from southern and southeastern Europe, and later from Turkey, was largely marginalized. The possibility of the long-term presence of these migrants and their active integration into German society was openly rejected. From the 1970s to the 1990s, almost every democratic party failed to effectively address migration as a social reality and economic necessity. No political party provided leadership to initiate the active integration of migrants who for years had made West Germany their home. Even worse, at the peak of the debate, the Christian Democratic government under Chancellor Kohl developed a scheme to support a broad return migration of so-called "guest workers," promising financial rewards to those who were willing to relocate after long-term residence in Germany.[8] Rather than developing a political strategy for integration, this policy whipped up populism in debates about migration and political asylum, often described as the "abuse" of political asylum. This interpretation sanctioned a negative perception of immigration, pluralism, multiculturalism, and diversity. Such politics set the tone for a broadly prevalent "cultural code"[9] for an otherwise democratic middle class, which justified xenophobic sentiment in German society and allowed candidates in leading democratic catch-all parties such as the CDU to campaign as recently as 2000 with slogans that employed discriminatory and exclusionary vocabulary such as "Kinder statt Inder."[10] Even Germany's special commitment to provide political asylum for victims of political and religious persecution under article 16 GG, originally based on its experience with Nazism, was compromised by Cold War-era political goals. The political asylum provision was finally curtailed, as it provided a loophole for immigrants who, in the absence of standard immigration legislation, saw the political asylum law as the sole opportunity to enter the country and gain permanent residence.[11]

The German reunification in October 1990 and the end of Cold War Europe offered an unexpected opportunity to develop a different perspective on migration and diversity in Germany. Both events challenged Germany in many ways, but also allowed the nation to depart from its temporary postwar status that had lasted for forty-five years, to reunite, and to negotiate a permanent peace treaty with the Allies. This peace treaty, the Two-Plus-Four Treaty of 1990, settled the de facto territorial losses of Germany to Poland and allowed the two Germanys to reunite. The end of the Cold War in Europe also called for an effort to reconstruct relations with Germany's eastern neighbors, who were deeply affected by Germany's former occupation and atrocities.[12]

In short, the reunification of Germany in a newly united Europe not only raised major concerns about Germany's future role as a nation among the former victims of Nazi atrocities, but also uniquely challenged the united Germany to live up to the ideals it had developed as a country that had learned the lessons of history. Unification provided a stepping stone for the reconsideration of what it meant to be German at the new millennium, more than fifty years after Nazism. The reality was that there were over seven million resident "foreigners" living in Germany at that time. Many of them had been part of West German society for decades, had been born and socialized there, and had little access to outdated Germanness, German citizenship, and civil society.[13] In addition, the seventeen million Germans who had spent forty-five years behind the Iron Curtain, and who had been considered ideological enemies, faced substantial difficulties adjusting to West German society. Such integration problems were also common among the more than 1.5 million ethnic Germans who had seized the unexpected opportunity to emigrate to West Germany after 1989/90. These "Germans" failed to blend in with West German society as easily as had been projected. In the midst of such integration problems, xenophobia and arson attacks against migrants in Hoyerswerda, Rostock,

Mölln, and Solingen brought back images of a racism that had been considered part of the Nazi past.[14] Such racism put unified Germany in the spotlight and shattered the high expectations that the international community had placed on it. Rather, it raised great skepticism as to whether the Germans had really found their place among democratic nations. These circumstances compelled Germans to demonstrate civic responsibility, for example by holding large public demonstrations and "chains of lights" against racism. These events also forced the political leadership to address the issues of *integration* and *diversity* in Germany and to pave the way toward a new understanding of Germanness, in addition to passing new citizenship and naturalization laws, as well as a formal immigration law. It was essential for Germany's image to underscore the role that united Germany would take in a united Europe, and to start to address inclusion in German society in the context of migration.[15]

Germany's central geographic position in Europe, the absence of limitations to free movement within Europe, and the demographic need for immigration indicated that migration would soon constitute a central challenge and potential conflict in this society. A long declining birthrate, fears that labor migration could lead to an imbalance in Germany's social systems, as well as Germany's diminished image as an internationally minded and open place for business and enterprise, all pointed to the need to deal with immigration. Besides these concrete reasons, unification and the end of the Cold War in Europe also offered a unique opportunity to embark on a new conversation about "self" and "other," and allowed a readjustment of what immigration and diversity might mean in the cultural memory of the nation.[16] Although the transition has not been easy, Germany has managed to institute two significant legal changes. First, in January 2000 an amendment to the nationality act provided for the first time a departure from the use of *jus sanguinis* as the sole basis upon which German citizenship was granted, and introduced *jus soli* as a principle, which allowed those born in Germany, irrespective of their ethnic or family background, to claim German citizenship.[17] Second, early in 2005, Germany put into effect its first immigration law, creating a legal framework for future immigration and, more importantly, acknowledging that immigration was a central feature of German society and polity while underscoring the centrality of social and political integration among the goals of the immigration process.[18]

Although the concepts of *nation* and *integration* have constituted the focal points in this transition, the larger European perspective has played an essential role as a "reflective surface" in this process. Not only has Germany attracted large numbers of *European* immigrants, and continues to do so, but the social, legal, political, and economic realities of united

Germany must be understood within the larger context of Europe and its history. For example, while the growth of the European Union and European integration have provided for the assimilation of some post–World War II immigrants from EU countries, other migrants have been excluded from this process, such as the large group of immigrants from Turkey. Also, the emerging Eurozone, intended to provide access to a common currency and thus wealth, has in fact created economic inequalities and migrations as a result.[19] More importantly, the end of the Cold War and the reemergence of free movement in Europe has allowed—and sometimes even forced—reunified Germany to see how its Nazi past was and still is directly related to lingering racism, xenophobia, and difficulties in understanding the migrations and increasing diversity of the postwar period. After 1990, Germans were able, and almost forced, to enter a more expansive European communicative framework to deal with aspects of a past that had been sealed off by the ideological conflict of the postwar period—aspects that stood at the heart of patterns of social exclusion and racism. This new encounter with its European neighbors was sometimes painful and difficult, but it has opened up new ways of understanding "self" and "other," which are in turn opening up opportunities for a new, more inclusive understanding of Germanness and of Germany's role as a destination for immigrants.[20]

Since Germany has increasingly acted within a European and postnational framework, this book will likewise approach Germany's postwar immigration history and its memory within a broader comparative framework. It will also examine how the German experience of immigration was, and continues to be, affected by larger European developments and will consider whether Germany faces similar, different, or competing challenges in relation to other European nations. Finally, this volume seeks to explore whether problems with diversity and memory are uniquely "German," or if and where similar problems are reflected in the larger European context, how Germany's experience corresponds with a larger European context and must be addressed in such a context, rather than by a national approach.

In the first section we will examine the history, demographics, status, perceptions, and memory of the major immigrant groups in West Germany from 1945 until 2010, starting with the German expellees from the territories occupied by the Red Army who found refuge mostly in the western zones of occupied Germany during the postwar years.

Martin Schulze Wessel addresses the difficulties Germans had in understanding expulsion as a result of Nazi expansion, and the atrocities committed by Germans in occupied Poland and former Czechoslovakia, and explores the tensions that developed around the politics of memory after 1990 in united Europe, when Germany, Poland, and the Czech Republic were encountering their past as EU partners.

The end of the Cold War also allowed a different understanding of displaced persons in West Germany. Anna Holian argues that while their presence generated strong xenophobia, with little recognition that their displacement was closely connected to the expansion of Nazism, and the inability to interpret their history as a result of the Nazi expansion into eastern Europe suppressed the notion that a number of these immigrants had permanently settled in West Germany, it was only the end of the Cold War that spurred new research on this immigration and consequently allowed a new understanding of this migrant group as an essential part of the German postwar experience.

Still today, the labeling of labor migrants shows massive discrepancies regarding their potential for inclusion and exclusion. Asiye Kaya explores this practice and compares the rejection of Turkish labor migrants with the attitude displayed toward the immigration of ethnic Germans from Eastern Europe during the same period. She explains that although Germany embarked on a transformation of some of its exclusionary patterns from the 1960s to the 1980s, the policy of negatively labeling immigrant groups has continued and is reflected in the differentiation between those "young, well qualified Europeans" who embark on the "German dream" and those, such as the Sinti and Roma from new EU member Romania, who experience public rejection as a "social burden," and whose migration is seen as "poverty migration."

Patrice Poutrus evaluates the unique position Germany had as a place in which to seek political asylum, and examines whether or not Germany lived up to its high moral goals in its asylum practices. Did German society embrace refugees and asylum seekers as a group that deserved *special* solidarity? How did Germany differ from other European nations in the admission and integration of asylum seekers, and how did it react to their rising numbers in the past?

The second section will mainly focus on the institutionalized memory of immigration and diversity in Germany, its commemoration in museums, the accessibility of archival materials for research, the place that immigration has found in school curricula and textbooks, and the language used in the discussion of "race" in Germany, which is committed to a political correctness that separates the past from the present.

Simone Lässig highlights curricula and school textbooks as central vehicles for raising the historical consciousness of immigration. She explores how and if immigration and immigrants were and are part of the curriculum, and how immigration and diversity were explained in a framework that connects to the Nazi past. Lastly, she asks how Germany's efforts compare to the approaches of other European nations to make immigration and diversity a central topic in their education systems.

In like fashion, museums educate the public on the place of immigration in German history and society. Katharzyna Nogueira and Dietmar Osses trace the discussion concerning the need for a national immigration museum in Germany, a conversation that has gained momentum within a larger European context as other European nations, for example France, have moved forward and created such a national memorial. Based on their observations of the French Musée Nationale de l'Histoire de l'Immigration, the authors put forward the advantages of the absence of such a memorial, which include maintaining the polyphonic diversity of the representation of migration in Germany, whose individuality and connection with grassroots movements might suffer from the "streamlining" and "homogenizing" effects of one singular national museum. Rather, they argue, competing regional perspectives on migration might enhance the understanding of mobility, as well as the transnational and even global connections and their consequences within the public sphere, in which migrants and non-migrants meet.

Institutional archives and archival collections have long neglected to identify and make accessible the immigrant experience for research in Germany. Klaus Lankheit discusses where and why records central to tracking the immigrant experience might be found in national and supranational European archival repositories today, and in particular develops a roadmap for a larger transnational European perspective on the study of immigration.

German postwar political correctness and the fear of using "race" as an analytic category in public discourse on immigration and diversity have made it difficult to understand contemporary "racism" and how it affects German society today, as racism has persisted, but it is sometimes difficult to address, as Rita Chin is demonstrating in her chapter on the epistemological use of the term "race".

The third part of the volume focuses on the changes and new challenges occurring in the years since 1989/90, after the end of the Cold War and the reunification of Germany in the midst of a united and steadily growing Europe. Growing diversity and a changing framework not only placed Germany at the center of an increasingly mobile Europe, but also spurred a redefinition of Germany's relationship with its immigrants and its history. The new place that Germany found in Europe challenged and still challenges it to integrate the memory of its past with its future in a united Europe, and also demonstrates the *painful* lessons of what it means to be German to its immigrant groups.[21]

Dietmar Schirmer sets the stage for this section with a systematic analysis of nationalism, citizenship, integration, and exclusion that defines reunification as a turning point in how Germany dealt with immigration. He stresses the contributory impact of the growing European Union, which put pressure on Germany to comply with EU laws and directives in an effort to craft its own legislation redefining citizenship, to pass a new citizenship and naturalization law in 1999 and an immigration law in 2004.

Kathrin Bower discusses what it meant to be "German," or "foreign" in the postunification period with an analysis of *Wende* migrants such as German *Ausländer*; she highlights the arbitrariness of such terminology and calls for a reconsideration of existing hierarchies of belonging.

Karen Körber explains how the unexpected migration of roughly 200,000 Russian Jews played a major role in the discourse of migration in Germany. Its symbolism could not be misunderstood: Germany was again a country of Jewish immigration, a fact that not only secured the survival of the relatively small and demographically declining postwar Jewish community, but also involved them in a larger public debate on inclusion and exclusion in Germany. This in turn challenged Germany's Jews to take on a significant role in translating the lessons of the past in a pluralistic future.[22]

How important it is to prevent the erosion of meaningful memory of the Holocaust as part of a "German" identity is explained by Annette Seidl-Arpaci. She warns of an ethnicization of memory in an increasingly pluralistic society that prevents the inclusion of immigrants' own memories of German occupation, atrocities, and family stories about their past in German Nazi-occupied Europe or North Africa. She also highlights how pointing to "imported" anti-Semitism among immigrants bears the danger of forgetting to reflect on Germany's own anti-Semitism and racism. More than ever, it is the task of German society to highlight that "Germanness" today must be deeply linked with embracing the lessons of Germany's past in order to build a future.

## Notes

1. The fear of *Überfremdung* (foreign infiltration) originated in the Prussian territories annexed from Poland, such as Posen, which kept attracting Polish agricultural workers from Russia while the native population of these areas, including the German Poles, increasingly migrated to the Ruhr area to take industrial jobs there. Although based on false assumptions, it was believed that the influx of Russian Poles would drive the native population westward into the industrialized areas of Prussia and thereby undermine the Prussian effort to tie the region in the long term to Prussia. Ulrich Herbert, *A History*

*of Foreign Labor in Germany, 1880–1980* (Ann Arbor: University of Michigan Press, 1990), 24–25. See also Jeffrey Peck, Mitchell Ash, and Christiane Lemke, "Natives, Strangers and Foreigners," *After Unity: Reconfiguring German Identities*, ed. Konrad Jarausch (New York/Oxford: Berghahn Books, 1997), 61–102.

 2. Cornelia Wilhelm, "Diversity in Germany: A Historical Perspective," *German Politics and Society* 31 (2013): 13–29.

 3. "OECD-Migrationsstudie: Jeder Dritte Einwanderer kommt nach Deutschland," *Spiegel Online*, 1 December 2014, accessed 29 April 2015, http://www.spiegel.de/politik/deutschland/migration-deutschland-laut-oecd-fast-so-wichtig-wie-usa-a-1005912.html.

 4. Rita Chin, Heide Fehrenbach, and Geoff Ely, eds., *After the Nazi Racial State: Difference and Democracy in Germany and Europe* (Ann Arbor: University of Michigan Press, 2009).

 5. Anselm Doering-Manteuffel, "Dimensionen von Amerikanisierung in der deutschen Gesellschaft," *Archiv für Sozialgeschichte* 35 (1995): 1–34; and Dieter Gosewinkel, "Reflections: Dominance of Nationality? Nation and Citizenship from the Late Nineteenth Century Onwards," *German History* 26 (2008): 92–108.

 6. Constantin Goschler, "The Attitude Towards Jews in Bavaria after the Second World War," *Leo Baeck Insititute Yearbook* 36 (1991): 443–58.

 7. Mary Fulbrook, *German National Identity after the Holocaust* (Cambridge: Polity Press, 1999), 183–85.

 8. Matthias Bartsch, Andrea Brandt, and Daniel Steinvorth, "Turkish Immigration to Germany: A Sorry History of Self-Deception and Wasted Opportunities," *Spiegel Online*, 7 September 2010, accessed 7 April 2015, http://www.spiegel.de/international/germany/turkish-immigration-to-germany-a-sorry-history-of-self-deception-and-wasted-opportunities-a-716067.html.

 9. This term is "borrowed" from Shulamit Volkov, who explained how anti-Semitic attitudes found broad acceptance and "respectability" among imperial Germany's middle class. Shulamit Volkov, "Antisemitism as a Cultural Code: Reflections on the History and Historiography of Antisemitism in Imperial Germany," *Leo Baeck Institute Yearbook* 23 (1978): 25–46. See also Benedikt Erenz, "Lehrer Rühe," *Die Zeit*, 4 June 1993, accessed 28 April 2015, http://www.zeit.de/1993/23/lehrer-ruehe.

10. "Children Instead of [Asian] Indians" (translated by the author); "Kinder statt Inder – die Parolen eines gescheiterten Zukunftsministers," *Das Erste* – Panorama, accessed 23 April 2015, https://daserste.ndr.de/panorama/archiv/2000/erste7444.html.

11. Patrice Poutrus, "Asylum in Postwar Germany," *Journal of Contemporary History* 49 (2014): 115–33.

12. Volker A. Berghahn, Gregory Flynn, and Paul Michael Lützeler, "Germany and Europe: Finding an International Role," in *After Unity: Reconfiguring German Identities*, ed. Konrad Jarausch (New York/Oxford: Berghahn Books, 1997), 173–200.

13. Helga Welsch, Andreas Pickel, and Dorothy Rosenberg, "East and West German Identities: United and Divided?" in *After Unity: Reconfiguring German Identities*, ed. Konrad Jarausch (New York/Oxford: Berghahn Books, 1997), 103–36.

14. "20 Jahre Brandanschlag in Solingen," Bundeszentrale für Politische Bildung, accessed 1 May 2015, http://www.bpb.de/politik/hintergrund-aktuell/161980/brandanschlag-in-solingen.

15. Douglas B. Klusmeyer and Demetrios G. Papademetriou, *Immigration Policy in the Federal Republic of Germany* (New York/Oxford: Berghahn Books, 2009), 144–156.

16. Jan Assmann, "Collective Memory and Cultural Identity," *New German Critique* 65 (1995): 125–33.

17. "German Nationality Act, last amended 13 Nov. 2014," Bundesministerium des Inneren, accessed 25 April 2015, http://www.bmi.bund.de/SharedDocs/Gesetzestexte/EN/Staats angehoerigkeitsgesetz_englisch.pdf?__blob=publicationFile.

18. "Act on the Residence, Economic Activity and Integration of Foreigners in the Federal Territory Residence Act, last amended 6 Sept. 2013," Bundesministerium der Justiz und für Verbraucherschutz, accessed 25 April 2015, http://www.gesetze-im-internet.de/ englisch_aufenthg/.

19. Klusmeyer and Papademetriou, *Immigration Policy*, 159–67, 216–25.

20. On the persisting difficulties of what it means to "be German" see also for example Zafer Senocak, *Deutschsein: Eine Aufklärungsschrift* (Hamburg: Körber-Stiftung, 2011); or see "Deutschland als Einwanderungsland, Wir sind besser als wir glauben," tagesschau.de, 28 April 2015, accessed 28 April 2015, http://www.tagesschau.de/inland/einwanderung-gutachten-deutschland-101.html.

21. "German Chancellor Receives Abraham Geiger Prize," World Union for Progressive Judaism, accessed 9 January 2016, http://wupj.org/News/NewsItem. asp?ContentID=1040.

22. Ibid.

# Works Cited

Assmann, Jan. "Collective Memory and Cultural Identity." *New German Critique* 65 (1995): 125–33.

Bartsch, Matthias, Andrea Brandt, and Daniel Steinvorth. "Turkish Immigration to Germany: A Sorry History of Self-Deception and Wasted Opportunities." *Spiegel Online*, 7 September 2010. Accessed 7 April 2015. http://www.spiegel.de/international/germany/ turkish-immigration-to-germany-a-sorry-history-of-self-deception-and-wasted-opportunities-a-716067.html

Berghahn, Volker A., Gregory Flynn, and Paul Michael Lützeler. "Germany and Europe: Finding an International Role." In *After Unity: Reconfiguring German Identities*, edited by Konrad Jarausch, 173–200. New York/Oxford: Berghahn Books, 1997.

Bundesministerium der Justiz und für Verbraucherschutz. "Act on the Residence, Economic Activity and Integration of Foreigners in the Federal Territory Residence Act, last amended 6 September 2013." Accessed 25 April 2015. http://www.gesetze-im-internet. de/englisch_aufenthg/.

Bundesministerium des Inneren. "German Nationality Act, last amended 13 November 2014." Accessed 25 April 2015. http://www.bmi.bund.de/SharedDocs/Gesetzestexte/EN/ Staatsangehoerigkeitsgesetz_englisch.pdf?__blob=publicationFile.

Bundeszentrale für Politische Bildung."20 Jahre Brandanschlag in Solingen." Accessed 1 May 2015. http://www.bpb.de/politik/hintergrund-aktuell/161980/brandanschlag-in-solingen.

Chin, Rita, Heide Fehrenbach, and Geoff Ely, eds. *After the Nazi Racial State: Difference and Democracy in Germany and Europe*. Ann Arbor: University of Michigan Press, 2009.

Doering-Manteuffel, Anselm. "Dimensionen von Amerikanisierung in der deutschen Gesellschaft." *Archiv für Sozialgeschichte* 35 (1995): 1–34.

Erenz, Benedikt. "Lehrer Rühe." *Die Zeit*, 4 June 1993. Accessed 28 April 2015. http://www. zeit.de/1993/23/lehrer-ruehe.

Das Erste–Panorama. "Kinder statt Inder – die Parolen eines gescheiterten Zukunftsministers." Accessed 23 April 2015. https://daserste.ndr.de/panorama/archiv/2000/erste7444.html.

Fulbrook, Mary. *German National Identity after the Holocaust*. Cambridge: Polity Press, 1999.

Goschler, Constantin. "The Attitude Towards Jews in Bavaria after the Second World War." *Leo Baeck Insititute Yearbook* 36 (1991): 443–58.

Gosewinkel, Dieter. "Reflections: Dominance of Nationality? Nation and Citizenship from the Late Nineteenth Century Onwards." *German History* 26 (2008): 92–108.

Herbert, Ulrich. *A History of Foreign Labor in Germany, 1880–1980*. Ann Arbor: University of Michigan Press, 1990.

Klusmeyer, Douglas B. and Demetrios G. Papademetriou. *Immigration Policy in the Federal Republic of Germany*. New York/Oxford: Berghahn Books, 2009.

Peck, Jeffrey, Mitchell Ash, and Christiane Lemke. "Natives, Strangers and Foreigners." In *After Unity: Reconfiguring German Identities*, edited by Konrad Jarausch, 61–102. New York/Oxford: Berghahn Books, 1997.

Poutrus, Patrice. "Asylum in Postwar Germany." *Journal of Contemporary History* 49 (2014): 115–33.

Senocak, Zafer. *Deutschsein: Eine Aufklärungsschrift*. Hamburg: Körber-Stiftung, 2011.

*Spiegel Online*. "OECD-Migrationsstudie: Jeder Dritte Einwanderer kommt nach Deutschland." 1 December 2014. Accessed 29 April 2015. http://www.spiegel.de/politik/deutschland/migration-deutschland-laut-oecd-fast-so-wichtig-wie-usa-a-1005912.html.

tagesschau.de. "Deutschland als Einwanderungsland – Wir sind besser als wir glauben." 28 April 2015. Accessed 28 April 2015. http://www.tagesschau.de/inland/einwanderung-gutachten-deutschland-101.html.

Volkov, Shulamit. "Antisemitism as a Cultural Code: Reflections on the History and Historiography of Antisemitism in Imperial Germany." *Leo Baeck Institute Yearbook* 23 (1978): 25–46.

Welsch, Helga, Andreas Pickel, and Dorothy Rosenberg. "East and West German Identities: United and Divided?" In *After Unity: Reconfiguring German Identities*, edited by Konrad Jarausch, 103–36. New York/Oxford: Berghahn Books, 1997.

Wilhelm, Cornelia. "Diversity in Germany: A Historical Perspective." *German Politics and Society* 31 (2013): 13–29.

World Union for Progressive Judaism. "German Chancellor Receives Abraham Geiger Prize." Accessed 9 January 2016. http://wupj.org/News/NewsItem.asp?ContentID=1040.

**Cornelia Wilhelm** is currently professor of modern history at Ludwig-Maximilians-Universität, Munich. From 2010 to 2016 she has been DAAD Visiting Professor in the Department of History and the Jewish Studies Program at Emory University in Atlanta and had also held visiting positions at Rutgers University, New Brunswick, and Leopold-Franzens-University of Innsbruck, Austria. She is author of *Bewegung oder Verein? Nationalsozialistische Volkstumspokitik in den USA* (1998); and *Deutsche Juden in America: Bürgerliches Selbstbewusstsein und Jüdische Identität in den Orden B'nai B'rith und True Sisters* (2007), also published in English translation (2011). She is currently working on an in-depth study on German refugee rabbis in the United States after 1933.

# PART I
## Postwar Migrations: History, Memory, and Diversity

*Chapter 1*

# THE COMMEMORATION OF FORCED MIGRATIONS IN GERMANY

*Martin Schulze Wessel*

The German attack on Poland in 1939 marked the beginning of the period during which the most extensive expulsions of ethnic minorities in Europe took place. From the beginning, Hitler pursued his monstrous program of a general reorganization of eastern Europe. The Shoah was part of that program; another element was the general "reorganization of the ethnographic situation" in central and eastern Europe by resettlement, as demanded by Hitler in his Reichstag speech of 6 October 1939.[1] Between twenty-five and thirty-one million people of "alien ethnicity" were removed from their homes by the German authorities, and between 5.6 and 12.2 million ethnic Germans from abroad were resettled into German-occupied eastern Europe. The connection between the Shoah and the anti-Polish policy can be shown, for instance, in the region of Zamość: Jewish Poles were murdered systematically while the non-Jewish Polish population was put through a selection process to decide if they were to be Germanized or deported into the General Governorate.[2]

This was the immediate background of the expulsions that affected the "German" population at the end of the war. During the later stages of World War II, German citizens in the eastern provinces of the Reich fled from Soviet troops. This process was followed by the expulsion of Germans from the territories captured by the Red Army. In literature it is common to distinguish between the phase of "wild expulsions" in the last months of the war and its immediate aftermath on the one hand, and the regulated expulsions that began in August 1945 and were sanctioned by the international Potsdam Agreement on the other. Violence and the thirst for revenge following the cruel occupation regime were typical for the wild phase of expulsions. Pogroms against Germans were a phenomenon in some places in Czechoslovakia (Brno, Ústí nad Labem), though in Poland there is no record of larger excesses.[3] After the legalization of forced migrations by the Potsdam Agreement, the expulsion of Germans and other minorities generally became more regulated and humane.

Germans were expelled from former German territories that were transferred to the Soviet Union and Poland after the war, as well as from territories of other central and eastern European states with ethnic German minorities, such as Poland, Czechoslovakia, Hungary, Romania, and northern Yugoslavia. About seven million Germans were expelled from the former eastern provinces of the Reich that belonged to the Soviet Union and postwar Poland after 1945, and approximately three million Germans were forced to leave Czechoslovakia. Thus, the total number of Germans who were expelled from the East to postwar Germany or to Austria was twelve million. Besides Germans, other ethnic groups were expelled, for example, Poles from the eastern parts of prewar Poland and the Magyars from Czechoslovakia, Romania, and Yugoslavia. However, the Germans constituted the largest group of expellees in Europe after 1945.

The expulsions can be seen as a consequence of the geopolitical reconfiguration of postwar Europe, as the culmination of exclusive nationalism, or as punishment of a nation in whose name unprecedented crimes had been committed during World War II—including plans to Germanize, eradicate, or enslave the entire Slavic population of central and eastern Europe. The expulsion had retrospective and prospective dimensions. Expulsions were a form of taking revenge for the crimes committed by the Wehrmacht and the SS. At the same time, the planners of the expulsions sought to solve fundamental political problems of the postwar European order. The British government believed that problems concerning minorities had contributed considerably to the crisis of interwar Europe and that a stable new European order could only be brought about by the establishment of strong nation states without minorities. Since the Treaty of Lausanne, which regulated a population transfer between Greece and Turkey in 1923, expulsion seemed to have gained acceptance as an appropriate method for solving the internal problems of nation states once and for all.

The flight and expulsion of about twelve million Germans from former eastern Germany and ethnically mixed areas in east central Europe to postwar Germany, was a fundamental break in the lives of the expellees. Being uprooted, and in many cases also traumatized, the expellees suffered much more from the results of the war than most other Germans. Expulsion meant the loss of attachment to their country of origin, which was difficult to rebuild in a new home. Beginning new lives in one of the four occupied zones of Germany, many expellees had to adapt to the habits of their new neighbors. Having lost nearly all their property, many middle-class expellees had to hire themselves out as unskilled workers on farms. The integration process depended upon various factors, such as age, gender, and the confessional and regional identities of the expellees.[4] Moreover, the question of where the expellees were settled affected their chances of integration. Rhineland-Palatinate, belonging to the zone occupied by France, accepted almost no refugees or expellees, whereas in 1946, almost half of Schleswig-Holstein's population consisted of Germans who had been expelled from the East. In some villages the number of new citizens was even higher than the number of native residents. Under such conditions, a new form of xenophobia arose in defense of the regional heritage, directed against the newly arrived Germans, who were equated with Poles or other eastern peoples. Many German farmers perceived and treated the expellees in a similar fashion to the Polish seasonal workers of the late nineteenth century and the Russian, Ukrainian, or Polish forced workers of World War II.[5] Marginalized by their western German compatriots, expellees complained that they alone had to pay the price of a lost war. This was especially an imposition for the German expellees who came originally from regions that had not belonged to the German Reich before World War II and who bore no responsibility for the rise of National Socialism in Germany. While the inhabitants of the four German zones sometimes articulated fears of foreign infiltration and antipathy against the German foreigners, the expellees were offended by treatment they felt to be unjust. The poverty of the immigrant population and the social and cultural tensions between the resident population and the immigrants created an explosive atmosphere. Therefore, the expulsion created a significant political challenge for the four powers and for German politics. These entities tried to solve the problems by forcing the resident population to house the expellees. The West German policy was to try to calm the expellees with revisionist rhetoric. Especially in the 1950s, West German politicians nourished hopes that the expellees would reclaim their homes in the East, which kept the issue of expulsion alive. In their election campaigns, each democratic party pledged not to acknowledge the eastern border. Symbolic actions, such as the erection of memorials for expulsions, also had the political function of integrating the expellees.[6] Only in the 1960s, and especially in the era of Willy Brandt's new *Ostpolitik* (Eastern Policy), did the political rhetoric in West Germany become more realistic and were revisionist promises withdrawn. Nevertheless, the official discourse of the German expellees had already been framed by the discourse of the 1950s with long-lasting effects on the political orientation of the German expellees. Remembrance of the expulsion became a polarizing issue in the debates of the 1960s and 1970s, in which the political representatives of the expellees played a distinctly conservative or even revisionist role. As a result, expulsion became a non-issue in large segments of the liberal and left public sphere. Only after the reunification of Germany in 1989 did the situation change due to the final settlement of Germany's eastern borders in the Two-Plus-Four Treaty of 1990.

Against the backdrop of the forced migration of Germans after World War II and their integration into West and East Germany after the war, this chapter will deal with the memory of forced migration during the Cold War period as well as after 1989. The text will illuminate in detail a well-known project of the official German memory policy, the "Flight, Expulsion, Reconciliation Foundation," which was established by the German Bundestag (Lower House of the Federal Republic of Germany, FRG) in 2008. The foundation plans a permanent exhibition about forced migrations in twentieth-century Europe in which the expulsion of Germans will have a central place. This chapter will also highlight how this discourse reaches far beyond Germany's borders in a newly united Europe and will primarily explain Polish and Czech positions on the German commemoration of a period of joint history.

Discourse about the memory of forced migrations can have a national, transnational, and universal dimension. Recently, memory has shown a tendency towards transnationalization. The causes of this trend are numerous, including the communication revolution, the transformations of transnational public spheres, and the end of the Cold War system, which divided memory along ideological lines.[7] Memory claims have become increasingly transnational and even universal. The Israeli historian Tom Segev postulates: "The Holocaust no longer exclusively belongs to Israel and the Jews. Today it belongs to the whole world."[8]

Yet, it is reasonable to argue in a similar fashion to Jan Assmann that memory and globalization work in opposite directions. While globalization tends to erode the markers of cultural specificity, memory is inherently divisive and shapes distinct cultural identities.[9] This is especially true for the memory of forced migrations. Forced migrations tend to be commemorated in the form of an archetypical narrative, as expulsion—a tragedy caused by an irresistible fate which strikes a whole community, old and young, male and female, guilty and innocent alike. Expulsions are community builders because all sorts of social, gender, and generational distinctions are overshadowed by the collective fate of the community of expellees. The expellers are perceived as a collective, homogeneous force as well. The transnational commemoration of expulsions creates clear distinctions of the "expeller state" or expeller ethnicity on the one hand, and the community of the expellees on the other. This can be exemplified by an analysis of the discourse of the German expellees in the 1950s, when the image of the expelled as victim was invented. Even the transnationalization of the discourse about expulsions, which can be observed in the German-Polish and German-Czech contexts since 1989, does not necessarily challenge the dichotomy of national interpretations.[10] In the heated Polish/German debates about the role of the German Federation of Expellees (Bund der Vertriebenen) and its president Erika Steinbach, it became evident that the emergence of a transnational public sphere on the issue of expulsions does not necessarily mean a common interpretation of this issue.[11] Quite the contrary: the transnational attention—which both sides attributed to the media debates in the other country—led to a dynamic memory conflict between the German and Polish media.

A transnational interest in the debates in Germany, Poland, and Czechoslovakia already existed in the 1950s and 1960s, but at that time there was still very little direct dialogue between the German media and the Polish or Czechoslovakian media.[12] The memory of expulsion was a national issue. In Germany, an important precondition for social services for the expellees and the cultural memory of expulsion was created by the German Federal Expellee Law of 1953, which defines as expellees all German nationals and ethnic Germans having a primary residence outside postwar Germany and who lost their residences in the course of World War II-related flight or expulsions.[13] This definition embraced people with manifold experiences of flight, expulsion, and forced migration. Some of them had German citizenship; others, such as expellees from Czechoslovakia or Romania, had never been German in the legal sense. The notion of the "expellee," created by this law, focused on ethnicity and on the fate of having lost one's own home, and suppressed important distinctions between the various groups. The primary historiographical work reflecting this notion was the *Dokumentation der Vertreibung der Deutschen aus Ost-Mitteleuropa*[14] (Documentation of the Expulsion of the Germans from East Central Europe), which was intended to ward off claims for reparations against Germany. Knowledge about the expulsions was politically important because the suffering of German expellees and their material losses had to serve as a potential counterargument against possible demands for reparations by the Allied powers.

The transnational dimension of the commemoration of expulsion consisted only in the transnational blaming of the so-called expeller states. There were no efforts toward creating a shared memory of expulsions. The purpose of the ideologues of the Federation of Expellees was to stress the extent of the crime that had been committed against ethnic Germans in the former eastern parts of Germany and in east central and south-east Europe. Though a considerable number of them had been perpetrators under the Nazi regime or had profited from it in some way,[15] the Federation of Expellees pursued a strategy of victimization that reflected the self-understanding of the German expellees. From the beginning, the fact that Poles and other people in eastern Europe were the first victims of expulsions was blotted out in the self-image of the German expellees. Under the conditions of the Cold War, critics of the victim narrative of the Federation of Expellees could easily be blamed for having sympathies with communist Eastern Europe. This practice of politicization and emotionalization of the expulsion issue had high costs.[16] When the German public, especially under the influence of the TV mini-series *Holocaust*, which was broadcast in Germany in January 1979, began to voluntarily address the Shoah, comparisons between Jewish and German victims became less acceptable. The Shoah was established as a singular crime in German memory, at least during the German *Historikerstreit* of 1987. This limited the memory strategies of the Federation of Expellees. Their members were now seen not only as victims but also as perpetrators and were therefore placed in a relatively minor position in the hierarchy of victim groups. Consequently, German memory culture was divided between the inner group of the expellees, their organizations, and their political structures on the one hand, and a liberal and leftist public that was ignoring or refusing the victim narratives of the expellees on the other. While the Federation of Expellees and its twenty-one constituent regional groups, the *Landsmannschaften*—among them, the big Silesian and the Sudeten German *Landsmannschaft*—continued staging their mass gatherings, which attracted hundreds of thousands of participants, the significance of the expulsion issue decreased in the German memory culture, for example in school curricula. The German historian Manfred Kittel overestimated and misinterpreted this aspect by advocating the thesis that the expellees were expelled for a second time in the 1960s and 1970s—this time out of the German memory.[17] It was the politicization and emotionalization of the expulsion issue—fostered by the Federation of Expellees itself—that made their claims less attractive in an era of East-West détente.

Moreover, the official self-image of the expellees was questioned by professional historical scholarship that stressed the logic of causes and consequences in World War II and the postwar period. At that time—the period of the new Eastern Policy of Willy Brandt and Walter Scheel—the commemoration of the expulsion became less prominent. The topic came back after the reunification of Germany and the final settlement of the border questions in the so-called Two-Plus-Four Treaty between

Germany and the World War II victors: the United States, the Soviet Union, Great Britain, and France.

In historiography, most research about the expulsions was conducted in the decades after 1989. This meant not only progress in empirical research, but in many cases a gain in multinational perspectives as well. Important documentation of the expulsions was produced in international historical commissions; important debates took place in the German-Polish Schoolbook Commission and the German-Czech and German-Slovak Historical Commissions. Young scholars started researching the intersections of German, Polish, and Czech historical debates about the expulsions.[18]

Since 1989, commemoration of the expulsion has not regained the political relevance of the 1950s. The Federation of Expellees' antagonism toward Willy Brandt's Eastern Policy and his idea of reconciliation isolated the political representatives of the expellees and harmed the commemoration of the expulsion in the political culture of West Germany. After reunification the memory of expulsion reappeared as an issue in Günter Grass's book *Im Krebsgang*. Grass was one of the first intellectuals who touched on the history of the expellees. Documentary TV series and popular publications about "Hitler's last victims" followed. Although the commemoration of the expellees was, of course, never suppressed by the state, the pioneers of the new memory boom claimed that there had been a "taboo" against the remembrance of the expulsion. This taboo never existed, but the climate for remembrance of the expulsion did indeed become much more favorable than it had been in the 1960s and 1970s. One consequence of this change was the new state interest in the commemoration of expellees.

This state initiative had a great impact on the whole topic: the commemoration of expulsion was becoming an element of a national memory with a universal pathos. This was a major difference from the commemorations of the 1950s, which had an international element only in blaming the so-called "expeller states" for the expulsion of the Germans. The new German memory policy conserved the victim image of the expellees, but put it in a row with other victim groups of the Nazi regime and World War II. Memorials were built for the following groups:

- Memorial to the Murdered Jews of Europe (Berlin 2004)
- Memorial for Persecuted Homosexuals during the Nazi Period (2008)
- Memorial to the Sinti and Roma Victims of National Socialism (Berlin 2012)
- Flight, Expulsion, Reconciliation Center with a permanent exhibition in the Deutschlandhaus (Berlin, opening planned 2016)

The rationale of state memorials is of course different from the rationale of historiography. While the latter focuses on the timeline and the causes and consequences, state memorials do not tell a story of causes and consequences, but privilege certain events and victim groups by visibility in the cityscape. The attack on Poland, for example, is not visible in the Berlin cityscape.

There is also another effect to be observed: though all commemorated groups were victims of the Nazi regime and of World War II, the memorials do not focus on the historical context (with the exception of the documentation center, which is situated beneath the Memorial to the Murdered Jews of Europe), and thus the universal claim of the memorials is stressed.

The problem with the Center for the Commemoration of German Expellees is the tension between the national interest on the one hand and the universal pathos on the other. The center is to be established by the Stiftung Flucht, Vertreibung, Versöhnung (Flight, Expulsion, Reconciliation Foundation) founded by the German Bundestag in 2008. The foundation is the best-known project of German national memory policy in recent years. The official purpose of the foundation is "to keep the commemoration and remembrance of flight and expulsion alive in a spirit of reconciliation and in the historical context of World War II and the National Socialist policy of expansion and elimination and its consequences."[19]

The high significance of the project emanates from the members of the foundation board. Members are the president of the foundation Deutsches Historisches Museum (German Historical Museum), bureaucrats of the Ministry of Foreign Affairs, the Ministry of the Interior, and the Federal Commissioner for Culture and Media. In addition, the board is composed of high-ranking representatives of religious groups (Catholic and Protestant churches and the Central Council of Jews) and the German Bundestag with the parliamentary groups of the Christian Democrats, Social Democrats, and the Liberals, but without a representative of the Green Party.

The composition of the foundation board, which was elected by the Bundestag in July 2010, was a highly political issue because the Federation of Expellees claimed representation in that body and nominated its chair, Erika Steinbach, for that function. Steinbach was known for her heated rhetoric arousing suspicion in Poland; therefore, after public protest by the Polish Foreign Minister Wladislaw Bartoszewski, she was not nominated.

This was the highly politicized situation in which the discussion around the permanent exhibition about the expulsion of the Germans developed. How to memorialize the forced migration was a question that concerned the understanding of twentieth-century European history as a whole.

Generally speaking, there were two main approaches. One of these, the exhibition *Erzwungene Wege: Flucht und Vertreibung im Europa des*

*20 Jahrhunderts* (Forced Paths: Flight and Expulsion in Twentieth-Century Europe), tested as a temporary exhibition in 2006 at the Kronprinzenpalais in Berlin, was organized by the Foundation Center Against Expulsions, a non-governmental organization set up by the Federation of Expellees in September 2000.[20] The exhibition had the underlying assumption that the forced migration of the Germans at the end of World War II was a typical event of the twentieth century, which in this context is often called "the century of expulsions."[21] In this sense, the forced migration of ethnic Germans should be understood and commemorated as one link in a chain of expulsions that started in the Ottoman Empire and ended in the post-Yugoslav wars. This perspective on the expulsion of the Germans is far from the narrative of the German expellees of the 1950s, who blamed concrete states and ethnicities for the expulsion of ethnic Germans, which, in their eyes, was a singular event, not to be compared with the expulsion of Greeks or Armenians.

In contrast, the narrative of the exhibition of 2006 was very abstract. It did not blame a concrete group of people or states but "modernity" for the phenomenon of expulsions. Nationalism as a modern phenomenon was responsible for the exclusion of ethnic minorities from the body politic. This tendency led in the end to the expulsions. Thus, from this perspective, National Socialism was just one example among many of exclusive nationalism. In that sense, World War II and the German occupational regime only had a triggering effect on the expulsions. They had only enforced an exclusive tendency that was inherent in Polish or Czech nationalism before 1938/39.

This approach is inevitably connected to a negative interpretation of the interwar period in Poland and Czechoslovakia, which can be observed in the exhibition *Erzwungene Wege* and is also notable in the plans for the permanent exhibition of the Flight, Expulsion, Reconciliation Foundation. One very typical example is the presentation of Kaaden Day, which has become a Sudeten German historical symbol, a *lieu de mémoire*. On 4 March 1919, the German population of the village of Kaaden demonstrated for the "right of self-determination," i.e., for secession from Czechoslovakia. This led to a conflict with local troops in which seventeen Sudeten Germans died. This was a tragedy in the local history of Kaaden. Yet it is remarkable that Kaaden Day is used in the context of explaining the expulsions. In general it cannot be proved that the republic of Czechoslovakia was a government of injustice. As a national state, it made distinctions between the majority of Czechoslovaks and various national minorities, among them the three million Sudeten Germans, but it guaranteed democratic rights for all citizens. The so-called Kaaden Day in the turbulent first year of the republic was far from typical of the political culture of the new state. Nevertheless, Kaaden plays a role not only in the manifestations of the historical identity of the Sudeten Germans up to the present time, but also in the official German memory policy. Kaaden and similar events in Poland serve as evidence for the exclusive and violent character of nationalism in east central Europe. In principle, this exclusiveness and violence makes the states comparable to Germany in the 1930s and suggests Czech and Polish responsibility for the expulsions. This bias in the exhibition follows a certain tradition in German historiography, which overstresses the exclusively nationalist character of the east central European states. In the older German historiography, migration of ethnic Germans from Poland to Germany after World War I was often depicted as a form of expulsion.[22] A key text is an article by Horst Möller, the former director of the Institute for Contemporary History in Munich (Institut für Zeitgeschichte), and Manfred Kittel, who in 2009 became the first director of the Flight, Expulsion, Reconciliation Foundation Center. Comparing western European nationalism with Eastern European nationalism, the authors identified Polish and Czech nationalism and their exceptional cultural exclusiveness as one of the main causes for ethnic cleansing after World War II.[23] Their dichotomous view on "good" political nationalism in the West and "evil" cultural nationalism in the East ignored the fact that French nationalism after World War I was quite aggressive, too. Teachers and other officials of ethnic German origin had to leave retaken France (i.e., Alsace-Lorraine) within two weeks.[24] Moreover, Möller and Kittel overemphasized the exclusiveness of east central European nationalism by hinting again at the "massacre of Kaaden." The Federation of Expellees' biased interpretation of the interwar period went so far that the spokesman of the organization, Erika Steinbach, blamed Poland for the outbreak of World War II because Warsaw had mobilized its troops in expectation of a German attack.[25] This is the framework of the discourse about the Flight, Expulsion, Reconciliation Foundation founded by federal law in May 2010. In contrast to the Foundation Center against Expulsions, it is not a non-governmental institution, but a dependent foundation. Its main purpose is to create a permanent exhibition on expulsions in the twentieth century.

An alternative concept to the permanent exhibition about expulsions was presented by the binational historical commissions that exist between Germany and Poland, and between Germany and the Czech Republic and Slovakia.[26] The primary idea of this alternative concept is, first of all, to focus on the logic of the violence that was initiated by Germany's war and occupational regime in east central Europe. The expulsions should be seen, first of all, in this context of cause and effect, not in the abstract context of the history of nationalism. The historical commissions propose local perspectives on the history of World War II and the expulsions. The whole complexity of the expulsions that were initiated by the Germans and Soviets, and also the Germans and Magyars captured at the end of the war, can be presented on the local level of cities with multiethnic populations—in local histories of cities such as Breslau/Wroclaw, Aussig/Ústí or Vilnius/Wilna/Wilno/Wilne. Only on this level is it possible to illuminate the connections between the social engineering of the states and the agency of local actors and to abandon simplified schemes of "perpetrators" and "victims." A sophisticated presentation of the issue of war and expulsion is only possible provided that the general connection between the causes and effects is not questioned. Another claim in the alternative concept is to stress the history of the integration of the expellees in both German states and the history of the memory of expulsions itself, including the role of the Federation of Expellees.

A first programmatic draft for the permanent exhibition of the Flight, Expulsion, Reconciliation Foundation was published by the director Manfred Kittel in September 2010. In contrast to the paper of the German-Polish and German-Czech and German-Slovak Historical Commissions, it professed an emotional way of presenting the history of expulsions. Like the alternative paper it took a topographical approach, but included highly controversial places like Bromberg/Bydgoszcz in the planned exhibition. Bromberg showed Germans as victims not only at the end of the war, but at its very beginning in 1939. In Bromberg, a Polish city with a sizable German minority, a series of killings of German inhabitants took place two days after the beginning of the German invasion of Poland. This incident, which is still debated among historians, was used in Nazi propaganda to justify cruelty against the Poles during World War II. The notion of "bloody Sunday" was intentionally shaped for propagandistic reasons.[27] The plan to integrate Bromberg into the permanent exhibition was almost provocative for Poles.

The Foundational Council was very hesitant to adopt the draft, calling it a "basis" for further planning. Indeed, in 2012 the more concrete planning of the permanent exhibition departed from the highly controversial form of history telling of the first draft and adopted some concepts from the alternative paper of the historical commissions.[28]

So far, the Flight, Expulsion, Reconciliation Foundation has not yet realized its permanent exhibition. In 2014 the temporary exhibition *Schlaglichter auf die künftige Dauerausstellung der Stiftung Flucht, Vertreibung, Versöhnung* (Flashlights on the Future Permanent Exhibition of the Flight, Expulsion, Reconciliation Foundation) was opened. Though the foundation has internationalized its advisory board in recent years, integrating, for example, Krzysztof Ruchniewicz, Marina Cattaruzza, Piotr Madajczyk, and Norman Naimark, the general tendency of the project seems to remain the same: to interpret expulsions as a hallmark of modernity and to tell the story, first of all, of the German victims.[29] The tensions between the international advisory board and the director of the foundation culminated in November 2014 when the latter brought a temporary exhibition to Berlin, which had been produced in Greek, and which showed the expulsion of the Germans from Poland without the historical context of World War II. After a heated public controversy, director Manfred Kittel was forced to resign from his position in the foundation.[30] Since then, public quarrel about positions has characterized the foundation: the Federal Secretary of Culture, Monika Grütters, together with the board of the foundation, nominated Wilfried Halder as the new director of the foundation. From the very beginning Halder was contested in the public sphere. He lacked scholarly experience in the field of expulsion studies but was supported by the German Federation of Expellees. Most of the members of the scientific board resigned after his appointment, including Halder himself half a year later. As an interim arrangement Uwe Neumärker, the director of the Memorial to the Murdered Jews of Europe, took over the directorship of the Flight, Expulsion, Reconciliation Foundation.[31]

In the last years, the exhibition project has been intensively and controversially discussed not only by the German public, but also in Poland, the Czech Republic, and Slovakia. In all four states, discussions about the project of the Flight, Expulsion, Reconciliation Foundation have had a nationalizing effect. This effect is, paradoxically, a result of the universalizing claim. What is unacceptable to the public spheres in Poland, the Czech Republic, and Slovakia is not the commemoration of the expulsions as such, but the effort to present the expulsions as a paradigmatic crime of the twentieth century. A "memory without borders," "based on the universal norms of human rights," as claimed by Jan-Werner Müller, can only be achieved if the dimension of preconditions and consequences is respected and visualized by the means of memory policy.[32] The universal trend of memory claims is problematic for two reasons: first, it simplifies memory because it reduces individual and collective tragedies to simple lessons such as "Nationalism leads to genocide and exclusion." Second, in the case of the expulsion of ethnic Germans, the universal claim is harmful in terms of international relations. To put it positively: if the expulsion of the Germans is commemorated as a specific event and if the specific historical conditions are not ignored, commemoration of expulsion will be acceptable to neighboring countries like Poland and the Czech Republic. The more precise the commemoration of expulsions becomes in terms of historical contexts, the higher the chances are for a common European memory of World War II.

# Notes

1. *Verhandlungen des Reichstages*, Vol. 460, Stenographische Protokolle 1939–1942, 4th Session, 6 October 1939, 51–63, here 56, accessed 29 October 2014, http://www.reichstagsprotokolle. de/Blatt2_n4_bsb00000613_00052.html.
2. Czesław Madajczyk, *Die Okkupationspolitik Nazideutschlands in Polen 1939–1945* (Cologne: Pahl-Rugenstein, 1988).
3. Tomáš Staněk, *Internierung und Zwangsarbeit: das Lagersystem in den böhmischen Ländern 1945–1948* (Munich: Oldenbourg, 2007).
4. Karen L. Gatz, "East Prussian and Sudeten German Expellees in West Germany 1945–1960. A Comparison of their Social and Cultural Integration," (PhD diss., Bloomington: Indiana University; Ann Arbor: UMI, 1989); Wolfram Wette, "Eine Gesellschaft im Umbruch: 'Entwurzelungserfahrungen' in Deutschland 1943–1948 und sozialer Wandel," in *Flucht und Vertreibung: Zwischen Aufrechnung und Verdrängung*, ed. Robert Streibel (Vienna, Picus-Verlag, 1994), 257–84; Philipp Ther, "The Integration of Expellees in Germany and Poland after World War II: A Historical Reassessment," *Slavic Review* 55, no. 4 (1996): 779–805.
5. Andreas Kossert, *Kalte Heimat: die Geschichte der deutschen Vertriebenen nach 1945* (Munich: Siedler, 2008), 71–86.
6. Matthias Stickler, *"Ostdeutsch heißt gesamtdeutsch." Organisation, Selbstverständnis und heimatpolitische Zielsetzungen der deutschen Vertriebenenverbände 1949–1972* (Düsseldorf: Droste, 2004); Christian Lotz, *Die Deutung des Verlusts. Erinnerungspolitische Kontroversen im geteilten Deutschland um Flucht, Vertreibung und die Ostgebiete 1948–1972* (Cologne: Böhlau 2007).
7. Aleida Assmann and Sebastian Conrad, "Introduction," in *Memory in a Global Age: Discourses, Practices and Trajectories*, eds. Aleida Assman and Sebastian Conrad (Basingstoke: Palgrave Macmillan, 2010), 7.
8. Tom Segev in an interview with the *Wiener Zeitung*, 27 May 2006, in Assmann and Conrad, "Introduction," 8.
9. Jan Assmann, "Globalization, Universalism, and the Erosion of Cultural Memory," in *Memory in a Global Age*, eds. Assmann and Conrad, 121–37.
10. Peter Haslinger, K. Erik Franzen, and Martin Schulze Wessel, eds., *Diskurse über Zwangsmigrationen in Zentraleuropa: Geschichtspolitik, Fachdebatten, literarisches und lokales Erinnern seit 1989* (Munich: Oldenbourg, 2008).
11. Maren Röger, *Flucht, Vertreibung und Umsiedlung. Mediale Erinnerung und Debatten in Polen und Deutschland seit 1989* (Marburg: Herder-Institut, 2011), 129.
12. Anna Jakubowska, *Der Bund der Vertriebenen in der Bundesrepublik Deutschland und Polen (1957–2004): Selbst- und Fremddarstellung eines Vertriebenenverbandes* (Marburg: Herder-Institut, 2012).
13. "Gesetz über die Angelegenheiten der Vertriebenen und Flüchtlinge (1953)", Bundesministerium der Justiz und für Verbraucherschutz, accessed 8 November 2014, http://www.gesetze-im-internet.de/bvfg/BJNR002010953.html.
14. Bundesministerium für Vertriebene, ed., *Dokumentation der Vertreibung der Deutschen aus Ost-Mitteleuropa*, bearbeitet von Theodor Schieder, 6 volumes, Bonn: Bundesministerium für Vertriebene, 1955–1963.
15. Michael Schwartz, *Funktionäre mit Vergangenheit: das Gründungspräsidium des Bundes der Vertriebenen und das "Dritte Reich"* (Munich: Oldenbourg, 2013).
16. Christian Lotz, *Die Deutung des Verlusts*; Constantin Goschler, "'Versöhnung' und 'Viktimisierung.' Die Vertriebenen und der deutsche Opferdiskurs," *Zeitschrift für Geschichtswissenschaft* 53 (2005): 873–84.

17. Manfred Kittel, *Vertreibung der Vertriebenen? Der historische deutsche Osten in der Erinnerungskultur der Bundesrepublik (1961–1982)* (Munich: Oldenbourg, 2007).

18. Madlen Benthin, *Die Vertreibung der Deutschen aus Ostmitteleuropa. Deutsche und tschechische Erinnerungskulturen im Vergleich* (Hannover: Hahn, 2007); Maren Röger, *Flucht, Vertreibung und Umsiedlung*; Anna Jakubowska, *Der Bund der Vertriebenen.*

19. Law for the establishment of a foundation "German Historical Museum," 21 December 2008 (Bundesgesetzblatt 2008, I, 2891), amended by article 1 of the law 14 June 2010 (Bundesgesetzblatt 2010, I, 784), "Stiftung Flucht Vertreibung Versöhnung", Stiftung Grundlagenpapiere, accessed 29 October 2014, http://sfvv.e-fork.net/stiftung/grundlagenpapiere/gesetz-2010.

20. Piotr Madajczyk, "'Das Zentrum gegen Vertreibungen' das polnische und das deutsche historische Gedächtnis und die deutsch-polnischen Erinnerungen," in *Definitionsmacht, Utopie, Vergeltung. "Ethnische Säuberung," im östlichen Europa des 20. Jahrhundert*, ed. Ulf Brunnbauer (Berlin: Lit-Verlag, 2006), 240–80; K. Erik Franzen, "Der Diskurs als Ziel? Anmerkungen zur deutschen Erinnerungspolitik am Beispiel der Debatte um ein 'Zentrum gegen Vertreibungen 1999–2005,'" in *Diskurse über Zwangsmigrationen in Zentraleuropa*, eds. Peter Haslinger, K. Erik Franzen and Martin Schulze Wessel, 1–30.

21. Wilfried Rogasch, Katharina Klotz, Doris Müller-Toovey, *Erzwungene Wege: Flucht und Vertreibung im Europa des 20. Jahrhunderts* (Ausstellung im Kronprinzenpalais, Berlin; eine Ausstellung der Stiftung Zentrum gegen Vertreibungen) (Wiesbaden: Zentrum gegen Vertreibungen, 2006).

22. Philipp Ther, *Die dunkle Seite der Nationalstaaten: "Ethnische Säuberungen" im modernen Europa* (Göttingen: Vandenhoeck & Ruprecht, 2011), 85.

23. Manfred Kittel and Horst Möller, "Die Beneš-Dekrete und die Vertreibung der Deutschen im europäischen Vergleich" (The Beneš Decrees and the Expulsion of the Ethnic Germans Seen from a European Perspective), in *Vierteljahrshefte für Zeitgeschichte* 54, no. 4 (2006): 541–81.

24. Ther, *Die dunkle Seite der Nationalstaaten*, 86.

25. Sven Felix Kellerhoff, "Hitler-Deutschland trieb die Polen zur Mobilmachung. Erika Steinbach hat Recht: Die polnische Armee machte im März 1939 mobil. Doch Hitler hatte die Polen monatelang provoziert, weil er den Krieg wollte," *DIE WELT*, 9 September 2010, accessed 4 November 2014, http://www.welt.de/politik/deutschland/article9501550/Hitler-Deutschland-trieb-die-Polen-zur-Mobilmachung.html.

26. Martin Schulze Wessel, "Forum: Konzeptionelle Überlegungen für die Ausstellungen der Stiftung Flucht, Vertreibung, Versöhnung," *H-Soz-u-Kult Diskussionen*, 10 September 2010, accessed 4 November 2014, http://hsozkult.geschichte.hu-berlin.de/forum/id=1355&type=diskussionen. Tim Völkering, *Flucht und Vertreibung im Museum: Zwei aktuelle Ausstellungen und ihre geschichtskulturellen Hintergründe im Vergleich*, (Berlin: Lit-Verlag, 2008).

27. Andrzej Krzysztof Kunert and Zygmunt Walkowski, eds., *Kronika kampanii wrześniowej 1939, Wydawnictwo Edipresse Polska* (Warsaw: Edipresse Książki, 2005), 35.

28. Stiftung Flucht, Vertreibung, Versöhnung, ed., *Conceptual Framework for the Flight, Expulsion, Reconciliation Foundation and Guidelines for the Planned Permanent Exhibition* (Stiftung Flucht, Vertreibung, Versöhnung: no place, 2012), accessed 29 October 2014, http://www.sfvv.de/sites/default/files/downloads/conceptual_framework_sfvv_2012.pdf.

29. "Schlaglichter auf die künftige Dauerausstellung der Stiftung Flucht, Vertreibung, Versöhnung," Stiftung Flucht Vertreibung Versöhnung, accessed 12 October 2014, http://sfvv.de/de/temporare-ausstellungen/schlaglichter-auf-die-kunftige-dauerausstellung-der-stiftung-flucht.

30. Jürgen Kaube, "Bundesstiftung in der Krise: Flucht, Vertreibung, Verwirrung," *FAZ. net*, 15 November 2014, accessed 12 October 2014, http://www.faz.net/stiftung-flucht-vertreibung-versoehnung-13264349.html.
31. Sven Felix Kellerhoff, "Chefsache für die Vertriebenenstiftung ist ein Debakel," *DIE WELT*, 4 November 2015, accessed 25 November 2015, http://www.welt.de/geschichte/article148412008/Chefsuche-fuer-Vertriebenenstiftung-ist-ein-Debakel.html.
32. Jan-Werner Müller, "Constitutional Patriotism beyond the Nation-Sate: Human Rights, Constitutional Necessity, and the Limits of Pluralism," in *Cardozo Law Review* 33 (2012): 1926–1933.

# Works Cited

Assmann, Aleida and Sebastian Conrad. "Introduction." In *Memory in a Global Age: Discourses, Practices and Trajectories*, edited by Aleida Assmann and Sebastian Conrad, 1–16. Basingstoke: Palgrave Macmillan, 2010.

Assmann, Jan. "Globalization, Universalism, and the Erosion of Cultural Memory." In *Memory in a Global Age: Discourses, Practices and Trajectories*, edited by Aleida Assmann and Sebastian Conrad, 121–37. Basingstoke: Palgrave Macmillan, 2010.

Benthin, Madlen. *Die Vertreibung der Deutschen aus Ostmitteleuropa. Deutsche und tschechische Erinnerungskulturen im Vergleich*. Hannover: Hahn, 2007.

Bundesministerium für Vertriebene, ed., *Dokumentation der Vertreibung der Deutschen aus Ost-Mitteleuropa*, bearbeitet von Theodor Schieder, 6 volumes, Bonn: Bundesministerium für Vertriebene, 1955–1963.

Bundesministerium der Justiz und für Verbraucherschutz. "Gesetz über die Angelegenheiten der Vertriebenen und Flüchtlinge (1953)." Accessed 8 November 2014. http://www.gesetze-im-internet.de/bvfg/BJNR002010953.html.

Franzen, K. Erik. "Der Diskurs als Ziel? Anmerkungen zur deutschen Erinnerungspolitik am Beispiel der Debatte um ein 'Zentrum gegen Vertreibungen' 1999–2005." In *Diskurse über Zwangsmigrationen in Zentraleuropa: Geschichtspolitik, Fachdebatten, literarisches und lokales Erinnern seit 1989*, edited by Peter Haslinger, K. Erik Franzen, and Martin Schulze Wessel, 1–30. Munich: Oldenbourg, 2008.

Gatz, Karen L., "East Prussian and Sudeten German Expellees in West Germany 1945–1960: A Comparison of their Social and Cultural Integration." PhD diss., Indiana University, Bloomington. Ann Arbor: UMI, 1989.

Goschler, Constantin. "'Versöhnung' und 'Viktimisierung'. Die Vertriebenen und der deutsche Opferdiskurs." *Zeitschrift für Geschichtswissenschaft* 53 (2005): 873–84.

Haslinger, Peter, K. Erik Franzen, and Martin Schulze Wessel, eds. *Diskurse über Zwangsmigrationen in Zentraleuropa: Geschichtspolitik, Fachdebatten, literarisches und lokales Erinnern seit 1989*. Munich: Oldenbourg, 2008.

Jakubowska, Anna. *Der Bund der Vertriebenen in der Bundesrepublik Deutschland und Polen (1957–2004): Selbst- und Fremddarstellung eines Vertriebenenverbandes*. Marburg: Herder-Institut, 2012.

Kaube, Jürgen. "Bundesstiftung in der Krise: Flucht, Vertreibung, Verwirrung." *FAZ. net*, 15 November 2014. Accessed 12 October 2014. http://www.faz.net/stiftung-flucht-vertreibung-versoehnung-13264349.html.

Kellerhoff, Sven Felix. "Hitler-Deutschland trieb die Polen zur Mobilmachung. Erika Steinbach hat Recht: Die polnische Armee machte im März 1939 mobil. Doch Hitler hatte die Polen monatelang provoziert, weil er den Krieg wollte." *DIE WELT*, 9 September 2010. Accessed 4 November 2014. http://www.welt.de/politik/deutschland/article9501550/Hitler-Deutschland-trieb-die-Polen-zur-Mobilmachung.html.

Kellerhoff, Sven Felix. "Chefsache für die Vertriebenenstiftung ist ein Debakel." *DIE WELT*, 4 November 2015. Accessed 25 November 2015. http://www.welt.de/geschichte/article148412008/Chefsuche-fuer-Vertriebenenstiftung-ist-ein-Debakel.html.

Kittel, Manfred. *Vertreibung der Vertriebenen? Der historische deutsche Osten in der Erinnerungskultur der Bundesrepublik (1961–1982)*. Munich: Oldenbourg, 2007.

Kittel, Manfred, and Horst Möller. "Die Beneš-Dekrete und die Vertreibung der Deutschen im europäischen Vergleich" (The Beneš Decrees and the Expulsion of the Ethnic Germans Seen from a European Perspective). *Vierteljahrshefte für Zeitgeschichte* 54, no. 4 (2006): 541–81.

Kossert, Andreas. *Kalte Heimat: die Geschichte der deutschen Vertriebenen nach 1945*. Munich: Siedler, 2008.

Kunert, Andrzej Krzysztof, and Zygmunt Walkowski, eds. *Kronika kampanii wrześniowej 1939, Wydawnictwo Edipresse Polska*. Warsaw: Edipresse Książki, 2005.

Lotz, Christian, *Die Deutung des Verlusts. Erinnerungspolitische Kontroversen im geteilten Deutschland um Flucht, Vertreibung und die Ostgebiete (1948–1972)*. Cologne: Böhlau, 2007.

Madajczyk, Czesław. *Die Okkupationspolitik Nazideutschlands in Polen 1939–1945*. Cologne: Pahl-Rugenstein, 1988.

Madajczyk, Piotr. "'Das Zentrum gegen Vertreibungen,' das polnische und das deutsche historische Gedächtnis und die deutsch polnischen Erinnerungen." In *Definitionsmacht, Utopie, Vergeltung. "Ethnische Säuberung" im östlichen Europa des 20. Jahrhundert*, edited by Ulf Brunnbauer, 240–280. Berlin: Lit-Verlag, 2006.

Müller, Jan-Werner. "Constitutional Patriotism beyond the Nation-State: Human Rights, Constitutional Necessity, and the Limits of Pluralism." *Cardozo Law Review* 33 (2012): 1926–1933.

Rogasch, Wilfried, Katharina Klotz, and Doris Müller-Toovey. *Erzwungene Wege: Flucht und Vertreibung im Europa des 20. Jahrhunderts* (Ausstellung im Kronprinzenpalais, Berlin; eine Ausstellung der Stiftung Zentrum gegen Vertreibungen). Wiesbaden: Zentrum gegen Vertreibungen, 2006.

Röger, Maren. *Flucht, Vertreibung und Umsiedlung. Mediale Erinnerung und Debatten in Polen und Deutschland seit 1989*. Marburg: Herder-Institut, 2011.

Schulze Wessel, Martin. "Forum: Konzeptionelle Überlegungen für die Ausstellungen der Stiftung Flucht, Vertreibung, Versöhnung." *H-Soz-u-Kult Diskussionen*, 10 September 2010. Accessed 4 November 2014. http://hsozkult.geschichte.hu-berlin.de/forum/id=1355&type=diskussionen.

Schwartz, Michael. *Funktionäre mit Vergangenheit: das Gründungspräsidium des Bundes der Vertriebenen und das "Dritte Reich."* Munich: Oldenbourg, 2013.

Staněk, Tomáš. *Internierung und Zwangsarbeit: das Lagersystem in den böhmischen Ländern 1945–1948*. Munich: Oldenbourg, 2007.

Stickler, Matthias. *"Ostdeutsch heißt gesamtdeutsch." Organisation, Selbstverständnis und heimatpolitische Zielsetzungen der deutschen Vertriebenenverbände 1949–1972*. Düsseldorf: Droste, 2004.

Stiftung Flucht, Vertreibung, Versöhnung. Stiftung Grundlagenpapiere. "Law for the Establishment of a Foundation 'German Historical Museum.'" 21 December 2008 (Bundesgesetzblatt 2008, I, 2891), amended by article 1 of the law 14 June 2010

(Bundesgesetzblatt 2010, I, 784). Accessed 29 October 2014. http://sfvv.e-fork.net/stiftung/grundlagenpapiere/gesetz-2010.

Stiftung Flucht, Vertreibung, Versöhnung, ed. *Conceptual Framework for the Flight, Expulsion, Reconciliation Foundation and Guidelines for the Planned Permanent Exhibition.* Stiftung Flucht Vertreibung Versöhnung: no place, 2012. Accessed 29 October 2014. http://www.sfvv.de/sites/default/files/downloads/conceptual_framework_sfvv_2012.pdf.

Stiftung Flucht, Vertreibung, Versöhnung. "Schlaglichter auf die künftige Dauerausstellung der Stiftung Flucht, Vertreibung, Versöhnung." Accessed 12 October 2014. http://sfvv.de/de/temporare-ausstellungen.

Ther, Philipp. "The Integration of Expellees in Germany and Poland after World War II: A Historical Reassessment." *Slavic Review* 55 (1996): 779–805.

Ther, Philipp. *Die dunkle Seite der Nationalstaaten: "Ethnische Säuberungen" im modernen Europa.* Göttingen: Vandenhoeck & Ruprecht, 2011.

*Verhandlungen des Reichstages.* Vol. 460. Stenographische Protokolle 1939–1942, 4th Session, 6 October 1939. 51–63. Accessed 29 October 2014. www.reichstagsprotokolle.de/Blatt2_n4_bsb00000613_00052.html.

Völkering, Tim. *Flucht und Vertreibung im Museum: Zwei aktuelle Ausstellungen und ihre geschichtskulturellen Hintergründe im Vergleich.* Berlin: Lit-Verlag, 2008.

Wette, Wolfram. "Eine Gesellschaft im Umbruch: 'Entwurzelungserfahrungen' in Deutschland 1943–1948 und sozialer Wandel." In *Flucht und Vertreibung: Zwischen Aufrechnung und Verdrängung,* edited by Robert Streibel, 257–84. Vienna: Picus-Verlag, 1994.

**Martin Schulze Wessel** holds the chair of eastern and southeastern European history at the Ludwig-Maximilians-Universität (LMU), Munich. He is speaker at the Graduate School of Eastern and Southeastern European Studies of the LMU and the University of Regensburg, director of the research institute Collegium Carolinum, member of the Bavarian Academy of Science, and president of the German Historical Association. His main research interests are the history of religion in eastern central Europe and eastern Europe and the history of international relations between Germany, eastern Europe, and Russia. Among his publication are the monographs *Russlands Blick auf Preußen. Die polnische Frage in der Diplomatie und politischen Öffentlichkeit des Zarenreiches und des Sowjetstaates 1697–1947* (1995), and *Revolution und religiöser Dissens. Der römisch-katholische und der russisch-orthodoxe Klerus als Träger religiösen Wandels in den böhmischen Ländern und in Russland 1848–1922* (2011).

# Chapter 2

# A MISSING NARRATIVE
Displaced Persons in the History of Postwar West Germany

*Anna Holian*

Writing about displaced persons (DPs) in West German narratives of migration poses a number of problems. In the early postwar period, Germany was home to hundreds of thousands of DPs. They represented the remnants of Nazi Germany's continental policies of exploitation, deportation, and murder. However, DPs were entirely marginal to discussions about migration in West Germany, which instead focused on German refugees and expellees and, in later decades, on "guest workers," asylum seekers, and post-wall migrants from Eastern Europe. Today, a large scholarly literature on DPs exists. Still, it would be a stretch to say that marginality has been overcome. DPs continue to have little purchase on the public imagination in Germany. The narrative of displaced persons thus remains in many respects a missing narrative.

How does one locate something that is missing? What clues or traces of the missing object can be found? And how does one explain such an absence? These are the questions I address in this chapter. Drawing on newspaper articles, public speeches, government reports, and scholarly studies, I trace the contours of popular and scholarly discussion about DPs in Germany from the late 1940s to the present. I especially consider how West German narratives about DPs reproduced anti-Semitic and anti-Slav stereotypes. I situate these narratives in a broader European and North American context, examining in particular how conceptions of the "DP problem" were affected by the Cold War.

I identify three periods of German engagement with DPs, corresponding roughly to three periods in West Germany's postwar history: the years of postwar reconstruction, the long period of West German statehood in a divided Europe, and the waning years of the Cold War and

---

postunification period. During the first period, from 1945 until the early 1950s, displaced persons did in fact receive regular attention. However, this attention was overwhelmingly negative. In narratives colored by anti-Semitic and anti-Slav sentiments, DPs were depicted as an undue burden on a country struggling with its "own" refugee population. After the mid-1950s, negative interest was replaced by almost total silence. While the plight of German refugees remained a central issue, DPs became a footnote in Germany's migration history. Finally, the period since the mid-1980s has been characterized by newfound scholarly interest in DPs, but limited efforts at incorporating their history into broader migration narratives. Outside the scholarly context, Germany's DP history remains largely unknown.

## Displaced Persons in West(ern) Germany: An Overview

An administrative novelty, the term "displaced persons" was coined by the Allies in the context of planning for the postwar. It referred to "civilians outside the national boundaries of their country by reason of the war."[1] The goal was to return these individuals to their home countries as quickly as possible. The Allies further distinguished between "United Nations," "enemy," and "ex-enemy" DPs. Only UNDPs—that is, citizens of the victorious Allied states—were eligible for Allied assistance in the form of food, shelter, medical care, and help returning home.[2] Thus many refugees—including the millions of Germans who had fled or been expelled from Eastern Europe—did not qualify for assistance. Consequently, the term "DP" became attached to those displaced Europeans receiving Allied assistance, that is, UNDPs.

When the war ended, there were more than eight million (UN)DPs in Germany, out of a European total of about eleven million.[3] They included six million foreign civilian workers, two million prisoners of war, and 700,000 surviving concentration and extermination camp prisoners.[4] They also included a large but difficult to determine number of foreigners who had fled to Germany before the advancing Red Army. Most DPs quickly and willingly returned home. However, large numbers of displaced Eastern Europeans, principally from Poland, the Baltic countries, and the USSR, were unwilling or unable to return home. The reasons for this were multiple. Many DPs, especially concentration and extermination camp survivors, were initially too weak or sick to return home. They were also uncertain about the desirability of doing so. The changing political order in Eastern Europe played an important role here, as did general concerns about economic insecurity. For Jewish DPs, especially those from Poland, the primary concerns were the resurgence of anti-Semitism and the over-whelming sense that there was no one and nothing to come home to. Many DPs did in fact face the prospect of returning to homes that were no longer in the same country, and, in many cases, of being displaced yet again. For Soviet citizens, fear of being treated as collaborators was paramount. Finally, as noted above, many DPs were refugees of the first hour, having fled before the Red Army. Some had collaborated with the Germans and feared retribution, while others were simply trying to avoid ending up under Soviet rule, in most cases for the second time.

In September 1945, after the great wave of repatriations had concluded, there were still about 1.2 million DPs in the western occupation zones of Germany.[5] They formed the basis of a long-term DP population. They received Allied assistance via the United Nations Relief and Rehabilitation Administration (UNRRA) and later the International Refugee Organization (IRO). They were a growing source of tension between the USSR and the western Allies. In accordance with the Yalta Agreement, the American and British militaries assisted in the compulsory repatriation of more than two million displaced Soviet citizens. Over time, however, they became uneasy about the use of force and eventually withdrew their coopera-tion.[6] Soviet authorities nonetheless continued to insist on the return of their citizens. They complained bitterly about anti-Soviet propagandizing among DPs and accused the western Allies of protecting collaborators and war criminals.

Given the diversity of paths by which it was possible to become a dis-placed person, it should come as no surprise that DPs often had little in common. Indeed, the DP camps were riven by conflicts. The most visible ones were ethnonational. Although the camps were originally organized by citizenship status for the purposes of repatriation, this soon proved to be unworkable. The Nazis had ruthlessly exploited ethnonational ten-sions to divide, conquer—and, in the case of Jews, destroy—populations. It was unreasonable to expect groups with such a history to live together peacefully. Enforced identification with citizenship categories especially angered Jews, who had been persecuted and murdered by their fellow citizens; they demanded their own camps and recognition of Jews as a distinct group. Initially unwilling to accommodate such requests, the western Allies eventually relented.

DPs were also divided by politics, religion, class, regional origins, and wartime experiences. Ukrainian DPs offer a good example of these divisions. Coming from at least five countries—the USSR, Poland, Czechoslovakia, Romania, and Hungary—they had vastly different prewar histories, wartime experiences, and reasons for rejecting repatria-tion. They included both Soviet Ukrainian labor deportees who wanted to return home but feared the consequences, and staunch Polish Ukrainian anticommunists who had voluntarily collaborated with the Germans.

As the Allies sought to convince the remaining DPs to return home, new groups of Eastern Europeans began to arrive, fleeing many of the same things that kept those already in Germany from repatriating. Coming principally from Poland, Hungary, Romania, and Czechoslovakia, these people were not DPs in the original sense of the term, since their arrival in Germany postdated the end of hostilities. Nonetheless, in the political atmosphere of the early postwar, in which both antifascism and anticommunism were relevant, the western Allies, especially the Americans, were generally willing to help them. Jews escaping a resurgence of anti-Semitism in Poland and other Eastern European countries began arriving in the second half of 1945, their numbers increasing dramatically as Polish Jews evacuated or deported to the USSR returned home. By the spring of 1947, the Jewish DP population in western Germany had reached about 200,000.[7] Smaller numbers of non-Jews also began arriving shortly after the war, their numbers swelling as Sovietization intensified. The largest group came from Czechoslovakia; in the early 1950s, some 45,000 Czechoslovak refugees were reportedly living in the Federal Republic.[8]

At the end of 1947, there were still at least 560,000 DPs in the three western occupation zones, and probably many more.[9] By this point, the boundary between wartime and postwar displacement, and between DPs and refugees, had become significantly blurred. This state of affairs was officially acknowledged when the IRO replaced UNRRA in June 1947. As Daniel Cohen notes, "the IRO expanded the notion of displaced persons and brought it closer to the concept of political refugees."[10] All DPs, including former Nazi deportees (i.e., the vast majority of the original population), were offered the opportunity to express "valid objections" against returning home. Not surprisingly, this development further alienated the Soviet Union, which ultimately refused to sign on to the IRO.

With the transition from UNRRA to the IRO, efforts to resolve the so-called DP problem shifted. Eager to minimize their costs, the western Allies now looked to third-country resettlement as the solution. By the second half of 1947, real opportunities for emigration began to open up. Key moments in this process were the Canadian government's initiation of a labor migration program in June 1947, the proclamation of the state of Israel in May 1948, and the passage of the U.S. Displaced Persons Act in June 1948. Displaced persons began to leave in large numbers. By the end of 1951, the IRO had resettled 719,000 people from Germany.[11]

Nonetheless, the DP problem did not completely disappear, as many people were rejected for immigration or decided that they did not want to be uprooted again. At the end of 1951, there were still at least 140,000 and perhaps as many as 254,000 DPs in Germany, almost half of whom had arrived since the end of the war.[12] In April 1951, after much back-and-forth with the western Allies, the Federal Republic passed the Homeless Foreigners Law, and displaced persons officially became a West German responsibility. Relabeled *heimatlose Ausländer* (homeless foreigners), they enjoyed most of the same civil, social, and economic rights as West German citizens. They did not, however, have political rights. Similarly, they were not offered a special path to German citizenship and were not eligible for the kinds of generous financial assistance available to German refugees. They thus existed in a kind of twilight status, as semi-permanent guests. Continuing a process set in motion by the IRO, the German authorities closed numerous DP camps. The last of these, the Jewish camp of Föhrenwald on the outskirts of Munich, closed in February 1957, but many DPs continued living in German "refugee camps" for some time. The United Nations High Commissioner for Refugees (UNHCR) was entrusted with providing homeless foreigners with legal protection. Since many remained because they did not qualify for labor migration, and since the German government did little to help them find work or otherwise integrate, it is unlikely that DPs benefited much from the economic boom of the 1950s and 1960s. However, this issue has yet to be researched in any depth.

## The DP Problem circa 1950: Criminal Menace, Illegitimate Burden

Part of the difficulty in talking about displaced persons in German narratives of migration is the confusing nature of the term itself. As we have seen, it was an administrative innovation of the war years. It encompasses people with vastly different identifications and experiences. It thus obscures more than it reveals, swallowing up the complexity of wartime and postwar displacement in two small and undemonstrative words.

When looking at German DP narratives, it is important to keep this tendency towards "obscurantism" in mind. In early postwar Germany, the term "DPs" often functioned as a euphemism, masking German antipathy towards Jews, Poles, and other "Eastern" and "Asiatic" peoples. These groups had been the focus of German nationalist and racist anxieties since the late nineteenth century, with anti-Semitism an especially potent force. Building on these anxieties, the Nazis had defined Jews and Slavs as racial inferiors, to be subjugated, exploited, and, in the case of Jews, systematically murdered. In Germany and German-occupied territories, an elaborate set of regulations governed relations between Germans and their racial others, enforcing physical and social distance.

After 1945, discussions of race underwent a significant shift. As Nazi racial thinking was officially delegitimized, expressions of anti-Semitism became more muted. Germans became increasingly unwilling to "speak openly about Jews using racialized terms."[13] Public discussions of race instead centered on black occupation soldiers and their relationships with German women. At the same time, animosity towards Jews hardly disappeared. Privately, Germans continued to talk about Jews in the old anti-Semitic ways, and acts of violence against Jews and Jewish spaces (synagogues, cemeteries) were a regular occurrence.[14] Animosity towards Slavs and other "Eastern" peoples was not as virulent; nonetheless, many Germans continued to view Poles, Russians, etc. as inferiors.

In this context, the term "displaced person" served a useful purpose. It made it possible to circumvent the social taboo against open displays of anti-Semitism and anti-Slavism by offering ostensibly neutral language. In effect, it provided an alibi. The writer Ruth Andreas-Friedrich commented on this phenomenon at the time. "Displaced persons!" she wrote. "The lowest rank in the hierarchy of mankind. The papers complain about immorality in the relocation camps, the black marketeering in the barracks of the UNRRA. 'Asocial elements,' they criticize, and most likely they would like to add: There you are, it's the Jews again!"[15]

Other terms also served an alibi function. Frequently, Germans talked about *Ausländer* (foreigners) rather than "DPs." Indeed, the two terms were used interchangeably in the early postwar years, suggesting that Germans viewed DPs as mere outsiders with no claims on Germany. Sometimes Jews were included in the category of foreigners and sometimes they were separated out. Publicly, Jews were often referred to as *jüdische Mitbürger* (Jewish fellow citizens), since the term "Jews" itself had become problematic. An invention of the early postwar period, the phrase "Jewish fellow citizens" is generally associated with postwar German philosemitism. However, it could also be used to hide unreconstructed attitudes: consider, for example, a 1949 Munich police report about the black market, where the word "Jew" is crossed out and replaced by "Jewish fellow citizen."[16] Other terms tainted by association with Nazism continued to be openly employed. One of these, as the quotation from Andreas-Friedrich suggests, was "asocials," long used to refer to individuals who did not conform to social norms and now unavoidably laden with racial connotations.

In looking at German discussions of DPs, we therefore need to continuously look beneath the surface of language. Who do the terms "DPs" or "foreigners" really refer to in any given utterance? Does the use of such generic terms suggest an unwillingness to think about displaced persons as individuals with a specific history? Or do these terms function as code? To what extent are they used to hide anti-Semitic, anti-Polish, anti-Russian, etc., sentiments?

During the late 1940s and early 1950s, German engagement with the issue of migration focused overwhelmingly on ethnic Germans. Their flight and expulsion figured as one of the major tragedies of the war. As Robert Moeller writes, "it was the story of German suffering and the 'loss of the German east' that filled the halls of parliament, thick volumes of 'contemporary history,' movie screens, and the pages of daily newspapers and mass-circulation illustrated magazines."[17] Indeed, the focus on the German refugee problem was so single-minded that the term *Flüchtlinge* (refugees) became a synonym for specifically *German* refugees and expellees.[18] Together with German POWs in Soviet captivity, German refugees and expellees demonstrated that Germans—more precisely, non-Jewish and non-anti-Nazi Germans—were *also* victims of the war, by some accounts just as much so as the victims of German criminality.

Less frequently but nonetheless regularly, Germans also engaged with the DP presence. However, this engagement was by and large negative.[19] From the German perspective, displaced persons were an undesirable mass of foreigners burdening a country already struggling with its "own" refugee problem. This conception of the DP problem had two interrelated themes: criminality and the illegitimacy of DP claims to German assistance. Both focused on the material costs of the DP presence but aimed to alleviate the psychological burden of responsibility for wartime deportation, exploitation, and murder. Both played on anti-Semitic and anti-Slav stereotypes and aimed at discrediting DPs as recipients of assistance and as human beings.

Before examining these narratives, it is important to outline the circumstances from which they drew nourishment. During the occupation period, and to some extent beyond, Germans were forced to pay the major share of the costs of maintaining the DP population. Displaced persons also enjoyed certain advantages over Germans, such as higher food rations and priority access to housing. Although these advantages were limited in practice, they were deeply resented by the German population. Resentment at being forced to support DPs was augmented by the fact that the German authorities had little control over DPs (e.g., limited police power) and by the aforementioned Allied refusal to assist German refugees and expellees.

The narrative of DP criminality was the main means by which Germans apprehended the DP presence. The focal point of the general grumbling about DPs during the early postwar period, it was promoted by the

German press and the German authorities. It was not for the most part promoted by academics, although there were exceptions. Thus the Bonn legal scholar Walter Schätzel claimed in 1955 that the foreign refugees in Germany included "a disproportionate number of criminals, asocials, and people incapable of working."[20] Various illicit and immoral activities came under the heading of DP criminality, including petty thievery, robbery, and murder. Although all groups of DPs were identified with these crimes, a kind of racial typecasting also operated. Thus Jews were primarily associated with the black market, while Poles, Russians, and other non-Jews were primarily associated with violent crimes. According to Wolfgang Jacobmeyer, German officials deliberately exaggerated DP criminality. However, many officials were genuinely convinced of the DP threat. Reporting internally on crime in Bavaria, a Munich police official noted in 1950 that "the fact that *50% of DPs* [i.e., DP offenders] are involved in capital crimes like murder and robbery is especially noteworthy."[21] Regardless of whether or not this number is reliable, the author seemed to think it was.

Significantly, the narrative of DP criminality was also promoted by the Allied occupation forces. While the first cohorts of Allied soldiers (those who had fought their way into Germany) demonstrated a good deal of sympathy for the DPs, their post-hostilities replacements tended to see only layabouts and lawbreakers. Reports are legion of soldiers mistreating and falsely arresting DPs. The narrative of DP criminality was thus a shared German-Allied framework, in which the prejudices of each group reinforced and justified those of the other.[22]

The main focus of concern about criminal activity was the black market. Indeed, the black market was synonymous with DP criminality.[23] While most DPs entered the black market on a small scale, stories about DP criminality gave a very different impression. German newspapers and news magazines offered sensationalistic accounts about "wheeler dealers" and "career refugees."[24] Although all DPs were associated with the black market, the association was strongest in the case of Jewish DPs. For postwar Germans, the black market was first and foremost the domain of Eastern European Jews. The West German press played a significant role in promoting this idea. Drawing on the long-standing association of Jews with money, newspapers and news magazines told fantastical stories about Jewish DPs making millions off the misery of Germans. This was often done covertly, without referring to Jews as such. As David Heredia notes in his study of *Der Spiegel*, "anti-Semitic code words such as 'raking it in' and 'haggling,' 'profiteer' and 'war profiteer' [we]re used frequently conjuring up the image of the (East European) Jewish 'profiteers' and 'war profiteers' which had been hawked around after the First World War."[25]

Displaced persons' tendency towards criminality was explained in a number of ways. In some cases, it was defined situationally, as the product of wartime and postwar circumstances. Misguided Allied policies were held especially to blame. Special rights and privileges, so the argument went, "had led to idleness and produced the black market and other kinds of criminality."[26] In other cases, it was defined as the product of inherent criminal tendencies. Thus the Bavarian Central Office for Criminal Identification, Police Statistics, and Police Intelligence argued "that the 'social-ethical background' of many DPs was 'most seriously compromised' by previous convictions in their countries of origin and thus before their term of forced labor."[27] Similarly, the West German press presented Jewish DPs' supposed predominance on the black market as the product of their inherently money-grubbing nature. Indeed, the press suggested, Jewish DPs' desire for profit was so great that they treated the assistance they received as a tool for criminal activity.[28] In different ways, each of these arguments aimed at discrediting displaced persons, either by defining them as individuals unworthy of assistance or by defining assistance itself as part of the problem.

While the narrative of criminality focused on the everyday means by which displaced persons exploited the German population, the narrative of illegitimate claims to assistance focused on the larger institutional structures of the occupation. Displaced persons were defined as a burden arbitrarily foisted upon Germany by the Allies, whose refugee policies were driven by a "revenge mentality"[29] and whose conception of DP assistance "went far beyond the norms of international refugee law and the practices of other countries."[30] This narrative rested on the contention that the DP phenomenon had little to do with National Socialism. It drew sustenance from many of the same postwar circumstances as the narrative of criminality, but did not have the same level of popularity. Indeed, it was a minor narrative, articulated primarily by academics, but it is nonetheless important as part of a larger effort to define a West German politics free of Allied constraints.

There were three main variants of the illegitimacy argument. The first claimed that the connection between displacement and Nazism had ended when displaced persons refused to return home. The key exponent of this position was the legal scholar Eberhard Jahn, who wrote a number of studies about DPs for the *Institut für Besatzungsfragen* (Institute for Occupation Questions), a German think tank created in 1949 to advise the state of Württemberg-Hohenzollern (later Baden-Württemberg) on relations with the Allies.[31] Jahn and the institute acknowledged that millions of foreigners had been brought to Germany or German-controlled territory "more or less involuntarily" during the war.[32] However, they contended that Germany was no longer responsible for their fate:

> If, since the founding of the IRO [in December 1946], only 65,000 DPs have in fact decided to return to their homelands, one may presume that the DPs still remaining in Germany are no longer real DPs but rather people who will not or cannot return home on account of considerations of a political, social, or religious nature. The reasons for staying away cannot however be traced back to German actions during the Second World War, and the DP problem has with this shift lost its immediate connection to the events of the Second World War.[33]

From this perspective, displaced persons who refused to return home could no longer be defined as victims of National Socialism; they were postwar refugees. More precisely, they were refugees from communism.[34] The Munich legal scholar Heinrich Rogge concurred. In his estimation, the original "Nazi deportees" had become "refugees from countries behind the Iron Curtain."[35] Thus Germany was no longer responsible for them. Indeed, as Jahn stressed, the DP problem had become "a part of the general European refugee problem which has haunted the continent again and again since 1912."[36] It thus had to be resolved on a European or international level.

The second variant of the argument of illegitimate claims contended that there had never been a connection between DPs and National Socialism. This variant focused on Eastern Europeans who had fled to Germany and again hinged on anticommunism. According to Jahn, it was inappropriate to call these people DPs. If, in the case of deportees, "a certain connection to the National Socialist regime" could still be identified,

> [such a connection] is entirely missing in the case of those people who left their country after the end of the war on account of internal political upheavals, as is the case with many Poles, Hungarians, Yugoslavs, Bulgarians, and Czechs. Jews who use Germany as a stop along the road to Palestine, or who have been driven from the Eastern European states by new persecutions, are also cared for by the IRO and receive the same benefits as "displaced persons" in the narrower sense of the term.[37]

From Jahn's perspective, social and political events in postwar Eastern Europe were strictly "internal" matters. Even the postwar persecution of Jews had no connection to Nazism. The jurist Heinrich Rogge articulated a similar position, though he chose his words less carefully. In his view, the postwar Eastern European refugees were "fake" DPs who sought to make their cases more plausible through "emphatic hatred of all things German."[38] Like wartime deportees who refused to return home, then, postwar DPs were defined as part of a larger international refugee problem for which Germany bore no particular responsibility.

Finally, a third variant of the illegitimacy argument suggested that the DP problem was largely the fault of the DPs themselves or, more precisely, of their collaborationist activities. Here the connection between displacement and National Socialism was reframed to make DPs the agents of wartime criminality. Part of the more general association of DPs with criminality, this argument was normative in the Soviet bloc. However, it also occasionally surfaced in the West. Thus a 1965 book about the Friedland refugee transit camp noted that "all those who collaborated [at home] with National Socialism want to avoid their homeland."[39] The argument about wartime criminality could also be turned around, so that DPs appeared as anti-German rather than pro-German forces. Playing on the Nazi association of Slavs with a violent hatred of Germans, Walter Schätzel argued that the foreign refugees in Germany were the same people "who in their former homelands often took part in the expulsion of the Germans and in brutalities against them."[40]

Arguments about the illegitimacy of making Germany pay for the maintenance of displaced persons were not entirely wrong. As I have already suggested, the DP presence in Germany could not always be directly traced back to the Nazis. It is also true that many DPs were former collaborators. Nonetheless, there is no overlooking the fact that scholars like Jahn, Schätzel, and Rogge argued in bad faith. Their arguments were driven by the desire to minimize German responsibility for the DP phenomenon by simplifying or obscuring the relationship between displacement and National Socialism. They ignored or minimized a number of inconvenient facts. They refused to acknowledge a connection between Nazification and Sovietization in Eastern Europe. To quote Theodor Adorno, they ignored the fact that "the destiny of political entanglements involves a nexus of guilt."[41] They also vastly oversimplified why displaced persons did not return home. In particular, they obscured the fact that opposition to communism was not the main factor among Jewish DPs. Indeed, precisely because the Jewish DP presence was difficult to explain without invoking German responsibility, it was rarely mentioned in such arguments. This is not to say that the authors in question made an *exception* for Jewish DPs. Rather, playing on the ambiguities of the term "DP," they employed arguments that had little to do with Jews to explain why *all DPs* constituted an unfair burden.

Interestingly, none of these authors suggested that accepting refugees from communism was a good thing. Anticommunism was a key "integrating ideology" of the early Federal Republic.[42] One might therefore have expected the status of displaced persons to have improved as the Cold War developed. In the United States, for example, Eastern European refugees were the focus of crisscrossing projections. On the one hand, they were the subject of elaborate fantasies of escape and salvation; on the other, many Americans did not want to see them let into the country.[43] In Germany, however, the projections were more straightforward—that is, more straightforwardly negative. Perhaps because the German image of communism was so tightly bound with a racialized image of "the East," it was difficult to imagine Eastern Europeans as *victims* of communism.[44] The German authorities did occasionally find it useful, however, to support anticommunist refugees. For example, until the 1990s, the West German and Bavarian governments underwrote the Ukrainian Free University, an institution created by anticommunist Ukrainians. Still, support for such projects did not translate into more open general policies towards DPs.

It has often been noted that after 1945, Germans demonstrated a deep unwillingness to acknowledge the consequences of Nazi aggression.[45] This unwillingness expressed itself in a stubborn focus on German suffering and in halfhearted efforts at making amends. If further confirmation of this thesis is needed, early postwar narratives about displaced persons provide it. These narratives aimed not only at eliminating the material costs associated with the DP population but also at removing the psychological burden implied by these costs.[46] The DP presence was an unhappy reminder of the fact that the Nazis had persecuted, exploited, and murdered millions of people. Many Germans were willing to acknowledge that these things had happened, but they did not feel personally responsible for them. Nor did they feel much sense of connection to the victims, defined for many years as national and racial "others." Hence their deep resentment of being forced to pay for the care and maintenance of the DPs. Hence also their efforts to cast doubt on the credibility of DPs and to reframe the DP problem as part of a larger European or international one.

In her book on "the long shadow of the past," Aleida Assmann identifies five strategies of denial common in postwar Germany: cancellation, externalization, elimination, silence, and falsification.[47] At least three of these strategies were central to German narratives about DPs. First, displaced persons' postwar criminality was presented as *cancelling out* whatever crimes had been committed against them during the war and demonstrating that they were unworthy of assistance. Second, the DP problem was *externalized* as a product of misguided Allied policies or as a postwar Eastern European phenomenon. Third, the relationship between displacement and Nazism was *falsified* in that the DPs themselves were identified as agents of Nazism or wartime criminality more generally.

One can also identify a further strategy of denial: minimization. Here the relationship between displaced persons and National Socialism was not denied, but the violence inherent in the relationship was downplayed.

Frequently, a Nazi-Soviet comparison—in other words, a framework convenient to the Cold War context—helped achieve the desired effect. The jurist Heinrich Rogge took this strategy to the extreme, suggesting that many DPs "were happy to have escaped the Soviet regime through German deportation."[48] The Institute for Occupation Questions was more subtle. It began its discussion of Polish DPs with a long preamble about flight and deportation to the Soviet Union. Only afterwards did it note—briefly—that 3.5 million Poles were deported to Germany.[49] It thus suggested that Nazi policies were not much different from Soviet ones. The institute was also evasive regarding Jews. It noted that Jews had suffered the "hardest fate" of all foreigners deported to Germany but had difficulty explaining what had happened to them. It made no mention of extermination camps or industrial murder.[50]

To be sure, not all West Germans participated in minimizing the relationship between displacement and National Socialism or promoting the myth of DP criminality. Leading politicians such as Kurt Schumacher and Theodor Heuss repeatedly drew the West German public's attention to the persecution and murder of Jews, though they were also careful to define these crimes as the work of a minority.[51] Similarly, newspapers in both West and East Germany occasionally sought to show their readers what displaced persons were "really" like.[52] However, such efforts had a difficult time competing with the much larger stream of negative propaganda and with people's everyday perceptions, which reinforced the sense that it was the Germans and not the DPs who were the real victims of the war.

## The Disappearance of the Displaced Person

According to Konrad Jarausch, the departures of displaced persons from Germany "were greeted with mutual relief" and thus "left little trace in collective recollections."[53] In point of fact, many DPs remained in Germany semi-permanently. However, with the end of the occupation and its structures of assistance, the DP remnant became less visible and hence less "problematic." Jarausch's general conclusion is thus correct. By the mid-1950s, the negative discourse surrounding displaced persons had more or less disappeared, to be replaced by almost total silence. One thus has to dig rather deep to find any traces of their presence.

An obvious place to look for such traces is in material focusing on refugees. However, this turns out to be disappointing. During the late 1950s and 1960s, both popular and scholarly discussions about refugees continued to focus on ethnic Germans. Displaced persons were rarely mentioned. While German refugees and expellees were the subject of an extensive, intensely emotional discourse, there was a complete lack of interest in the situation of DPs.

A few examples will illustrate my point. The first is a 1957 English-language booklet entitled *After Ten Years*, published by the Bundesministerium für Vertriebene, Flüchtlinge und Kriegsgeschädigte (Federal Ministry for Expellees, Refugees, and War Victims).[54] Filled with articles by prominent West German politicians, government officials, and academics, it focuses on German refugees and prisoners of war. Through both text and image, it seeks to elicit sympathy for their plight. Only two pages (out of almost fifty) are devoted to the subject of "non-German refugees." These two pages provide a solid factual assessment of the situation of foreign refugees in Germany, but they are not very moving and do not include photographs. Interestingly, they were written by a representative of the UNHCR—in other words, a third party. The use of an outsider might suggest a new West German willingness to take responsibility for DPs and to accept criticism about their treatment. However, it can also be seen as evidence of a continued *unwillingness* to view DPs as a German issue. Despite incorporation into the West German state, rhetorically, DPs continued to be kept at arm's length.

This pessimistic interpretation is borne out by a comparison between the booklet and its German predecessor, the much weightier *10 Jahre nach der Vertreibung* (Ten Years after the Expulsion). Coming in at almost five hundred pages and consisting largely of newspaper extracts, it is a completely different text. It focuses exclusively on the flight and expulsion of Germans. There is no mention of DPs. The only traces of their existence are a few anxious newspaper articles about Polish exiles being lured home with the promise of land in Pomerania.[55] To the extent that one can locate a "DP presence," then, it is the menacing presence of Polish DPs stealing German land.

The inclusion of an article about DPs in the English-language version thus seems to have been largely for show. It was a performance, for the international community, of West Germany's goodwill towards foreigners. This goodwill, it was hoped, would be reciprocated with assistance for German refugees. In other words, even the article about displaced persons can be seen as part of a larger discourse about Germans.

My second example is the above-mentioned 1965 book about the Friedland transit camp, also published by the Federal Ministry for Expellees. Like my first example, the Friedland book devotes only a few pages to DPs. It does so in a decidedly schizophrenic manner. In a two-page section entitled "The Foreigners," displaced persons are alternately described as victims of Nazism and Nazi collaborators, and their presence in Germany is alternately presented as helpful and burdensome. Most peculiarly, the book tries to *incorporate* DPs into the story of German refugees. It notes that the two groups shared the common experience of westward flight. It also suggests, rather fancifully, that displaced persons helped Germans along the way. "All [the foreigners]," the author writes, "helped the manless German families in their flight, sometimes in a moving way."[56] It thus appears that the only path to emotional investment in the plight of displaced persons is through the story of ethnic Germans.

These few references are about all I have been able to find for the late 1950s and 1960s. By the mid-1960s, as the German refugee problem itself became much less urgent—and lost political traction—displaced persons disappeared more or less completely. To be fair, however, the situation was not much different elsewhere. After the mid-1950s, DPs no longer commanded the interest of government officials, scholars, or publics outside Germany. The DP problem had been seemingly resolved through resettlement, and there seemed to be no reason to recall it.

## The Return of the Displaced Person

For many years, then, displaced persons were more or less absent from German and international consciousness. Since the 1980s, however, there has been a surge of scholarly interest in DPs, which has only grown stronger since the collapse of the Soviet bloc.

It is difficult to know what initially stimulated this new interest, which developed almost simultaneously in the United States, Canada, Germany, and Israel. The waning of the Cold War no doubt played some role, although many early publications were still, as one author admits, "immersed in East-West tensions."[57] Perhaps more significant was the growth of interest in migrants, refugees, and ethnic identities. As migration and displacement became important issues on the contemporary political scene, and as ethnicity reemerged as a key category of self-identification, the study of DPs became compelling from the perspectives of both policy and experience. Indeed, much of the new research was carried out by DPs and their descendants; thus it often represented an effort to write one's "own" history—and to make this history a legitimate part of larger national narratives. The growth of interest in the Holocaust also played a significant role, overlapping with the developments outlined above to draw attention to the fate of Jewish DPs.

After 1990, the reconsideration of the Cold War era also came into the picture. In the context of a larger reconsideration of the postwar period, displaced persons came to be seen as a key focal point of Cold War tensions and as the main group around which the Cold War-era international refugee regime took shape.[58] For scholars from the former Soviet bloc, DPs also represented a lost chapter in the wartime and postwar history of their countries. From the late 1940s onwards, displaced persons had been a taboo topic, privately remembered but publicly "forgotten." To date, other previously restricted topics, in particular forced labor and POWs, have received more sustained attention, no doubt because they are more viscerally connected to the war. However, a number of scholars from Eastern Europe—and Eastern Europe specialists from other countries—have also investigated the DP question, often as part of a larger study of forced repatriation and its aftermath.[59]

Germany was central to the new scholarly interest in DPs that developed during the 1980s. Here an emerging consciousness of migration as a social force—connected to the transformation of "guest workers" into permanent members of West German society—converged with a strong interest in the history of Nazism. Wolfgang Jacobmeyer was the first of a new generation of German scholars to write about displaced persons.[60] Since the publication of his 1985 book, the German-language literature on DPs has grown enormously.[61] The history of Jewish DPs, central to any effort to understand Jewish life in Germany after 1945, has been especially well researched. There have also been a number of museum exhibits focusing on (or incorporating) DPs, thus bringing the subject to a wider audience.[62] Finally, one must also mention scholarly and public discussions about Nazi criminality. Although they usually end where the story of displaced persons begins, they have done a great deal to bring the Nazi treatment of Jews and foreigners to the attention of the German public.[63]

The new literature on displaced persons has not, however, been well integrated into mainstream German scholarship on migration. This is due in part to the fragmentation that plagues migration studies more generally, but it also seems to reflect the belief that displaced persons, for the most part temporary migrants, are not important subjects of German history.[64] The new literature on migration that has developed since the 1980s has tended to focus on the largest and most permanent groups of migrants. It thus moves from German refugees to "guest workers" to asylum seekers and beyond. Sometimes displaced persons are included, but more often they are not.[65] In particular, they are often excluded from discussions about *refugees*. For example, in an essay about refugees in Nordrhein-Westfalen since 1945, Uwe Kleinert reserves the term "refugees" for ethnic Germans, "in keeping," he states, "with the new research in contemporary history."[66] Similarly, in an essay about migration in

Niedersachsen during the late 1940s, Peter Marschalk distinguishes between "real refugees," on the one hand, and DPs and evacuees, on the other hand.[67] He makes no effort to explain what makes the refugee status of ethnic Germans any more real than that of DPs. This is quite striking, as German narratives of the early postwar period, however much they sought to absolve Germans of responsibility, had no problem identifying DPs as bona fide refugees.

The German difficulty in thinking about displaced persons as refugees is confirmed by my own experiences. My dissertation focused on politics and ideology among DPs. Whenever anyone in Germany asked me about my research, I would usually say that I was working on *Flüchtlinge* after World War II. I assumed most people would not be familiar with the concept of the displaced person, and in any case, I considered "refugee" a perfectly acceptable synonym. Inevitably, however, my interlocutors assumed I was working on German refugees and expellees. I, in turn, was puzzled by their assumption, since the history of the expulsions at that time occupied only a small place in my vision of the postwar refugee crisis. Indeed, it was through these encounters that I first realized how large a place the history of the expulsions occupies in German conceptions of postwar migration.

It is difficult to say what the future will bring. On the one hand, there is now a large German-language scholarly literature on DPs and some effort being made to bring their history to the attention of broader publics. The topic continues to attract young scholars. From an academic perspective, then, displaced persons are no longer a missing narrative. On the other hand, what is most striking about the contemporary moment is the resurgence of interest in German refugees and expellees. Contemporary presentations of their history are often uncannily reminiscent of the discourse of the early postwar period, with its highly emotive linguistic and visual style.[68] A key task for scholars of DP history is thus not only to critique the resurgence of deeply problematic narratives of German victimhood, but also to clarify why DPs are important to our understanding of German history. How did policies toward displaced persons set the stage for the later development of migration and refugee policies in Germany? How did German encounters with DPs shape postwar conceptions of "foreigners"? What happened to former DPs during the "economic miracle" of the 1950s and 1960s, when foreign labor again began to be imported? In short, DP scholars will themselves have to work harder at integrating displaced persons into Germany's migration history and at following DPs further into the postwar period, tracing what happened to "homeless foreigners" after they disappeared from German consciousness.[69]

# Notes

1. "Outline Plan for Refugees and Displaced Persons," 3 June 1944, Institut für Zeitgeschichte, Munich (IfZ), Fi 01.84.
2. Stateless persons and victims of Nazi persecution from "enemy" and "ex-enemy" countries were also given assistance.
3. Wolfgang Jacobmeyer, *Vom Zwangsarbeiter zum Heimatlosen Ausländer. Die Displaced Persons in Westdeutschland 1945–1951* (Göttingen: Vandenhoeck & Ruprecht, 1985), 42.
4. Ulrich Herbert, "Nicht entschädigungsfähig? Die Wiedergutmachungsansprüche der Ausländer," in *Arbeit, Volkstum, Weltanschauung. Über Fremde und Deutsche im 20. Jahrhundert* (Frankfurt a.M.: Fischer, 1995), 157–58.
5. Jacobmeyer, *Vom Zwangsarbeiter*, 82–4.
6. Nicholas Tolstoy, *The Secret Betrayal* (New York: Charles Scribner's Sons, 1977); Mark R. Elliott, *Pawns of Yalta: Soviet Refugees and America's Role in Their Repatriation* (Urbana: University of Illinois Press, 1982); Jacobmeyer, *Vom Zwangsarbeiter*, chap. 5.
7. Atina Grossmann, "From Victims to 'Homeless Foreigners': Jewish Survivors in Postwar Germany," in Rita Chin et al., *After the Nazi Racial State: Difference and Democracy in Germany and Europe* (Ann Arbor: University of Michigan Press, 2009), 55.
8. Jacques Vernant, *The Refugee in the Post-War World* (New Haven: Yale University Press, 1953), 80.
9. Jacobmeyer, *Vom Zwangsarbeiter*, 173. Many DPs were not captured by the statistics until they registered for resettlement. Those who feared repatriation typically preferred to live "under the radar."
10. Gerard Daniel Cohen, *In War's Wake: Europe's Displaced Persons in the Postwar Order* (New York: Oxford University Press, 2011), 33.
11. Vernant, *The Refugee in the Post-War World*, 145.
12. Ibid., 145–46. Even after the resettlement period, many DPs remained unaccounted for in official statistics.
13. Heide Fehrenbach, "Black Occupation Children and the Devolution of the Nazi Racial State," in Rita Chin et al., *After the Nazi Racial State*, 32.
14. Frank Stern, *The Whitewashing of the Yellow Badge: Antisemitism and Philosemitism in Postwar Germany* (Oxford: Pergamon Press, 1992).
15. Ruth Andreas-Friedrich, *Battleground Berlin: Diaries, 1945–1948*, trans. Anna Boerresen (New York: Paragon House, 1990), 159–60. See also Klaus Schulte, "'Was ist denn das überhaupt, ein Jude?': Anna Seghers' Einspruch anlässlich der antisemitischen Hetze gegen die Insassen der Berliner Transitlager für 'Displaced Persons' in der Presse der Vier-Sektoren-Stadt im Jahre 1948: Rekonstruktion, Lektüre, Kommentar," *Jahrbuch für Kommunikationsgeschichte* 4 (2002): 196; David Heredia, "*Der Spiegel* and the Image of Jews in Germany: The Early Years, 1947–1956," *Leo Baeck Institute Yearbook* 53 (2008): 84.
16. Stadtrat der Landeshauptstadt München, Polizeipräsidium, Kriminaluntersuchungsabteilung, "Schwarzer Markt (Sammelbericht)," 24 October 1949, Staatsarchiv München (StM), Polizeidirektion München (PolDir) 11367. On philosemitism, see Michael Brenner and Norbert Frei, "Zweiter Teil: 1950–1967. Konsolidierung," in *Geschichte der Juden in Deutschland von 1945 bis zur Gegenwart. Politik, Kultur und Gesellschaft* (Munich: C.H. Beck, 2012), 239; Grossmann, "From Victims to 'Homeless Foreigners,'" 76.
17. Robert G. Moeller, *War Stories: The Search for a Usable Past in the Federal Republic of Germany* (Berkeley: University of California Press, 2001), 13.
18. As in the following article, devoted exclusively to German refugees: Friedrich Edding, "Das Flüchtlingsproblem in Westdeutschland," *Weltwirtschaftliches Archiv* 62 (1949).

19. On this issue, see also Jacobmeyer, *Vom Zwangsarbeiter*, chap. 8.
20. Walter Schätzel, "Die Staatsangehörigkeit der politischen Flüchtlinge," *Archiv des Völkerrechts* 5, no. 1–2 (March 1955): 77.
21. K1, "Mitgliederversammlung des Bayerischen Landesverbandes für Gefangenen-fürsorge," 16 May 1950, StM, PolDir 11418. Emphasis in original.
22. Jacobmeyer, *Vom Zwangsarbeiter*, 208–9; Michael Berkowitz, *The Crime of My Very Existence: Nazism and the Myth of Jewish Criminality* (Berkeley: University of California Press, 2007), 198–205.
23. Jacobmeyer, *Vom Zwangsarbeiter*, 211.
24. Heredia, "*Der Spiegel* and the Image of Jews in Germany," 83.
25. Ibid., 83–4. See also Schulte, "'Was ist denn das überhaupt, ein Jude?,'" 196.
26. Jacobmeyer, *Vom Zwangsarbeiter*, 204.
27. Ibid., 212.
28. Heredia, "*Der Spiegel* and the Image of Jews in Germany," 85.
29. Heinrich Rogge, "Zum internationalen Abkommen über die Rechtsstellung der Flüchtlinge vom 28. Juli 1951," *Integration* 1 (1954): 200.
30. Eberhard Jahn, "Das DP-Problem in Deutschland," in *Das deutsche Flüchtlingsproblem*, ed. Institut für Raumforschung (Bielefeld: F. Eilers, 1950), 102.
31. Jahn seems to have authored all of the institute's DP studies. However, the official author is in most cases the institute itself.
32. Institut für Besatzungsfragen, *Sechs Jahre Besatzungslasten. Eine Untersuchung des Problems der Besatzungskosten in den drei Westzonen und in Westberlin, 1945–1950* (Tübingen: J.C.B. Mohr, 1951), 193.
33. Institut für Besatzungsfragen, *Das DP-Problem. Eine Studie über die ausländischen Flüchtlinge in Deutschland* (Tübingen: J.C.B. Mohr, 1950), 2. See also Institut für Besatzungsfragen, *Sechs Jahre Besatzungslasten*, 197–98.
34. Jahn, "Das DP-Problem in Deutschland," 102.
35. Rogge, "Zum internationalen Abkommen," 203.
36. Jahn, "Das DP-Problem in Deutschland," 102.
37. Institut für Besatzungsfragen, *Sechs Jahre Besatzungslasten*, 194.
38. Rogge, "Zum internationalen Abkommen," 203.
39. Günther Meinhardt, *20 Jahre Lager Friedland* (Bonn: Bundesministerium für Vertriebene, Flüchtlinge und Kriegsgeschädigte, 1965), 48.
40. Schätzel, "Die Staatsangehörigkeit der politischen Flüchtlinge," 77.
41. Theodor W. Adorno, "What Does Coming to Terms with the Past Mean?" in *Bitburg in Moral and Political Perspective*, ed. Geoffrey H. Hartman (Bloomington: Indiana University Press, 1986), 120.
42. Eric D. Weitz, "The Ever-Present Other: Communism in the Making of West Germany," in *The Miracle Years: A Cultural History of West Germany, 1949–1968*, ed. Hanna Schissler (Princeton: Princeton University Press, 2001).
43. Susan L. Carruthers, *Cold War Captives: Imprisonment, Escape, and Brainwashing* (Berkeley: University of California Press, 2009).
44. Moeller, *War Stories*.
45. Hannah Arendt, "The Aftermath of Nazi Rule: Report from Germany," *Commentary* 10 (January 1950); Adorno, "What Does Coming to Terms with the Past Mean?"; Alexander Mitscherlich and Margarete Mitscherlich, *The Inability to Mourn: Principles of Collective Behavior* (New York: Grove Press, 1975).
46. See also Jacobmeyer, *Vom Zwangsarbeiter*, 215; Heredia, "*Der Spiegel* and the Image of Jews in Germany," 79.

47. Aleida Assmann, *Der lange Schatten der Vergangenheit. Erinnerungskultur und Geschichtspolitik* (Munich: C.H. Beck, 2006), chap. 6.
48. Rogge, "Zum internationalen Abkommen," 203.
49. Institut für Besatzungsfragen, *Das DP-Problem*, 16.
50. Ibid., 19.
51. Brenner and Frei, "Zweiter Teil: 1950–1967. Konsolidierung," 239.
52. For the West, see M.W., "Polacken?," *Der Ruf*, 15 November 1947; for the East, see Schulte, "'Was ist denn das überhaupt, ein Jude?'"
53. Konrad Hugo Jarausch and Michael Geyer, *Shattered Past: Reconstructing German Histories* (Princeton: Princeton University Press, 2003), 209.
54. Bundesministerium für Vertriebene, Flüchtlinge und Kriegsgeschädigte, *After Ten Years: A European Problem, Still No Solution* (Frankfurt a.M.: Wirtschaftsdienst Verlag und Druckerei, 1957), 34–5. See also Bundesministerium für Vertriebene, Flüchtlinge und Kriegsgeschädigte, *Care and Help for Expellees, Refugees, Victims of Material War Damage, Evacuees, Prisoners of War and Civilian Prisoners of War and Civilian Prisoners, Repatriated Persons [and] Non-German Refugees.* (Bonn: Bundesministerium für Vertriebene, Flüchtlinge und Kriegsgeschädigte, 1964).
55. Bundesministerium für Vertriebene, Flüchtlinge und Kriegsgeschädigte, *10 Jahre nach der Vertreibung. Äusserungen des In- und Auslandes und eine Zeittafel* (Bonn: Bundesministerium für Vertriebene, Flüchtlinge und Kriegsgeschädigte, 1956), 305–6.
56. Meinhardt, *20 Jahre Lager Friedland*, 48.
57. Mark Wyman, *DP: Europe's Displaced Persons, 1945–1951* (Ithaca: Cornell University Press, 1998), 1.
58. Kim Salomon, *Refugees in the Cold War: Towards a New International Refugee Regime in the Early Postwar Era* (Lund: Lund University Press, 1991); Cohen, *In War's Wake*.
59. Viktor Nikolaevich Zemskov, "Rozhdenie 'vtoroi emigratsii' 1944–1952," *Sotsiologicheskie issledovaniia* 4 (1991); Czesław Łuczak, *Polacy w okupowanych Niemczech 1945–1949* (Poznań: Pracownia Serwisu Oprogramowania, 1993); Viktor Nikolaevich Zemskov, "Repatriatsiia sovetskikh grazhdan i ikh dal'neishaia sud'ba (1944–1956 rr.)," *Sotsiologicheskie issledovaniia* 6 (1995); Pavel Polian, *Against Their Will: The History and Geography of Forced Migrations in the USSR* (Budapest: Central European University Press, 2004); Ulrike Goeken-Haidl, *Der Weg zurück. Die Repatriierung sowjetischer Zwangsarbeiter und Kriegsgefangener während und nach dem Zweiten Weltkrieg* (Essen: Klartext, 2006).
60. Jacobmeyer, *Vom Zwangsarbeiter.*
61. Important works include Juliane Wetzel, *Jüdisches Leben in München 1945–1951. Durchgangsstation oder Wiederaufbau?* (Munich: Kommissionsverlag UNI-Druck, 1987); Ulrich Müller, *Fremde in der Nachkriegszeit. Displaced persons—zwangsverschleppte Personen—in Stuttgart und Württemberg-Baden 1945–1951* (Stuttgart: Klett-Cotta, 1990); Michael Brenner, *After the Holocaust: Rebuilding Jewish Lives in Postwar Germany* (Princeton: Princeton University Press, 1997); Patrick Wagner, *Displaced Persons in Hamburg. Stationen einer halbherzigen Integration 1945 bis 1958* (Hamburg: Dölling und Galitz, 1997); Angelika Königseder, *Flucht nach Berlin. Jüdische Displaced Persons 1945–1948* (Berlin: Metropol, 1998); Angelika Eder, *Flüchtige Heimat. Jüdische Displaced Persons in Landsberg am Lech 1945 bis 1950* (Munich: Kommissionsverlag UNI-Druck, 1998); Tamar Lewinsky, *Displaced Poets. Jiddische Schriftsteller im Nachkriegsdeutschland, 1945–1951* (Göttingen: Vandenhoeck & Ruprecht, 2008).
62. For example, the new permanent exhibit at the Dachau Concentration Camp Memorial Site, installed in 2003, contains extensive material about DPs. There have also been two recent exhibits about Jewish DPs: "Juden 45/90. Von da und dort – Überlebende

aus Osteuropa," Jüdisches Museum München (November 2011–June 2012); "Jüdisches Leben in Augsburg nach der Katastrophe, Teil 1. GEHEN? oder BLEIBEN! Lebenswelten osteuropäischer und deutscher Juden in der Nachkriegszeit, 1945–1950," Jüdisches Kulturmuseum Augsburg Schwaben (May–December 2012).

63. Works that make the connection to DPs explicit include Ulrich Herbert, *Fremdarbeiter. Politik und Praxis des "Ausländer-Einsatzes" in der Kriegswirtschaft des Dritten Reiches* (Berlin: J.H.W. Dietz, 1985); Ulrich Herbert, *Arbeit, Volkstum, Weltanschauung. Über Fremde und Deutsche im 20. Jahrhundert* (Frankfurt a.M.: Fischer, 1995); Andreas Heusler, *Ausländereinsatz. Zwangsarbeit für die Münchner Kriegswirtschaft 1939–1945* (Munich: Hugendubel, 1996).

64. Jarausch and Geyer, *Shattered Past*, 199.

65. They are well integrated in Klaus J. Bade, *Deutsche im Ausland, Fremde in Deutschland. Migration in Geschichte und Gegenwart* (Munich: C.H. Beck, 1992).

66. Uwe Kleinert, "Die Flüchtlinge als Arbeitskräfte – zur Eingliederung der Flüchtlinge in Nordrhein-Westfalen nach 1945," in *Neue Heimat im Westen. Vertriebene, Flüchtlinge, Aussiedler*, ed. Klaus J. Bade (Münster: Westfälischer Heimatbund, 1990), 58 fn 1.

67. Peter Marschalk, "Bevölkerung und Wanderung im Raum Niedersachsen seit dem Zweiten Weltkrieg," in *Fremde im Land. Zuwanderung und Eingliederung im Raum Niedersachsen seit dem Zweiten Weltkrieg*, ed. Klaus J. Bade (Osnabrück: Rasch, 1997), tables 3 and 5.

68. This is most obvious in the work of the Stiftung Flucht, Vertreibung, Versöhnung. See their website, accessed 8 September 2013: http://www.sfvv.de/.

69. Two recent books that pursue the aim of integration are Atina Grossmann, *Jews, Germans, and Allies: Close Encounters in Occupied Germany* (Princeton: Princeton University Press, 2007) and Adam Seipp, *Strangers in the Wild Place: Refugees, Americans, and a German Town, 1945–1952* (Bloomington: Indiana University Press, 2013). An important earlier article is Frank Stern, "The Historic Triangle: Occupiers, Germans, and Jews in Postwar Germany," *Tel Aviver Jahrbuch für deutsche Geschichte* 19 (1990).

# Works Cited

Adorno, Theodor W. "What Does Coming to Terms with the Past Mean?" In *Bitburg in Moral and Political Perspective*, edited by Geoffrey H. Hartman. Bloomington: Indiana University Press, 1986.

Andreas-Friedrich, Ruth. *Battleground Berlin: Diaries, 1945–1948*. Translated by Anna Boerresen. New York: Paragon House, 1990.

Arendt, Hannah. "The Aftermath of Nazi Rule: Report from Germany." *Commentary* 10 (January 1950).

Assmann, Aleida. *Der lange Schatten der Vergangenheit. Erinnerungskultur und Geschichtspolitik*. Munich: C.H. Beck, 2006.

Bade, Klaus J. *Deutsche im Ausland, Fremde in Deutschland. Migration in Geschichte und Gegenwart*. Munich: C.H. Beck, 1992.

Berkowitz, Michael. *The Crime of My Very Existence: Nazism and the Myth of Jewish Criminality*. Berkeley: University of California Press, 2007.

Brenner, Michael. *After the Holocaust: Rebuilding Jewish Lives in Postwar Germany*. Princeton: Princeton University Press, 1997.

Brenner, Michael, and Norbert Frei. "Zweiter Teil: 1950–1967. Konsolidierung." In *Geschichte der Juden in Deutschland von 1945 bis zur Gegenwart. Politik, Kultur und Gesellschaft*. Munich: C.H. Beck, 2012.

Bundesministerium für Vertriebene, Flüchtlinge und Kriegsgeschädigte. *10 Jahre nach der Vertreibung. Äusserungen des In- und Auslandes und eine Zeittafel*. Bonn: Bundesministerium für Vertriebene, Flüchtlinge und Kriegsgeschädigte, 1956.

Bundesministerium für Vertriebene, Flüchtlinge und Kriegsgeschädigte. *After Ten Years: A European Problem, Still No Solution*. Frankfurt a.M.: Wirtschaftsdienst Verlag und Druckerei, 1957.

Bundesministerium für Vertriebene, Flüchtlinge und Kriegsgeschädigte. *Care and Help for Expellees, Refugees, Victims of Material War Damage, Evacuees, Prisoners of War and Civilian Prisoners of War and Civilian Prisoners, Repatriated Persons [and] Non-German Refugees*. Bonn: Bundesministerium für Vertriebene, Flüchtlinge und Kriegsgeschädigte, 1964.

Carruthers, Susan L. *Cold War Captives: Imprisonment, Escape, and Brainwashing*. Berkeley: University of California Press, 2009.

Cohen, Gerard Daniel. *In War's Wake: Europe's Displaced Persons in the Postwar Order*. New York: Oxford University Press, 2011.

Edding, Friedrich. "Das Flüchtlingsproblem in Westdeutschland." *Weltwirtschaftliches Archiv* 62 (1949).

Eder, Angelika. *Flüchtige Heimat. Jüdische Displaced Persons in Landsberg am Lech 1945 bis 1950*. Munich: Kommissionsverlag UNI-Druck, 1998.

Elliott, Mark R. *Pawns of Yalta: Soviet Refugees and America's Role in Their Repatriation*. Urbana: University of Illinois Press, 1982.

Fehrenbach, Heide. "Black Occupation Children and the Devolution of the Nazi Racial State." In Rita Chin et al., *After the Nazi Racial State: Difference and Democracy in Germany and Europe*. Ann Arbor: University of Michigan Press, 2009.

Goeken-Haidl, Ulrike. *Der Weg zurück. Die Repatriierung sowjetischer Zwangsarbeiter und Kriegsgefangener während und nach dem Zweiten Weltkrieg*. Essen: Klartext, 2006.

Grossmann, Atina. *Jews, Germans, and Allies: Close Encounters in Occupied Germany*. Princeton: Princeton University Press, 2007.

Grossmann, Atina. "From Victims to 'Homeless Foreigners': Jewish Survivors in Postwar Germany." In Rita Chin et al., *After the Nazi Racial State: Difference and Democracy in Germany and Europe*. Ann Arbor: University of Michigan Press, 2009.

Herbert, Ulrich. *Fremdarbeiter. Politik und Praxis des "Ausländer-Einsatzes" in der Kriegswirtschaft des Dritten Reiches*. Berlin: J.H.W. Dietz, 1985.

Herbert, Ulrich. *Arbeit, Volkstum, Weltanschauung. Über Fremde und Deutsche im 20. Jahrhundert*. Frankfurt a.M.: Fischer, 1995.

Heredia, David. "*Der Spiegel* and the Image of Jews in Germany: The Early Years, 1947–1956." *Leo Baeck Institute Yearbook* 53 (2008).

Heusler, Andreas. *Ausländereinsatz. Zwangsarbeit für die Münchner Kriegswirtschaft 1939–1945*. Munich: Hugendubel, 1996.

Institut für Besatzungsfragen. *Das DP-Problem. Eine Studie über die ausländischen Flüchtlinge in Deutschland*. Tübingen: J.C.B. Mohr, 1950.

Institut für Besatzungsfragen. *Sechs Jahre Besatzungslasten. Eine Untersuchung des Problems der Besatzungskosten in den drei Westzonen und in Westberlin, 1945–1950*. Tübingen: J.C.B. Mohr, 1951.

Jacobmeyer, Wolfgang. *Vom Zwangsarbeiter zum Heimatlosen Ausländer. Die Displaced Persons in Westdeutschland 1945–1951*. Göttingen: Vandenhoeck & Ruprecht, 1985.

Jahn, Eberhard. "Das DP-Problem in Deutschland." In *Das deutsche Flüchtlingsproblem*, edited by Institut für Raumforschung. Bielefeld: F. Eilers, 1950.

Jarausch, Konrad Hugo, and Michael Geyer. *Shattered Past: Reconstructing German Histories*. Princeton: Princeton University Press, 2003.

Kleinert, Uwe. "Die Flüchtlinge als Arbeitskräfte – zur Eingliederung der Flüchtlinge in Nordrhein-Westfalen nach 1945." In *Neue Heimat im Westen. Vertriebene, Flüchtlinge, Aussiedler*, edited by Klaus J. Bade. Münster: Westfälischer Heimatbund, 1990.

Königseder, Angelika. *Flucht nach Berlin. Jüdische Displaced Persons 1945–1948*. Berlin: Metropol, 1998.

Lewinsky, Tamar. *Displaced Poets. Jiddische Schriftsteller im Nachkriegsdeutschland, 1945–1951*. Göttingen: Vandenhoeck & Ruprecht, 2008.

Łuczak, Czesław. *Polacy w okupowanych Niemczech 1945–1949*. Poznań: Pracownia Serwisu Oprogramowania, 1993.

M.W. "Polacken?" *Der Ruf*, 15 November 1947.

Marschalk, Peter. "Bevölkerung und Wanderung im Raum Niedersachsen seit dem Zweiten Weltkrieg." In *Fremde im Land. Zuwanderung und Eingliederung im Raum Niedersachsen seit dem Zweiten Weltkrieg*, edited by Klaus J. Bade. Osnabrück: Rasch, 1997.

Meinhardt, Günther. *20 Jahre Lager Friedland*. Bonn: Bundesministerium für Vertriebene, Flüchtlinge und Kriegsgeschädigte, 1965.

Mitscherlich, Alexander, and Margarete Mitscherlich. *The Inability to Mourn: Principles of Collective Behavior*. New York: Grove Press, 1975.

Moeller, Robert G. *War Stories: The Search for a Usable Past in the Federal Republic of Germany*. Berkeley: University of California Press, 2001.

Müller, Ulrich. *Fremde in der Nachkriegszeit. Displaced persons—zwangsverschleppte Personen—in Stuttgart und Württemberg-Baden 1945–1951*. Stuttgart: Klett-Cotta, 1990.

Polian, Pavel. *Against Their Will: The History and Geography of Forced Migrations in the USSR*. Budapest: Central European University Press, 2004.

Rogge, Heinrich. "Zum internationalen Abkommen über die Rechtsstellung der Flüchtlinge vom 28. Juli 1951." *Integration* 1 (1954).

Salomon, Kim. *Refugees in the Cold War: Towards a New International Refugee Regime in the Early Postwar Era*. Lund: Lund University Press, 1991.

Schätzel, Walter. "Die Staatsangehörigkeit der politischen Flüchtlinge." *Archiv des Völkerrechts* 5, no. 1–2 (March 1955).

Schulte, Klaus. "'Was ist denn das überhaupt, ein Jude?': Anna Seghers' Einspruch anlässlich der antisemitischen Hetze gegen die Insassen der Berliner Transitlager für 'Displaced Persons' in der Presse der Vier-Sektoren-Stadt im Jahre 1948: Rekonstruktion, Lektüre, Kommentar." *Jahrbuch für Kommunikationsgeschichte* 4 (2002).

Seipp, Adam. *Strangers in the Wild Place: Refugees, Americans, and a German Town, 1945–1952*. Bloomington: Indiana University Press, 2013.

Stern, Frank. "The Historic Triangle: Occupiers, Germans, and Jews in Postwar Germany." *Tel Aviver Jahrbuch für deutsche Geschichte* 19 (1990).

Stern, Frank. *The Whitewashing of the Yellow Badge: Antisemitism and Philosemitism in Postwar Germany*. Oxford: Pergamon Press, 1992.

Tolstoy, Nicholas. *The Secret Betrayal*. New York: Charles Scribner's Sons, 1977.

Vernant, Jacques. *The Refugee in the Post-War World*. New Haven: Yale University Press, 1953.

Wagner, Patrick. *Displaced Persons in Hamburg. Stationen einer halbherzigen Integration 1945 bis 1958*. Hamburg: Dölling und Galitz, 1997.

Weitz, Eric D. "The Ever-Present Other: Communism in the Making of West Germany." In *The Miracle Years: A Cultural History of West Germany, 1949–1968*, edited by Hanna Schissler. Princeton: Princeton University Press, 2001.

Wetzel, Juliane. *Jüdisches Leben in München 1945–1951. Durchgangsstation oder Wiederaufbau?* Munich: Kommissionsverlag UNI-Druck, 1987.

Wyman, Mark. *DP: Europe's Displaced Persons, 1945–1951*. Ithaca: Cornell University Press, 1998.

Zemskov, Viktor Nikolaevich. "Rozhdenie 'vtoroi emigratsii' 1944–1952." *Sotsiologicheskie issledovaniia* 4 (1991).

Zemskov, Viktor Nikolaevich. "Repatriatsiia sovetskikh grazhdan i ikh dal'neishaia sud'ba (1944–1956 rr.)." *Sotsiologicheskie issledovaniia* 6 (1995).

**Anna Holian** is associate professor of modern European history at Arizona State University. She is the author of *Between National Socialism and Soviet Communism: Displaced Persons in Postwar Germany (2011)*. She is currently working on a book about "war children" in European films of the 1940s and 1950s. She is also a member of the Holocaust Geographies Collaborative, which studies the Holocaust from a spatial perspective.

# Chapter 3

# INCLUSION AND EXCLUSION OF IMMIGRANTS AND THE POLITICS OF LABELING

Thinking Beyond "Guest Workers," "Ethnic German Resettlers," "Refugees of the European Crisis," and "Poverty Migration"

*Asiye Kaya*

"Poor, young, smart immigrant"[1] was the title of an article in the prestigious weekly German newspaper *Die Zeit*, suggesting a positive outlook on the fresh wave of skilled immigrants from member countries of the European Union (EU).[2] According to the article, the predominantly young and highly qualified new immigrants were citizens of the EU and came to Germany mainly from Greece, Spain, Italy, Portugal, Romania, Bulgaria and Hungary.[3] It highlighted the record number of new immigrants in 2012. After taking arrivals and departures into account, the total number of immigrants in 2012 was 340,000, the highest since the 1990s.[4] Despite presenting this new immigration as a positive development; the article nevertheless underscored a warning by Hans-Peter Friedrich, then federal minister of the interior from the conservative Christian Social Union (CSU). Addressing the movement of people from Romania and Bulgaria within the EU, Friedrich cautioned against possible "poverty migration" and raised the "fear of poor Roma." The article underlined Friedrich's concern that the new immigrants and their families, "driven by poverty," might be coming to Germany with their families to apply for welfare, and in Friedrich's words, might "destroy the social peace" in Germany.[5] Earlier, in 2013, Friedrich, in his position as the minister of the interior, had requested that the EU control the borders and reinstitute bans on "some" EU citizens. His request for a selectively restrictive policy was targeted mostly at the Roma population from the member states of Bulgaria, Romania, and Hungary.[6] This group would have had work restrictions

**FIGURE 3.1** "Die neuen Gastarbeiter: Europas junge Elite für Deutschlands Wirtschaft,"
*Der Spiegel*, 9 September 2013, cover page.

removed after 2014, which would have resulted in the same freedom of movement within the EU as that of other EU citizens.[7] This discriminatory policy request provoked a debate on the new waves of immigration to Germany, and on the double standards in the integration and migration policies applied for decades to various immigrant groups in Germany. Moreover, the new immigration wave, Germany's response to it, and the related debates show that Germany can no longer see immigration solely as an internal issue, but must consider it in the context of the European Union.

Historically, Germany has used selective integration measures for different immigrant groups. Furthermore, both politically and sociohistorically, immigrants in West Germany have been categorized in various ways since the beginning of each wave of immigration in the aftermath of

World War II. This policy of labeling,[8] along with differentiated integration policies, has caused structures of inclusion and exclusion, which in turn have determined the experiences of immigrants in German society. The clearest examples of this double standard were the policies developed for ethnic German resettlers versus those for post–World War II labor migrants. Symbolically, "guest workers"[9] from Turkey and their offspring were considered to be representatives of the latter category in West Germany. Related policies are rooted in the perceived non-assimilation of this population and its descendants, and, more bluntly, in the notion that labor migrants are unquestionably different and incongruous with German society, and that their integration is not possible. Furthermore, they are largely viewed as "the most problematic" immigrant group in post–World War II immigration history in Germany. Considered homogenously as both non-European and Islamic, they are labeled as Muslims, a group suspected of posing a threat to the German democratic order and the nation. In contrast, the immigration—or rather "returning home"—of ethnic German resettlers is characterized by institutional structures that help a group exhibiting perceived "sameness" in ethnicity, religion, and language settle in Germany. As a result of favorable migration policies and extensive integration policies, ethnic German resettlers, especially those who arrived before the 1990s and who could not return during the Cold War, as well as some who arrived following the end of the Cold War in 1991 and the collapse of the Soviet Union until 1993 are today seen as relatively integrated when compared to those whose families migrated from Turkey. The different treatment of these immigrant groups existed until the state's declaration in 2005 that Germany was in fact an immigration country, and the introduction of its first official integration programs. However, as I explore in this chapter, the outcomes for ethnic German resettlers differed from those of immigrants from Turkey. While the perceived sameness of ethnic German resettlers resulted primarily in the experience of social and structural inclusion as well as privilege, the perceived difference of immigrants from Turkey and their descendants resulted for the most part in social and structural exclusion and institutionalized discrimination.

More precisely, this chapter discusses how structural inclusion and exclusion of immigrants and their descendants in Germany is intertwined with the politics of sameness and difference, which is discursively (re) produced in both the public and political spheres.

Against this backdrop, I examine what role the differentiated treatment of these two immigrant groups and their descendants by way of German migration and integration policies played in their representations in Germany. I furthermore examine the new wave of migration from established and new EU member countries. I am also interested in how related public and political debates repeat older structures of West German migration and integration policies since the 1950s.

The chapter is divided into three sections, each focusing mainly on a group or groups and correlated integration policies. The first deals with the post–World War II labor migration period with a focus on immigrants from Turkey, and how the non-integration policies in Germany affected this immigrant group and their descendants. Beginning with a brief illustration of the labor recruitment programs between 1955 and 1973, I discuss how all stakeholders (companies that invited workers, states, and immigrants) dealt with the uncertainty of the labor recruitment programs during their first decades. I also discuss how the politics of labeling based on ethnocultural and religious differences was practiced in public and political discourse since the beginning of the 1960s. This politics of exclusion was reproduced and implemented in relation to the succeeding generation as well. The second section focuses on the experience of ethnic German resettlers and the advantageous integration policies implemented due to their status as belonging to the German people (*Volksdeutsche*). Following a brief legal and historical contextualization of this group of immigrants, I focus mainly on the integration policies applied particularly in the 1980s and 1990s. I discuss how the inclusionary integration policies had an impact on the position and perceptions of this immigrant group in German society at large. These two sections should illustrate the divergent treatment and experience of both immigrant groups in regard to integration policy. The final section deals with the current migration wave from EU member countries, discussing the conditions of arrivals of Roma and "Europe's young elite" in Germany. It examines how contradictory public and political sentiments about these immigrants illustrate the patterns of migration and integration policies in Germany.

## Post–World War II Labor Migration: Immigrants from Turkey and German Non-Integration Policies

Labor migration models, such as "foreign worker" (*Fremdarbeiter*)[10] and "guest worker" (*Gastarbeiter*),[11] symbolize specific perceptions of migrant labor forces during different periods in German history, specifically before and after the establishment of the Federal Republic of Germany (FRG or West Germany) as a liberal democratic polity in 1949.

In 1955, shortly after becoming a member of NATO, the FRG launched a labor recruitment program with neighboring NATO member Italy to address the emerging need for a large number of unskilled workers that had resulted in part from the economic growth known as the German economic miracle. This agreement, concluded in the aftermath of World War II, marked the official beginning of the guest worker era (1955–73). Some scholars trace the choice of partner countries to Germany's foreign policy concerns, arguing that the FRG sought to enhance its international standing by stabilizing moderate governments in southern Europe.[12] Others account for the decision to engage with those select countries as due to the fact that labor forces from those countries were already present in Germany. According to their accounts, by the end of the 1960s there were already 13,000 people from Greece, 9,000 from Spain, 2,500 from Turkey, and 9,000 from what was then Yugoslavia contributing to a strong labor force in the West German market.[13] By the time Germany signed further labor recruitment agreements with Greece and Spain in 1960, more than 100,000 Italian laborers had already been recruited for the labor market.[14] It should be noted that while the recruitment of foreign nationals and related labor migration policies focused mainly on the economic needs of West Germany and not those of the neighboring countries, those countries sending labor were also involved and eager to secure recruitment agreements in order to help shed excess labor and improve trade balances through the receipt of remittances.[15]

Following the building of the Berlin Wall in 1961, West Germany signed a labor recruitment agreement with Turkey, an ally during World War I and a NATO member country. Because of the timing of this decision, "guest workers" from Turkey were considered compensation for the loss of labor resulting from the division of Germany. Further agreements were signed with Morocco in 1963, Portugal in 1964, and finally with Yugoslavia in 1968. The numbers illustrate a rapid increase of more than one million people after 1968. By the end of the recruitment efforts in 1973, "guest workers" and their families numbered around 2.5 million, a majority of more than 600,000 of whom hailed from Turkey. The number of migrants from Turkey rose further to 1.5 million people in 1984, and thus came to represent the most prominent symbol of the "foreigner" (*Ausländer*) in the eyes of the West German public.

Although the labor recruitment program from its beginning in 1955 was mostly believed to have the aim of attracting of male workers, it also targeted women, both single and married, skilled and unskilled. Married couples in Turkey often responded positively, as many young women were already married and preferred to emigrate together with their husbands.[16] Female workers, mostly from Spain, Greece, Turkey, and Yugoslavia, made up thirty percent of the foreign workforce between 1960 and 1973, i.e., until the end of the labor requirement program.[17] Among immigrants from Turkey the proportion of skilled female workers was higher than that from other countries—by 21 percent in 1966 and by 14 percent in

1968.[18] This, however, had little impact on changing classical gender roles. In general, where women assumed the role of the breadwinner, the existing gender wage differentials in industries and the West German recruitment policy and its work restrictions for invited spouses into the 1990s, helped to sustain and stabilize a hierarchical and gender-segregated labor market. While wages for female workers were 30 to 40 percent lower than those of men, in those cases where it was the man who came to Germany as the dependent spouse, restrictions on his work permit were imposed for the first four years.[19] At the same time, the recruitment of workers from abroad changed the distribution of labor among ethnic German and foreign workers by bringing upward mobility to ethnic German workers and allowing about three million blue-collar native German workers to move up to positions as white-collar employees.[20]

German labor recruitment policy focused on short-term and temporary solutions, with the government making as little commitment as possible and exhibiting no intention of future planning. Scholars have criticized Germany's policy of denying that it was a country of migration, and its accompanying failure to respond to integration-related responsibilities.[21] Despite some important policy changes, such as the citizenship law in 1999, the situation remained largely constant until the declaration of Germany as a country of immigration (*Zuwanderungsland*) in 2005. Since then, the Merkel government has performed its obligation to develop integration policies as encouraged by the Council of the European Union, which in 2004 agreed on common basic principles for immigrant integration policy within the EU.[22]

Since 2010, the Migrant Integration Policy Index[23] has assessed the comparative success of the integration policies of the forty countries listed in the index based on the following seven policy areas: long-term residency, labor market mobility, family reunion for third nation countries, education, political participation, access to nationality, and antidiscrimination. Germany is currently ranked thirteenth and has "halfway favorable integration policies,"[24] mostly thanks to EU-driven policy improvements since 2007. In the following section of this chapter, special attention will be paid to German integration policies put in place regarding some MIPEX policy areas following the labor requirement agreement in 1955.

Germany, historically and politically, has been reluctant to integrate immigrants with different ethnic and religious backgrounds into its societal system. In the beginning of the new guest worker era of the 1950s, Germany applied a policy of non-integration, intending to ease the return of "guest workers" to their home countries. Work agreements with imported laborers were based on short-term contracts, which would be extended based on the needs of the companies. It was more practical for companies to keep the same workers instead of hiring non-trained work-ers, which within a few years led to the option of long-term residency for the "guest worker."[25]

Against the background of this short-term labor migration policy focus-ing solely on labor, the cultural and integration needs of the imported laborer were intentionally ignored from the start. As the inviting compa-nies were also responsible for housing laborers, this allowed for the segre-gation and isolation of "guest workers" from German society. Due to the fact that housing was a cost factor for the inviting companies, primitive housing conditions for labor migrants was commonplace.

Company housing was typically organized near the workplace and often far from urban centers, which resulted in exclusion from social, educational, and political structures, and was a central experience for most "guest workers." This method of organizing living conditions for the imported laborer based on the initial short-term nature of their stays created long-term isolation. Since "guest workers" were given marginal public attention during the first half of the 1960s, it was primarily their living conditions in media reports that awakened public interest in them, and not their working conditions or status under German law.[26] The pub-licly accepted and legitimizing argument for this overall treatment was that the government called for labor, not people.

Germany's first severe postwar economic crisis in 1973 led to the end of labor recruitment efforts. Many immigrants put a priority on bringing members of their families to Germany before it was too late to do so. This was a critical turning point, as the policy of non-integration became a major issue both for the migrants and their families, and for the German state. Germany's foreigner policy did not change in its structural non-inte-gration approach, which also applied to the children of immigrants. The increasing number of immigrant children and concern about the long-term impact of the "second generation" on German society, often discussed in conjunction with the declining German birth rate, became apparent in the 1970s. The historically reproduced fear that Germans would eventually be overrun by a foreign population,[27] along with the economic crisis, moti-vated the majority of the German population to support the politics of anti-integration and the institutional and social exclusion of non-Germans in society.

Despite similar conditions of recruitment, there were distinct images of "guest workers" based on their respective cultural, religious, ethnic, and national differences. From the late 1960s on, economic worries, and ethnic and racist labeling of migrant groups created a class of those seen as potential problems in general that included Yugoslav, Italian, Greek, and Turkish workers. There was an especially strong ethnic and partly religious label for "the Turkish guest worker."[28] In the following years and into the 1980s, immigrants from Italy, Spain, Greece, and Portugal increasingly gained rights due to their countries' memberships in the European Economic Community (EEC). In contrast, "the Turkish guest worker" became the "Turkish issue" expertly exploited by political parties and a topic in public discourse, with arguments citing cultural, religious, and educational differences, as well as an ascribed inability to integrate into German society. This approach characterized the migration debates of the 1970s and 1980s. In the beginning of the 1980s, the government, then led by the Christian Democratic Union (CDU), added to the debate and sought to reduce the number of immigrants from Turkey by promising financial benefits to all those who left Germany. The government's politics of marginalization and exclusion gained public support. Public backing for the decision to send foreigners back to their countries of origin rose from 39 percent in 1978 to 68 percent in 1982.[29]

In addition, the government stigmatized and punished immigrants by constructing a threatening difference—that was threatening for the German society—and labeling the immigrants as a "problem." The government failed to address integration as a political goal; rather, it misused its power by introducing a non-integration policy in order to structurally exclude these immigrants from society, instead of paving a path for the immigrants' social integration. Peter Katzenstein observes similarities between these labeling policies and those used a century earlier towards immigrants from Poland, underlining the parallel discourses concerning the "Polish Question" of the 1890s and the "Turkish Question" of the 1980s.[30] Labeling and stigmatizing a group of immigrants as a "problem" based on their difference is a structural mode in Germany.

Immigrants from Turkey and their descendants have reacted to the various labeling practices in different ways. Xenophobia/racism and unemployment encouraged over one hundred thousand people to opt for the financial benefits offered by the government of Chancellor Helmut Kohl (CDU) and to return to Turkey. The results of this political offensive can be observed in migration statistics: between 1976 and 2008 there was a consistent surplus of migration from Turkey to Germany, with the exception of the years 1982–84, which mark the only deficit.[31]

Many of the migrant laborers who remained in Germany established immigrant organizations in cooperation with political refugees and students, primarily from Turkey. This cultural and political mobilization helped to increase feelings of security.[32] After the mid-1980s, some of these immigrant organizations, as well as other non-governmental organizations, designed non-systematic integration projects in cooperation with local governments. Furthermore, the politics of non-integration and exclusion motivated many immigrants from Turkey to keep strong ties with Turkey, preventing them from investing economically, politically, educationally, or socially in Germany.

Equally, the Turkish state was interested in not losing ties with its nationals, and provided them with various services. These included sending imams for religious services and teachers to German schools to teach the Turkish language and culture to the second generation.

Against this backdrop, some immigrants reacted to the social, economic, and political insecurity they were experiencing, and to conflicts with educational and other institutions, by sending their children to schools in Turkey. In the long run, the lack of perspective about the future has had a particularly negative impact on the education of these children. Most of the second generation inherited the experience of marginalization, non-recognition, and exclusion, as well as the structural non-integration in German institutions based on the given sociopolitical conditions, particularly in the 1970s and 1980s. Those experiences and their effects continue to impact the educational experiences of subsequent generations.[33]

Economic determinants and the long-term impacts of migration policy on the descendants of immigrants is, in the main, ignored or neglected when it comes to discussions about integration and education. A study by Maurice Crul and Jens Schneider based on comparative integration context theory in diverse European cities shows that differences in integration contexts, including institutional arrangements in education, the labor market, housing, religion, and legislation, as well as differences in the social and political context are especially important for social and cultural participation and the sense of belonging by immigrants. They explain the predominantly negative educational situation of second-generation immigrants with Turkish backgrounds in Germany as generated, to a significant degree, by their low socioeconomic background. According to them, some remaining minor elements can then usually be attributed to cultural differences. Comparing the second generation with Turkish backgrounds across several European countries, the study finds them doing much better in countries other than Germany: whereas only three percent enter higher education in Germany, the number increases to almost forty percent in Sweden and France.[34]

In like fashion, a rigid naturalization law and the denial about Germany being a country of immigration kept access to citizenship out of reach for non-ethnic German and non-European immigrants.[35] The federal government discouraged immigration and further integration into German society by intensifying the requirements and the naturalization process. Politics of exclusion based on restrictive citizenship rights remained in effect for non-ethnic German immigrants until the reformation of the

Nationality Act established a right to naturalization in 1993.[36] With this revision, naturalization decisions were left to the discretion of the authorities. Shortly after the fall of the Berlin Wall, when the entry of almost seventeen million East Germans into West Germany increased unemployment, the flow of ethnic German resettlers, mostly from the former Soviet Union, also reached its peak. This situation created a decisive, structural, and institutional discriminatory policy, when compared with the integration policies applied to the ethnic German resettlers who received German citizenship upon arrival until 1993. Strong societal change and identity debates on "Germanness" in the 1990s, racist attacks from far-right extremist groups and individuals against immigrants, along with the ever-present issues of belonging, identity, nationality, and security became central issues for immigrants and their children, particularly those from Turkey.[37] These encouraged some among the youth to build their own subcultures, or even to form street gangs as a method of self-defense.[38] In the 1990s, a generation labeled "Turkish youth" and "Russian youth" (i.e., ethnic German resettler youth) attracted public and political attention through deviant and violent incidents perpetrated as a reaction to ethnicization, discrimination, and stigmatization, as well as rivalry between the two groups.[39] However, based on their different residency and citizenship rights, the groups experienced different consequences, a factor that I will further highlight in the next section in the context of ethnic German resettlers.

The citizenship law of 1999 symbolizes a radical change in thinking, from the descent-based (*jus sanguinis*) understanding of German citizenship law into civic rights-based citizenship (*jus soli*) that non-European immigrant children born in Germany could claim German citizenship with some restrictions (*Optionspflicht*). In April 2014, the grand coalition of the SPD and CDU removed the criticized restrictions,[40] and agreed upon the right to dual citizenship for second-generation children who had been born in Germany to immigrant parents. This is particularly significant in regard to equal treatment for the younger generation with parents from non-EU countries such as Turkey.

At the end of 2011 the estimated number of people of Turkish background in Germany was 2.95 million; today almost half of them have German citizenship, either through naturalization or by birth (after 2000).[41] In recent years, the number of people arriving in Germany from Turkey has shrunk, while the number of those leaving Germany increases.[42] Those leaving are mostly well-educated, highly skilled descendants of immigrants from Turkey, born in Germany, seeking better social and economic conditions in other countries, including Turkey. A recent study from the Turkish-German Foundation for Education and Scientific Research

(TAVAK)[43] has found that, increasingly, young well-educated people of Turkish origin are moving to Turkey because of unemployment and discrimination in Germany. Between 2007 and 2011 about 190,000 returned to Turkey, according to TAVAK Chairman Faruk Sen. It is expected that up to 65,000 will leave Germany for Turkey annually.[44] Nonetheless, increasing economic collaborations between the two countries open new business opportunities for the younger generation.

In sum, despite the positive turn against ethnicity- and nationality-based discrimination,[45] differences based on religion and culture continue to be the accepted central argument for justification of discrimination of "the non-Christian other" in public and political spheres. Predominantly since 9/11, the image of "violent Turkish youth" of the 1990s has been transformed as "violent Muslim males."

This, and the aftermath of the attacks on the World Trade Center, marked the transformation of the discourses related to immigrants from Turkey and their descendants from a "foreigner problem" to debates on "Muslim immigrants." Islam is now increasingly associated with a transnational "war on terror," "oppressive and violent gender relations," "securitization of migration," which has produced rigid border politics in the EU. At the same time, in the 2015 census report Islam is not even mentioned in the statistics of the officially recognized religious communities, despite the statements from both then President Christian Wulff (CDU) in 2010 and current Chancellor Angela Merkel (CDU) in 2015 that "Islam belongs to Germany."[46]

## Ethnic German Resettlers and Specific Integration Policies

The term "ethnic German resettler" (*Aussiedler*), or "returning settlers of German descent" refers to:

> those immigrants of German ethnic origin who have come to Germany since the 1950s. These immigrants are either descendants of the German settlers who had migrated to Russia mostly during the eighteenth century and were forced to resettle in Kazakhstan during the Stalin era (mainly the "Wolga-Germans"), and Germans who had made homes in other Eastern and Southeastern European regions. Also included in this category are those former German citizens who had lived in German territories that were under Polish administration until 1990 but were finally ceded to Poland in that year by a peace treaty that concluded the territorial questions Germany had kept open until then.[47]

Klusmeyer and Papademetriou trace the history of ethnic German resettlers back to the twelfth century and consider them to be "the descendants of colonists, who first begun to migrate eastward from German lands."[48] According to the authors, the issue of German resettlers arose from the diasporic character of historic German settlement patterns throughout central and eastern Europe, where there were varying concepts of national belonging. German state policies toward external German minorities as well as the national self-understandings of these minorities have continuously changed since the establishment of the Second Reich in 1871. In other words, when we consider the issue of German resettlers in the twentieth century we ought to bear these three different perspectives in mind.[49]

Immigration of ethnic German resettlers is referred to as "ethnic-priority immigration."[50] Since 1949, the privileged admittance of *Aussiedler*, *Übersiedler* and expellees to Germany has been rooted in article 116 in the German Basic Law (*Grundgesetz*), the 1953 Federal Expellee Law (*Bundesvertriebenengesetz*), and the 1955 Law on Regulating Questions of Citizenship (*Gesetz zur Regelung von Fragen der Staatsangehörigkeit*), based on the 1913 Imperial and State Citizenship Act ("RuStaG": *Reichs- und Staatsangehörigkeitsgesetz*). According to the Basic Law, a person is considered German if they possess German citizenship, or if they were admitted to the territory of the German Reich within the 31 December 1937 borders as a refugee or expellee of German ethnic origin or as the spouse or descendant of such a person. An ethnic German resettler was defined by article 1(2) and (3) of the Federal Expellee and Refugee Law as a German citizen or as German *Volkszugehörige* (ethnic Germans) who had his or her home residence prior to 8 May 1945 in the former eastern territories, Poland, the former Soviet Union, Danzig [the Baltic states], Czechoslovakia, Hungary, Romania, Bulgaria, Yugoslavia, Albania, or China and between the end of the general expulsion measures and 31 December 1992.[51]

Thus, "ethnic German resettler" denoted a special legal status, which emerged after 1949. This category has been applied mainly to those of German descent in the former communist countries. Their privileged admission to Germany was based on the assumption that they ethnically belong to the German people (*deutsche Volkszugehörigkeit*), and that they therefore experienced forced resettlement, ethnic discrimination, and persecution during World War II and the Cold War in the Eastern Bloc and the Soviet Union.[52] Since their "victimhood" on the basis of their perceived German ethnicity was central, it was sufficient to provide proof of German descent to be admitted to Germany, even if the notion of the ethnocultural German nation included shared cultural, linguistic, religious, ethnic, and national ties.[53] Upon arrival, the ethnic German resettlers were granted all German legal, economic, and social welfare rights—including German citizenship. After 1991 and the fall of the Iron Curtain, a series of laws were passed, such as the introduction of an annual quota system, that gradually increased the requirements and limited the privileges and quotas for ethnic German resettlers.

Between 1950 and 1987, a total of 1.4 million ethnic German resettlers came to Germany, primarily from Poland and Romania.[54] Following the removal of exit restrictions in the declining communist states of Eastern Europe and the Soviet Union, their numbers reached almost 1.65 million in 1989. After the fall of the Iron Curtain the number of ethnic German resettlers rapidly increased, reaching its peak at nearly 400,000 in 1990. The Soviet Union became the major sending country after 1989. Between 1988 and 1999 a total of 2.6 million resettlers migrated to Germany, mostly (69 percent) from Kazakhstan, Russia, and Kyrgyzstan, followed by Poland (22 percent) and Romania (8 percent). Despite steadily decreasing numbers since 1990, and limitations since 1993, the total admission of ethnic German resettlers since 1950 reached 4.5 million in 2011.[55] Currently, resettlers migrate exclusively from the former Soviet Union countries. A significant characteristic of current resettler immigration is that German language competencies are progressively decreasing and the share of mixed families (German-Russian) is increasing. In 1993, 74 percent of the resettlers were of German ethnic descent; in 2004 this share declined to just 19 percent. Furthermore, since 1989 the motivation of ethnic migration has shifted from ethnic and family motivations to political and economic migration.[56]

Depending on their former place of residence, ethnic German resettlers came with differing German language abilities and cultural and religious perceptions.[57] In addition to citizenship rights, they were immediately included in structural, economic, and social benefits in terms of housing, subsidized loans for furnishing apartments, compensation for lost property, immediate unemployment benefits, schooling, assistance, generous pension schemes for the elderly, and more.[58] This practice of privilege toward the ethnic German resettlers compared to that of the labor immigrants and their descendants symbolized a unique form of inequality. As Joppke and Roshenhek stated, "it pointed to a discriminated group in, rather than outside, society."[59] In other words, in terms of inclusionary and exclusionary politics, the insider/outsider constructions were perceived conversely. Ludger Pries comments critically on the privileged treatment of the resettler particularly after 1993: "In terms of language use, identity, socio cultural beliefs, and behaviour [*sic*] they differed as much or even more from the 'majority society' than Italian, Spanish or Turkish immigrants of second or third generation—although the latter had no German citizenship."[60]

Despite decades of gradually gaining more and more privileges compared to domestic Germans, the ethnic German resettlers first became an issue of conflict for the West German population toward the end of the 1980s, primarily due to economic issues. By the time of German unification in 1990, over 80 percent of the West German public was in favor of restricting ethnic immigration.[61] Now that the Cold War was over, many Germans considered it time to cut back on the privilege of ethnic Germans returning to Germany, since part of why they were so privileged no longer existed. Even as ethnic German resettlers became increasingly seen as a burden on the German economy, and sentiments against the privileges they received upon their arrival grew strong, the German state continued to actively support their integration into the German economy and society. As indicated earlier, the state was marginally inclusive towards labor immigrants and their offspring until 2005. Barbara Dietz points out that despite the continuous reduction since 1989, the integration incentives for ethnic German resettlers in 2006 included financial assistance for unemployment (which could be obtained during attendance of state-sponsored language courses), language encouragement, support for integration into the labor market (by enabling advanced training and retraining), and support for the social integration and the professional advancement of ethnic German immigrant youth.[62]

As stated above, issues of social cohesion and integration became central after the unification of both Germanys. Many young ethnic German resettlers lacked German language and sociocultural adaption skills, were confronted with increased unemployment, had problems in school, and experienced the majority society as stigmatizing and discriminating. "Integration" and "violence" became central buzzwords related to the young resettler. Conflicts with ethnic German resettler youth provoked their ethnicization as "Russian-German." Their Germanness (regarding language, culture, and behavior) was questioned in response to conflict potential. Interestingly, both "Russian-German" and "Turkish" youth were being compared—and even to a certain extent considered equal—in terms of integration problems and deviance issues, primarily with regards to (gang) violence.[63] This largely age-specific rebellion against the majority society, which they experienced as stigmatizing and discriminating, and reaction to racist attacks, were labeled as ethnic characteristics (Russian and Turkish). Despite the similarities in their age-specific experiences, consequences of their period of social rebellion were very different. This was mainly because of their varying legal, i.e., citizenship rights. Born and raised in Germany, but without German citizenship, youth with Turkish background could be threatened with deportation and would actually be deported, as in the deportation case of underage "Mehmet," a fourteen-year-old youth born in Germany, where he lived but did not have citizenship. He was sent "back" to Turkey in 1998.[64] His case was used as a political issue by the Christian Social Union (CSU) in Bavaria to raise political and public attention to the integration problems of "the Turkish second generation" in Germany. Despite public and legal debates surrounding questions as to how justice should enable the deportation of a young teenager, who was born and socialized in Germany, without his parents, to a country where he does not have proper command of the language, and which he knows mainly from summer vacations, Mehmet was deported to Turkey. Local Bavarian authorities suggested deportation after finding him guilty of committing numerous crimes. In other words, although he was a product of German society, the German authorities did not consider him to be their responsibility. While integration programs for ethnic German resettler youth were to enhance their German identity and foster their inclusion in societal, educational, and labor systems, similar efforts for youth with migrational backgrounds were not working towards that goal anything like as intensively or effectively.

Following the "integration" concerns of the German government, in 1996, a language test requirement came into force for people applying for ethnic German resettler status.[65] The language test was decisive for the determination of status and could be taken just once. Strong willingness on the part of the German government to facilitate "ethnic return" for ethnic Germans, and to ensure that their integration into German society be as successful as possible, motivated the government to subsidize language courses and tests in Russia. Joppke and Roshenhek observe the contradiction in the new language policy and the action of the government. They argue, "The German government-financed language courses in Russia, quite literally, helped produce the co-ethnics that are then subjected to a (paradoxically language-centered) status test."[66] Since 2005, accompanying family members have also been required to prove fluency in German.[67] German financing of language courses in the immigrants' country of origin/residence also sends a clear message of privilege in contrast to the immigration bill of 2007 for spouses from Turkey, who must finance their own language courses, symbolizing further unequal treatment by the German state of both immigrant groups.

Despite the structural break at the end of the 1980s, and thanks to various intensified welcoming and integration programs before and after the ethnic German resettlers arrived in Germany, today when compared to non-European immigrants and their offspring who have been living in Germany for decades, the resettlers are generally perceived as having "melted" into German society.[68] The *Datenreport* 2013 indicates that ethnic German resettlers earn more on average than the Turkish population, are much better integrated into the education system, and have lower rates of unemployment. Since 2005, ethnic German resettlers have been included in research on the integration of immigrants in Germany. According to the controversial 2009 study, "Unused Potential," conducted by the Berlin Institute for Population and Development, the resettlers are much better integrated than the "guest worker immigrants," especially those with Turkish backgrounds. Reiner Kliengholz, who directed the study, states in an interview that the reason for this is the special treatment given to the resettlers compared with other immigrant groups. He explains that from the moment they arrive in Germany, due to political interests, they are treated not as immigrants, but as Germans, and they are provided with the same rights as well as with special integration programs. He states further that they look physically like Germans and that this lack of visual difference also eased their lives. According to Kliengholz, his study demonstrates the responsibility of integration politics to enable the participation of every person without ethnic or religious discrimination. As he states, "it [his study] shows, that one [the State] could also achieve similar success for the others if one [the State] wanted to."[69]

Prior to 2005, ethnic German resettlers were considered both in public and political discourse and statistically as "home returnees." Since the first population census following the new migration law in 2005, ethnic German resettlers have been included in the group of "persons with migrational background" and with that have returned to the public memory with their migration and integration experiences. According to the *Datenreport* 2013, with 3.2 million in total, and 97 percent holding German citizenship in 2011, they not only represent the largest immigrant group in Germany, but also have significantly increased the proportion of immigrants in society. Currently, the more than fifteen million people with migrational backgrounds make up over nineteen percent of the total population. The focus of new immigration debates is on the new wave of immigration of young, skilled, but poor European citizens from southern and southeastern European countries, including the marginalized Roma population.

## The New Immigration Wave and the (New) Politics of Inclusion and Exclusion: The European Young Elites vs. Roma

In February 2013, *Der Spiegel*, the most popular weekly magazine in Germany, celebrated the arrival of well-educated, highly skilled young European immigrants to Germany with a special issue titled "The New Guest Workers: Europe's Young Elites for the German Economy."[70] According to *Der Spiegel*, almost half of the newcomers from southern

Europe and a third of those from eastern Europe had an academic background. The cover page of this special issue showed attractive young people next to Berlin's Brandenburg Gate, the symbol of the new, united Germany.[71] The group of four females and three males evoked an image of youth, leisure, and modernity—a carefree crew of professionals. They came from Greece, Italy, Spain, Poland, Romania, Bulgaria, and Hungary. *Der Spiegel* referred to them as part of a new generation of EU-internal guest workers, the so-called "refugees of the European economic crisis." Built around short vignettes about the selected seven young individuals, the article primarily underlined the similarities between these "Europe's young elites," and the image of the Berliner, which in the last decades has come to represent a new image of Germany, particularly for the young and mobile generation in Europe. By constructing similarities based on an image of Berlin and Berliners, *Der Spiegel* depicted these young individuals as "of us" and as belonging to "us." Centered around the perception of sameness based on European belonging, or rather a collective Europeanness, the article outlined an overly positive reaction from economists as well as from the German Liberals (Freie Demokratische Partei or FDP), who welcomed the young, highly skilled new guest workers, and asked that the government modernize immigration law.

By focusing mainly on this European elite, the article in *Der Spiegel*, together with the article from *Die Zeit* discussed in the introduction, which additionally highlights the political debates labeling the arrival of Roma in Germany as "poverty migration," reveal public and political debates about the arrivals of two different groups of immigrants: Roma, depicted as an outside threat to social peace, and the young elite of Europe, who are highly welcome in Germany. They are seen as strengthening the German economy, and as young European individuals; they do not represent a threat either to social peace or to the idea of a new Germanness.

Paradoxically, Roma in public debates are decoupled—or rather detached—from any sociohistorical ties with Germany or German-Sinti, while being perceived as a homogenous ethnic group despite their different national backgrounds. As Markus End argues, the public disinformation and misrecognition enables denial of the historical past of Sinti-Roma in relation to Germany, and warns Germans of an invasion of (poor) Roma.[72] However, the stigmatizing media perceptions of Roma as a "social problem" (through such images as the deviant, antisocial, poor, uncultivated, rootless, and non-European alien) and "undesirable foreigners," harkens back to public associations with Nazi Germany.[73] Although the Roma from Europe have been part of German daily life since the 1990s, Roma mostly became a "problematic issue" in political debates when they obtained EU citizenship and with that the right to travel to Germany.

Their position and social practice has been complicated since 1990 due to the multiple positions they hold in Germany: as EU citizens, as tourists, and as a group desiring to become asylum seekers. Their life experiences in Germany and other European countries show that they have all the necessary conditions to apply for asylum, but even today they are subject to systematic discrimination and persecution, they have been made homeless in their country of origin, and they are traumatized,[74] even if this, due to their existing rights as EU citizens, is apparently not conceivable.

In the *Der Spiegel* article mentioned previously, the "the European young elite," particularly from Italy, Greece, and Spain are thought of as having existing ties to Germany through their grandparents, who served Germany during the 1950s and 1960s as "guest workers." Moreover, they are seen as different from their "guest worker" grandparents because of their education, higher qualifications, and language skills, as well as their willingness to be part of social life in Germany. Since the term "guest worker" in the public consciousness tends to include all immigrants from Turkey and even their descendants, the statement above refers to integration debates regarding the larger group, suggesting that Turkish immigrants themselves are responsible for their situation in society if they have decided to stay in Germany without making a strong commitment to be part of it. Furthermore, the article brings up popular arguments urging integration indicators for the "new European guest workers" in order to guide them toward integrating into the economic and social life of Germany.

Additionally, with its subsequent article titled "The German Dream," *Der Spiegel* encouraged its readers to connect with the notion of "the American dream": the ideals of freedom, equality, and opportunity traditionally held as available to every individual in the United States. This notion of "the German dream" is a desired new image of Germany, at least within the European context: a country that opens its doors wide for young, highly skilled, mostly European, ambitious, cosmopolitan individuals, who want to be successful through hard work.[75]

Politicians such as the former labor secretary Ursula von der Leyen regarded this new quality of immigration as a "lucky situation" for Germany, and hoped that highly qualified young people would bring about long-term change for the average German citizen. *Der Spiegel* quotes her as saying, "It helps our country, makes it younger, more creative and more international." Moreover, she declared that Germany must establish a "welcoming culture" not just for the newcomers alone, but also for their families. This is a plea for a new migration policy that indicates that, unlike "the guest worker" migration wave after 1955, "Europe's young elite" should be considered long-term residents. She states, "The republic has opened for these people a 'welcome center' to greet them. Now it should offer them a house so that they stay."[76] Media coverage, as well as political and public voices, indicated that the government should take responsibility for these new immigrants, who deserve to be part of German life.

As noted above, political voices for Roma are not yet welcoming. The plea, in sharp contrast, is to keep them outside Germany's borders. Within the internally borderless European Union, however, that is not possible. They are not considered to be "the new guest workers, Europe's young elites for the German economy," but of lesser "value" to the country, or as not even belonging to Europe. They are certainly not perceived as being part of "the German dream," but are rather regarded as a current "social problem" for Germany.[77]

The construction of similarity based on Europeanness and sociohistorical ties through grandparents having served Germany as "guest workers," enables arguments for a new politics of openness and a welcoming culture towards "Europe's new elite." This in turn serves to ease their integration into German life, thus enabling them to become part of society. The perception of Roma as immigrants "driven by poverty" without any sociohistorical or cultural ties to Germany, and lacking signs of European identity, however, serves to exclude them from both the political and public spheres. It seems reasonable to indicate that despite their presence in Europe since the thirteenth century, historically, Roma have not been recognized as part of modern Christian Western civilization. In European thinking, they have always represented as "the rest," as defined by Stuart Hall.[78] In other words, they have been recognized by the EU as a European minority group since 2012, and they have long held the position of "the established outsiders in Europe."[79] Despite the EU offering a series of recommendations for improving the quality of life of Roma in Europe in terms of housing, education, employment, and health issues in 2012, some EU member countries, like Germany, continue to enact legislation harmful to Roma. The supranational European identity seems to result in the Roma's further marginalization, while the "European young elite" have become the European cosmopolitans.[80] A current representative study "Between Ignorance and Denial—the Public Attitude towards Sinti and Roma," funded by the Anti-Discrimination Agency in Germany, shows the impact of policies on public opinion. The study finds that ignorance, public denial, and the exclusion of Roma shape people's perceptions of them: more than eighty percent of the population do not want to have Sinti and/or Roma as neighbors and regard them as personally responsible for the existing perceptions of these groups in Germany.[81]

# Conclusion

I argue in this chapter that the politics of labeling, along with perceptions of cultural sameness and difference regarding ethnicity, culture, and religion, impact immigrants' lives and their experiences of legal and institutional inclusion and exclusion in German society and vice versa. Examination of different immigration waves and concepts in West Germany since 1950 reveals that immigration and integration policies in Germany are shaped by the politics of labeling newcomers as "one of us" or "other" based on the perception of sameness and difference, together with economic concerns.

The experiences of ethnic German resettlers show that ethnic and presumed cultural sameness results in the experience of social, institutional, and structural inclusion and privilege. The experiences of immigrants from Turkey and their descendants indicate, however, that ethnic, cultural, and religious difference results in decades-long unequal treatment: discrimination, and institutional and structural exclusion. Structures of inclusion and exclusion are discursively (re)produced in both the public and political spheres. The differentiated experiences of immigrant groups regarding integration policies of the German state imply a relationship between perceptions of difference, ethnicism/racism, and inequalities.[82]

Current immigration cases of Roma and the European young elite reflect historical perceptions of Europeanness/the new European identity, and Germany's—as well as Europe's—discomfort with the recognition of Roma as belonging to Christian European modernity. The emergence of a new European identity based on the othering/foreignization and stigmatization of the Muslim and Roma minorities is not only a German phenomenon, but rather a European one in general. However, it can be argued that in Germany, difference has been perceived as a threatening problem that must be overcome in order to protect social cohesion. Through the many overlapping discourses, stereotypes emerge in the process of "othering" different minority groups in the sociohistorical context of Germany. The most recent narrative of "Roma as a problem" symbolizes a discourse of "difference as a problem" that has been reproduced in Germany since the nineteenth century in relation to different groups: in the 1890s as a "Polish problem," in the 1930s as a "Jewish problem" (though it emerged initially in the 1870s), in the 1980s as a "Turkish problem," and finally since the 2000s as a "Muslim problem." Marking a minority group as a "problem" in order to stigmatize it is a structural problem in Germany. The labeling of a minority group as a "problem" involves the production of public representations of the labeled group.

The examination of some minority and immigration experiences during the late nineteenth and twentieth centuries indicates that historically,

Germany has performed poorly in integrating non-ethnic German minorities and immigrants into society. In recent years, it has begun to provide them and/or their descendants with a path to upward economic and social mobility. Together with the guidance of the European Union, constructive changes in immigration and integration policies in recent years give reason to hope for a future with more inclusive migration and integration policies for minorities in Germany. The call for a welcoming culture, and structural and social incorporation of the new European immigrants, is a positive step. It should not, however, intensify the existing hierarchies between immigrant groups. The German government has, with its special integration policies for the ethnic German resettler, proven that it is possible to include immigrants in social, political, and institutional structures. This should be practiced for all individuals in Germany, regardless of their ethnicity or religion. That will be the fulfilling of "the German dream," both for those who have been in the country for decades and for those who would like to live there.

# Notes

1. Petra Pinzler, "Arme, junge, kluge Einwanderer: Der Bundesinnenminister warnt vor Armutsmigranten. Aber wer kommt wirklich nach Deutschland?" *Die Zeit*, 4 May 2013, accessed 5 May 2013, http://www.zeit.de/2013/19/einwanderung-armutsmigranten.
2. Ibid., Pinzler reported findings of an OECD study in her article in *Die Zeit*. Correspondingly, because of demographic reasons affecting the retirement and social security balance, Germany requires a yearly surplus of approximately 400,000 immigrants in order to keep its status as a social state.
3. This chapter focuses on the migration policies of the Federal Republic of Germany (West Germany). I will use both terms interchangeably, as well as the term Germany, to refer to the same country.
4. According to the Federal Census Bureau (*Statisches Bundesamt*), the number of immigrants rose from 1,081,000 in 2012 to 1,226,493 in 2013, which meant a surplus of 428,607, the highest since 1993. "Migration," Statistisches Bundesamt, accessed 1 September 2014, https://www.destatis.de/EN/FactsFigures/SocietyState/Population/Migration/Tables/MigrationGermanTotal.htm.
5. Pinzler, "Arme, Junge kluge Einwanderer."
6. I will use the term Roma as an umbrella term for all diverse groups related to Roma in various European countries. This includes Sinti, a term which is especially significant in relation to the German sociohistorical context.
7. These politics of exclusion were not just a German phenomenon, but rather, were reproduced cooperatively with politicians from France and Denmark, and recently the UK also joined in on the debates. Countries even attempted to set up their own border regimes to control the immigration of Roma from other EU member countries.

8. I use the term "labeling" in the sense of naming, or categorizing, a group of people in the social and political sense. It has no connection with the concept of labeling as used in deviance studies.

9. I will use quotation marks when I refer to the "guest workers" from the 1955 to 1973 labor recruitment period. The term is used to characterize some immigrant groups, partly in a pejorative sense.

10. For the term *Fremdarbeiter* and earlier policies of labor recruitment see Ulrich Herbert, *A History of Foreign Labor in Germany 1880–1980. Seasonal Workers/Forced Laborers/Guest Workers* (Michigan: The University of Michigan Press, 1990), 4–87. "Überblick über die Zuwanderung nach Deutschland seit 1945," Friedrich Ebert Stiftung, Digital Bibliothek, last modified November 1998, accessed 26 October 2014, http://library.fes.de/fulltext/asfo/00227001.htm. See also Douglas B. Klusmeyer and Demetrios G. Papademetrios, *Immigration Policy in the Federal Republic of Germany* (New York: Berghahn Books, 2009), 531–44.

11. The term *Gastarbeiter* refers to a member of the foreign labor force recruited through the labor recruitment program first launched in 1955 as a result of an agreement between Italy and Germany. According to Herbert, this term was introduced because Germans were reluctant to use the term *Fremdarbeiter* due to its historic connotations. Herbert, *A History of Foreign Labor in Germany 1880–1980*, 3.

12. Triadafilos Triadafilopoulos and Karen Schönwälder, "How the Federal Republic Became an Immigration Country: Norms, Politics and the Failure of West Germany's Guest Worker System," *German Politics and Society* 24, no. 3 (2006): 1–19.

13. Friedrich Ebert Stiftung, "Überblick über die Zuwanderung nach Deutschland seit 1945."

14. The recorded number of workers recruited from Italy varies from 120,000 to 144,000. The initial number is based on sources from the *Datenreport* 2013 of the Statistisches Bundesamt (German Federal Statistics Agency), accessed 20 October 2014, https://www.destatis.de/DE/Publikationen/Datenreport/Downloads/Datenreport2013.pdf?__blob=publicationFile. The second number noted above is from Klusmeyer and Papademetrios, *Immigration Policy in the FRG*, 92.

15. Triadafilopoulos and Schönwälder, "How the Federal Republic Became an Immigration Country," 7.

16. Aytac Eryilmaz, "Frauen als Arbeitsmigrantinnen," in *Fremde Heimat. Yaban Silan olur. Eine Geschichte der Auswanderung aus der Türkei*, eds. Aytac Eryilmaz and Mathilda Jamin (Essen: Klartext Verlag, 1998), 33–137. Monica Mattes, "Gender and Migration in Germany: The Case of Female Labour Migration from the 1950s to the 1970s," *Netzwerk Migration* 4 (2009), accessed 30 January 2015, http://migrationeducation.de/fileadmin/uploads/MattesGenderMigration_01.pdf.

17. Rita Chin, *The Guest Worker Question in Postwar Germany* (Cambridge: Cambridge University Press, 2007), 39–40. Also Klusmeyer and Papademetrios, *Immigration Policy in the FRG*, 92.

18. Mattes, "Gender and Migration in Germany," 4.

19. Eryilmaz, "Frauen als Arbeitsmigrantinnen."

20. Herbert, *A History of Foreign Labor in Germany*, 217. Chin, *The Guest Worker Question*, 92.

21. Herbert, *A History of Foreign Labor in Germany*, 235–37.

22. Eric Leise, "Germany Strives to Integrate Immigrants with New Policies," Migration Policy Institute, 9 July 2007, accessed 30 September 2014, http://www.migrationpolicy.org/article/germany-strives-integrate-immigrants-new-policies. For different integration projects see "Focus on People–Support and Integrate," Bundesamt für Migration und Flüchtlinge (German Federal Office for Migration and Refugees), accessed 30 September

2014, http://www.bamf.de/EN/Willkommen/willkommen-node.html. For a comprehensive discussion of immigration and integration policies from 2000 to 2009 see Rita Süssmuth, "The Future of Migration and Integration Policy in Germany," Migration Policy Institute, MPI Reports, October 2009, accessed 30 September 2014, http://www.migrationpolicy.org/research/future-migration-and-integration-policy-germany. And lastly, for a current perception of integration see Frauke Miera, "Not a One-way Road? Integration as a Concept and as a Policy," in *European Multiculturalisms: Cultural, Religious and Ethnic Challenges*, ed. Anna Triandaftllidou et al. (Edinburgh: Edinburgh University Press, 2012), 192–212.

23. Migrant Integration Policy Index, accessed 10 August 2014, http://www.mipex.eu/about.
24. Migrant Integration Policy Index, accessed 10 August 2014, http://www.mipex.eu/key-findings.
25. See Klusmeyer and Papademetrious, *Immigration Policy in the FRG*; and Chin, *The Guest Worker Question*.
26. Herbert, *A History of Foreign Labor in Germany*, 217–20.
27. Ruth Mandel, *Cosmopolitan Anxieties: Turkish Challenges to Citizenship and Belonging in Germany* (Durham: Duke University Press, 2008). For a historical perspective see Cornelia Wilhelm, "Diversity in Germany: A Historical Perspective," *German Politics & Society* 31, no. 2 (2013): 13–29.
28. An example of newspaper and magazine headlines "Die Türken kommen – rette sich, wer kann" [The Turks are coming save yourself if you can], *Der Spiegel*, 30 July 1973, in *Transit Deutschland: Debatten zu Nation und Migration*, eds. Deniz Göktürk, David Gramling, et al. (Konstanz: Konstanz University Press, 2007), 153–54. According to Deniz Göktürk and her co-editors, and Ruth Mandel, this perception was partly due to the historically established image of the Ottoman Turks, which was perceived as a threat by Europe.
29. In 2013, unsealed confidential British documents based on statements by Margaret Thatcher in 1982 revealed that the then German chancellor Helmut Kohl planned to reduce the number of Turks living in Germany by fifty percent within the following years. Claus Hecking, "Secret Thatcher Notes: Kohl Wanted Half of Turks out of Germany," *Der Spiegel*, 1 August 2013, accessed 20 September 2014, http://www.spiegel.de/international/germany/secret-minutes-chancellor-kohl-wanted-half-of-turks-out-of-germany-a-914376.html.
30. Noted in Klusmeyer and Papademetriou, *Immigration Policy in the FRG*, 95.
31. "Facts & Figures," Statistisches Bundesamt, accessed 1 October 2014, https://www.destatis.de/EN/FactsFigures/SocietyState/Population/Migration/Migration.html.
32. See for example the Türkischer Bund Berlin-Brandenburg (TBB) [Turkish union in Berlin-Brandenburg]. For more information, see their homepage, accessed 30 October 2014, http://tbb-berlin.de.
33. Kathrin Erdmann, "Rütli-Schule: Vom Brennpunkt zur Vorzeigeschule," NDR.de, 3 July 2014, accessed 4 November 2014, http://www.ndr.de/info/sendungen/reportagen/Abitur-am-Ruetli-Gymnasium,ruetlischule100.html. Teresa Dapp, "Rütli-Schule. Die gleichen Schüler mit neuen Perspektiven," *Die Zeit*, 27 February 2014, accessed 25 November 2014, http://www.zeit.de/gesellschaft/schule/2014-02/ruetli-schule-berlin-brandbrief.
34. Maurice Crul and Jens Schneider, "Comparative Integration Context Theory: Participation and Belonging in New Diverse European Cities," *Ethnic and Racial Studies* 33, no. 7 (March 2010): 1249–68.
35. Despite some amendments in 1965, until 1993 the naturalization law was mainly based on the 1913 perception of ethnocultural Germanness, and because of that, it was quite exclusionary to labor immigrants.

36. Prior to reform of the citizenship law, the requirement was fifteen years of legal and permanent residency in the Federal Republic, or eight years for people between 16 and 23 years of age.

37. For various constructions of local, religious, transnational, and hyphenated belongings expressing their experience of inclusion/exclusion in Germany as well as in their country of ancestry, see Czarina Wilpert, "Identity Issues in the History of the Postwar Migration from Turkey to Germany," *German Politics and Society* 31, no. 2 (2013): 108–31. See also Asiye Kaya, *Mutter-Tochter-Beziehungen in der Migration: Biographische Erfahrungen im alevitischen und sunnitischen Kontext* (Wiesbaden: VS-Verlag, 2009).

38. Ayse Caglar, "Popular Culture, Marginality and Institutional Incorporation German-Turkish Rap and Turkish Pop in Berlin," *Cultural Dynamics* 10, no. 3 (1998): 243–61. Mandel, *Cosmopolitan Anxieties*. See also Thom Shanker, "Neo-Nazi Attacks Call Turk Gangs to Arms: Germans Promise to 'Hit Back Hard'," *Chicago Tribune*, 30 August 1993, accessed 10 February 2015, http://articles.chicagotribune.com/1993-08-30/news/9308300132_1_turks-right-radical-attacks.

39. Elmar G.M. Weitekamp, Kerstin Reich, et al., "Why Do Young Male Russians of German Descent Tend to Join or Form Violent Gangs?" in *European Street Gangs and Troublesome Youth Groups*, ed. Scott H. Decker (Lanham/New York/Oxford: Altamira Press, 2005), 81.

40. Until April 2014 it included some restrictions (*Optionspflicht*) regarding potential dual citizenship, and required that naturalized young people choose between their parents' citizenship and German citizenship until they reached the age of twenty-three. According to the new bill, the children of foreign parents are exempt from the obligation to choose between German citizenship and the citizenship of their parents and can obtain dual citizenship. Statistisches Bundesamt, "Doppelte Staatsbürgerschaft: Rund eine halbe Million Optionskinder," Archiv im Focus vom 9 April 2014, accessed 1 October 2014, https://www.destatis.de/DE/ZahlenFakten/GesellschaftStaat/Bevoelkerung/MigrationIntegration/MigrationIntegration.html.

41. Roland Preuß, "Wundersamer Zuwachs," *Süddeutsche Zeitung*, 2 Febuary 2013, accessed 1 October 2014, http://www.sueddeutsche.de/politik/zahl-der-deutschtuerken-wundersamer-zuwachs-1.1589719.

42. "Rekord Zuzug von Ausländern. Viele Türken verlassen Deutschland," *Focus Online*, 4 April 2012, accessed 1 October 2014, http://www.focus.de/finanzen/news/wirtschaft-sticker/roundup-rekord-zuzug-von-auslaendern-viele-tuerken-verlassen-deutsch-land_aid_732881.html. "Zahl der Ausländer auf Rekordhoch," *Handelsblatt Deutschland*, 7 March 2014, accessed 1 October 2014, http://www.handelsblatt.com/politik/deutschland/deutschland-zahl-der-auslaender-auf-rekordhoch/9585708.html.

43. "Weg aus Deutschland: fast 200.000 Türken gehen in vier Jahren," *Deutsch-Türkische Nachrichten*, 14 March 2013, accessed 15 March 2013, http://www.deutsch-tuerkische-nachrichten.de/2013/03/470905/weg-aus-deutschland-fast-200-000-tuerken-gehen-in-vier-jahren/.

44. According to the *Datenreport* 2013 of the Statistisches Bundesamt, about 40 percent of the descendants of immigrants from Turkey have concerns regarding xenophobia and racism, 14 percent report perceived discrimination, and only 75 percent want to remain in Germany in the future.

45. The positive steps include declaring Germany a country of immigration in 2005, the involvement of some Muslim communities in a dialogue on integration by assembling the Islamkonferenz (Islamic Conference) in 2006, the development of the National Integration Plan (NIP), and the German General Act on Equal Treatment (*Allgemeines Gleichbehandlungsgesetz* – AGG), known as the Anti-Discrimination Law.

46. *Die Zeit*, "Der Islam gehört zu Deutschland," 12 January 2015, accessed 12 January 2015, http://www.zeit.de/politik/deutschland/2015-01/angela-merkel-islam-deutschland-wulff.
47. Ludger Pries, "Changing Categories and the Bumpy Road to Recognition in Germany," in *Shifting Boundaries of Belonging and New Migration Dynamics in Europe and China*, ed. Ludger Pries (Hampshire/New York: Pelgrave Macmillan, 2013), 63. For the history of ethnic Germans, see Klusmeyer and Papademetriou, *Immigration Policy in the FRG*, 53–75. For a historical perspective see also Klaus J. Bade, *Ausländer, Aussiedler, Asyl. Eine Bestandaufnahme* (Munich: Beck'sche Reihe, 1994), 147–74.
48. Klusmeyer and Papademetriou, *Immigration Policy in the FRG*, 54.
49. Ibid., 53–54.
50. Christian Joppke and Zeev Roshenhek, "Ethnic Priority Immigration in Israel and Germany: Resilience versus Demise," Online working paper 45, The Center for Comparative Immigration Studies, 2001, accessed 10 February 2013, http://ccis.ucsd.edu/?s=Ethnic+Priority+Immigration+in+Israel+and+Germany.
51. Bade, *Ausländer, Aussiedler, Asyl*, 285. See also Joppke and Roshenhek, "Ethnic Priority Immigration in Israel and Germany," 19.
52. Barbara Dietz, "Aussiedler in Germany: From Smooth Adaptation to Tough Integration," in *Paths of Integration: Migrants in Western Europe (1880–2004)*, eds. Leo Lucassen, David Feldman, and Jochen Oltmer (Amsterdam: Amsterdam University Press, 2006), 116.
53. Some scholars also underline the regime and ideology aspect, as only ethnic Germans under communism would qualify for resettler status. See Joppke and Roshenhek, "Ethnic Priority Immigration in Israel and Germany," 19–20; and Amanda Klekowski von Koppenfels, "From Germans to Migrants. Aussiedler Migration to Germany," in *Diasporic Homecomings. Ethnic Return Migration in Comparative Perspective*, ed. Takeyuki Tsuda (Stanford: Stanford University Press, 2009), 103–32.
54. Veysel Ozcan, "Germany Country Profile," *Focus Migration* 1 (2007), accessed 25 August 2014, http://focus-migration.hwwi.de/Germany.1509.0.html?L=1.
55. Bundeszentrale für politische Bildung, "(Spät-)Aussiedler. Die soziale Situation in Deutschland," 28 November 2012, accessed 30 January 2015, http://www.bpb.de/nachschlagen/zahlen-und-fakten/soziale-situation-in-deutschland/61643/.
56. Dietz, "Aussiedler in Germany," 123. Dietz notes that the resettler settlement was influenced partly by chain and also by distribution by the German authorities' quota system. This led resettler concentration from Romania to Bavaria and from Poland to North Rhine Westphalia. 132.
57. According to Dietz, resettlers from Romania were more successful at preserving German language, culture, and religion. German language abilities diminished in Poland and the Soviet Union after the Second World War. Resettlers from former Soviet republics have the highest rate of mixed marriages. Ibid., 125.
58. Joppke and Roshenhek, "Ethnic Priority Immigration in Israel and Germany," 40.
59. Ibid., 38.
60. Pries, "Changing Categories and the Bumpy Road to Recognition in Germany," 66.
61. Joppke and Roshenhek, "Ethnic Priority Immigration in Israel and Germany," 41.
62. Dietz, "Aussiedler in Germany," 121.
63. See Frieder Dünkel, "Migration and Ethnic Minorities in Germany: Impacts on Youth Crime, Juvenile Justice and Youth Imprisonment," University of Greifswald, 20 December 2006, accessed 20 October 2014, http://www.rsf.uni-greifswald.de/fileadmin/mediapool/lehrstuehle/duenkel/Germany_youngMig.pdf.
64. The name Mehmet is a pseudonym. He has been living in Turkey since the deportation and has been involved in various forms of criminal behavior both in

Germany and in Turkey. His case is still discussed today, since it remains relevant to political debates on immigration. Jörg Burger, "Der Mann, der Mehmet war," *Die Zeit*, 6 October 2013, accessed 10 September 2014, http://www.zeit.de/2013/41/mehmet-abschiebung-tuerkei-beckstein.

65. Special integration programs for ethnic German resettlers include a culture and identity focus. This is different than for any other immigrants. For an example of an integration course plan see "Ergänzende Maßnahmen für Spätaussiedler. Identität und Integration plus," Bundesamt für Migration und Flüchtlinge, October 2011, accessed 10 October 2014, https://www.bamf.de/SharedDocs/Anlagen/DE/Downloads/Infothek/Integrationsprojekte/spa1-konzept-foerderangebot-spaetaussiedler.pdf?__blob=publicationFile.

66. Joppke and Roshenhek, "Ethnic Priority Immigration in Israel and Germany," 38.

67. Ozcan, "Germany Country Profile."

68. Susanne Worbs, et al., "(Spät)Aussiedler in Deutschland. Eine Analyse aktueller Daten und Forschungsergebnisse," Bundesamt für Migration und Flüchtlinge, 2013, accessed 10 October 2014, http://www.bamf.de/SharedDocs/Anlagen/DE/Publikationen/Forschungsberichte/fb20-spaetaussiedler.html.

69. Fabian Grabowsky, "'Diese Integration ist erstaunlich gut gelaufen.' Interview zur Lage der Aussiedler," tagesschaue.de, 12 January 2011, accessed 1 October 2014, http://www.tagesschau.de/inland/aussiedlerinterview100.html.

70. "Die neuen Gastarbeiter: Europas junge Elite für Deutschlands Wirtschaft," *Der Spiegel*, 25 February 2013, accessed 25 February 2014, http://www.spiegel.de/spiegel/print/d-91203388.html.

71. For the cover picture of *Der Spiegel* see Figure 3.1 at the beginning of this chapter.

72. Markus End provides a comprehensive analysis of anti-Roma sentiment in the media and public communication in recent years in Germany. Markus End, *Antiziganizmus in der deutschen Öffentlichkeit: Strategien und Mechanismen medialer Kommunikation* (Heidelberg: Neuman Druck, 2014).

73. Milan Pisarri, "The Suffering of Roma in Serbia during the Holocaust" (Belgrade: Forum for Applied History, 2014), accessed 27 November 2014, http://romagenocide.com.ua.

74. Ayse Caglar and Sebastian Mehling, "Sites and Scales of the Law: Third Country Nationals and EU Roma Citizens," in *Enacting European*, eds. Engin F. Isin and Michael Saward, (Cambridge University Press, 2013), 169.

75. For a new concept of cosmopolitanism based on European experiences of transnational European identity see Ulrich Beck and Edgar Grande, "Cosmopolitanism. Europe's Way out of Crisis," *European Journal of Social Theory* 10, no. 1 (2007): 67–85. In this context see also Feyzi Baban and Kim Rygiel, "Snapshots from the Margins: Transgressive Cosmopolitanisms in Europe," *European Journal of Social Theory* 17, no. 4 (February 2014): 461–78. Klaus Eder, "The EU in Search of its People: The Birth of a Society out of the Crisis of Europe," *European Journal of Social Theory* 17, no. 3 (2014): 219–37.

76. See Sven Becker, Markus Dettmer, et al., "Der deutsche Traum", *Der Spiegel*, 25 February 2013, accessed 25 February 2014, http://www.spiegel.de/spiegel/print/d-91203388.html.

77. For a comprehensive analysis of media images of Roma in Germany, see End, *Antiziganismus in der deutschen Öffentlichkeit*.

78. Stuart Hall, "The West and the Rest: Discourse and Power," in *Modernity: An Introduction to Modern Societies*, ed. Stuart Hall (Cambridge, MA: Blackwell Publishers, 1996), 184–227.

79. Norbert Elias and John L. Scotson, *The Established and the Outsiders: A Sociological Enquiry into Community* (London: SAGE, 1994).

80. For a comprehensive discussion on the impact of European cosmopolitanism on minority groups in Europe, see Baban and Rygiel, "Snapshots from the Margins."
81. "Zwischen Ablehnung und Gleichgültigkeit: Bevölkerungseinstellungen gegenüber Sinti und Roma," Antidiskriminierungsstelle des Bundes, 3 September 2014, accessed 30 September 2014, http://www.antidiskriminierungsstelle.de.
82. Patricia H. Collins and John Solomos, "Introduction: Situating Race and Ethnic Studies," in *The Sage Handbook of Race and Ethnic Studies*, ed. Patricia H. Collins (London: SAGE, 2010), 9.

# Works Cited

Antidiskriminierungsstelle des Bundes. "Zwischen Ablehnung und Gleichgültigkeit: Bevölkerungseinstellungen gegenüber Sinti und Roma." 3 September 2014. Accessed 30 September 2014. http://www.antidiskriminierungsstelle.de.

Baban, Feyzi, and Kim Rygiel. "Snapshots from the Margins: Transgressive Cosmopolitanisms in Europe." *European Journal of Social Theory* 17, no. 4 (February 2014): 461–78.

Bade, Klaus J. *Ausländer, Aussiedler, Asyl. Eine Bestandaufnahme.* Munich: Beck'sche Reihe, 1994.

Beck, Ulrich, and Edgar Grande. "Cosmopolitanism. Europe's Way out of Crisis." *European Journal of Social Theory* 10, no. 1 (2007): 67–85.

Becker, Sven, Markus Dettmer, et al. "Der deutsche Traum." *Der Spiegel*, 25 February 2013. Accessed 25 February 2014. http://www.spiegel.de/spiegel/print/d-91203388.html.

Bendel, Petra. "Coordinating Immigrant Integration in Germany. Mainstreaming at the Federal and Local levels." Migration Policy Institute, Washington, DC, 1 August 2014. http://www.migrationpolicy.org/about/staff/petra-bendel.

Bundesamt für Migration und Flüchtlinge. "Ergänzende Maßnahmen für Spätaussiedler. Identität und Integration plus." October 2011. Accessed 10 October 2014. https://www.bamf.de.

Bundesamt für Migration und Flüchtlinge. "Focus on People—Support and Integration." Accessed 30 September 2014. http://www.bamf.de/EN/Willkommen/willkommen-node.html.

Bundeszentrale für politische Bildung. "(Spät-)Aussiedler. Die soziale Situation in Deutschland," 28 November 2012. Accessed 30 January 2015. http://www.bpb.de/nachschlagen/zahlen-und-fakten/soziale-situation-in-deutschland/61643/.

Burger, Jörg. "Der Mann, der Mehmet war." *Die Zeit*, 6 October 2013. Accessed 10 September 2014. http://www.zeit.de/2013/41/mehmet-abschiebung-tuerkei-beckstein.

Caglar, Ayse S. "Popular Culture, Marginality and Institutional Incorporation: German-Turkish Rap and Turkish Pop in Berlin." *Cultural Dynamics* 10, no. 3 (1998): 243–61.

Caglar, Ayse, and Sebastian Mehling. "Sites and Scales of the Law: Third Country Nationals and EU Roma Citizens." In *Enacting European*, edited by Engin F. Isin and Michael Saward, 155–77. Cambridge: Cambridge University Press, 2013.

Chin, Rita. *The Guest Worker Question in Postwar Germany.* Cambridge: Cambridge University Press, 2007.

Collins, Patricia H., and John Solomos. "Introduction: Situating Race and Ethnic Studies." In *The Sage Handbook of Race and Ethnic Studies*, edited by Patricia H. Collins. London: SAGE, 2010.

Crul, Maurice, and Jens Schneider. "Comparative Integration Context Theory: Participation and Belonging in New Diverse European Cities." *Ethnic and Racial Studies* 33, no. 7 (2010): 1249–68.

Dapp, Teresa. "Rütli-Schule. Die gleichen Schüler mit neuen Perspektiven." *Die Zeit*, 27 February 2014. Accessed 25 November 2014. http://www.zeit.de/gesellschaft/ schule/2014-02/ruetli-schule-berlin-brandbrief.

*Deutsch Türkische Nachrichten.* "Weg aus Deutschland: fast 200.000 Türken gehen in vier Jahren." 14 March 2013. Accessed 15 March 2013. http://www.deutsch-tuerkische-nachrichten. de/2013/03/470905/weg-aus-deutschland-fast-200-000-tuerken-gehen-in-vier-jahren/.

Dietz, Barbara. "Aussiedler in Germany: From Smooth Adaptation to Tough Integration." In *Paths of Integration: Migrants in Western Europe (1880–2004)*, edited by Leo Lucassen, David Feldman, and Jochen Oltmer, 116–36. Amsterdam: Amsterdam University Press, 2006.

Dünkel, Frieder. "Migration and Ethnic Minorities in Germany: Impacts on Youth Crime, Juvenile Justice and Youth Imprisonment." University of Greifswald, 20 December 2006. Accessed 20 October 2014. http://www.rsf.uni-greifswald.de/fileadmin/mediapool/ lehrstuehle/duenkel/Germany_youngMig.pdf.

Eder, Klaus. "The EU in Search of its People: The Birth of a Society out of the Crisis of Europe." *European Journal of Social Theory* 17, no. 3 (2014): 219–37.

Elias, Norbert, and John L. Scotson. *The Established and the Outsiders: A Sociological Enquiry into Community*. London: SAGE, 1994.

End, Markus. *Antiziganizmus in der deutschen Öffentlichkeit: Strategien und Mechanismen medialer Kommunikation*. Heidelberg: Neuman Druck, 2014.

Erdmann, Kathrin. "Rütli-Schule: Vom Brennpunkt zur Vorzeigeschule." NDR.de. 3 July 2014. Accessed 4 November 2014. http://www.ndr.de/info/sendungen/reportagen/ Abitur-am-Ruetli-Gymnasium,ruetlischule100.html.

Eryilmaz, Aytac. "Frauen als Arbeitsmigrantinnen." In *Fremde Heimat.Yaban Silan olur. Eine Geschichte der Auswanderung aus der Türkei*, edited by Aytac Eryilmaz and Mathilda Jamin, 33–137. Essen: Klartext Verlag, 1998.

Friedrich Ebert Stiftung, Digital Bibliothek. "Überblick über die Zuwanderung nach Deutschland seit 1945." Last modified November 1998. Accessed 26 October 2014. http:// library.fes.de/fulltext/asfo/00227001.htm.

Göktürk, Deniz, David Gramling, et al., eds. *Transit Deutschland: Debatten zu Nation und Migration*. Konstanz: Konstanz University Press, 2007.

Grabowsky, Fabian. "'Diese Integration ist erstaunlich gut gelaufen.' Interview zur Lage der Aussiedler." tagesschau.de, 12 January 2011. Accessed 1 October 2014. http://www. tagesschau.de/inland/aussiedlerinterview100.html.

Hall, Stuart. "The West and the Rest: Discourse and Power." In *Modernity: An Introduction to Modern Societies*, edited by Stuart Hall, 184–227. Cambridge, MA: Blackwell Publishers, 1996.

*Handelsblatt Deutschland.* "Zahl der Ausländer auf Rekordhoch." 7 March 2014. Accessed 1 October 2014. http://www.handelsblatt.com/politik/deutschland/deutschland-zahl-der-auslaender-auf-rekordhoch/9585708.html.

Hecking, Claus. "Secret Thatcher Notes: Kohl Wanted Half of Turks out of Germany." *Der Spiegel*, 1 August 2013. Accessed 20 September 2014. http://www.spiegel.de/ international/germany/secret-minutes-chancellor-kohl-wanted-half-of-turks-out-of-germany-a-914376.html.

Herbert, Ulrich. *A History of Foreign Labor in Germany 1880–1980. Seasonal Workers/Forced Laborers/Guest Workers*. Michigan: The University of Michigan Press, 1990.

Joppke, Christian, and Zeev Roshenhek. "Ethnic Priority Immigration in Israel and Germany: Resilience versus Demise." Online working paper 45, The Center for Comparative Immigration Studies, 2001. Accessed 10 February 2013. http://ccis.ucsd.edu/?s=Ethnic+Priority+Immigration+in+Israel+and+Germany.

Kaya, Asiye. *Mutter-Tochter-Beziehungen in der Migration: Biographische Erfahrungen im alevitischen und sunnitischen Kontext.* Wiesbaden: VS-Verlag, 2009.

Kaya, Asiye. "Introduction: (Re)Considering the Last Fifty Years of Migration and Current Immigration Policies in Germany." *German Politics and Society* 31, no. 2 (2013): 1–12.

Klekowski von Koppenfels, Amanda. "From Germans to Migrants. Aussiedler Migration to Germany." In *Diasporic Homecomings. Ethnic Return Migration in Comparative Perspective*, edited by Takeyuki Tsuda, 103–32. Stanford: Stanford University Press, 2009.

Klusmeyer, Douglas B., and Demetrios G. Papademetrios. *Immigration Policy in the Federal Republic of Germany.* New York: Berghahn Books, 2009.

Leise, Eric. "Germany Strives to Integrate Immigrants with New Policies." Migration Policy Institute. 9 July 2007. Accessed 30 September 2014. http://www.migrationpolicy.org/article/germany-strives-integrate-immigrants-new-policies.

Mandel, Ruth. *Cosmopolitan Anxieties: Turkish Challenges to Citizenship and Belonging in Germany.* Durham: Duke University Press, 2008.

Mattes, Monica. "Gender and Migration in Germany: The Case of Female Labour Migration from the 1950s to the 1970s." *Netzwerk Migration* 4 (2009). Accessed 30 January 2015. http://migrationeducation.de/fileadmin/uploads/MattesGenderMigration_01.pdf.

Miera, Frauke. "Not a One-way Road? Integration as a Concept and as a Policy." In *European Multiculturalisms: Cultural, Religious and Ethnic Challenges*, edited by Anna Triandaftllidou et al., 192–212. Edinburgh: Edinburgh University Press, 2012.

Migrant Integration Policy Index. "Key Findings—Strengths and Weakness." Accessed 10 August 2014. http://www.mipex.eu/key-findings.

Ozcan, Veysel. "Germany Country Profile." *Focus Migration* 1 (2007). Accessed 25 August 2014. http://focus-migration.hwwi.de/Germany.1509.0.html?L=1.

Pinzler, Petra. "Arme, junge, kluge Einwanderer: Der Bundesinnenminister warnt vor Armutsmigranten. Aber wer kommt wirklich nach Deutschland?" *Die Zeit*, 4 May 2013. Accessed 5 May 2013. http://www.zeit.de/2013/19/einwanderung-armutsmigranten.

Pisarri, Milan. "The Suffering of Roma in Serbia during the Holocaust." Belgrade: Forum for Applied History, 2014. Accessed 27 November 2014. http://romagenocide.com.ua.

Preuß, Roland. "Wundersamer Zuwachs," *Süddeutsche Zeitung*, 2 February 2013. Accessed 1 October 2014. http://www.sueddeutsche.de/politik/zahl-der-deutschtuerken-wundersamer-zuwachs-1.1589719.

Pries, Ludger. "Changing Categories and the Bumpy Road to Recognition in Germany." In *Shifting Boundaries of Belonging and New Migration Dynamics in Europe and China*, edited by Ludger Pries, 55–84. Hampshire/New York: Palgrave Macmillan, 2013.

"Rekord Zuzug von Ausländern. Viele Türken verlassen Deutschland." *Focus Online*, 4 April 2012. Accessed 1 October 2014. http://www.focus.de/finanzen/news/wirtschaftsticker/roundup-rekord-zuzug-von-auslaendern-viele-tuerken-verlassen-deutschland_aid_732881.html.

Shanker, Thom. "Neo-Nazi Attacks Call Turk Gangs to Arms: Germans Promise to 'Hit Back Hard.'" *Chicago Tribune*, 30 August 1993. Accessed 10 February 2015. http://articles.chicagotribune.com/1993-08-30/news/9308300132_1_turks-right-radical-attacks.

*Der Spiegel.* "Die neuen Gastarbeiter: Europas junge Elite für Deutschlands Wirtschaft." 25 February 2013. Accessed 25 February 2014. http://www.spiegel.de/spiegel/print/d-91203388.html.

Statistisches Bundesamt—Bundeszentrale für Politische Bildung, ed. *Datenreport 2013: Ein Sozialbericht für die Bundesrepublik Deutschland*. Bonn: bpb, 2013. Accessed 20 October 2014. https://www.destatis.de/DE/Publikationen/Datenreport/Downloads/Datenreport2013. pdf?__blob=publicationFile.

Statistisches Bundesamt. "Doppelte Staatsbürgerschaft: Rund eine halbe Million Optionskinder." Archiv im Focus vom 9 April 2014. Accessed 1 October 2014. https://www. destatis.de/DE/ZahlenFakten/GesellschaftStaat/Bevoelkerung/MigrationIntegration/ MigrationIntegration.html.

Statistisches Bundesamt. "Migration." Accessed 1 September 2014. https://www.destatis.de/ EN/FactsFigures/SocietyState/Population/Migration/Tables/MigrationTotal.html.

Statistisches Bundesamt. "Facts & Figures." Accessed 1 October 2014. https://www.destatis. de/EN/FactsFigures/SocietyState/Population/Migration/Migration.html.

Süssmuth, Rita. "The Future of Migration and Integration Policy in Germany." Migration Policy Institute. MPI Reports, October 2009. Accessed 30 September 2014. http://www. migrationpolicy.org/research/future-migration-and-integration-policy-germany. Türkischer Bund Berlin-Brandenburg (TBB). "Startseite." Accessed 30 October 2014. http://tbb-berlin.de.

Triadafilopoulos, Triadafilos, and Karen Schönwälder. "How the Federal Republic Became an Immigration Country: Norms, Politics and the Failure of West Germany's Guest Worker System." *German Politics and Society* 24, no. 3 (2006): 1–19.

Weitekamp, Elmar G.M., Kerstin Reich, et al. "Why Do Young Male Russians of German Descent Tend to Join or Form Violent Gangs?" In *European Street Gangs and Troublesome Youth Groups*, edited by Scott H. Decker and Frank M. Weerman, 81–104. Lanham/New York/Oxford: Altamira Press, 2005.

Wilhelm, Cornelia. "Diversity in Germany: A Historical Perspective." *German Politics & Society* 31, no. 2 (2013): 13–29.

Wilpert, Czarina. "Identity Issues in the History of the Postwar Migration from Turkey to Germany." *German Politics and Society* 31, no. 2 (2013): 108–31.

Worbs, Susanne, Eva Bund, Martin Kohls, and Christian Babka von Gostomski. "(Spät)Aussiedler in Deutschland. Eine Analyse aktueller Daten und Forschungsergebnisse." Bundesamt für Migration und Flüchtlinge, 2013. Accessed 10 October 2014. http://www.bamf.de.

*Die Zeit*. "Der Islam gehört zu Deutschland." 12 January 2015. Accessed 12 January 2015. http://www.zeit.de/politik/deutschland/2015-01/angela-merkel-islam-deutschland-wulff.

**Asiye Kaya** is a social scientist and a former visiting DAAD Professor at Georgetown University currently teaching Diversity Studies at Hochschule Magdeburg-Stendal. Her work focuses on migration, diversity, critical race studies, social inequalities, belonging, gender, generational relations, and qualitative research methodologies. Among other published works are *Mutter-Tochter-Beziehungen in der Migration* (2009) and "The Fiftieth Anniversary of Migration from Turkey to Germany," a special issue of *German Politics and Society* (2013).

*Chapter 4*

# REFUGEE REPORTS
Asylum and Mass Media in Divided Germany during
the Cold War and Beyond

*Patrice G. Poutrus*

Without a doubt, the provision on refugees, article 16, paragraph 2 in the West German constitution (the Basic Law) passed by the Parliamentary Council in 1949 underscoring that "Persons persecuted on political grounds have the right of asylum," is unique in refugee law, and marked the beginning of a West German *Sonderweg* (alternative path) in asylum policy. Until the legislation was changed by the so-called Constitutional Compromise of 1993,[1] West Germany's provision for asylum seekers offered foreign citizens and stateless persons seeking asylum protection against being turned away at the border, against expulsion, and against extradition.[2] It also offered labor, social, and family rights similar to those granted to West German citizens.[3] This liberal law went against traditional definitions of German citizenship, which included only people of German descent. It also acknowledged a change in patterns of migration in Germany, which for more than a hundred years had been a point of departure, not entry.[4] Moreover, it contradicted European immigration practices in the immediate postwar period, which were generally a continuation of policies that sought to solve social and political problems by expelling foreigners/minorities.[5] The parents of the constitution, then, clearly had a liberal, generous asylum law in mind.[6]

## The Postwar Years in West Germany

However, in the newly founded Federal Republic of Germany (West Germany) neither the public nor politicians regarded foreign refugees as a symbol distancing the new state from the Third Reich. Instead, foreign

Notes for this chapter begin on page 98.

refugees represented a threat to inner peace and stability and a burden forced upon West Germans.[7] For example, Bohumil Laušman, the anti-communist Vice Prime Minister of Czechoslovakia, was not welcome in Germany in 1950 because he felt the expulsion of German minorities from Bohemia and Moravia after World War II was justified. His published statement called into question the postwar myth that Germans were themselves victims of World War II.[8] The furious public reaction this caused contradicted the principles of the 1949 asylum provision, but this did not seem to strike anyone at the time. Because the confrontation with communism was not yet a dominant issue, Laušman was not considered a "natural" ally and was forced to live in exile in Austria.[9]

In clear contrast to this case, the West German public and judicial system showed sympathy for a group of seven convicted Dutch Waffen SS troopers who had escaped prison and crossed the border illegally to seek refuge in West Germany under the 1949 law.[10] The Dutch government insisted on their deportation, but the West German police demonstrated a clear reluctance to find the war criminals. In the end, one of the refugees was turned over to Dutch authorities only because of the direct intervention of the British occupying power — a move that the West German chancellor considered a public affront to the country's sovereignty.[11] Both episodes show an obvious reluctance to break with the Nazi past.

If we keep these cases in mind, it is no surprise that such postwar attitudes were more influential in the practice of granting asylum than what the constitution provided for. Three and a half years after the enactment of the 1949 provision, the first rules governing the procedures for granting asylum, the so-called Asylum Ordinance of 1953, came into effect. This ordinance, which circumvented parliamentary approval, was based on the highly restrictive 1938 National Socialist Police Decree on Foreigners, the *Ausländerpolizeiverordnung* (APVO), and granted local police authorities broad discretion in immigration decisions, which were often made based on current political interests rather than on the merit of individual cases. Granting asylum, then, became increasingly distant from the original notion set out in the constitution.[12] Although asylum numbers were limited, the process was still very lengthy. Indeed, the 1953 ordinance was used to reject foreign refugees and to circumvent the 1949 provision.[13]

## Refugees from the Hungarian Revolution of 1956

The self-referential attitude of West Germans and their government was challenged by the crises in the Soviet bloc after the death of Stalin in 1953.[14] The arrival of hundreds of thousands of refugees from the GDR presented a significant social burden; however, as the Cold War escalated, these East German refugees quickly began to symbolize the superiority of "the West" in the battle of ideologies. This background helps explain the reaction of the ministries of the Federal Republic responsible for questions of migration in the face of increasing refugee movement towards the west after the violent suppression of the Hungarian Revolution of November 1956. Initially, they treated requests for assistance from Austria in dealing with the Hungarian refugees with studied rejection.[15] And yet, for the first time in postwar history, this sentiment found no backing from either the federal government or the public.[16]

Even before the repression of the revolution, the *Frankfurter Allgemeine Zeitung* (*FAZ*) reported on the increasing admission of Hungarian refugees into Austria and asked whether Hungarians had been abandoned by the free world, given the slow pace of humanitarian aid and the perception among some refugees that the Hungarian revolutionaries had little public or state support.[17] The newspaper *Münchner Merkur* picked up this theme a week later in a full-page report comparing the fates of Hungarian refugees in Austria with that of Germans fleeing the Red Army at the end of World War II:

> On Sunday, things at the border looked like ours in the East in 1945. The lines of refugees with their covered horse-drawn farmers' carts, omnibuses, trucks, farm tractors, bicycles, motorcycles, baby carriages, all packed to the hilt with people or the refugees' few belongings, pushing into Austria before the Soviets closed the border. Many children came without their parents. In other places, you could see sobbing parents who had lost their children. Images of misery and desperation, just as they remain in memory from those grim days eleven years ago.[18]

Such self-identification with the Hungarian refugees corresponded with the mood of West Germans and especially the self-perception of the West Berlin population. On the same day, 6 November 1956, the *Berliner Kurier* reported on a rally in West Berlin where more than 100,000 citizens of the divided city showed up with posters, banners, and torches. Because of the reported "excited" state of the demonstrators, the local representatives of the Sozialdemokratische Partei Deutschlands (Social Democratic Party of Germany, SPD), the Christlich Demokratische Union Deutschlands (Christian Democratic Union, CDU), and the Freie Demokratische Partei (Free Democartic Party, FDP) saw the need to call repeatedly upon the assembled Berliners to support the Hungarian revolutionaries with respect and admiration, instead of expressing anger in the face of feelings of helplessness. Before the actual rally, students had gathered at the Soviet memorial and threatened the Soviet soldiers on duty with cries of "Freedom for Hungary!" "Freedom for the zone [GDR]!" and "Ivan, go home!" Demonstrators threw rocks at a bus arriving with military reinforcements, and only the actions of the West Berlin police prevented an escalation of the situation. According to the newspaper article, the spontaneous outbreaks of desire to take some kind of action ended with increased support for the victims of the Soviet invasion of Hungary.[19]

The extreme reactions of the West Berlin populace cannot be explained away as the result of the city's particular front-line status in the noncommunist half of postwar Germany. As the Hamburg newspaper *Die Welt* reported on 6 November 1956, impressive demonstrations broke out across Germany. The multiple voices of the pro-Hungarian demonstrations—which comprised a mixture of a fear of "the Russians," alarm at the possibility of war, and the love of freedom—could now be seen as a sign of West German integration into the international movement against Soviet aggression in Hungary.[20] In this atmosphere, the Federal Republic declared itself ready to grant asylum to 3,000 Hungarian refugees from Austrian refugee camps.[21] This decision prevented local police authorities from rejecting the Hungarian asylum seekers who were leaving Austria, a relatively safe country of refuge. The legal basis for this policy came in the form of an interesting and creative interpretation of the situation, which stated that the Hungarian Revolution was the result of events brought about by the communist takeover in 1948/49, in essence backdating the beginning of the refugees' need for asylum before 1 January 1951 and the signing of the Geneva Convention on Refugees.[22]

The rather symbolic nature of this decision—accepting 3,000 people from the 180,000 to 200,000 Hungarians in Austrian refugee camps[23]— nonetheless redirected public awareness away from events in Hungary and toward the fate of the refugees themselves. Consequently, West German newspapers began to report on the general willingness to help refugees. Sentimental and emotionally stirring stories circulated among West German readers, who learned of the danger-laden flights from Soviet troops and the difficult living conditions in the Austrian refugee camps.[24] It quickly became clear that the West German public not only had a much higher tolerance for carrying the burden of incoming refugees but also a stronger desire to help out than local politicians and other authorities had previously believed.[25]

The change in refugee admission policy and practice coincided with a transformation in mass media representations of the flight from the "Eastern Bloc." The acceptance of refugees no longer served to legitimize West Germans' self-perception as victims of Nazi Germany and the turbulence of the postwar period; instead, political refugees now pushed the issue of the communist threat to the foreground.

The protest movements of early November had resulted in a number of assistance programs on the part of the West German public. The *Welt am Sonntag* of 11 November 1956, for instance, reported that thousands of people throughout the entire country had tried to donate blood for the Hungarian freedom fighters, but that some regional hospitals had not been prepared for the unanticipated rush of donors and had had to turn away several disappointed Germans who had hoped to show their support for the refugees.[26] The *Kölner Stadt-Anzeiger* wrote on 14 November about the tragic situation of Hungarian refugee children, many of whom had been separated from their parents, or else had been sent west with only their mothers. Such reports pushed individual financial donations in West Germany to record highs. The Red Cross received six million Deutschmarks within days, and the equally impressive number of in-kind donations pushed the organization to the limits of its ability to make use of all the items.[27] In light of this self-sacrificing spirit, the Düsseldorf newspaper *Mittag* repeated criticism made in the Bundestag (Lower House of the Federal Republic of Germany) regarding the attitude of some federal states that did not want to take part in finding accommodation for the Hungarian refugees who were already in the Federal Republic, contrasting this reluctance to help with the aid provided by other parts of West German society.[28]

By 20 November, *Die Welt* reported that Bavarian state politicians, given the worsening situation for Hungarians, had demanded that the number of refugees accepted be doubled.[29] A day later, the *Hannoversche Allgemeine Zeitung* warned of catastrophe and worsening conditions for emigration after the definitive failure of the Hungarian Revolution.[30] On 22 November, the Secretary for Refugees (Bundesminister für Vertriebene, Flüchtlinge und Kriegsgeschädigte) Theodor Oberländer announced that he would lift the quota for admitting Hungarian refugees. He did so only after reminding his audience of the continuing burden of the massive influx of GDR refugees and immigrants and the ongoing challenges of integrating them into West German society.[31]

Similar attempts to discuss the hardships of German migrants alongside the difficulties of Hungarian refugees elicited no response from the West German press. No discussions took place about the flagging support of West Germans for refugees brought about by an overburdening of the sociopolitical infrastructure.[32] Instead, the combination of the aid measures of the German Red Cross and the admission of refugees to the Federal Republic appeared repeatedly and demonstratively as a collaborative effort on the part of west European countries with a common goal of relief for refugees.[33] In light of the increasingly dramatic conditions in the Austrian refugee camps, the federal government decided to admit up to 10,000 Hungarians.[34] These refugees would receive the same rights and help guaranteed only to expellees and refugees from the GDR.[35] This policy of an active integration program is itself remarkable because it illustrates—assuming a positive interpretation of the presence of foreigners in West German society—the increased scope of political maneuverability available to authorities responsible for policy in this field.

Mass media representations in the subsequent weeks of the flight of Hungarian refugees can be divided into two clear tendencies. In some, they appeared as a part of an imagined community of immigrants intending to return home. The emphasis ceased to be on the consequences of the war, and turned towards the communist dictatorship in Central and Eastern Europe. The experience of Hungarian revolutionaries verified and strengthened the idea that Germans who migrated from east to west had been the victims of persecution as a result of communism and especially the Soviet Union's violent dictatorship.[36] The other picture painted by the mass media was one of "helper's pride," expressed repeatedly in reports about West German aid projects that outdid themselves in the desire to support refugees. Indeed, this self-image led to the conclusion that, of all the western countries, the Federal Republic was the real champion in helping Hungary.[37] This characterization even found acknowledgement abroad, as evidenced by an article in the *Neue Züricher Zeitung*.[38]

In December 1956 the Austrian-Hungarian border westwards became impossible to cross because of its definitive closure from the eastern side. Although the situation in refugee camps in Austria slowly eased, the largely unified and positive portrayals of Hungarian refugees in West German newspapers dissolved. Arguments about overburdening the West German sociopolitical system reappeared without comment in a number of regional newspapers. This time, the press often and loudly repeated the fear that the attention paid to Hungarian refugees would unjustly result in a loss of status for Germans migrating from east to west.[39] Regardless of the assumption that some sort of competition even existed, the West German press followed policymakers closely over the next months in order to evaluate how the admission of Hungarian refugees unfolded. These reports demonstrated that, despite the high symbolic value of Hungarian refugees for the changing self-perception of the Federal Republic, the Hungarians faced the same challenges that other immigrant communities did in their efforts to integrate into daily life in West Germany.[40]

Even though the employment situation improved in the Federal Republic, living conditions for some Hungarians were marked by enough alienation and disappointment that in 1957 *Die Welt* discovered—with some degree of dismay and astonishment—that a number of refugees desired a quick return to their communist-ruled homeland.[41] Against the background of continuous refugee movement from the GDR, this decision must have seemed like a slap in the face for West German readers. Nonetheless, it is interesting that in this context, as in the question of admitting foreign refugees from the communist-ruled countries of Central and Eastern Europe, the East German SED-State was never a point of reference. As far as the West German public was concerned, the ideological conflict regarding the communist threat in Europe occurred primarily via the policies of the Soviet Union and a strict geopolitical demarcation from them.

Even if, as noted above, the acceptance of Hungarian refugees was not free of friction, Hungarians initially represented the type of "good refugee" who could find a safe haven in the "free West."[42] Reasons for this perception did not rest on a willingness to assimilate, but rather, because it had been possible to establish and maintain a small Hungarian diaspora based on the clear ethnic identity of refugees from 1956. In West German society, just as among Hungarian migrants, the accepted wisdom was that Hungarians would be able to return to Hungary. The other similarity between West German society and the small Hungarian minority lay in the anticommunist sentiments of both groups during the Cold War.[43]

The worries of federal authorities about internal stability in the face of uncontrolled admission of refugees faded into the background as worries about security in foreign affairs increased—especially regarding the threat of the Soviet bloc. The West German public found it inappropriate in these circumstances to return to a fundamental policy of exclusion regarding foreigners, and especially political refugees. Even so, unconditional protection of political refugees, albeit foreseen in the Basic Law (the West German constitution) never materialized.[44]

## Future Developments in West and East Germany

Nonetheless, the public clamor and policies that had resulted in the admission of political refugees into the Federal Republic marked a new era of reforms that contributed to the codification of the unrestricted right of asylum in the Basic Law. In 1959, the Constitutional Court ruled that the right to asylum for political refugees could not be based solely on the Geneva Convention.[45] This decision marked the beginning of a debate in the country's legal history whose implications extended far beyond the question of a generous or restrictive asylum policy. Instead, the legal issue of asylum came to stand for the question of whether the state's interests should be allowed to limit the authority of the Basic Law, or whether all matters of state should conform to constitutional norms.[46] Not until 1975 did the Federal Administrative Court decide that the right to asylum as guaranteed under article 16, paragraph 2.2 should have no immanent restrictions.[47] Thus, the interests of the state and its national security concerns could no longer play a role in awarding asylum, the only decisive factor being establishing of political persecution.

This development, however, was accompanied by public debates in which refugees and persons fleeing from political persecution received extremely ambivalent treatment in mass media representations of their experiences. The debates about the admission of North African refugees during the Algerian War (1959)[48] and the case of politically motivated violence against Croatian separatists (1962)[49] showed that the West German public had again picked up the clearly self-protective discourse about the "misuse of asylum rights" — as would be standard practice twenty years later in debates on asylum, albeit under different auspices.[50]

These very different cases demonstrate undisputedly that protection from deportation, so fundamental to asylum rights, is publically called into question whenever domestic and foreign interests are affected, whether only apparently or in actuality.[51] The Federal Republic never ceased to fear that the admission of refugees would disturb its internal stability and endanger the newly won credibility that it enjoyed among other nations.[52] Mass media representations found their equivalent in what amounted to a practice of granting asylum in the early Federal Republic, which Karin Hunn and Ulrich Herbert have accurately described as "as liberal as necessary and as restrictive as possible."[53]

With the invasion of Warsaw Pact troops into Czechoslovakia in 1968, the West German public reactions of 1956 seemed to repeat themselves under the sign of the Cold War.[54] Because of their proximity to the dramatic events, Austria and Bavaria again became centers of admission for a new wave of refugees.[55] West German reports did not fail to draw parallels between the end of the Prague Spring and the suppression of the 1956 Hungarian Uprising.[56] This time, however, no one needed any "emergency reports" to move the state and federal governments to allow immediate admission of refugees. Instead, the 1968 reports spoke of aid and support for Czechoslovakian emigrants as though such engagement had long been routine in West Germany.[57]

In an article for the *FAZ*, the unconditional readiness on the part of the public to help the 15,000 refugees from their neighboring country meant more than just humanitarian support for political refugees from countries ruled by a communist dictatorship. The growing distance in time from the National Socialist past made it possible to see this behavior as a sign of reconciliation between Germans and Czechs.[58] In contrast to the mass media representations of Hungarian refugees, the press did not portray the admission of Czechoslovakian refugees as evidence of collaborative effort with other Western democracies. If it was mentioned at all, it was only in passing and as a self-evident state of affairs.[59]

Thus, it is evident that, at least for the Federal Republic, it was not only the international constellation of the Cold War that influenced or even determined the kind and degree of admission of political refugees from Central and Eastern Europe. The mass media reports on political refugees in West Germany, though not free of contradiction, were key in making the dynamic transformations in the political culture of the Federal Republic visible. The status of the internal constitutionality ultimately centered on which refugee groups West Germans decided to welcome. In this context, the immediate vicinity of the communist threat was a necessary precondition—together with other developments described here—that marked the limits of the inner-societal willingness to admit refugees.

The acceptance of communist refugees from military dictatorships from South America in the early 1970s started a controversy that anticipated the lines of conflict in future asylum debates of the 1980s and early 1990s.[60] The debates about the acceptance of Chilean refugees demonstrated that the anticommunist consensus at the public and policy levels of the early Federal Republic could not simply be transformed into a universal consensus regarding the protection of political refugees. More importantly, the question of whether or not communist refugees should be granted asylum ignited a heated political debate.[61] Additionally, the internal stabilization of West German society and the successful foreign policies of the social-liberal coalition after 1969 affected another aspect of the asylum law: it lost its function as evidence of a commitment to Western democratic values.[62]

In the mid-1970s, refugee and asylum questions increasingly became part of public debates about policies regarding foreigners and immigration. One key point became the epicenter of a multidimensional transformation of attitudes about migration: the rising number of asylum seekers. In the early 1970s between 2,500 and 5,600 people submitted petitions for asylum. In 1976, the number of petitions had risen to 10,000. By 1980, the Federal Republic was receiving over 100,000 petitions annually. The origin of applicants also changed. Up until the 1970s, refugees came primarily from the communist dictatorships of Central and Eastern Europe. The proportion of so-called Eastern Bloc refugees fell in the early 1970s, but the entirety of asylum seekers rose, as did the percentage of non-European refugees.[63] The late 1970s also saw a current of political change: the opposition party, the CDU, enjoyed strong support in the federal states, and the social-liberal coalition government practiced a cautious, even hesitant, policy regarding foreigners. This situation afforded the CDU a unique opportunity to improve its political profile by accusing the coalition of doing nothing about the issue of asylum.[64]

The conservative media and tabloids supported this position. After all, from 1978 to 1993, the asylum debates had resulted in seventeen major legislative changes and legally binding decisions for the Standing Council of the Ministers of the Interior and the Federal Government. Despite this flood of regulations, however, the CDU, which came to power in 1982, had not been able to reduce the rising numbers of asylum applications.[65] In public debates the burden that refugees and asylum seekers put on the crisis-laden welfare state and the purported threat of this new demographic of foreigners influenced the ways in which mass media represented both the people involved and the sociopolitical issues. Indeed, no one seemed to care about or, in many cases even believe, the refugees' reasons for fleeing their homelands or their stories of political persecution.[66]

The debates about the fundamental right of asylum in the Federal Republic took place in a highly charged political atmosphere.[67] The extraordinary mobilization of public politics on the issue of asylum from the late 1970s to the early 1990s cannot be fully explained by the unfortunate experiences of many foreign refugees[68] or by the accompanying challenges faced by the country's welfare state, perceived to have already reached its limits.[69] Rather, the issues of refugee and asylum policies were always connected to fundamental questions about the political and moral foundations of (West) German society. Some groups saw a broad refugee and asylum policy as a symbol for definitive rupture with the history of a racially oriented Germany. Others regarded such a generous policy as unthinkable, since it would mean a break with the paradigm of a Germany that was not an immigration country, and the loss of a historical, cultural, and ethnic identity.[70] Up until the early 1990s, neither side could give their position enough political weight to result in much movement, resulting in a stalemate, which—paradoxically—dissipated with the end of the GDR.

In its interactions with political refugees and their representation in mass media, the East German State was "freed" from the ambivalences and dynamics of the near omnipresent asylum discussions in the democratic half of Germany.[71] The overall contradictory attitude of the leadership of the Sozialistische Einheitspartei Deutschlands (SED) and the East German population regarding foreigners became particularly clear when the GDR admitted the Chilean "polit. emigrants." After the bloody military coup against the elected leftist government of President Salvador Allende, 2,000 of them sought asylum in the GDR. The mass media representations of the staged public appearances of prominent SED officials with Chilean emigrants at protest movements against the Chilean military dictatorship not only served to enhance the GDR's image in "capitalist," i.e., Western, countries—especially West Germany—but also displayed a fundamental consensus between the East German Party leadership and its populace.[72] The SED presented the Chilean emigrants to its walled-in citizens as freedom fighters in need of solidarity. In East German mass media, the GDR portrayed the refugees as more proof of the extremely humanistic mission of the SED and of the continuing promise of a fulfilling life in the GDR.[73] As a result, the East German public viewed political refugees as emissaries of the SED and treated them accordingly.[74] After the events of 1989 had shown that the majority of East Germans had fundamentally rejected "socialism in GDR colors," it was not surprising that a majority had no sympathy for the rising number of asylum seekers in unified Germany.

## After German Unification

In the early 1990s this shared German attitude provided the momentum for liberal-conservative politicians to bring about constitutional reform in the fundamental right to asylum. That the proponents of a generous and unrestricted right to asylum did not succeed either at the governmental or public level might make the asylum compromise look like a defeat. Yet this compromise also speaks to the depth of human rights as part of the political culture of unified Germany.[75] Ultimately, many voices wanted to eliminate the right to asylum entirely, thus demonstrating that issues surrounding the principle of a nation state and human rights in the field of migration policy had not disappeared. On the contrary, there is much that points to the fact of a continuing conflict, even if that conflict will likely be dealt with more and more at the European level.[76] Still, the continuing conflicts about asylum rights cannot be explained as a consequence of this one development. Against the background of a latent tension between the principle of sovereignty of the modern nation state and universal human rights that have historically been linked to this claim,[77] the Federal Republic's right to asylum—from the state's foundation to the constitutional change of 1993—was constantly subjected to new interpretations.[78] But, at the same time, the 1993 amendment was a compromise between liberal asylum laws with an emphasis on human rights, and traditional political notions of belonging to the German nation based on ethnicity. In this sense it was a fundamental act in founding a unified Germany.

With respect to content, the compromise was based on the premise that the right to asylum would remain in the constitution, but that the access to that right would be to a large extent limited by the inclusion of the so-called "third-state rule" into the reformulated article 16a of the Basic Law. This was possible because it was assumed that potential asylum seekers had already had the possibility to apply for asylum in reunified Germany's neighboring countries and that therefore, this did not have to be checked by Germany. In the following years, all German governments strove to steer European asylum regulations towards such a model in which the responsibility for asylum decisions was shifted to countries at the borders of the European Union (EU).

Since 1993, Germany has reduced the very infrastructure of the humane and legally founded processing of asylum requests that is needed in the current crisis. The reason for this development was the temporary decrease in the number of asylum seekers in Germany, which fell below the "magic" 100,000 application mark in 2003—ten years after the asylum compromise.[79] This begs the question of whether the constitutional amendment is really to blame. In the public perception, as well as in the actions of the responsible politicians, this development has kept alive the illusion that one's own society can be protected from the effects of international crises by regulating migration. As long as the masses of asylum seekers remained in southern and southeastern Europe, the German government also rejected the idea at the European level of distributing asylum seekers on a quota-based system and was only willing to offer financial compensation.

Due to the developments in the Middle East and in the west Balkan countries, by the summer of 2015 at the latest, this system of blocking asylum seekers at the borders of the EU broke down. Germany, the geographic, economic, and political core country of the EU, has again become the target destination of hundreds of thousands of refugees seeking asylum there. The German public's reactions are in many ways reminiscent of the developments before 1993: panic-stricken reactions in politics and the media, the mobilization of xenophobic and racist movements, and acts of violence aimed at refugee accommodations and at refugees themselves. However, this time it is apparent that emerging problems can be overcome where the readiness of citizens and initiative groups to help meets an executive branch ready to take action. And where administrative bodies are incompetent or unwilling, the commitment of helpers can save the state from failing to fulfill a humanitarian task. Still, at its essence, the conflict is the same as it was decades ago. Will the Germans and the Europeans choose to act in solidarity and uphold the principles of human rights,[80] or will they go back to a life behind fences, walls, and other barriers and set their hopes on the return of the European nation state of the nineteenth century?

# Notes

1. Hans-Peter Schneider, "Das Asylrecht zwischen Generosität und Xenophobie: Zur Entstehung des Artikels 16 Absatz 2 Grundgesetz im Parlamentarischen Rat," *Jahrbuch für Antisemitismusforschung* 1 (1992): 217–36.

2. Ursula Münch, *Asylpolitik in der Bundesrepublik Deutschland: Entwicklung und Alternativen* (Opladen: Leske + Budrich, 1993), 22–35. Bertold Huber, *Ausländer–und Asylrecht* (Munich: Ch. Beck, 1983).

3. Reinhard Marx, "Die Definition politischer Verfolgung in der Bundesrepublik Deutschland," in *Flucht und Asyl. Berichte über Flüchtlingsgruppen*, eds. Andreas Germershausen and Wolf-Dieter Narr (Freiburg i.Br: Lambertus, 1988), 148–58.

4. Dittmar Dahlmann, ed., *Unfreiwilliger Aufbruch. Migration und Revolution von der Französischen Revolution bis zum Prager Frühling.* (Essen: Klartext-Verlag, 2007). Jochen Oltmer, *Migration und Politik in der Weimarer Republik* (Göttingen: Vandenhoeck & Ruprecht, 2005), 219–69.

5. Göran Therborn, *Die Gesellschaften Europas 1945–2000. Ein soziologischer Vergleich* (Frankfurt a. M.: Campus, 2000), 55–60. Rainer Münz, "Phasen und Formen der europäischen Migration," in *Migration und Flucht: Aufgaben und Strategien für Deutschland, Europa und die internationale Gemeinschaft*, ed. Steffen Angenendt (Bonn: Bundeszentrale für politische Bildung, 1997), 34–47.

6. Peter Steinbach, "Die Verpflichtung zur Beheimatung politisch Verfolgter: Der Weg zum Asylrecht des Grundgesetzes," *UNIVERSITAS* 50, no. 12 (1995): 1126–45.

7. Ulrich Herbert and Karin Hunn, "Beschäftigung, soziale Sicherung und soziale Integration von Ausländern," in *Geschichte der Sozialpolitik in Deutschland seit 1945, Vol. 3*, ed. Bundesministerium für Arbeit und Soziales (Baden-Baden: Nomos, 2005), 779–801.

8. *DPA Report*, 9 January 1950, retrieved from the Press Archive of the German Bundestag (Presse Archiv des Deutschen Bundestags), a parliamentary news service, under the keyword "asyl".

9. Patrice G. Poutrus, "Flüchtlingsberichte: Öffentlichkeit und Asylpolitik im geteilten Deutschland während des Kalten Krieges," in *Flüchtlingslager im Nachkriegsdeutschland. Migration, Politik, Erinnerung*, eds. Henrik Bispinck and Katharina Hochmuth (Berlin: Ch. Links, 2014), 90–112.

10. Memorandum, "Justitzminister des Landes Nordrhein-Westfalen an Bundesministerium der Justiz, betr: Grenzübertritt holländischer Kriegsverbrecher," 2 January 1953, Bundesarchiv Koblenz (hereafter BArch), B 106, No. 47456.

11. Harald Fühner, *Nachspiel: Die niederländische Politik und die Verfolgung von Kollaborateuren und NS-Verbrechern, 1945–1989* (Münster: Waxmann Verlag, 2005).

12. Patrice G. Poutrus, "The Right to Asylum in West Germany: Refugee Policies in the Federal Republic of Germany, 1949–1975," in *Human Rights and History: A Challenge for Education*, ed. Rainer Huhle (Berlin: FATAMorgana Verlag, 2010), 106–12, especially 108.

13. Fritz Franz, "Verhältnis der Verheißung des Grundgesetzes zur Flüchtlingskonvention und zum Ausländergesetz," in *Grenzfragen des innerdeutschen Asylrechts*, ed. Otto-Beneke-Stiftung (Bonn: Otto.Beneke-Stiftung, 1976), 28–40.

14. Jan Foitzik, "Enstalinierungskrise in Ostmitteleuropa: Verlauf, Ursachen und Folgen," in *Kommunismus in der Krise. Die Entstalinisierung 1956 und die Folgen*, eds. Roger Engelmann, Thomas Großbölting, and Hermann Wentker (Göttingen: Vandenhoeck & Ruprecht, 2008), 35–60.

15. Patrice G. Poutrus, "Zuflucht im Nachkriegsdeutschland. Politik und Praxis der Flüchtlingsaufnahme in Bundesrepublik und DDR von den späten 1940er bis zu den 1970er Jahren," *Geschichte und Gesellschaft. Zeitschrift für Historische Sozialwissenschaft* 35, no.1 (2009): 135–75.

16. Sándor Csík, "Die Flüchtlingswelle nach dem Ungarn-Aufstand 1956 in die Bundesrepublik," *Almanac II (2003–2004)*, ed. Deutsch-Ungarische Gesellschaft (Berlin: Deutsche-Ungarische Gesellschaft, 2005), 207–46.

17. "Mehr Flüchtlinge aus Ungarn. Österreich gewährt jedem Hilfesuchenden Asyl," *FAZ*, 31 October 1956.

18. Hans-Georg Rambousek, "Flüchtlingstreck wie vor elf Jahren. Ein gewaltiger Strom verzweifelter Ungarn erreicht rechtzeitig die österreichische Grenze," *Münchner Merkur*, 6 November 1956.

19. "Steinwürfe gegen sowjetischen Autobus," *Der Tagesspiegel*, 6 November 1956.

20. "Die freie Welt gedenkt Ungarns Freiheitskämpfer. Gedenkminuten und Protestmärsche," *Frankfurter Neue Presse*, 7 November 1956.

21. Csík, "Die Flüchtlingswelle," 208.

22. Reinhardt Marx, "Vom Schutz vor Verfolgung zur Politik der Abschreckung. Zur Geschichte des Asylverfahrensrechtes in der Bundesrepublik Deutschland," *Kritische Justiz* 18, no. 4 (1985): 379–95.

23. Ibolya Murber, "Ungarnflüchtlinge in Österreich 1956. Grenzübertritt der Flüchtlinge," in *Die ungarische Revolution und Österreich 1956*, eds. Ibolya Murber and Zoltán Fónagy (Vienna: Czernin, 2006), 335–86.

24. Karin Friedrich, "Eine Mutter, die vor den Panzern floh. Mit drei Kindern von Ungarn nach München–Vater an der Grenze zurückgehalten," *Süddeutsche Zeitung*, 9 November 1956. Alois Euler, "Mit Totengebeten kamen sie über die Grenze. Volk auf der Flucht– Säugling am Schlagbaum niedergelegt–Brief an den Vater in Budapest–Erinnerungen an furchtbare Stunden," *Generalanzeiger für Bonn und Umgebung*, 10 November 1956.

25. "Ungarische Flüchtlinge wollen der Heimat nahe bleiben. 500 Volksdeutsche in Bayern erwartet–Appell an die Bundesländer," *Stuttgarter Nachrichten*, 10 November 1956.

26. Erich Richtenberg, "Viele wollen ihr Blut spenden. Hunderte von 'Konserven' wurden hergestellt," *Welt am Sonntag*, 11 November 1956.

27. Hans Jürgen Kramer, "Vater blieb drüben, um zu kämpfen. Bisher 10000 ungarische Kinder auf österreichischen Boden," *Kölner Stadt-Anzeiger*, 14 November 1956.

28. "Kein Platz für Ungarnflüchtlinge? Einige Bundesländer weigern sich–Erster Transport eingetroffen," *Der Mittag*, 17 October 1956.

29. "Aufnahme von 6000 Ungarn?" *Die Welt*, 20 November 1956.

30. Raimund Hörhager, "Ein Steg war der Weg in die Freiheit. Neuer Flüchtlingsstrom aus Ungarn über die Grenze. Andau–unvollkommene Herberge der Not," *Hannoversche Allgemeine Zeitung*, 21 November 1956.

31. "Bonn erweitert Hilfe für Ungarn. Bundeskabinett streicht die Begrenzung auf 3000 Flüchtlinge," *Die Welt*, 23 November 1956.

32. "Mit dem Gedanken noch in Ungarn. Über 3000 ungarische Flüchtlinge wurden durch Ungarn geschleust–Neue Heimat in Belgien–Ergreifende Szenen auf dem Hauptbahnhof – Freiwillige Hefter lindern die größte Not," *Aachener Nachrichten*, 24 November 1956.

33. "Die gemeinsame Hilfe für die Ungarn-Flüchtlinge. Bisher sechs Hilfszüge für Budapest– Tätigkeit des Deutschen Roten Kreuzes," *Stuttgarter Nachrichten*, 27 November 1956.

34. "Bonn will 10000 Ungarn aufnehmen. Bundesregierung schickt weitere Lebensmittel nach Ungarn," *Die Welt*, 29 November 1956.

35. "Keine Auslese ungarischer Flüchtlinge. Bundesregierung betont die Gleichstellung mit allen Vertriebenen." *FAZ*, 4 December 1956.
36. Josef Schmidt, "Vom Ostwind verweht ... Lager Friedland in diesen Tagen – Flüchtlinge aus Ungarn, schlesische Aussiedler, Heimkehrer aus Russland," *Süddeutsche Zeitung*, 5 December 1956.
37. "20 Millionen für Ungarn," *Die Welt*, 20 December 1956. "Bundesrepublik an erster Stelle. Der deutsche Anteil an der Ungarnhilfe beträgt 60 Prozent," *Die Welt*, 29 December 1957.
38. "Die Ungarnhilfe der Deutschen Bundesrepublik," *NZZ*, 21 December 1956.
39. Rudolf Richter, "Vorsitzender des Flüchtlingsausschusses im Durchgangslager Hamburg-Wandsbek, Die Arbeitshose geht zurück. Sind die Deutschen jetzt Flüchtlinge zweiten Ranges?" *Hamburger Anzeiger*, 10 December 1956. O.A. "Es werden mehr kommen. Minister Fiedler: Bei aller Hilfsbereitschaft – vergeßt die deutschen Flüchtlinge nicht," *Badische Zeitung*, 19 December 1956. Bert Schnitzler, "Deutsche Flüchtlinge im Schatten. Strom der Nächstenliebe fließt vor allem für die 10 000 Ungarn-Flüchtlinge im Bundesgebiet," *Neue Rhein-Zeitung*, 20 December 1956.
40. Walter Schallies, "Nach dem Straßenkampf das Abitur. Einziges ungarisches Gymnasium auf westdeutschen Boden in Not – Kein Platz für 250 geflüchtet Schüler," *Stuttgarter Nachrichten*, 21 January 1957. Helmut Alt, "Wir sind nichts als Menschen – bietta schön! Die Ungarn-Hilfe steht vor dem Abschluß – wenn nicht noch neue kommen," *Frankfurter Rundschau*, 26 January 1957.
41. Helmuth Rüttner, "Die Helden sind schnell vergessen. Ungarn kehren zurück – Hat der Westen versagt?" *Die Welt*, 27 March 1957.
42. Jan Molitor, "Drei Ungarn von tausend. Das neue Leben nach der Flucht – Was den Fremdling glücklich macht," *Die Zeit*, 31 October 1957.
43. Claus Gennrich, "Ungarn in Deutschland," *FAZ*, 21 May 1966.
44. Karen Schönwälder, "'Ist nur Liberalisierung Fortschritt?' Zur Entstehung des ersten Ausländergesetzes der Bundesrepublik," in *50 Jahre Bundesrepublik – 50 Jahre Einwanderung. Nachkriegsgeschichte als Migrationsgeschichte*, eds. Motte et al. (Frankfurt a.M.: Campus, 1999) 127–44.
45. See BVerfGE 9, 174 (181) vol. 4, February 1959, cited in Münch, *Asylpolitik*, 53.
46. Otto Kimminich, *Grundprobleme des Asylrechts* (Darmstadt: Wissenschaftliche Buchgesellschaft, 1983), 99–106.
47. See BVerwGE 49, 202 vol. 7, October 1975, cited in ibid., 103.
48. "Schärfere Kontrolle der Algerier. Länder wollen ihre Maßnahmen koordinieren," *Die Welt*, 28 October 1959.
49. "Bombenanschlag auf die jugoslawische Mission in Bad Godesberg," *FAZ*, 30 November 1962.
50. Astrid Bröker and Jens Rautenberg, *Die Asylpolitik in der Bundesrepublik Deutschland unter besonderer Berücksichtigung des sogenannten "Asylmissbrauchs"* (Berlin: Express Edition, 1986).
51. Simone Wolken, "Asylpolitik in der Bundesrepublik Deutschland. Politik gegen politische Flüchtlinge?" in *Flucht und Asyl. Informationen, Analysen, Erfahrungen aus der Schweiz und der Bundesrepublik Deutschland*, eds. Dietrich Thränhardt and Simone Wolken (Freiburg i.Br.: Lambertus, 1988), 62–97.
52. "Wer erhält in Zirndorf Asyl? Das Bundessammellager für ausländische Flüchtlinge," *Stuttgarter Zeitung*, 16 November 1965.
53. Ulrich Herbert and Karin Hunn, "Beschäftigung, soziale Sicherung und soziale Integration von Ausländern," in *Geschichte der Sozialpolitik in Deutschland seit 1945*, vol. 5, ed. Bundesministerium für Arbeit und Soziales (Baden-Baden: Nomos, 2006), 791.

54. "Tschechen: Überwältigt von der Anteilnahme. Von Anteilnahme im Ausland überraschte Feuerwehrleute in Frankfurt." *Frankfurter Rundschau*, 26 August 1968.

55. Jiri Prenes, "Das tschechoslowakische Exil 1968. Exilanten, Emigranten, Landleute: Diskussion über Begriffe," in *Unfreiwilliger Aufbruch. Migration und Revolution von der Französischen Revolution bis zum Prager Frühling*, ed. Dittmar Dahlmann (Essen: Klartext, 2007), 187–96.

56. László Ziermann, "Schande – Skandal – Gemeinheit," *Die Rheinlandpfalz* (Ludwigshafen), 22 August 1968.

57. "Die Arbeiterwohlfahrt hilft den Tschechoslowaken, Stuttgart bietet jetzt Quartiere an – Pässe der Heimreisende werden verlängert – Keine Schwierigkeiten an der Grenze," *Stuttgarter Zeitung*, 29 August 1968.

58. Claus Gennrich, "Zehntausend kamen seit dem 21 August. Die deutsche Hilfe für tschechoslowakische Flüchtlinge," *FAZ*, 30 October 1968.

59. Thomas Pampusch, "CSSR-Bürger – Wohnort München. Rund 2000 leben in der Landeshauptstadt," *Süddeutsche Zeitung*, 21 August 1969.

60. Michael Stolle, "Inbegriff des Unrechtsstaates. Zur Wahrnehmung der chilenischen Diktatur in der deutschsprachigen Presse zwischen 1973 und 1989," *Zeitschrift für Geschichtswissenschaft (ZfG)* 51, no. 9 (2003): 793–813.

61. Ibid.

62. Dietrich Thränhardt, "'Ausländer als Objekte deutscher Interessen und Ideologien," in *Der gläserne Fremde. Bilanz und Kritik der Gastarbeiterforschung und der Ausländerpädagogik*. ed. Hartmut M. Griese (Opladen: Leske + Budrich, 1984), 115–32.

63. Doris Dickel, *Einwanderungs- und Asylpolitik der Vereinigten Staaten von Amerika, Frankreichs und der Bundesrepublik. Eine vergleichende Studie der 1980er und 1990er Jahre* (Opladen: Leske + Budrich, 2002), 283.

64. Margit Stöber, *Politisch Verfolgte genießen Asylrecht. Positionen und Konzeptionen von CDU/CSU zu Artikel 16 Absatz 2 Satz 2 Grundgesetz 1978 bis 1989* (Berlin: Verlag für Wissenschaft und Bildung, 1990), 88.

65. Klaus J. Bade, "Politisch Verfolgte genießen …: Asyl bei den Deutschen: Idee und Wirklichkeit," in *Deutsche im Ausland–Fremde in Deutschland*, ed. Klaus J. Bade (Berlin: Bertelsmann-Club, 1992), 411–22, here 413.

66. Jürgen Link, "Medien und Asylanten: Zur Geschichte eines Unworts," in *Flucht und Asyl*, eds. Dietrich Thränhardt and Simone Wolken, 50–61.

67. "Universal" in this case referred only to men. See Peter Graf Kielmansegg, *Nach der Katastrophe. Eine Geschichte des geteilten Deutschland* (Berlin: Siedler, 2000), 319–32.

68. Johannes Müller, ed., *Flüchtlinge und Asyl. Politisch handeln aus christlicher Verantwortung* (Frankfurt a.M.: J. Knecht, 1990).

69. Hans F. Zacher, "Sozialer Einschluß und Ausschluß im Zeichen von Nationalisierung und Internationalisierung," in *Koordinaten deutscher Geschichte in der Epoche des Ost-West-Konflikts*, Schriften des Historischen Kollegs, Kolloquien 55, ed. Hans Günter Hockerts (Munich: Oldenbourg, 2004), 103–52.

70. Klaus J. Bade, *Ausländer – Aussiedler – Asyl, Eine Bestandsaufnahme* (Munich: Ch. Beck, 1994), 91–146.

71. Patrice G. Poutrus, "Zuflucht im Ausreiseland. Zur Geschichte des politischen Asyls in der DDR," *Jahrbuch für Historische Kommunismusforschung 2004* (Berlin: Aufbau, 2004) 355–78.

72. Patrice G. Poutrus, "Teure Genossen. Die 'polit. Emigranten' als 'Fremde' im Alltag der DDR-Gesellschaft," in *Ankunft – Alltag – Ausreise. Migration und interkulturelle*

*Begegnungen in der DDR-Gesellschaft*, eds. Christian Müller, Th. Christian, and Patrice G. Poutrus (Cologne: Böhlau, 2005), 221–66.

73. Jost Maurin, "Flüchtlinge als politisches Instrument – Chilenische Emigranten in der DDR," *TuD* 2, no. 3 (2005): 345–74.

74. Dagmar Henke, "Fremde Nähe – nahe Fremde: Ein Beitrag zur Ausländerarbeit der Kirchen in der ehemaligen DDR," *Berliner Theologische Zeitschrift* 9, no. 1 (1992): 121.

75. Mathias Hong, *Asylgrundrecht und Refoulementverbot* (Baden-Baden: Nomos, 2008).

76. Elisabeth Haun, *The Externalisation of Asylum Procedures. An Adequate EU Refugee Burden Sharing System?* (Frankfurt a.m.: Peter Lang, 2007).

77. Günter Renner, "Aktuelle und ungelöste Probleme des Asyl- und Flüchtlingsrechts," in *Migrationsreport 2002. Fakten – Analysen – Perspektiven*, eds. Klaus J. Bade and Rainer Münz (Frankfurt a.m.: Campus, 2002), 179–206.

78. Olaf Köppe, "MigrantInnen zwischen sozialem Rechtsstaat und nationalem Wettbewerbsstaat. Zur Bedeutung von Justiz und Politik bei der Vergabe von 'bürgerlichen' und sozialen Rechten an MigrantInnen unter sich verändernden sozialen, politischen und ökonomischen Bedingungen" (PhD diss., Universität Duisburg, 2003).

79. Peter Schimany, "Asylmigration nach Deutschland," in *20 Jahre Ayslkompromiss. Bilanz und Perspektiven*, eds. Stefan Luft and Peter Schimany (Bielefeld: transcript, 2014), 33–66.

80. Jannis Panagiotidis, Patrice G. Poutrus, and Frank Wolff, "Integration ist machbar, Nachbar! Der Historiker Jörg Baberowski wirft der Politik den Verlust des Unterscheidungsvermögens in der Flüchtlingsdebatte vor. Kennt er die Unterschiede? Eine Antwort aus der historischen Migrationsforschung," *FAZ*, 2 October 2015.

# Works Cited

*Aachener Nachrichten*. "Mit dem Gedanken noch in Ungarn. Über 3000 ungarische Flüchtlinge wurden durch Ungarn geschleust–Neue Heimat in Belgien–Ergreifende Szenen auf dem Hauptbahnhof – Freiwillige Hefter lindern die größte Not." 24 November 1956.

Alt, Helmut, "Wir sind nichts als Menschen – bietta schön! Die Ungarn-Hilfe steht vor dem Abschluß – wenn nicht noch neue kommen." *Frankfurter Rundschau*, 26 January 1957.

Bade, Klaus J. "Politisch Verfolgte genießen …: Asyl bei den Deutschen: Idee und Wirklichkeit." In *Deutsche im Ausland–Fremde in Deutschland*, edited by Klaus J. Bade, 411–22. Berlin: Bertelsmann-Club, 1992.

Bade, Klaus J. *Ausländer – Aussiedler – Asyl, Eine Bestandsaufnahme*. Munich: Ch. Beck, 1994.

Bröker, Astrid, and Jens Rautenberg. *Die Asylpolitik in der Bundesrepublik Deutschland unter besonderer Berücksichtigung des sogenannten "Asylmissbrauchs."* Berlin: Express Edition, 1986.

Csík, Sándor. "Die Flüchtlingswelle nach dem Ungarn-Aufstand 1956 in die Bundesrepublik." In *Almanac II (2003–2004)*, edited by Deutsch-Ungarische Gesellschaft, 207–46. Berlin: Deutsch-Ungarische Gesellschaft, 2005.

Dahlmann, Dittmar, ed. *Unfreiwilliger Aufbruch. Migration und Revolution von der Französischen Revolution bis zum Prager Frühling*. Essen: Klartext-Verlag, 2007.

Dickel, Doris. *Einwanderungs- und Asylpolitik der Vereinigten Staaten von Amerika, Frankreichs und der Bundesrepublik. Eine vergleichende Studie der 1980er und 1990er Jahre*. Opladen: Leske + Budrich, 2002.

Euler, Alois. "Mit Totengebeten kamen sie über die Grenze. Volk auf der Flucht–Säugling am Schlagbaum niedergelegt–Brief an den Vater in Budapest–Erinnerungen an furchtbare Stunden." *Generalanzeiger für Bonn und Umgebung*, 10 November 1956.

Foitzik, Jan. "Enstalinierungskrise in Ostmitteleuropa: Verlauf, Ursachen und Folgen." In *Kommunismus in der Krise. Die Entstaliniserung 1956 und die Folgen*, edited by Roger Engelmann, Thomas Großbölting and Hermann Wentker, 35–60. Göttingen: Vandenhoeck & Ruprecht, 2008.

*Frankfurter Allgemeine Zeitung (FAZ)*. "Mehr Flüchtlinge aus Ungarn. Österreich gewährt jedem Hilfesuchenden Asyl." 31 October 1956.

*Frankfurter Allgemeine Zeitung (FAZ)*."Keine Auslese ungarischer Flüchtlinge. Bundesregierung betont die Gleichstellung mit allen Vertriebenen." 4 December 1956.

*Frankfurter Allgemeine Zeitung (FAZ)*. "Bombenanschlag auf die jugoslawische Mission in Bad Godesberg." 30 November 1962.

*Frankfurter Neue Presse*. "Die freie Welt gedenkt Ungarns Freiheitskämpfer. Gedenkminuten und Protestmärsche." 7 November 1956.

*Frankfurter Rundschau*. "Tschechen: Überwältigt von der Anteilnahme. Von Anteilnahme im Ausland überraschte Feuerwehrleute in Frankfurt." 26 August 1968.

Franz, Fritz. "Verhältnis der Verheißung des Grundgesetzes zur Flüchtlingskonvention und zum Ausländergesetz." In *Grenzfragen des innerdeutschen Asylrechts*, edited by Otto-Beneke-Stiftung, 28–40. Bonn: Otto-Beneke-Stiftung, 1976.

Friedrich, Karin. "Eine Mutter, die vor den Panzern floh. Mit drei Kindern von Ungarn nach München–Vater an der Grenze zurückgehalten." *Süddeutsche Zeitung*, 9 November 1956.

Führner, Harald. *Nachspiel: Die niederländische Politik und die Verfolgung von Kollaborateuren und NS-Verbrechern, 1945–1989*. Münster: Waxmann Verlag, 2005.

Gennrich, Claus. "Ungarn in Deutschland." *Frankfurter Allgemeine Zeitung (FAZ)*, 21 May 1966.

Gennrich, Claus. "Zehntausend kamen seit dem 21 August. Die deutsche Hilfe für tschechoslowakische Flüchtlinge." *Frankfurter Allgemeine Zeitung (FAZ)*, 30 October 1968.

Haun, Elisabeth. *The Externalisation of Asylum Procedures. An Adequate EU Refugee Burden Sharing System?* Frankfurt a.M.: Peter Lang, 2007.

Henke, Dagmar. "Fremde Nähe – nahe Fremde: Ein Beitrag zur Ausländerarbeit der Kirchen in der ehemaligen DDR," *Berliner Theologische Zeitschrift* 9, no. 1 (1992): 121.

Herbert, Ulrich, and Karin Hunn. "Beschäftigung, soziale Sicherung und soziale Integration von Ausländern." In *Geschichte der Sozialpolitik in Deutschland seit 1945. Vol. 3*, edited by Bundesministerium für Arbeit und Soziales, 779–801. Baden-Baden: Nomos, 2005.

Herbert, Ulrich, and Karin Hunn. "Beschäftigung, soziale Sicherung und soziale Integration von Ausländern." In *Geschichte der Sozialpolitik in Deutschland seit 1945. Vol. 5*, edited by Bundesministerium für Arbeit und Soziales, 783-809. Baden-Baden: Nomos, 2007.

Hong, Mathias. *Asylgrundrecht und Refoulementverbot*. Baden-Baden: Nomos, 2008.

Hörhager, Raimund. "Ein Steg war der Weg in die Freiheit. Neuer Flüchtlingsstrom aus Ungarn über die Grenze. Andau–unvollkommene Herberge der Not." *Hannoversche Allgemeine Zeitung*, 21 November 1956.

Huber, Bertold. *Ausländer–und Asylrecht*. Munich: Ch. Beck, 1983.

Kielmansegg, Peter Graf. *Nach der Katastrophe. Eine Geschichte des geteilten Deutschland*. Berlin: Siedler, 2000.

Kimminich, Otto. *Grundprobleme des Asylrechts*. Darmstadt: Wissenschaftliche Buchgesellschaft, 1983.

Köppe, Olaf. "MigrantInnen zwischen sozialem Rechtsstaat und nationalem Wettbewerbsstaat. Zur Bedeutung von Justiz und Politik bei der Vergabe von ›bürgerlichen‹ und sozialen

Rechten an MigrantInnen unter sich verändernden sozialen, politischen und ökonomischen Bedingungen." PhD diss., Universität Duisburg, 2003.

Kramer, Hans Jürgen. "Vater blieb drüben, um zu kämpfen. Bisher 10000 ungarische Kinder auf österreichischen Boden." *Kölner Stadt-Anzeiger*, 14 November 1956.

Link, Jürgen. "Medien und Asylanten: Zur Geschichte eines Unworts." In *Flucht und Asyl*, edited by Dietrich Thränhardt and Simone Wolken, 50–61. Opladen: Leske + Budrich, 1984.

Marx, Reinhardt. "Vom Schutz vor Verfolgung zur Politik der Abschreckung. Zur Geschichte des Asylverfahrensrechtes in der Bundesrepublik Deutschland." *Kritische Justiz* 18, no. 4 (1985): 379–95.

Marx, Reinhard. "Die Definition politischer Verfolgung in der Bundesrepublik Deutschland." In *Flucht und Asyl. Berichte über Flüchtlingsgruppen*, edited by Andreas Germershausen and Wolf-Dieter Narr, 148–58. Freiburg i.br: Lambertus, 1988.

Maurin, Jost. "Flüchtlinge als politisches Instrument – Chilenische Emigranten in der DDR." *TuD* 2, no. 3 (2005): 345–74.

*Der Mittag*. "Kein Platz für Ungarnflüchtlinge? Einige Bundesländer weigern sich–Erster Transport eingetroffen." 17 October 1956.

Molitor, Jan. "Drei Ungarn von tausend. Das neue Leben nach der Flucht – Was den Fremdling glücklich macht." *Die Zeit*, 31 October 1957.

Müller, Johannes, ed. *Flüchtlinge und Asyl. Politisch handeln aus christlicher Verantwortung.* Frankfurt a.M.: J. Knecht, 1990.

Münch, Ursula. *Asylpolitik in der Bundesrepublik Deutschland: Entwicklung und Alternativen.* Opladen: Leske + Budrich, 1993.

Münz, Rainer. "Phasen und Formen der europäischen Migration." In *Migration und Flucht: Aufgaben und Strategien für Deutschland, Europa und die internationale Gemeinschaft*, edited by Steffen Angenendt, 34–47. Bonn: Bundeszentrale für politische Bildung, 1997.

Murber, Ibolya. "Ungarnflüchtlinge in Österreich 1956. Grenzübertritt der Flüchtlinge." In *Die ungarische Revolution und Österreich 1956*, edited by Ibolya Murber and Zoltán Fónagy, 335–86. Vienna: Czernin, 2006.

*NZZ*. "Die Ungarnhilfe der Deutschen Bundesrepublik." 21 December 1956.

O.A. "Es werden mehr kommen. Minister Fiedler: Bei aller Hilfsbereitschaft – vergeßt die deutschen Flüchtlinge nicht." *Badische Zeitung*, 19 December 1956.

Oltmer, Jochen. *Migration und Politik in der Weimarer Republik*. Göttingen: Vandenhoeck & Ruprecht, 2005.

Panagiotidis, Jannis, Patrice G. Poutrus, and Frank Wolff. "Integration ist machbar, Nachbar! Der Historiker Jörg Baberowski wirft der Politik den Verlust des Unterscheidungsvermögens in der Flüchtlingsdebatte vor. Kennt er die Unterschiede? Eine Antwort aus der historischen Migrationsforschung." *Frankfurter Allgemeine Zeitung (FAZ)*, 2 October 2015.

Poutrus, Patrice G. "Zuflucht im Ausreiseland. Zur Geschichte des politischen Asyls in der DDR." *Jahrbuch für Historische Kommunismusforschung* 11, 355–78. Berlin: Aufbau, 2004.

Poutrus, Patrice G. "Teure Genossen. Die 'polit. Emigranten' als 'Fremde' im Alltag der DDR-Gesellschaft." In *Ankunft – Alltag – Ausreise. Migration und interkulturelle Begegnungen in der DDR-Gesellschaft*, edited by Christian Müller, Th. Christian, and Patrice G. Poutrus, 221–66. Cologne: Böhlau, 2005.

Poutrus, Patrice G. "Zuflucht im Nachkriegsdeutschland. Politik und Praxis der Flüchtlingsaufnahme in Bundesrepublik und DDR von den späten 1940er bis zu den 1970er Jahren." *Geschichte und Gesellschaft. Zeitschrift für Historische Sozialwissenschaft* 35, no.1 (2009): 135–75.

Poutrus, Patrice G. "The Right to Asylum in West Germany: Refugee Policies in the Federal Republic of Germany, 1949–1975." In *Human Rights and History: A Challenge for Education*, edited by Rainer Huhle, 106–112. Berlin: FATAMorgana Verlag, 2010.

Poutrus, Patrice G. "Flüchtlingsberichte: Öffentlichkeit und Asylpolitik im geteilten Deutschland während des Kalten Krieges." In *Flüchtlingslager im Nachkriegsdeutschland. Migration, Politik, Erinnerung*, edited by Henrik Bispinck and Katharina Hochmuth, 90–112. Berlin: Ch. Links, 2014.

Prenes, Jiri. "Das tschechoslowakische Exil 1968. Exilanten, Emigranten, Landleute: Diskussion über Begriffe." In *Unfreiwilliger Aufbruch. Migration und Revolution von der Französischen Revolution bis zum Prager Frühling*, edited by Dittmar Dahlmann, 187–96. Essen: Klartext, 2007.

Rambousek, Hans-Georg. "Flüchtlingstreck wie vor elf Jahren. Ein gewaltiger Strom verzweifelter Ungarn erreicht rechtzeitig die österreichische Grenze." *Münchner Merkur*, 6 November 1956.

Renner, Günter. "Aktuelle und ungelöste Probleme des Asyl- und Flüchtlingsrechts." In *Migrationsreport 2002. Fakten – Analysen – Perspektiven*, edited by Klaus J. Bade and Rainer Münz, 179–206. Frankfurt a.M.: Campus, 2002.

Richtenberg, Erich. "Viele wollen ihr Blut spenden. Hunderte von 'Konserven' wurden hergestellt." *Welt am Sonntag*, 11 November 1956.

Richter, Rudolf. "Vorsitzender des Flüchtlingsausschusses im Durchgangslager Hamburg-Wandsbek, Die Arbeitshose geht zurück. Sind die Deutschen jetzt Flüchtlinge zweiten Ranges?" *Hamburger Anzeiger*, 10 December 1956.

Rüttner, Helmuth. "Die Helden sind schnell vergessen. Ungarn kehren zurück – Hat der Westen versagt?" *Die Welt*, 27 March 1957.

Schallies, Walter. "Nach dem Straßenkampf das Abitur. Einziges ungarisches Gymnasium auf westdeutschen Boden in Not – Kein Platz für 250 geflüchtet Schüler." *Stuttgarter Nachrichten*, 21 January 1957.

Schimany, Peter. "Asylmigration nach Deutschland." In *20 Jahre Ayslkompromiss. Bilanz und Perspektiven*, edited by Stefan Luft and Peter Schimany, 33–66. Bielefeld: transcript, 2014.

Schmidt, Josef. "Vom Ostwind verweht ... Lager Friedland in diesen Tagen – Flüchtlinge aus Ungarn, schlesische Aussiedler, Heimkehrer aus Russland." *Süddeutsche Zeitung*, 5 December 1956.

Schneider, Hans-Peter. "Das Asylrecht zwischen Generosität und Xenophobie: Zur Entstehung des Artikels 16 Absatz 2 Grundgesetz im Parlamentarischen Rat." *Jahrbuch für Antisemitismusforschung* 1 (1992): 217–36.

Schnitzler, Bert, "Deutsche Flüchtlinge im Schatten. Strom der Nächstenliebe fließt vor allem für die 10 000 Ungarn-Flüchtlinge im Bundesgebiet." *Neue Rhein-Zeitung*, 20 December 1956.

Schönwälder, Karen. "'Ist nur Liberalisierung Fortschritt?' Zur Entstehung des ersten Ausländergesetzes der Bundesrepublik." In *50 Jahre Bundesrepublik – 50 Jahre Einwanderung. Nachkriegsgeschichte als Migrationsgeschichte*, edited by Jan Motte et al., 127–44. Frankfurt a.M.: Campus, 1999.

Steinbach, Peter. "Die Verpflichtung zur Beheimatung politisch Verfolgter: Der Weg zum Asylrecht des Grundgesetzes." *UNIVERSITAS* 50, no. 12 (1995): 1126–45.

Stöber, Margit. *Politisch Verfolgte genießen Asylrecht. Positionen und Konzeptionen von CDU/CSU zu Artikel 16 Absatz 2 Satz 2 Grundgesetz 1978 bis 1989*, 88. Berlin: Verlag für Wissenschaft und Bildung, 1990.

Stolle, Michael. "Inbegriff des Unrechtsstaates. Zur Wahrnehmung der chilenischen Diktatur in der deutschsprachigen Presse zwischen 1973 und 1989." *Zeitschrift für Geschichtswissenschaft (ZfG)* 51, no. 9 (2003): 793–813.

*Stuttgarter Nachrichten.* "Ungarische Flüchtlinge wollen der Heimat nahe bleiben. 500 Volksdeutsche in Bayern erwartet–Appell an die Bundesländer." 10 November 1956.

*Stuttgarter Nachrichten.* "Die gemeinsame Hilfe für die Ungarn-Flüchtlinge. Bisher sechs Hilfszüge für Budapest–Tätigkeit des Deutschen Roten Kreuzes." 27 November 1956.

*Stuttgarter Zeitung.* "Wer erhält in Zirndorf Asyl? Das Bundessammellager für ausländische Flüchtlinge." 16 November 1965.

*Stuttgarter Zeitung.* "Die Arbeiterwohlfahrt hilft den Tschechoslowaken, Stuttgart bietet jetzt Quartiere an – Pässe der Heimreisende werden verlängert – Keine Schwierigkeiten an der Grenze." 29 August 1968.

*Der Tagesspiegel.* "Steinwürfe gegen sowjetischen Autobus." 6 November 1956.

Therborn, Göran. *Die Gesellschaften Europas 1945–2000. Ein soziologischer Vergleich.* Frankfurt a. M.: Campus, 2000.

Thränhardt, Dietrich. "Ausländer als Objekte deutscher Interessen und Ideologien." In *Der gläserne Fremde. Bilanz und Kritik der Gastarbeiterforschung und der Ausländerpädagogik,* edited by Hartmut M. Griese, 115–32. Opladen: Leske + Budrich, 1984.

*Die Welt.* "Aufnahme von 6000 Ungarn?" 20 November 1956.

*Die Welt.* "Bonn erweitert Hilfe für Ungarn. Bundeskabinett streicht die Begrenzung auf 3000 Flüchtlinge." 23 November 1956.

*Die Welt.* "Bonn will 10000 Ungarn aufnehmen. Bundesregierung schickt weitere Lebensmittel nach Ungarn." 29 November 1956.

*Die Welt.* "20 Millionen für Ungarn." 20 December 1956.

*Die Welt.* "Bundesrepublik an erster Stelle. Der deutsche Anteil an der Ungarnhilfe beträgt 60 Prozent." 29 December 1957.

*Die Welt.* "Schärfere Kontrolle der Algerier. Länder wollen ihre Maßnahmen koordinieren." 28 October 1959.

Wolken, Simone. "Asylpolitik in der Bundesrepublik Deutschland. Politik gegen politische Flüchtlinge?" In *Flucht und Asyl. Informationen, Analysen, Erfahrungen aus der Schweiz und der Bundesrepublik Deutschland,* edited by Dietrich Thränhardt and Simone Wolken, 62–97. Freiburg i.Br.: Lambertus, 1988.

Zacher, Hans F. "Sozialer Einschluß und Ausschluß im Zeichen von Nationalisierung und Internationalisierung." In *Koordinaten deutscher Geschichte in der Epoche des Ost-West-Konflikts.* Schriften des Historischen Kollegs, Kolloquien 55, edited by Hans Günter Hockerts, 103–52. Munich: Oldenbourg, 2004.

Ziermann, László. "Schande – Skandal – Gemeinheit." *Die Rheinlandpfalz* (Ludwigshafen), 22 August 1968.

**Patrice G. Poutrus** is currently a member of the Refugee Research Network of the DFG (German Research Foundation). From 2013–15 he held a Lise-Meitner Fellowship at the Institute of Contemporary History, University of Vienna, and from 2008–14 held a lectureship at the Institute for History, Martin-Luther-University, Halle/Wittenberg. His research interests are European migration history, the history of modern media, and the history of communism in Europe, as well as the history of the Claims Conference, forced labor, and restitution. His most current publications on the subject of asylum are "Asylum in Postwar Germany: Refugee Admission Policies and Their Practical Implementation in the Federal Republic and the GDR Between the Late 1940s and the Mid-1970s" (2014) and "Zuflucht im Nachkriegsdeutschland. Politik und Praxis der Flüchtlingsaufnahme in Bundesrepublik und DDR von den späten 1940er Jahren bis zur Grundgesetzänderung im vereinten Deutschland von 1993" (2016).

# PART II
## Institutional Responses to Migration and Cultural Difference

# Chapter 5

# HISTORY, MEMORY, AND SYMBOLIC BOUNDARIES IN THE FEDERAL REPUBLIC OF GERMANY

Migrants and Migration in School History Textbooks

*Simone Lässig*

## Introduction

With the emergence of compulsory schooling in the nineteenth century, textbooks came to be regarded as powerful instruments for shaping collective memory and identity, and history textbooks were no exception. The idea of what history instruction should be was closely tied to, and a crucial part of, the evolution of modern nation states; for more than a century, the nation state has considered this field a domain in which it has the right and the duty to set the interpretive agenda. Most history textbooks of bygone eras thus reflected the past only inasmuch as it could be read as a prelude to the present of the nation in question, and their authors aimed at providing a logically consistent narrative to this end. In this context, school textbooks sometimes became a powerful means of marking symbolic boundaries between a nation and its counterparts or "enemies."

In the wake of World War II, however, nationalistic and chauvinistic concepts of history education invited serious criticism, particularly in the nation that had unleashed this war and that was responsible for mass murder and crimes against humanity of inconceivable dimensions. We might, in the light of this caesura, consider whether, why, and to what extent history education was denationalized or transnationalized, patterns of inclusion and exclusion changed, and symbolic boundaries underwent transformation in post-1945 Germany. Immediately after the war, the path of identification with their nation's history was to a considerable extent closed to Germans. Did this situation prove to be an opportunity to provide new generations of Germans with images of the past liberated from

---

the existing narrow conception of a national history deriving from an essentially exclusive norm of ethnic homogeneity?

With history textbooks as both our sources and our focus, this chapter will analyze this question in the context of historical representations of migrants. In this way, our discussion will center on social groups that, during certain periods of German history, have been perceived as internal "others" in an ethnic, religious, and/or cultural sense and whose depiction therefore implicitly reflects ideas and questions regarding inclusion and exclusion, both in society at large and in the images of history predominant within it.[1]

After a brief discussion of the value of school textbooks as historical sources, the chapter will explore when, how, and why, during the seven decades that have passed since 1945, new interpretations of the past and new approaches in history teaching have emerged or been propagated via textbooks. In view both of textbooks' specific potential for defining symbolic boundaries and of the fact that Germany today has often been described as a postnational nation, it seems heuristically stimulating to focus on schoolbook depictions of forms of migration and groups of migrants that are an integral part of our contemporary history but that have not always been part of our collective memory or that instead have been the subject of widely differing assessments.[2] This chapter will examine how textbooks have covered two broadly defined kinds of migration: first, forced migration, as epitomized by Jews and other Germans who fled Nazi Germany and by Germans who later fled or were expelled from Eastern Europe; second, migrant groups that contributed significantly to the transformation of Germany into a society characterized by migration (the so-called *Einwanderungsgesellschaft* or "immigration society"), i.e., victims and opponents of Nazism who returned to Germany after the war (*Remigranten*), labor migrants (so-called guest workers or *Gastarbeiter*), and asylum seekers fleeing persecution elsewhere. The discussion will conclude with a comparative international contextualization of the findings.

## School Textbooks as Media and as Sources for Historical Research

Because school textbooks reach the hands, if not always the minds, of more or less their entire intended audience, they can be viewed as ideal instruments by which states can shape "collective identities." The particular status of textbooks in comparison to that of other media and identity-building resources derives in part from the fact that the knowledge they contain is relatively slow to change and highly selective in nature. Produced by means of complex processes of content construction, they are generally authorized by the state and are therefore frequently perceived as particularly objective, accurate, and relevant.

The specific role of the state in this context does not imply, however, that textbooks are immune to the influence of scholarly or societal discourses. Quite the contrary, textbooks point to, but also help to create, conceptions of societal order, patterns of memory, and notions of the future, each in accordance with the times and either hegemonic or emerging from societal processes of negotiation.[3] The cultural, social, and political codes that textbooks unfailingly transmit can become subjects of political debate and reform activity, most markedly after the collapse of political systems, but also in situations marked by changing social and cultural contexts, including reworked cultures of memory. In most cases, textbooks eventually *reflect* such structural changes in societies. In some instances, however, they can *trigger* serious conflict around matters of memory, the recognition of specific interests, and cultural awareness.

In no field is this truer than in history. Textbooks on this subject are considered uniquely resonant instruments of memory politics, remembrance, and the promotion of social cohesion. In tracing specific self-images and images of "the other" back into the past, and in neglecting specific groups or excluding or eradicating them from representations of history, textbook authors, who are as deeply enmeshed as any other member of their society in the discourses reflected in textbooks, lend these images and the symbolic boundaries closely related to them a specific legitimacy, relevance, and validity for the present and the future of that society. It is not only in periods of hypernationalism or conflict that history textbooks contain, disseminate, or abet perceptions, interpretations, and stereotypes that support constructions of national superiority or collective victimhood. And it is beyond question that images of internal or external "others" are inscribed in such accounts or emanate from them. On the other hand, history teaching may also help to overcome prejudices or hostility and promote mutual respect and reconciliation between groups once joined only by enmity.[4]

From a historian's point of view, history textbooks are an appealing source for at least three other reasons. First, with some exceptions such as in Turkey, they are expected to be "up to date." Since textbook authors generally do not access archives in the course of their work and are therefore unaffected by the usual time-dependent prohibitions on the release of historical documents, the materials they produce for history *instruction* reach much closer to the present in their coverage than historical *research* does. Past and present, the experience of events and comprehending reflection on them, history and memory—all come very close in teaching and textbooks, almost merging into one. The "past" with which history education works is often still very "present" indeed.[5] Second, textbooks reveal the point at which and the form in which key issues, methodological approaches, and new findings in academic history have entered social and political discourse. Third, curricula and textbooks both reflect and generate canons of knowledge and views on the world that states and societies seek to implant into the cultural memory of successive generations, and thus cast a specific light on the zeitgeist shaping the period in which they were produced.

## Historical Narratives of a Postnational Nation? "Self" and "Other" in German History Textbooks since the 1950s

Nationalistic and chauvinistic methods of creating meaning and identity, once almost ubiquitous in Europe and applied to an extreme degree in Nazi Germany, lost their previously near-unquestioned status in the wake of the Shoah and the war of annihilation waged by the Germans. In all four occupation zones of defeated Germany, the Allies were greatly and urgently concerned with "decontaminating" and redesigning the nation's textbooks, which were henceforth—like the schools themselves—to expedite the process of democratization and promote understanding between nations. General Lucius D. Clay, U.S. Military Governor in Germany from 1947 to 1949, proposed that German textbook authors be equipped with every form of material and nonmaterial support, believing that re-education could not be expected to succeed without appropriate school textbooks.[6] Terence J. Leonard, the head of the British Textbook Section, which was part of the British Education Branch of the occupying authorities, shared this view. He considered school textbooks to be strategically the most decisive issue in the denazification of education, more important still than the re-education of teachers: "Cleanse the text in textbooks and all teachers, conscious of their duty, will pass the new contents on to their pupils!"[7]

From a medium-term perspective, the "coercive stimulus" to change provided by the occupying authorities in Germany might be viewed as effective. Although the Germans, unlike the Japanese, rejected a structural reform of their education system, they seemed—again in contrast to Japan[8]—relatively open to new concepts of teaching and to the idea of turning history education from a tool that justified "German superiority" and bellicosity into an instrument for the formation of a new self-image for the nation, at least in its western part. The struggle for democracy was becoming a central theme for civics and history education.[9] As early as 1949, officials from the U.S. Office of Military Government for Germany (OMGUS) stated that militarism, extreme nationalism, and racism had disappeared from German textbooks.[10] Revanchist tendencies appeared only occasionally in schoolbooks of the 1950s/1960s before likewise vanishing almost entirely, making way for a generally pacifist culture, which, over the ensuing two decades, evolved into a central element of the German postwar "self" as expressed in the Federal Republic's social and political values and in the beliefs of many individuals. Activities in the field of international textbook revision, initiated in the late 1940s with Anglo-German and Franco-German textbook dialog,[11] and the public debates on reconciliation that commenced in the late 1960s augmented these changes to West Germany's self-image—as reflected in history teaching—and left their mark on the way textbooks represented the country's neighbors and former enemies. Indeed, with such transnational textbook activities, especially in the German-Polish textbook commission (active since 1972), scholars,[12] teachers, and other individuals in the field of textbooks came to play a significant role not only in reflecting, but also in setting agendas and exerting a decisive directional influence on societal discourse. The controversies triggered by the German-Polish textbook recommendations published in 1975, of which 300,000 copies were distributed, initially presented a real challenge to mainstream German society and its customary interpretations of national history.[13] In the long run, however, even conservative German ministries of education, such as that of Bavaria, took the recommendations into account when authorizing textbooks. This shift, at least in part, arose from the fundamental changes that historical culture in German society underwent, beginning in the mid 1980s. The policy of "reconciliation" between Germany and those states and peoples that had suffered greatly at German hands, originally promoted by civil society stakeholders and the social democratic–liberal coalition government between 1969 and 1982, enjoyed increasing levels of acceptance in significant parts of West German society. Although representatives of the *Vertriebenenverbände*, the organizations promoting the interests of Germans expelled from Eastern Europe after the end of the war, continued to use revanchist rhetoric, "reconciliation" remained one of the major political objectives of the Federal Republic even after 1982, when Helmut Kohl's liberal-conservative coalition came to power.[14] While the politics of memory in general persisted as a controversial issue,[15] "reconciliation" seems to have become a rather inclusive concept, capable of transcending internal political divides and, from the 1990s onward, developing into an almost undisputed principle behind history textbook writing in unified Germany.[16]

The singularity of the genocide perpetrated against the Jews and of the German war of annihilation in Eastern Europe, and the role of these crimes in augmenting the extent to which German collective identity was shaken after the country's defeat, are likely to have been central factors in the disappearance of extreme nationalism and the emergence of a fundamentally pacifist attitude in textbooks. At this point, it was effectively impossible for most Germans to have a comfortable relationship with their national history. In general, nationalists were no longer welcome in the public arena, not least because Germany found itself during the Cold War (which itself left a significant mark on textbooks) in partnership with some of its erstwhile enemies and actively involved in processes of European integration.

The first teaching and learning materials to be published after the war, under Allied influence, favored European and global perspectives on various subjects, including history;[17] however, the curricula and textbooks of 1950s and 1960s West Germany did not, at least initially, continue along this path.[18] Instead, the dominant tone in history textbooks reflected adherence to a rather conservative, Western- and Christian-influenced concept of history. While these books did not promote war or nationalism, they did take as their apparently undisputed focal point a largely ethnically defined national historical narrative. From the 1970s onward, by contrast, history teaching and textbooks, in line with emerging tendencies in historical scholarship, began to critically analyze nationalism as a historical phenomenon with the idea of Europe becoming a key focus. The authors of a widely used history textbook of the 1970s stated in its introduction:

> This century has been an age of frequently excessive nationalist sentiment. Yet the rubble to which our towns and cities were reduced, the devastation wreaked upon vast parts of our world and the many millions of dead speak eloquently of the depths to which national egoism can lead us. The century of small nation states is over. The course of history continues to draw us toward alliances of nations spanning broad geographical spaces.[19]

Since the 1980s, the majority of textbooks examined in the research on which this chapter draws have reflected Germany's new self-image as a Western nation making committed efforts to Europeanize the interpretation of its national history.[20]

Nevertheless, this rejection of nationalism and embracing of a European identity does not mean that West German textbook authors consistently made an unambiguous effort to come to terms with Germany's recent and most challenging past. Indeed, at least initially, the reverse was true. It would take two decades after the end of the war until the Nazi period and the mass murder carried out by Germans became topics for public debate and for historical analysis in the classroom that went beyond brief mentions focusing on the responsibility of Hitler and his companions. During the 1950s and 1960s, most textbooks had, on the one hand, adopted interpretations in line with totalitarianism theory[21] and, on the other hand, constructed the "Third Reich" as a disruption of democratic traditions, as a "detour" on the path of German history. In this regard, they actively contributed to the culture of exculpating (ordinary) Germans from the crimes of Nazism, a response typical of West German society during the period of the "economic miracle." The elites who formed the backbone of civil society, such as teachers, education officials, and indeed textbook authors, carried their own personal stories of living under National Socialism and, like many of the Nazis' victims, consciously or unconsciously resisted engaging with this period in their lives. This phenomenon typified societies emerging from dictatorship and undergoing transformation. Germany's divergence from international patterns in this regard had less to do with the postwar generation's suppression of discussion of the period than its interest in attempting to come to terms with the past, whose late emergence contrasted with its striking intensity.

Almost all textbooks published in the 1950s and 1960s reflected this silence in the face of the most recent past and the concomitant refusal to engage with it. On the whole, West German society at the time tended to attribute a victim status to itself rather than seek out the stories of the actual victims of persecution and mass murder.[22] Although textbooks of the early Federal Republic mentioned crimes committed between 1933 and 1945, the issue of individual and collective responsibility was never raised beyond its application to a small group of high-ranking Nazi officials. In this, however, those in charge of curricula and of authoring and publishing textbooks took a position broadly similar to that of contemporary academic history, which likewise initially avoided the question of perpetrators, bystanders, victims, and those who resisted the regime, despite the fact that a significant amount of documentation had become available almost immediately after the end of World War II.[23]

A school textbook from 1967, which referred on one page to the emigration of German Jews and to *Synagogenbrand* (i.e., the pogroms of November 1938, literally "synagogue burning") was by no means exceptional in the message of exculpation it delivered: "Only a very small proportion of the German people took part in these excesses; the majority witnessed the events from the sidelines and responded passively, shrugging their shoulders or feeling a shiver of horror go down their spines."[24] Although this textbook, in its 1974 edition, refers to "foreign workers" (*"Fremdarbeiter"*, the National Socialist euphemism for forced laborers from outside Germany), points to "exploitation and [mass] abduction," and provides, in references to the massacres of Lidice and Oradour, unvarnished examples of the inhuman treatment meted out to the peoples in German-occupied territories, it attributes the "reprehensible and psychologically disastrous policy of occupation"—as, indeed, all crimes committed in Germany and Europe between 1933 and 1945—solely to "Hitler and his commissioners," or to the "monstrous blindness to reality of Hitler and of the SS that was firmly in thrall to him."[25]

The ambivalence is evident. On the one hand, curricula and textbook authors of the 1960s and early 1970s had begun to engage with the more recent past, including its dark side and its victims.[26] On the other hand, most textbooks of the period continued to focus on a small, powerful elite as the principal perpetrators. This approach was boosted by the continued dominance of traditional political history, not only in curricula and school textbooks but also in academic teaching and scholarship until at least the late 1970s, when social history and the history of everyday life came into their own. This last development received momentum from a simultaneously emerging direction in history teaching, which by now has gained broad acceptance in Germany, emphasizing critical thinking, the ability to approach a subject from a number of different perspectives, and the development of textbooks in line with this new emphasis.[27]

At the same time, the practice of silencing and suppressing the question of responsibility for the atrocities committed during the Nazi era came in for increasing criticism in West German society. This change in attitude was reflected to some degree in educational policy and officialdom, as is evident in the decision taken in 1978 by the Standing Conference of the West German State Education Ministers (KMK) to give National Socialism much more attention in schools in order to convey solid knowledge and embrace critical analysis.[28] Whether it was political elites, the media (especially the 1979 broadcast of the U.S. television series *Holocaust*), or civil society that proved the most significant factor in this direction, we can state with confidence that this development led to, while simultaneously being influenced by, an increasingly diverse textbook landscape. Further, this diversity and ambivalence was in line with the state of historical research at the time, although German academic historians, on the whole, at first proved reticent in their engagement with the critical approach that history workshops (*Geschichtswerkstätten*) and other citizens' initiatives, including the *Geschichtswettbewerb des Bundespräsidenten* (The Federal President's History Competition), had begun to establish toward the most recent past.[29] From this point of view, the impression arises that in this particular period a number of German textbook authors and others blazed a trail for new directions developed later by mainstream historical scholarship rather than, as is more typically the case in relation to the production of school textbooks, following research with a significant delay.[30] The landscape was altogether different in the 1980s, by which time West German politics and society had become sites of searching, passionate, and epoch-making debates on history and memory, a fount of new ideas in academic history and history teaching, and a manifestation of the direction that historical and civic education were to take in the future. The societal discourse of this period, which framed the production of history textbooks as much as it was influenced by concepts for textbooks that had emerged during the 1970s and 1980s, differed significantly from that of the 1950s and 1960s.

Let us now consider what changes, if any, have occurred in German ideas about who should be afforded which place in historical representations of German identity, how predominant patterns of belonging—of sharing in this identity—have changed, and how these changes are reflected in history textbooks. Questions about how those coming from "outside" (or those viewed as outsiders) have been integrated into Germany's self-image since the end of World War II, into German interpretations of the past and of the role of internal or external "others" in this history. These questions have gained previously unparalleled academic and political relevance in the context of a debate over Germany as a society of immigration that has been ongoing since the late 1990s. The section that follows will analyze these issues from both a contemporary and, importantly, a historical perspective as they have manifested themselves in textbooks past and present. In this context, the discussion will turn first to two very different types of *forced* migration, that of Jewish emigrants and refugees from the Nazis, on the one hand, and that of those expelled from formerly German-controlled regions of Eastern Europe, on the other. For all the evident differences between these two groups, core elements of their representation and depiction in school textbooks, particularly those produced in the first two decades after the war, feature striking parallels.

## *Forms of Forced Migration from and to Germany: German Victimhood and German Loss*

With few exceptions, both the genocide committed against European Jewry and the emigration and exile imposed upon people by National Socialism were distinctly marginal topics in textbooks during the 1950s and 1960s.[31] If they were mentioned at all, then in a context that minimized the experience of those who had been forced to leave their countries due to a background targeted by Nazi racial policies or because of opposition to the regime. A related approach was to subsume emigration and exile under a narrative of German loss, bringing to the fore representations of suffering endured by Germans during and after the war. In this period, refugee movements, flight, and expulsion received extensive and highly emotional treatment that focused almost exclusively on ethnic Germans from Eastern Europe, in particular on their fate during the war's final stages and after. Almost unanimously, textbook authors described the situation of those fleeing parts of Eastern Europe formerly under German control as miserable, detailing their fear of an enemy who "knew no mercy with women, children or the elderly … Thousands died of frostbite, starvation, dehydration, and exhaustion. Others bled to death in the hail of gunfire from Russian planes … The sufferings endured by these people were unimaginable."[32] These textbooks frequently featured photographs of endless refugee treks, with women, children, and elderly people often shown exposed to bitter cold and in desperate situations. At a time when textbooks generally contained few illustrations of any kind, such images added significant and very emotional emphasis to the discourse of victimhood produced in the text.[33] The flight of Germans across the Vistula Lagoon or the Baltic Sea that many claimed, after the publication of Günter Grass's novel *Crabwalk* in 2002,[34] had been swept under the rug for decades, was detailed in dramatic terms in many textbooks of the Federal Republic until the mid 1960s—and in some books even longer. The mass nature of these events was emphasized by supplementing absolute figures with comparisons, asserting, for instance, that the numbers of Germans expelled from their erstwhile homes between 1945 and 1955 exceeded the populations of entire countries such as the Netherlands, Australia, Switzerland, or Denmark.[35]

By contrast, young Germans of the first postwar generation learned nothing of how many other Europeans had been forced to leave their homelands during or as a result of the war waged by Germans, and nothing of their sufferings. While the *Documentation of the Expulsion of Germans from Eastern and Central Europe* (commissioned by the German federal government in 1953 and produced by historians) found immediate mention in textbooks,[36] the fact that 300,000 *Poles* had been forced to leave their homes during the German occupation and more than an additional million were taken to Germany as forced laborers—with 1.5 million subsequently moved west between 1944 and 1946 in accordance with Allied decrees— received no such consideration in the discourse of self-victimization that dominated the interpretation of the war and its aftermath in the Federal Republic's early years and decades.[37]

This even applied to textbooks that at first glance seemed exemplary in their global contextualization of the history of "forced migration," if not in their wording of that contextualization, whether in headings such as "Our Age of Refugees and Displaced People"[38] or in discussions of the "greatest mass migration [*Völkerwanderung*] in human history,"[39] which they deemed to have begun either in 1912 with the Balkan wars or in

1917 with the Bolshevik Revolution. A textbook published in 1955 generalized victimhood, implicitly including Germans driven from Eastern Europe. Marking Europe and Asia as the world regions most affected, the authors provided a chart informing students that between 1917 and 1951, 55 million people, of whom 20 million were German, became victims of "forced European migration movements due to political events." There was no accompanying attempt to give specific detail about groups of forced migrants or refugees or to provide any reasonably precise historical explanation of these events.[40] Instead of offering historical facts or background information that would have aided students in interpreting these figures, many books of this period presented precise details of the rapid rise in population density in West Germany and charts portraying the "influx of refugees"—often including refugees from the GDR, still referred to as the "Soviet zone"—into the Federal Republic.[41]

The avoidance of historically substantive analysis by approaching forced migration from a thoroughly generalizing international perspective affected the image of history received by successive generations. As recently as 1981, a table titled "Refugees and Expulsions in Our *Century*" (emphasis added) in a textbook began with the expulsion and flight of Germans from Eastern Europe at the end of World War II. While continuing to completely ignore Jewish and Polish forced migrants, the authors of this textbook considered it essential to mention the "flight and expulsion of 800,000 Arabs from the newly founded State of Israel (1948)," "of 300,000 Arabs [from Israel] after the June war (1967) [i.e., the Six-Day War]," of French Algerians, and, entirely in line with the patterns of interpretation dictated by the Cold War, refugees from Hungary and Czechoslovakia after the crushing of the uprisings in 1956 and 1968.[42]

As startling as the picture evident here might appear from the perspective of our present, it needs to be considered in the light of a number of specific issues and developments. The pluralization of the West German textbook landscape that arose in the 1980s made room for divergent interpretations of historical events, which meant that the perspective cited above was neither an actual exception nor was it the only one available on the textbook market.[43] Further, as Gerhard Paul found in 2010, emigration, exile, and remigration had never taken a significant role in the Federal Republic's culture of history and memory. Paul observed that there is as little mention of these issues in major public history projects as there is in material cultures of memory.[44] Thus, it is important for us to be aware of the historical context in which an issue is mentioned or avoided and the context in which a society places a past event or a collective experience. In the 1980s, when the table cited above was published, the persecution and injustices perpetrated against Jews in Nazi Germany had long since ceased to be taboo topics. They were, however, virtually never approached in the context of forced migration but instead primarily treated as part of the history of National Socialism (which itself was semantically restricted to referencing Hitler and the NSDAP) or as one of the events making up the history of World War II. Further, these issues were generally discussed from the perspective of the perpetrators with little self-awareness evident in the use of some source materials. *Spiegel der Zeiten* (Mirror of History), to cite one example, which since 1961 had made mention of the campaign of denial of basic rights pursued against the Jews and its culmination in mass murder, observed in a tone intended as emphatically factual that Jewish families who in the face of burning synagogues and the successive loss of civil rights had decided to emigrate had "escaped a fate worse still."[45] Textbooks tended to obfuscate German responsibility for forced migration rather than throw light on it. There were just as few clear depictions of the interconnection between the National Socialist regime and movements of emigration and exile despite the inclusion of a plethora of statistics, which carry the implication of being reliable facts, and despite the increasing amount of space authors were dedicating to the issue of forced migration. A textbook first published in 1961 still carried the following passage word for word in the mid 1980s: "From 1933 onward, a third wave of refugees began their journeys [as a consequence of] the [de facto] expulsion from Germany of approximately 400,000 opponents of the Hitler regime and Jews. From 1912 to 1939, an approximate total of 13 million refugees and resettlers were recorded in Europe, 1.1 million of them Germans."[46] Whether or not this count classified the Jews forced to migrate as "German" was not indicated in the book,[47] which was anything but exceptional in the manner of its depiction of these matters. Many representations of emigration and exile from Germany in 1960s West Germany went unchanged or saw only minor amendments in successive editions of textbooks over decades.[48] In this way, generations of pupils who passed through German schools between the end of the 1960s and the late 1980s—and, to an extent, even into the 1990s—learned not only about the trials and hardships faced by those forced to leave Germany, but also about the "irreplaceable loss" inflicted on *German* culture, science, and academia by the emigration, flight, and persecution of Jews and opponents of the Nazi dictatorship.[49] Such a narrative conveyed the impression of a double German victimhood. First, pupils' attention was directed toward the negative effects of emigration from Nazi Germany on *German* society. In the case both of forced emigration *from* (Nazi) Germany and of refugee movements from Eastern Europe *to* Germany, the members of German society appeared as the principal victims, first as affected by the "loss" of a significant part of the former academic and cultural elite, and then as having to absorb millions of poor and culturally "other" immigrants at a time when German cities were still suffering from housing shortages as a result of Allied bombings. Second, the dominant narrative on emigration and exile focused almost exclusively on the fates of *elites*, i.e., on what happened to those who had been leading figures in German society, which, along with constituting an expression of the overall tendency of history at the time to focus nearly exclusively on "the great and the good," reiterated the theme of *German* loss. The majority of German and European Jews received little more than an obligatory mention in the margins until at least the late 1980s and 1990s.[50]

Over time, however, sensitivity to and awareness of the bitter plight of those forced to leave Germany and its occupied territories increased. By the late 1980s and early 1990s, the story of loss and victimhood originally told mainly from an ethnically defined *German* perspective had lost its status as the hegemonic narrative framework for the issue of forced migration and soon ceased to dominate history teaching in this area. People's emotional responses were now drawn not to Germans forced to leave Eastern Europe but to representations of Jews and non-German victims of the Nazis. The sufferings of the so-called *Fremdarbeiter* were now mentioned in almost every textbook, with new research findings such as those by Ulrich Herbert entering the texts with striking rapidity.[51] A significant number of textbooks published since the 1990s have discussed the discrimination, deprivation of fundamental rights, persecution, and genocide suffered by European Jews between 1933 and 1945. They both address the issue of the perpetrators and give voice—and thus historical agency—to the victims, including ordinary Jews such as those who have shared their memories of the *Kindertransporte*.[52] In these textbooks, the Holocaust is dealt with as extensively as it is in contemporary German and Western European cultures of memory.[53]

The evident change in emphasis toward a focus on the victims of National Socialism, particularly Jewish victims, and toward critical historical analysis of the causes and consequences of forced migration, doubtless represents a paradigm shift, one that recent debates on non-Jewish German victims of World War II have left intact.[54] At the same time, at the beginning of the new millennium it has become apparent that German history embedded in its European context continues to follow narratives distinct from those of Jewish history, even though an integrative approach has been well established in research on the history of European Jewry. Where these textbooks refer to Jews and German/European Jewry, it is—with few exceptions—largely in the overarching context of a history of anti-Judaism, anti-Semitism, and prejudice toward Jews.[55] Jews have rarely been depicted in such a way as to allow them to be perceived as "subjects of their own historicity." Instead, they are frequently discussed within the context of a traditional *Beitragsgeschichte* approach that underscores what Jews have "contributed" to *German* culture, the *German* economy, *German* science, or other fields. This approach has also been applied to other groups with a contested status of "belonging" to German society. In fact, we might venture to state that this contributionism is only a short step away from the manner in which German textbooks represented emigration until the 1980s.

Although some of the textbooks currently on the market in Germany[56] mention periods of history in which Jews and non-Jews lived side by side with little conflict and give this minority a historical voice by including Jewish sources in their accounts, the dominant narrative is nevertheless one of the near-essentializing attribution to Jews of a victim status with limited historical agency, effectively designating them as objects of a history shaped by non-Jews.[57] Whether intentionally or otherwise, this manner of proceeding promotes or confirms a perception of Jews historically as "others" or "outsiders," whose belonging to or centrality in the nation's history is in question.[58] Surveying German societal discourses as they appear reflected in textbooks, we cannot escape the observation that Jews have not yet been incorporated into the historical interpretive framework of reunited Germany as subjects of history in possession of agency. An approach to history that takes account of complex relationships and interconnections in this regard (*Verflechtungsgeschichte*) appears to remain primarily the domain of academic research. The current place of Jewish history in German historical culture is still that of a marginalized or excluded minority. At the same time, the empathy with Jewish victims of persecution—and the self-conscious claiming of collective responsibility for which this image of Jewish history allows—enables non-Jewish Germans to rest on the laurels of their fundamental notion, formed over decades, of modern Germany as a postnational society open to the rest of the world, a society that has attained the necessary maturity to reflect critically on its difficult past.

## *The Place of Labor Migration, Political Migration, and Voluntary Remigration in Textbooks and the German Memory Landscape*

Up until the early 1980s, it was only in exceptional cases that German textbooks related the issue of "migration" to immigration, diversity, and the enrichment of society through the presence of a variety of cultures and ethnicities. Where the topic was touched upon at all, it was mainly in reference to politically or socially motivated emigration to America in the late nineteenth century or the—seemingly successful—integration of German refugees in the Federal Republic. While interest in the latter declined from the mid-to-late 1970s onward, labor migrants, who had played a decisive role in driving the country's economic miracle, gradually entered the historical picture. The arrival of the children of so-called guest workers in German classrooms led a small number of textbook authors to respond to Germany's changing social realities and to the significance to German society of working migrants, who were still viewed as *Ausländer* or foreigners. In taking on the topic, these authors were considerably ahead of Germany's political elite, who in official statements continued until the turn of the millennium to vehemently deny that Germany was a country of immigration.

Even the short paragraph or chart on the country's more than two million working migrants with which a few textbooks of the mid 1970s initially referenced the issue represented a level of engagement we would not necessarily expect from *history* textbooks. In most cases, such references were part of a chapter on the social and economic history of the Federal Republic since 1949. Labor migrants thus "entered" the nation's history textbooks as an integral component of the postwar narrative of success built on the economic miracle.[59] This said, one 1974 textbook commented, in an observation clearly intended to be positive in tone, that full employment had been achieved "despite large numbers of immigrant workers."[60] Remarks such as these already transported the narrative of problematization, which "after the boom," as the Federal Republic faced the challenge of coping with the "structural rupture of modernity as expressed in industrial society" and with increasing rates of unemployment,[61] came to dominate discourse in this area for at least two decades.[62]

Starting at the end of the 1970s, historians' assessment of the labor migrants began to change in two respects. First, parts of the West German population, and therefore some textbook authors, developed greater awareness of the situation of migrant workers who had come to the Federal Republic under recruitment agreements entered into with eight other states, beginning in 1955,[63] and who had become increasingly visible in West German society over time, not least by virtue of the families who joined so many of them. Against this backdrop, some textbooks tended to take a critical tone when discussing how employers, the state, and society dealt with *Gastarbeiter*, a term now regarded as problematic, yet used very much without scare quotes at the time. Viewpoints of immigrant workers could occasionally be found in the historical sources provided in textbooks. One workbook published in 1978 contained an account by an anonymous "guest worker" who argued that the German economy, for all its dependence on the labor of migrants to the country, failed "in most cases [to treat them] as guests," consigning them instead to a position on the margins of society with low-status and dangerous work, low pay, and poor living conditions. These circumstances, in turn, caused problems with the German host population.[64]

The interpretive tendency behind using this account essentially stemmed from a sense of solidarity with migrant workers subjected to degrading treatment and therefore constituted a strand of social criticism.[65] The economic crisis unfolding at roughly the same time gave birth to a further interpretive framework in connection with this subject, which advanced to a dominant position when it became clear that many migrant workers would be staying in Germany for the foreseeable future, if not permanently, and therefore presented a challenge to Germany's self-understanding. This pattern of interpretation consisted of a specific image of those members of German society considered culturally foreign, an image that, as it was reflected in history textbooks, soon found itself reduced to the synecdochical "Turks," a group considered problematic on a number of levels: as Muslims in an environment dominated by secularism and cultural Christianity; as an uneducated underclass, slaves to traditions rooted in agrarian ways of life in an industrial society decisively influenced by its citizens' prizing of upwardly mobile ambition and by the expansion of educational opportunities; and as a group that appeared notably reluctant to embrace "German culture." Statistics cited in these textbooks bore the nimbus of "reliable" sources and seemed to supply robust proof that West Germany had acquired a new underclass with low levels of education and high crime rates.[66] This viewpoint increasingly gave the term "migration" negative connotations, with "migrant" becoming a word primarily associated with an existence on the margins of society. This association of migration with problematized and conflict-laden contexts was one manifestation of the insecurities that beset a post-"boom" Federal Republic faced with a growing migrant population. These migrants, whose presence was particularly felt in major cities, were perceived neither in the traditional ethnically based sense nor culturally as "belonging" to German society. Yet as distancing as the terms used to describe these workers were, the issues raised by the figure of the *Gastarbeiter*, "the Turk," could not be kept at bay.

The issues involved confronted schools at least as much as other areas of West German society, with the impact of increasing numbers of children with a migration background making itself felt in classrooms by the 1980s at the latest. In the late 1960s, educational research in the country had begun to develop what it called *Ausländerpägagogik* (foreigner pedagogy), which segued in the 1980s into *interkulturelle Pädagogik* (intercultural pedagogy). Nevertheless, it is almost certain that many teachers and textbook authors felt themselves to be insufficiently prepared for the challenges of teaching in multicultural settings, a task not made any simpler by the continued refusal of leading politicians to entertain the idea that Germany was a country substantially characterized by immigration.

In this context, the lead taken by education policy makers on these issues was of great significance. In 1964, the KMK (standing conference of the education ministers of Germany's states) made recommendations on "teaching [the] children of foreigners" (*Ausländer*) and, in 1985, on "culture and our foreign fellow citizens" (*ausländische Mitbürger*) with the aim of promoting "mutual understanding between migrants and native German inhabitants" (1985).[67] Later, in 1996, this key political institution went in a decisive new direction with its recommendations on "Intercultural Education in Schools,"[68] departing from the essentialist notions of culture that had dominated debate on *Ausländer* until then, and speaking of the emergence of change in value systems and ideas about the world produced by encounters between people of different cultural backgrounds.[69] Although the standing conference continued in its recommendations to shy away from the hotly contested term *Einwanderungsgesellschaft* (immigration society) in relation to the now unified Germany, it unambiguously defined cultural diversity and the immigrants' desire to remain in the country as a "cultural reality." The document's terminological spectrum continued to adhere to a structural dichotomy between "us" (the Germans) and the "others" (even the inclusive effect of the term "fellow citizen" was attenuated by the modifier "foreign"). Nevertheless, this was the first time that education officials had spoken clearly of the challenges of migration as challenges for "native German inhabitants" and migrants alike, thus defining the integration into Germany of those from outside the country (or whose parents fit that description) as a process connecting both groups, a challenge that society as a whole had to meet. The recommendations cited the idea of an intercultural "change of perspective" that results when "the familiar and the unfamiliar meet and interact," thus facilitating the emergence of "a mature, self-aware view of others … promot[ing] the development of a robust self-identity and contributing to the integration of society." It was this "change of perspective" that the standing conference wished to see in all schools and across the curriculum. This was what these education officials believed would meet the challenge posed by immigration.[70] These developments in policy raise the question of how and to what extent migration has been discussed as a *historical* phenomenon in textbooks published in reunited Germany. More broadly, how do immigrants who have arrived in Germany since 1945—in particular, migrant workers, asylum seekers, those returning from Nazi-era emigration or exile—figure in the collective memory of a society in which almost half of school students in the major cities are now first- or second-generation immigrants? Does Germany as an *Einwanderungsgesellschaft*, with many of its erstwhile immigrants long since in possession of a German passport, have a historical memory whose traces we can perceive in textbooks of the last two or three decades? If so, how has this memory manifested itself?

To return to the standing conference's recommendations, there was considerable variation in the extent and degree to which the German states and textbook publishers put these into practice. This meant that the curricula and textbooks of this period reflected virtually the entire spectrum of arguments and positions taken up in the occasionally antagonistic debates around legislation on immigration that took place in the public arena starting in the year 2000. A commission on migration led by the respected conservative politician Rita Süssmuth had at that time brought about a turning point in the discussion by acknowledging that Germany was indeed a country of immigration. Further, in a way not before seen in the history of the Federal Republic, it had concerned itself with the issue of how immigration might be handled in a manner that would be sustainable into the future. Change appeared to have been in the air even before this, however. A not insignificant number of textbooks showed evidence of a paradigm shift as early as the 1990s. This circumstance was notable because German historians did not begin publishing solid work on the history of labor migrants and asylum seekers in the Federal Republic until after the turn of the millennium. Again, as in the case of Nazi atrocities and their victims in the 1970s, some textbooks were ahead of the mainstream of academic history.

A 1997 edition of the textbook *Geschichte und Geschehen* illustrates, at least in part, the paradigm shift observable at this time. Introducing new interpretive perspectives, the authors first informed students that the German government had attempted via legislation to "get rid of" the erstwhile *Gastarbeiter* once the large-scale recruitment of workers from abroad had stopped in 1973 as a consequence of the oil crisis and economic downturn. Next, the authors pointed out that many former labor migrants and their families had long since come to regard Germany as their home and that 80 percent of all young people with non-German backgrounds had been born in Germany. Referencing research findings in support of this observation, the authors concluded that Germany was already a country of immigration, albeit one not officially acknowledged as such.[71] In line with this message, some textbooks now discussed the unintended consequences of labor migration. The observation made in 1965 by the author Max Frisch that "we called for workers, and we got people" ("*wir riefen Arbeitskräfte, und es kamen Menschen*") became at this time a quasi-iconic representation of how textbooks discussed migration.

Nevertheless, while textbooks increasingly dealt with the ambiguities surrounding migration from a range of perspectives, the wide variety of cultures of origin and ways of life among migrants remained largely unmentioned. Similarly, the discursive strategies that textbooks used to approach these issues evinced little nuance. The contemporary backdrop to these books was marked by individual and group acts of xenophobic violence, especially between 1991 and 1993, in regions of both former West and East Germany. Sensationalist media reporting at this time alleged educational failures, entrenched dependency on social welfare benefits, and high crime rates among immigrants and their offspring as well as other population groups labeled non-German (so-called *Ausländerkriminalität* or foreigner criminality). Operating under the shadow of these noxious events and discourses, supporters of migration, including those who authored textbooks, felt obligated to emphasize at every opportunity the work ethic and productivity of migrants and to point out that, far from having taken jobs away from Germans, *Gastarbeiter* had taken on work that Germans were reluctant to carry out and that they therefore filled an important gap in the labor market. This impulse produced textbooks that drew students' attention first and foremost to the economic usefulness of the first generation of *Gastarbeiter* and of those "foreigners" recruited by German states in earlier periods of history. Chapters entitled "Poland— *Gastarbeiter* in the 'Wild West' of Prussia" or "An Economic Boom Produced by Foreigners before 1914"[72] sought to encourage students to perceive migration and multicultural integration as the norm in human society and thus gain critical distance from the suggestion that migration represented a "problem." But this effort only succeeded in lending momentum to the subliminal discourse of utility that extended throughout public debate on the issue and set its tone. Some authors, however, found ways to avoid this trap and to critically reflect on this narrative. One example appears in a history book published in 2008 for the state of Saxony. A chapter headed "Religious Refugees Promoting [Economic] Development"[73] contained discussion, primary sources, and tables on how the Huguenots, driven from France, had aided the development of the Prussian and Saxon economies. It then juxtaposed this material with a cartoon from around 1987 by the well-known cartoonist Marie Marcks showing a family with several children, the mother's veil denoting their Turkish/Muslim background, being discussed by two German men. One of these men says, "Hmm, if they were *Huguenots* ...," to which the other rejoins, "... then a bit of tolerance wouldn't be a problem."[74]

There are notable parallels here with the discourse on emigration and exile from Germany discussed above. Where the societal groups driven from Germany from 1933 onward had been depicted in terms of what German society had lost with their departure, representations of migrants arriving in Germany since the 1950s revolved around the issue of what they had "given" to German society, primarily in an economic sense and with an implicit connection to the legitimacy or otherwise of their presence in the country. This is a new variant of *Beitragsgeschichte*, which for all its good intentions has the potential to strengthen patterns of interpretation that center on the "us" and "them" dichotomy and classify the former *Gastarbeiter* and their descendants as outsiders in German society. This interpretive framework tends to degrade migrants to the status of mere objects in historical processes that appear singular and isolated, principally controlled by the receiving society. This understanding of migration went hand in hand with the paternalism embodied in the iconic 1964 photograph of the "millionth guest worker." In this image, Rodrigues de Sá, a Portuguese worker dressed in slightly shabby clothes and wearing a somewhat overawed expression, sits astride a moped just presented to him upon his arrival in Cologne by besuited, confidence-exuding representatives of German employers' associations.[75]

The "othering" thus observable in German textbooks dealing with migration issues did not escape criticism, which increased from the 1990s onward and was no doubt justified in many respects. This said, the indications are that the programmatic reorientation undertaken by the standing conference in 1996 has amounted to more than a powerless piece of paper. Although substantial historical research on the interrelationship of education and migration in the actual educational practices of the Federal Republic is still in its early stages, it should be safe to state that the standing conference, in issuing its recommendations, was responding in part to bottom-up pressure from educational practitioners whose everyday working lives involved multicultural student bodies. As most German school textbook authors are teachers by profession, it comes as no surprise that some textbooks contained core elements of the new concept even before policymakers had officially issued recommendations on cross-curricular awareness of the "migration" perspective. The 1996 paper itself provided an additional important stimulus, which was taken up reasonably quickly by a number of curriculum planners and textbook authors, although not all history curricula and textbooks are yet fully in line with an integrative approach.

At the same time, social and cultural history were gradually making inroads into textbooks, and interest in global and transnational history was increasing at a similar pace. Both of these developments were facilitating factors in a trend toward the gradual subsiding of previously dominant patterns of the representation of migrants and "foreigners." Issues of cultural transfer, mutual perceptions of peoples, globalization, and migration were advancing in relevance. One innovation in textbooks was the inclusion of explicit questions to students on the causes and effects of mass migration processes or events.[76] Another entailed a global history approach differing in significant respects from that used between the 1960s and 1980s. In this vein, a growing number of history textbooks brought together very different migration movements in laterally and longitudinally structured chapters that explored the issue of migration in a number of its facets.[77]

It is doubtless the case that one effect of this approach could be to render invisible specific features of individual migrant groups and redefine or relativize attributions of victimhood.[78] Another, however, is to historicize migration, as perceived in textbook references to religious refugees of the early modern age, German emigration to America, and the Poles who migrated to Germany's Ruhr Valley in the late nineteenth century. This trend in textbooks also entails greater acknowledgement of the experience of those involved in migration, heightened awareness of transnational processes, and increased visibility of causal relationships in history. In this way, a space has emerged in isolated instances for the stories of migrants returning to Germany, whom history teaching had almost completely failed to acknowledge over a period of half a century—even in relation to Germany's successful postwar reconstruction. The *Forum Geschichte* textbook series, which has been pointing out since 2003 that the Jewish exodus from Germany was "never emigration, but always escape,"[79] incorporated a section on Jewish life after 1945 into its 2003 edition and expanded it in 2011. At the heart of this section is the question of what made people choose to rebuild their lives in the land of the perpetrators "after Auschwitz" (reworded in 2011 as "after the Shoah"). The book's guiding approach here revolves around allowing the voices of the Jewish "returnees" and their descendants to be heard as they communicate their experience of coming back to Germany. The book supplements this core with information on the experience of Jewish life in the GDR, its tone conveying respect for these people's decision to help build a socialist state.[80]

*Forum Geschichte*'s approach, however, remains a notable exception to the rule. The return to Germany of former emigrants is still covered as rarely in school history textbooks as Holocaust survivors are. Although historical research has over the last decade made a concerted and ultimately successful effort to shed light on postwar Jewish life in Europe in general and DP camps in particular,[81] only a handful of school textbooks discuss the return of Jewish émigrés to Germany,[82] the foundation or reestablishment of Jewish religious congregations in the country, and the immigration in significant numbers of Jews from Eastern Europe after 1990. Jews are almost completely absent from the vast majority of textbook chapters on postwar history, seemingly disappearing from European history, from German society, and from its historical memory at the "zero hour" of 1945. Chapters dealing with contemporary history associate Jews almost exclusively with the State of Israel, obscuring the plurality of ways of life characteristic of the modern Jewish diaspora, and thus effectively excluding Jews from German and European history.[83]

When it comes to the *Muslim* "other," the most significant finding is that even history textbooks tend to indulge in a degree of detemporalization. In other words, they depict Muslims as a social and religious group that has remained largely immune to change throughout the turbulences of history, at least since the "golden age" of Islam on the Iberian Peninsula (Al-Andalus) came to an end in the fifteenth century. This tendency appears in such phenomena as the use of present-day photographs of Muslim pilgrims to Mecca as illustrations for text on the emergence of Islam as a religious doctrine in the seventh century. Textbooks also frequently tend to essentialize Islam, paying little attention to the differences between religious doctrine and day-to-day practice of the faith.[84] Another, once highly evident tendency toward homogenizing the Muslim "other" is, however, no longer predominant and has in some respects been historicized. Although we still frequently find Muslims presented primarily as members of a "parallel society" of migrants with very little internal diversity and scant ties to "German culture," we also find icons of a multicultural Germany and hybrid identities as an unquestioned norm. A photograph of a stylishly dressed, smiling young woman wearing a headscarf and wrapped in a German flag during the soccer World Cup of 2006 appears, for example, in several recent history textbooks.[85]

Such new images complement and in some cases displace the more conventional one of *Kopftuchmädchen* or "headscarf girls" (with the item of religious clothing literally predefining the person), which for so long has symbolized foreignness and refusal to integrate. The new images are indicative of the fact that, in the context of demographic change, a growing number of Germans—including political decision makers—have begun to develop new attitudes toward migrants and their descendants. Textbook chapters entitled "Foreigners [*Ausländer*] in Germany" persist to this day; however, viewed in this context, they seem to be remnants of another, distant age. Teachers, too, are increasingly reluctant to pass on such outdated messages.[86] This said, not all history textbooks possess material indicating a significant understanding of "othering" practices, with textbooks frequently reiterating the stereotypes and "them and us" dichotomies that continue to appear in politicians' speeches and in the media. Nevertheless, many textbook authors and publishers have accepted the challenges posed by Germany's being an *Einwanderungsgesellschaft*. One suggestive indicator of this change is the disappearance of the now infamous "moped photo" discussed above from some textbook series that had still carried it as recently as the year 2000. Migrants, once passively "presented" to students, now speak to them through sources that—and this too represents an innovation—frequently consist of accounts by young people who either grew up in Germany as the children of immigrants or who arrived as asylum seekers or refugees and who in many cases hold German citizenship.[87]

Further, the most recently published textbooks reference a broad spectrum of countries of origin in their discussions of migrants, thus challenging and broadening the narrow perspective that had equated "migrants" with "Turks." Examples illuminating the historical continuity of migration both to and from German states for a wide range of economic, political, and religious reasons similarly help the discussion to achieve a factual and nuanced tone. Such examples cast light on people's motivations for leaving their homelands behind, posit migration as a legitimate way in which people have shaped their lives, and historicize fears of the cultural unknown. In calling attention to instances of migration in the past, textbook authors are evidently making connections, on the one hand, with the current debate on "parallel societies" that reject integration into mainstream society and, on the other hand, with concerns around *Überfremdung* (literally "overforeignization," that is, becoming "swamped" by foreigners). Apparently these authors are seeking to reduce the tension and hyperbole inherent in such discourses by calling attention to the history of migration with materials that point to the occurrence of similar discourses in entirely different temporal and regional contexts. The historical cases selected tend to be ones that today's young people would likely regard as shining examples of successful integration. Accordingly, *Expedition Geschichte* quotes from a speech given in 1849 by a U.S. congressman airing his concerns about the threat posed to American culture by the large numbers of German immigrants "continuously seeping into the northwestern states of our Union … They live there in complete isolation. They speak a foreign language, have strange ways and customs … They pass all this down to their children and their children's children; in less than fifty years, it will … literally be crawling with Germans [there]."[88] Such depictions of global migration in history textbooks also make clear to students that the migration of societal elites is only part of the picture. Today's textbooks feature migration in the past to North and South America that was driven to a considerable extent by poverty (and included large numbers of Germans). They point out further that not all French Protestants who came to Germany during the seventeenth and eighteenth centuries were wealthy and successful or became so.[89] Likewise, they show students that Polish immigrants to the Ruhr Valley, recruited to help drive the economy, did not turn their backs on the region when it fell into crisis. The self-help organizations they had formed and the language they used were never, despite the Prussian government's assimilationist claims, "a danger to German ways and customs." If new "immigrant groups [tend] to develop their own subcultures," then apparently not automatically or permanently. Today, as one of these textbooks continues, the descendants of these so-called *Ruhrpolen* are recognizable as such only by the endings of their surnames.[90]

Textbooks using a historically longitudinal perspective are now devoting more space to the issue of political asylum, which has been highly controversial in the Federal Republic's political and public arenas, especially since the late 1980s. This coverage is doing its part toward increasing the diversity of images of migrants available to young people in the present day. Alongside discussions of and sources relating to the German revolutionaries of 1848/49 who fled Germany and took refuge in the United States and other countries, such textbooks contain passages on asylum policies and practices during the Cold War, when opponents of the communist governments in Eastern Europe could count on receiving asylum in Germany. Further, they include the voices of those who fled war, violence, and ethnic conflict in southeastern Europe in the early 1990s, showing that Germany and other European countries became safe havens for these individuals.[91] The books address the water-related imagery frequently used in this context, which creates the idea of a "flood" of asylum seekers threatening to "swamp" Germany or speaks of "the boat," i.e., the country, being "full." They also engage critically with these metaphors by incorporating cartoons. Apart from books that take a longitudinal approach, however, the issue of asylum plays a startlingly marginal role in German history textbooks today. Even more unsettling given Germany's history, students only rarely receive information from textbooks on the experiences of those who, fleeing the National Socialist regime, either found a safe haven in other countries or were turned away.[92] Where textbooks do discuss policies relating to the admission of refugees from Nazi Germany held by key emigration destinations from 1933 onward, or provide accounts of the despair or worse experienced by those refused entry, the relevant passages are worryingly brief.[93]

Some recent textbooks have incorporated the *Spätaussiedler* (literally "late emigrants"), ethnic Germans from Eastern Europe who moved to Germany from 1993 onward, into the catalog of migrants they bring to students' attention. In so doing they explain that their (German) ancestors had left the German territories a very long time ago, drawn by ambitious regents' recruitment drives to seek their fortunes in the east of Europe, which meant that upon their arrival in the Federal Republic they possessed only rudimentary knowledge of the German language and way of life. This is an indirect way of stimulating classroom discussion on whether "being German" is principally a matter of ethnicity or culture.

The question of citizenship and participation in political processes as criteria of "belonging," however, receives very little historical contextualization. It is generally left to social studies textbooks, if it is tackled in teaching materials at all.

In other words, the socioeconomic inequalities, differing perceptions, distinct memory cultures, and other challenges of the German *Einwanderungsgesellschaft*, as well as its potential, have not yet found adequate expression in history textbooks across the board. As well, the landscapes of memory inhabited by "native" Germans, on the one hand, and "migrants," on the other hand, remain separate and distinct. At the same time, recent textbooks evince clear potential to create a common space in which both sides can tell their stories. These textbooks frequently reference the findings of school students who participated in the Federal President's history competitions of 1988 and 2002, which set migration and "foreignness" as topics for the young people's research projects.[94] The wider impact of these competitions, which reference a specific local context, has yet to be assessed. It seems, however, that the Körber Foundation, which backs the competition, and the academics and teachers who have worked with it over the years, have proved crucial to getting controversial questions, past or present, onto the agenda of both historical research and history teaching.

## German Textbooks in an International and Comparative Context

Overall, this analysis of German history textbooks has shown that recent and current works have increasingly begun to pay attention to the history of migration and to historicize diversity. It has also confirmed that over a period of decades, migrants—with the exception of ethnic Germans who fled or were expelled from Eastern Europe at the end of the war or in its aftermath—were excluded from West German cultural memory after 1945 or incorporated peripherally at best. Although the 1970s saw an increasing number of textbooks beginning to explore German history from a position of rather critical distance and to raise awareness of the fact that historical myths and legends are constructed and can therefore also be deconstructed, stereotypes around "foreigners" remained alive, as did corresponding notions of what "German culture" was. German elites and society have at best begun only recently to recognize the stories of (former) migrants and to place them historically in common frameworks that might form the basis of a shared space of memory and a new historical narrative, one that has yet to come into being.

The question remaining at this point is whether this development in German textbooks has been particular to German society. To avoid over-extending our conclusions in this regard, we should first recall that, with a few exceptions, even academic historical research has only acknowledged the place of migration as a constitutive element of German and European society for around a decade. Postcolonial and labor migration after 1945 in particular have been research topics long neglected by historians.[95] We would do well, moreover, to view this chapter's findings in a comparative framework. When did other Western societies, including countries with an imperial and/or colonial past, begin to address migration and diversity in their national memory landscapes, particularly in the teaching of history?

According to a comprehensive study based on a neoinstitutionalist world society approach and the quantitative analysis of a large data set (465 civics and history textbooks from 90 countries), the value placed on humanity and diversity in textbooks and on the cosmopolitan and multicultural emphases they contain has been increasing significantly across the globe since 1970.[96] The study included German textbooks, which the authors did not consider any less adequate in this regard than those of most other Western states. Qualitative studies, however, reveal a more complex picture. In most Western European states, even in countries such as the United Kingdom and Sweden, which are well known for their inclusive approach to education and for valuing diversity, the institutions predominantly involved in the construction of historical narratives with the potential to shape identities and national memory depict immigration and diversity primarily as a problem. Wherever in Europe scholars have examined important identity resources such as textbooks or museums, they have observed that migrants in general and immigrants in particular have largely been left out of the national and European historical narratives.

In Austria, where in 2010/11 about 25 percent of elementary school pupils used an everyday language other than German, a figure rising to over 50 percent in Vienna, scholars point to ongoing marginalization and stereotyping of migrants. In the view of Gerhard Paul, Austria treats emigration, exile, and remigration linked to National Socialism with still less importance than Germany does. Christiane Hintermann's findings complement this picture by suggesting that migration history has to this day been represented, if at all, as an addendum to the common national narrative and not as part of a set of connected histories. She also observes that remigration and transmigration processes receive scant attention in textbooks.[97] Studies on Swedish, French, and English textbooks corroborate the Austrian findings. Across Europe, we observe that connections are rarely made between the histories of migrant groups and the histories of the countries from which they originally came, leaving students without important contextualizing information on the background of migrations.[98] A common practice in Austrian textbooks is to present pictures of Muslim women wearing headscarves as symbols of "parallel societies" and an assumed refusal to integrate. In Austria and Sweden, the discourse of utility we identified in German textbooks of the 1980s and 1990s in particular, as well as in some more recent textbooks, has likewise been perpetuated over more than four decades. In the vast majority of Swedish and Austrian textbooks, the decisive question in relation to the evaluation of migration as positive or negative is whether or not immigrants, in specific periods of history, have been beneficial to the national economy or demographic development.[99] As Lozic and Hintermann concluded in 2010 with regard to the European countries mentioned here,[100] "the discursive exclusion of immigrants from national societies is still evident, as is the long-lasting tendency to depict immigration as problematic to the countries of destination and immigrants as a problem group."[101]

From this point of view, the approach to migration history taken by German textbooks comports with the European picture, at least as it has been since the 1960s.[102] A further parallel is observable in the fact that in all the European countries investigated here, with the exception of Greece, whose textbooks show a considerable level of ethnocentrism,[103] the issue of migration began finding its way into the canon in the mid 1990s, i.e., at exactly the time we have identified as a caesura in German educational policy and practice.[104] Within this European trend, textbooks from France and England seem to transcend the national framework of history with specific emphasis.[105] Soysal's and Sakács's research points to an increasing "cosmopolitanization" of French and English curricula and textbooks, including a shift toward a less negative connotation of "the other" and a more positive focus on the importance of intercultural exchange.[106] This corresponds with the observation made by Soysal and Schissler in 2005 that "national history has lost in importance practically everywhere" and "histories of social groups below the national level … and transnational entities … [have] gained in importance."[107] We can thus state as an initial conclusion that the developments described in this chapter are far from a specifically German phenomenon. The trajectory of the last few decades has instead been *European* in nature, although it unfolded within distinct national and historical frameworks and evinced specific features from country to country.[108]

This conclusion applies only partially, however, to representations of German and European Jews. The harrowing violence and genocide experienced by that group requires an exemplary transnational and migration-sensitive approach to the history of Europe and to forced migration in the twentieth century. Although most German textbooks still fail to use this topic to develop an integrative historical approach that comprehends Jews and Jewish history as paradigmatic, for instances, in the context of migration and the transnational, they nonetheless pay, for obvious historical reasons, much more attention to this subject than textbooks in most other countries. A comparison of German, U.S., Spanish, British, and French textbooks reveals emphatically that textbooks from none of the countries, with some exceptions in the United States, feature anywhere near as much Jewish history as those from Germany. Likewise, the approach taken to the topic in textbooks from the other European countries is even less nuanced than that in the German textbooks. Those books that feature the cultural achievements of Jewish citizens or Jewish communities living peacefully side by side with the majority group in society are clear exceptions, usually from the United States. Most depictions of Jewish history, where they appear at all, offer a history of victimhood.[109]

Although a number of international initiatives, such as that of UNESCO in 1974,[110] recommended at a relatively early stage that national history should be taught to pupils within a global framework and encouraged states to develop textbooks conducive to supporting familiarity with other cultures and understanding between peoples (including minorities and indigenous peoples), the response has generally remained rather limited. Seen in this light, limited attention to diversity and migrant groups in history textbooks was a widespread phenomenon until the 1990s and in many countries of the world thereafter. Indeed, the UN Special Rapporteur for cultural rights recently stated:

> In many societies, history teaching either altogether ignores, or carries, validates, or strengthens stereotypes about marginalized groups ... The dominant homogenizing narrative blanches out diversity, ignoring the cultural heritage of everyone outside the group in power, simultaneously depriving the majority of the opportunity to understand the complexity of their country ... The histories of migrant populations are also very commonly excluded.[111]

That said, most recent German textbooks do not display evident ignorance on the matter of cultural diversity; indeed they often overtly value it. At the same time, German textbooks are sometimes a site of striking collisions between the desire for inclusivity and the perceptions and ideas that persist as underlying assumptions in German cultural discourse. It might, nevertheless, be exactly this kind of inconsistency and internal contradiction that offer teachers and society in general opportunities to move beyond officially sanctioned knowledge as stipulated in curricula, which are themselves highly ambiguous and vague when it comes to diversity, frequently contradicting their own recommendations.[112] The shattering of previously unchallenged historical narratives and the intertwined nature of discourses in today's complex world may make orienting one's views toward defined sets of values or assumptions a less simple matter than it once was, but they may also allow the next generation to develop a more transnational, diverse, and inclusive understanding of history.

If we take the "practice turn" in current research seriously and therefore focus not only on text in a narrow sense (textbooks, curricula) but also on processes of translating, interpreting, and applying or failing to apply the content of these texts in the classroom, we might uncover a further dimension to our findings. In the teaching and learning process, "memory" is created in a complex interaction that entails negotiating, first, official narratives communicated in a top-down manner, second, pervasive representations of the past conveyed by the (traditional and new) media, and, finally, individual or group-specific experiences and memories expressed from the bottom up. The classroom becomes a potential arena for the narratives of today's European societies of immigration, narratives that sometimes converge, sometimes clash, and sometimes exist side by side in mutual isolation. Interviews conducted in 2012 by scholars from the Georg Eckert Institute for International Textbook Research with history teachers on the current relevance of the topic of migration to their teaching underline the unique opportunity that textbook analysis offers for investigating the zeitgeist and the most influential, if not hegemonic, perspectives in interpreting the past, present, and future of a society. Yet the interviews also caution us that textbooks should not be taken as a mirror of the actual historical consciousness of students or teachers. "Well," one of the teachers interviewed said,

> we do look at it [migration] briefly once, but at least—emigration to the U.S. That's not what you're referring to right now, is it [?], but it's migration, too, after all ... Yes, and then we get round to the guest workers, the so-called guest workers, and to be honest, at the moment my [grade] ten [class] are deep in the Nazi period, they've got work experience in January, so that means I hopefully need to be finished with that by Christmas. In February I'll do the Cold War, then I need to get the GDR founded, and the school year will be over in June and I want to have at least got Germany reunited. I won't be able to do it all— unless I race through it at a speed that means that in the final analysis we're just doing a history of events again, like in the olden days, "now children, learn this, this, this and this," but then we'd really be doing history like fifty years ago.[113]

Textbooks in the contemporary German classroom are at the sharp end of a dilemma that teachers face between the avoidance of cramming in facts "like fifty years ago" and the need to cover extensive material within a short space of time. They cannot, in other words, act as "transcripts" of what students are actually learning about migration. The implied reluctance of the teacher quoted above to treat the topic of *Gastarbeiter* in a Gradgrindian manner revolving around the learning of figures and dates might give us cause for cautious optimism, even if the place in history teaching of migration narratives seems threatened by the stampede through twentieth-century German history that the interviewee feels forced by time constraints to undertake. This emergent sensitivity toward such narratives among educational practitioners suggests that migrants may well in the future be able to put down roots in history curricula, as they have long since done in German society and cultural memory.

# Notes

1. Curricula and textbooks from the former GDR will not be included in the analysis because it is principally the Federal Republic of Germany, both before and after reunification, that has been the site of significant migration. While the GDR also counted migrants, who were largely returnees to Germany, among its population—ethnic Germans who had resettled from Eastern Europe (*Umsiedler*), students, or workers recruited from other socialist countries to ease labor shortages (*Vertragsarbeiter*)—it could hardly be defined as a society of immigration as such.

2. For existing studies see Barbara Christophe, "Migration in German Textbooks: Is Multiperspectivity an Adequate Response?" *The Journal of Educational Media, Memory, and Society (JEMMS)* 1 (2009): 190–202; Jan Motte and Rainer Ohliger, eds., *Geschichte und Gedächtnis in der Einwanderungsgesellschaft* (Essen: Klartext Verlag, 2004), esp. their introduction, and Bettina Alavi's chapter on textbooks, 199–212; Verena Radkau, "Vom Umgang mit Verschiedenheit und Vielfalt. Befunde aus deutschen und US-amerikanischen Schulbüchern," in *Interkulturelles Verstehen und kulturelle Integration durch das Schulbuch?*, eds. Carsten Heinze and Eva Matthes (Bad Heilbrunn: Klinkhardt, 2004), 301–20; and Dirk Lange, "Fremdheit und Akkulturation im historisch-politischen Schulbuch," in Heinze and Matthes, *Interkulturelles Verstehen*, 321–37.

3. Michael Apple, ed., *Ideology and Curriculum*, 3rd ed. (New York: Taylor & Francis, 2004); Linda Christian-Smith and Michael Apple, eds., *The Politics of the Textbook* (New York: Routledge, 1991); Simone Lässig, "Textbooks and Beyond. Educational Media in Context(s)," *JEMMS* 1 (2009): 1–20.

4. Falk Pingel, *UNESCO Guidebook in Textbook Research and Textbook Revision*, 2nd revised and updated edition (Paris/Braunschweig: UNESCO/Georg Eckert Institute for International Textbook Research, 2010).

5. The history textbook published in West Germany in 1974 featuring findings of a 1973 survey on "*Gastarbeiter*" is not an exceptional case: Joachim Immisch, *Zeiten und Menschen*, vol. B, no.4 (Paderborn/Hannover: Schoeningh/Schroedel, 1967), 158.

6. Karl-Ernst Bungenstab, "Die Schulbuchrevision in der US-Zone nach 1945 im Zusammenhang mit der amerikanischen Umerziehungspolitik," *Internationales Jahrbuch für Geschichtsunterricht* 11 (1968/69): 96–140, here: 135. See also Brian Puaca,

ed., *Learning Democracy. Education Reform in West Germany 1945–1965* (Oxford/New York: Berghahn Books, 2009).

7. Material from the estate of T.J. Leonard, Georg Eckert Institute Braunschweig, Library.

8. Beate Rosenzweig, ed., *Erziehung zur Demokratie? Amerikanische Besatzungs- und Schulreformpolitik in Deutschland und Japan* (Stuttgart: Franz Steiner Verlag, 1998); Masako Shibata, *Japan and Germany under the U.S. Occupation. A Comparative Analysis of Postwar Education Reform* (Lanham: Lexington Books, 2005); Julian Dierkes, ed., *Postwar History Education in Japan and the Germanys: Guilty Lessons* (London: Routledge, 2010).

9. See Puaca, *Learning Democracy*, 80–81.

10. Ibid.

11. "Deutsch französische Vereinbarung über strittige Fragen europäischer Geschichte," special issue, *Internationales Jahrbuch für Geschichtsunterricht* 2 (1953).

12. As in the Franco-German case, the recommendations were drawn up in the period between 1972 and 1976 by a number of historians, geographers, and political scientists who were or would become well known in their fields and who represented a broad spectrum of theoretical schools. The German academics involved included Karl Dietrich Bracher, Martin Broszat, Andreas Hillgruber, Eberhard Kolb, Susanne Miller, Gotthold Rhode, Rudolf von Thadden, Heide Wunder, and Klaus Zernack.

13. The thesis, for example, that German wartime policies in Poland "were not only geared towards the elimination of the Polish state, but also strove to destroy the Polish intelligentsia and culture, and to repress Polish people and transform Poland into a colonial space" was by no means accepted knowledge in mid-1970s Germany. Gemeinsame Deutsch-Polnische Schulbuchkommission, "Empfehlungen für Schulbücher der Geschichte und Geographie in der Bundesrepublik Deutschland und in der Volksrepublik Polen," *Internationales Jahrbuch für Geschichts- und Geographieunterricht* XVII (1976): 173.

14. Lily Gardner Feldman, ed., *Germany's Foreign Policy of Reconciliation: From Enmity to Amity* (Lanham: Rowman & Littlefield, 2012). On unintended effects: Anna Kochanowska-Nieborak, Hans Henning Hahn and Heidi Hein-Kircher, eds., *Erinnerungskultur und Versöhnungskitsch* (Marburg: Herder-Institut Verlag, 2008). For a sociological point of view on the German case, see Jeffrey K. Olick, ed., *The Politics of Regret. On Collective Memory and Historical Responsibility* (New York: Routledge, 2007).

15. Wulf Kansteiner, ed., *In Pursuit of German Memory: History, Television, and Politics after Auschwitz* (Athens: Ohio University Press, 2006).

16. Otto-Ernst Schüddekopf, ed., *History Teaching and History Textbook Revision* (Strasbourg: Council for Cultural Co-operation of the Council of Europe, 1967); Karina Korostelina and Simone Lässig, eds., *History Education and Post-Conflict Reconciliation. Reconsidering Joint Textbook Projects* (London: Routledge, 2013).

17. One of the first series of history textbooks produced in collaboration with an American Education Service Center was *Wege der Völker*. Appearing in 1948, the book had been approved in many German states by 1953. It had a high distribution rate in the early years of the Federal Republic before falling into disuse. Fritz Wuessing, *Geschichtsbuch für deutsche Schulen. Wege der Völker*, vol. D, no. 5 (Berlin/Frankfurt a.M.: Pädagogischer Verlag Schulz, 1948).

18. Falk Pingel, "Geschichtslehrbücher zwischen Kaiserreich und Gegenwart," in *Grenzgänger. Aufsätze von Falk Pingel*, ed. Falk Pingel (Göttingen: V&R Unipress, 2009), 403–24. Pingel cites one of the few exceptions to this trend, Hans Ebeling, *Reise in die Vergangenheit*, no. 3 (Braunschweig: Westermann, 1972), which incorporated viewpoints from global and universal history and emphasized cultural history instead of political history, albeit working from a rather antimodern idea thereof.

19. Ebeling, *Reise in die Vergangenheit*, no. 3 (1972), 314.

20. In some cases, textbook authors of the time also tried to strengthen global perspectives, for example, Hermann Meyer and Wilhelm Langenbeck, *Grundzüge der Geschichte, Mittelstufe* (Frankfurt a.M.: Diesterweg, 1970).

21. This was entirely in accordance with the party line prescribed by policymakers during the period; in 1962, for instance, the standing conference of the education ministers of West Germany's states (KMK) issued a "decree on totalitarianism" (*Totalitarismus-Erlaß*) that sought to establish National Socialism as a topic for teaching in schools, but viewed the regime as "structurally identical" to the Soviet system.

22. Gilad Margalit, *Guilt, Suffering, and Memory. Germany Remembers Its Dead of World War II* (Bloomington: Indiana University Press, 2010).

23. This documentation included documents on the Nuremberg trials and OMGUS documents as well as, for instance, Eugen Kogon, *Der SS-Staat. Das System der deutschen Konzentrationslager* (Munich: Heyne, 1946).

24. Immisch, *Zeiten und Menschen* (1967), 138.

25. Ibid. (1974), 106–7.

26. Friedrich J. Lucas and Heinrich Bodensieck, *Menschen in ihrer Zeit*, no. 4 (Stuttgart: Klett, 1969).

27. New ways of teaching were evident in, for instance, Lucas and Bodensieck, *Menschen in ihrer Zeit*, no. 4, (1969); Heinz Dieter Schmid, ed., *Fragen an die Geschichte* (Frankfurt a.M.: Hirschgraben-Verlag, 1974–78); Günther-Arndt Hilke, ed., *Geschichtsbuch. Die Menschen und ihre Geschichte in Darstellungen und Dokumenten*, no. 4 (Berlin: Cornelsen, 1986–88).

28. "Behandlung des Nationalsozialismus im Unterricht," Beschluss der Kultusminister-Konferenz vom 20.04.1978, Nr. 553; und "Empfehlungen zur Behandlung des Widerstandes in der NS Zeit im Unterricht," Beschluss der Kultusminister-Konferenz vom 04.12.1980, Nr. 561, in *Sammlung der Beschlüsse der Ständigen Konferenz der Kultusminister der Länder in der Bundesrepublik Deutschland*, ed. Kultusministerkonferenz der Länder (Darmstadt/Neuwied: Luchterhand, 1964).

29. Bodo von Borries, "The Third Reich in German History Textbooks since 1945," *Journal of Contemporary History* 38 (2003): 45–62; Norbert Frei and Volkhard Knigge, eds., *Verbrechen erinnern. Die Auseinandersetzung mit Holocaust und Völkermord* (Munich: C.H. Beck, 2002).

30. Falk Pingel, "From Evasion to a Crucial Tool of Moral and Political Education," in *What Shall We Tell the Children? International Perspectives on School History Textbooks*, ed. Keith A. Crawford and Stuart J. Foster (Greenwich: Information Age Publishing, 2006), 131–54. This phenomenon was reminiscent of the immediate postwar period when, under the influence of the Allies, some textbook authors had developed approaches, methods, and topics that from today's point of view appear innovative but that at the time, with few exceptions, were not adopted by the majority of textbook authors or academic historians.

31. Gerhard Paul, "Leerstelle im kulturellen Gedächtnis. Emigration, Exil und Remigration in deutschsprachigen Schulgeschichtsbüchern 1955–2007," in *Gedächtnis des Exils: Formen der Erinnerung*, ed. Claus-Dieter Krohn and Lutz Winckler (Munich: edition text + kritik, 2010), 1–23.

32. Wuessing, *Geschichtsbuch für deutsche Schulen* (1953), 120–21.

33. Without a specific interest in textbook images, but revealing: Maren Röger, "Bilder der Vertreibung: Propagandistischer Kontext und Funktionalisierung in erinnerungskulturellen Diskursen seit dem Ende des Zweiten Weltkrieges," in *Bilder*

*in historischen Diskursen*, ed. Franz X. Eder et al. (Wiesbaden: Springer Verlag, 2014), 261–82; Gerhard Paul, "Der Flüchtlingstreck. Bilder von Flucht und Vertreibung als europäische *lieux de mémoire*," in *Das Jahrhundert der Bilder*, ed. Gerhard Paul (Bonn: Vandenhoeck & Ruprecht, 2009), 666–73.

34. Günther Grass, *Im Krebsgang. Eine Novelle* (Göttingen: Steidl Verlag, 2002). In 2008, the textbook publisher Cornelsen devoted almost half a page of *Forum Geschichte* to a quotation from the historian Hans-Ulrich Wehler, who felt the debate sparked by Grass's novel to be "a liberation" due to the, as he put it, expectation placed on expelled Germans since 1945 to "privatize" their suffering; Hans-Otto Regenhardt and Claudi Tatsch, eds., *Forum Geschichte kompakt. Von der Nachkriegszeit bis zur Gegenwart*, no. 2/2, Nordrhein-Westfalen (Berlin: Cornelsen, 2008), 101. Textbooks published before 1960, among other sources, bear extensive witness to the inaccuracy of this statement for the first postwar generation of Germans at the least.

35. Wuessing, *Geschichtsbuch für deutsche Schulen* (1953), 130.

36. See, for example, the fifteen lines on the subject in ibid., 130.

37. Jerzy Kochanowski, "Gathering Poles into Poland. Forced Migration from Poland's Former Eastern Territories," in *Redrawing Nations. Ethnic Cleansing in East-Central Europe 1944–1948*, ed. Ana Siljak and Philipp Ther (Lanham, Boulder, New York and Oxford: Rowman & Littlefield, 2001), 135–54; Andrew Demshuk, ed., *The Lost German East. Forced Migration and the Politics of Memory 1845–1970* (Cambridge: Cambridge University Press, 2012); Pertti Ahonen, ed., *After the Expulsion. West Germany and Eastern Europe 1945–1990* (Oxford: Oxford University Press, 2003); Robert G. Moeller, "Germans as Victims? Thoughts on a Post-Cold War History of World War II's Legacies," *History and Memory* 17 (2005): 147–94; Pertti Ahonen et al., eds., *People on the Move: Forced Population Movements in Europe in the Second World War and its Aftermath* (Oxford: Bloomsbury Academic, 2008); Hahn and Hahn, eds., *Die Vertreibung im deutschen Erinnern. Legenden, Mythos, Geschichte* (Paderborn: Schöningh, 2010).

38. Ebeling, *Reise in die Vergangenheit*, no. 4, Baden-Württemberg (Braunschweig: Westermann, 1986).

39. While this translates as "the largest mass migration in human history," the romanticizing term *Völkerwanderung* does little to aid understanding of the topic; Hans Ebeling and Gustav Rüggeberg, *Deutsche Geschichte*, vol. A, no. 5 (Braunschweig: Westermann, 1955), 151.

40. Ebeling, *Deutsche Geschichte* (1955), 151; Eveling, *Reise in die Vergangenheit*, no. 4 (1961/86); Ebeling, *Reise in die Vergangenheit*, no. 3 (1981), 265–66, mentions in its text of "the driving from Germany of around 400,000 opponents of Hitler's regime and Jews;" an accompanying table, however, only features figures from 1945 onward and begins with expelled Germans and the "repatriation of around 3 million Japanese," neglecting to provide any further explanation of this information. Further examples primarily provide support to anticommunist interpretations of events. An exception is Israel, about which pupils are told that "by 1957, almost 1.8 million Jewish emigrants and refugees from all over the world had flocked [there], while around 0.9 million Arab refugees were forced to leave."

41. Ibid., 153–55.

42. Ebeling, *Reise in die Vergangenheit*, no. 3 (1981).

43. In a number of textbooks from this period, which eventually facilitated a paradigm shift in West German memory culture, the genocide committed against the Jews remained little more than a marginal note and even Jewish emigration and exile after 1933 was still a topic pushed to the margins, while others, almost immediately after the initial

broadcast of the television mini-series *Holocaust* in Germany in 1979, devoted considerably more space to the events, referring to them by the term that gave the iconic broadcast its title.

44. Paul cites, as an example, the regular issuance of sets of stamps commemorating the flight and expulsion of Germans from Eastern Europe and the lack of such sets on the subject of prewar emigration and exile. Gerhard Paul, "Leerstelle im kulturellen Gedächtnis," 20.

45. Martin Stellmann, *Spiegel der Zeiten. Geschichtsbuch für deutsche Schulen*, no. 4 (Frankfurt a.M.: Diesterweg, 1971), 89–90.

46. Ebeling, *Reise in die Vergangenheit* (1961), 265–66; (1981), 213–14.

47. Ibid. In an almost breathtaking demonstration of historical insensitivity, the text accompanying a map in the 1981 edition of *Erinnern und Urteilen* (which translates as "Remembering and Judging") showing movements of peoples in Europe after World War I refers to "migration movements of 'guest workers'" in the same metaphorical breath as expulsion and tourism; Peter Alter, *Erinnern und Urteilen: Unterrichtseinheiten Geschichte 4* (Stuttgart: Klett, 1981).

48. An example is *Zeiten und Menschen*, which appeared in 1967 with several pages on the Nazis' campaign of ostracism against the Jews, emigration, and the genocide perpetrated against European Jews; Immisch, *Zeiten und Menschen* (1967), 138–9; (1974), 81; (1980), 105–6; (1996), 104–6. The brief piece of text on Jewish emigration that appeared in *Geschichte und Geschehen* remained completely unchanged for a period of fifteen years; Karl-Heinz Menzel and Fritz Textor, *Geschichte und Geschehen. Kletts Geschichtliches Unterrichtswerk für die Mittelklassen*, vol. C. no. 4 (Stuttgart: Klett, 1968/1983), 109.

49. Immisch, *Zeiten und Menschen* (1967), 138–39; Rüdiger vom Bruch, *BSV Geschichte 4. Vom Zeitalter des Imperialismus bis zur Gegenwart* (Munich: Oldenbourg Schulbuchverlag, 1988/1993), 121; Wolfgang Hug, *Unsere Geschichte*, no. 4, Baden-Württemberg (Frankfurt a.M.: Diesterweg, 1988), 93–94, 102. Such passages were rarely concerned with gender awareness, referring, as in *Zeiten und Menschen*, to "men (*Männer*) whose research findings made Germany the scientific envy of the world;" Immisch, *Zeiten und Menschen* (1974), 104–7.

50. One exception was *Geschichtsbuch 4* (published by Cornelsen), whose 1988 and 1996 editions quoted from Marta Appel's memories of the year 1936; Hilke, ed., *Geschichtsbuch*, no. 4, 136–37. Immisch, *Zeiten und Menschen* (1967), 140, was more typical in its tone; here, the pogroms of November 1938 were reported as having caused "mass flight," while in 1981 Hans Ebeling and Wolfgang Birkenfeld simply stated that "[a]pproximately 150,000 German Jews left their homeland in 1938/39"; Ebeling, *Reise in die Vergangenheit* (1972), 140.

51. Ulrich Herbert, ed., *Fremdarbeiter: Politik und Praxis des "Ausländer-Einsatzes" in der Kriegswirtschaft des Dritten Reiches* (Berlin/Bonn: J.H.W. Dietz Nachf., 1985) was cited in, for instance, Hug, *Unsere Geschichte* (1988), 148.

52. See, for example, Immisch, *Zeiten und Menschen* (1974), 112. Textbooks' individualization and regionalization of such narratives frequently promoted student identification with the victims. A critical look at identification with victims can be found in Christian Schneider and Ulrike Jureit, eds., *Gefühlte Opfer. Illusionen der Vergangenheitsbewältigung* (Stuttgart: Klett-Cotta, 2010).

53. Bernhard Giesen, "Europäische Identität und transnationale Öffentlichkeit. Eine historische Perspektive," in *Transnationale Öffentlichkeiten und Identitäten im 20. Jahrhundert*, ed. Alexander Schmidt-Gernig, Hartmut Kaelble, and Martin Kirsch (Frankfurt a.M.: Campus Verlag, 2002), 67–84; Harald Welzer, ed., *Der Krieg der Erinnerung. Holocaust,*

*Kollaboration und Widerstand im europäischen Gedächtnis* (Frankfurt a.M.: Fischer Taschenbuch Verlag, 2007).

54. Bill Niven, ed., *Germans as Victims: Remembering the Past in Contemporary Germany* (Basingstoke: Palgrave, 2006).

55. Ernst Hinrichs, ed., *Deutsch-israelische Schulbuchempfehlungen: Zur Darstellung der jüdischen Geschichte sowie der Geschichte und Geographie Israels in Schulbüchern der Bundesrepublik Deutschland*, Studien zur internationalen Schulbuchforschung: Schriftreihe des Georg-Eckert-Instituts (Braunschweig/Hannover: Hahn, 1979).

56. Dirk Sadowski and Martin Liepach, eds., *Jüdische Geschichte im Schulbuch* (Göttingen: V&R Unipress, 2014).

57. The year 2003 saw the publication by the Academic Working Group of the Leo Baeck Institute of a guide to "German-Jewish History in the Classroom," which was reissued in an updated edition in 2011; LBI Kommission für die Verbreitung deutsch-jüdischer Geschichte, ed., *Deutsch-Jüdische Geschichte im Unterricht. Eine Orientierungshilfe für Schule und Erwachsenenbildung* (Bad Homburg: VAS-Verlag, 2011). Retrieved 12 May 2016 from http://www.stiftung-evz.de/fileadmin/user_upload/EVZ_Uploads/Handlungsfelder/Auseinandersetzung_mit_der_Geschichte_01/Leo_Back_Programm/orientierungshilfe-korrigiert.pdf.

58. See, e.g., the heading "The Jews – the Persecution Began in the Middle Ages," in Hans-Wilhelm Eckhardt, *Zeit für Geschichte* 5, Niedersachsen (Braunschweig: Schroedel, 2009), 138.

59. An example is Immisch, *Zeiten und Menschen* (1974), 158–59.

60. Ibid., 159.

61. Anselm Doering-Manteuffel and Lutz Raphael, eds., *Nach dem Boom. Perspektiven auf die Zeitgeschichte seit 1970* (Göttingen: Vandenhoeck & Ruprecht, 2008).

62. A 1997 edition of *Geschichtliche Weltkunde*, no. 3, for instance, contained passages on *Gastarbeiter* that were almost identical to those that appeared in the 1976 edition; Wolfgang Hug, Joachim Hoffmann, and Elmar Krautkrämer, *Geschichtliche Weltkunde*, no. 3 (Braunschweig: Diesterweg, 1976/1997).

63. Italy (1955), Spain (1960), Greece (1960), Turkey (1961), Morocco (1963), Portugal (1964), Tunisia (1965), and Yugoslavia (1968).

64. Schmid, *Fragen an die Geschichte*, 182.

65. Beginning in the late 1970s, the textbook landscape in West Germany grew increasingly diverse and showed politicized tendencies for various reasons, including the fact that under federalism education was and remains the most significant policy area under the control of the individual states. Therefore, the vigorous debate on the political direction of the Federal Republic ignited in 1968 and, continuing unabated into the 1970s and 1980s, extended into the realm of education and had a profound impact on educational materials and curricula.

66. Manfred Albrecht, *Expedition Geschichte* no. 6, Berlin (Braunschweig: Diesterweg, 2008); Immisch, *Zeiten und Menschen* (1974).

67. Ständige Konferenz der Kultusminister der Länder, ed., *"Interkulturelle Bildung und Erziehung in der Schule," Sammlung der Beschlüsse der Ständigen Konferenz der Kultusminister der Länder in der Bundesrepublik Deutschland* (Neuwied: Luchterhand, 1996), 2. In the 1970s, the standing conference issued a number of recommendations on promoting pupils' German skills, while in 1992, in response to a series of incidents of mob violence against asylum seekers and other immigrants, it issued a "Declaration on Tolerance and Solidarity."

68. Dated 25 October 1996.

69. Ständige Konferenz der Kultusminister der Länder, ed., *"Interkulturelle Bildung und Erziehung in der Schule,"* Sammlung der Beschlüsse der Ständigen Konferenz der Kultusminister der Länder in der Bundesrepublik Deutschland (Neuwied: Luchterhand, 1996), 4.

70. Ibid., 5.

71. Menzel and Textor, *Geschichte und Geschehen* (1997), 234.

72. Ibid., 225; Albrecht, *Expedition Geschichte*, 45.

73. In German: *"Glaubensflüchtlinge als Entwicklungshelfer"*; the term *Entwicklungshelfer* more commonly refers to someone from a developed country working in a developing or less developed country to provide support in its economic or humanitarian progress.

74. Albrecht, *Expedition Geschichte*; the competing publisher Klett had used the same cartoon in its 1997 textbook Menzel and Textor, *Geschichte und Geschehen* (1997), 222.

75. Susanne Grindel, "Das Bild von MigrantInnen im Schulbuch," in *Wirtschaften mit Migrationshintergrund: zur soziokulturellen Bedeutung "ethnischer Ökonomien" in urbanen Räumen,"* eds. Alexander Trupp and Maria Dabringer (Innsbruck: Studien Verlag, 2008), 120–29.

76. Examples are Stellmann, *Spiegel der Zeiten*, 143; Menzel and Textor, *Geschichte und Geschehen* (1997), 233.

77. Menzel and Textor, *Geschichte und Geschehen* (1997/2007); Xavier Adams and Leon Cuppes, *ANNO 4* (Lier: Uitgeverij Van In, 2000); Immisch, *Zeiten und Menschen* (2005).

78. One book from 1998 contains a one-and-a-half-page section on "prisoners of war and civilian victims of forced deportation: forgotten victims of war and aggression," whereas Jewish emigration is referred to in only the briefest of terms: "360,000 Jews had left Germany by October 1941." Jutta Stehling and Michael Guse, *Wir machen Geschichte* (Frankfurt a.M.: Diesterweg, 1998), 142, 229.

79. This is a quotation from Juliane Wetzel, herself quoting Adrienne Thomas. Regenhardt and Tatsch, eds., *Forum Geschichte. Vom Ende des Weltkriegs bis zur Gegenwart*, no. 4 (Berlin: Cornelsen, 2003), 94.

80. Regenhardt and Tatsch, eds., *Forum Geschichte* (2003), 252–55; (2008), 160–61; (2011), 201–5.

81. Atina Grossmann, ed., *Jews, Germans and Allies: Close Encounters in Occupied Germany* (Princeton: Princeton University Press, 2009); Michael Brenner, ed., *After the Holocaust: Rebuilding Jewish Lives in Postwar Germany* (Princeton: Princeton University Press, 1997); Anthony D. Kauders, *Unmögliche Heimat: Eine deutsch-jüdische Geschichte der Bundesrepublik* (Munich: Deutsche Verlags-Anstalt, 2007); Anthony D. Kauders, *Democratization and the Jews. Munich 1945–1965* (Nebraska/London: University of Nebraska Press, 2004); David Cesarani, *Survivors of Nazi Persecution in Europe after the Second World War* (London: Vallentine Mitchell, 2010).

82. Immisch, *Zeiten und Menschen*, no. 4, discusses Jewish returnees from its 1974 edition onward, making the following comment: "The strength of the love many emigrants held for Germany is evident in the fact that after the collapse [of the Nazi regime] they returned to the country in which they had suffered such great wrongs."

83. The chapter on Jewish remigration cited above stands out from others in this respect, with its iconographic reference to Jewish religious life in today's Germany, centering on the realization, presented in citations from sources, that it is possible to live a Jewish life outside Israel, and on this realization's transformation into practice; Regenhardt and Tatsch, eds., *Forum Geschichte* (2011), 210–11.

84. This was a finding of a study carried out at the Georg Eckert Institute for International Textbook Research (GEI); GEI, ed., *Keine Chance auf Zugehörigkeit? Schulbücher*

*europäischer Länder halten Islam und modernes Europa getrennt* (Braunschweig: roco druck, 2011); retrieved 12 May 2016 from http://www.gei.de/fileadmin/gei.de/pdf/presse/Islamstudie_2011.pdf; see also "Teaching about Islam and the Muslim World. Textbooks and Real Curriculum," special issue, *JEMMS* 3 (2011), esp. Gerdien Jonker's essay "Caught in a Nutshell: 'Islam' and the Rise of History Textbooks in Germany (1700–2005)," *JEMMS* 3 (2011): 61–80.

85. Most prominently in Albrecht, *Expedition Geschichte*, 30.

86. This said, almost all teachers surveyed in a study carried out by the GEI admitted that they had never thought about whether depictions of migration and migrants in textbooks were appropriate for use in classrooms with a high degree of migration-related heterogeneity. Dorte Huneke and Johanna Ahlrichs, "Sind unsere Schulbücher noch zeitgemäß?," in *Ziemlich deutsch: Betrachtungen aus dem Einwanderungsland Deutschland*, ed. Dorte Huneke (Bonn: Bundeszentrale für politische Bildung, 2013), 66–76.

87. In some exceptional cases, textbooks published as early as the end of the 1990s contained interviews conducted by migrants from one country with migrants from another, thus calling into question the underlying assumption of exclusively "German" agency in the depiction and interpretation of migrants and migration; Menzel and Textor, *Geschichte und Geschehen* (1997), 236.

88. Manfred Albrecht, *Expedition Geschichte*, 40. Gary Davis is the politician quoted here.

89. *Geschichte und Geschehen* already contains this point in its 1997 edition, Menzel and Textor, *Geschichte und Geschehen* (1997), 226.

90. Ibid., 222.

91. Eritrea and Vietnam also receive several mentions.

92. Textbooks on the subject allow students to weigh the various views on asylum legislation and the argumentation used to support them. Defensive attitudes and hurdles to cultural integration are not suppressed in these books and are sometimes voiced in statements by migrants or their children.

93. Although *Buchners Kolleg Geschichte* devotes a comparatively large amount of space to the topic, its seemingly factual presentation is undermined by the use of extremely loaded terms such as "streams" (of immigrants heading to Germany), "mass," and "dramatic" (immigration); Dieter Brückner, Harald Focke and Lorenz Maier, eds., *Buchners Kolleg Geschichte* (Bamberg: C.C. Buchner, 2010), 204–6.

94. The subjects of the competitions for these two years were *Our Hometown – a Home for Foreigners? (Unser Ort – Heimat für Fremde?)*, (Hamburg, 1988/89) and *Departing and Arriving: Migration in History (Weggehen-Ankommen: Migration in der Geschichte)*, (Hamburg, 2002/03).

95. The work of German authors such as Klaus Bade, Dirk Hoerder, Christiane Hartzig, and Jochen Oltmer, who were conducting research on the history of migration relatively early, received a hesitant response from mainstream academic history; empirical studies devoted to social and cultural history in the twentieth century, such as Maren Möhring, ed., *Fremdes Essen. Die Geschichte der ausländischen Gastronomie in der Bundesrepublik Deutschland* (Munich: Oldenbourg Wissenschaftsverlag, 2012), were a rarity before the turn of the millennium. The neglect of migration issues we have identified is primarily the case for Europe, less so for American academic history; Jan Logemann, "Europe – Migration – Identity: Connections between Migration Experiences and Europeanness," *National Identities* 1 (2013): 1–8; Karen Schönwälder, "Integration from Below? Migration and European Contemporary History," in *Conflicted Memories: Europeanizing Contemporary Histories*, ed. Konrad Jarausch (New York: Berghahn Books, 2007), 154–63.

96. According to the study, the number of textbooks discussing the rights of immigrants, for instance, roughly tripled, from 6 percent to 19 percent, between 1970 and 2009; Francisco Ramirez, Patricia Bromley, and Susan Garnett Russell, "The Valorization of Humanity and Diversity," *Multicultural Education Review (MER)* l.1 (2009): 29–54.

97. Gerhard Paul, "Leerstelle im kulturellen Gedächtnis," 17; C. Hintermann et al., "Debating Migration in Textbooks and Classrooms in Austria," *JEMMS* 1 (2014): 79–106.

98. C. Hintermann et al., "Texbooks, Migration and National Narratives: An Introduction," in *Migration and Memory: Representations of Migration in Europe since 1960*, ed. Christiane Hintermann (Innsbruck: Studien Verlag, 2010), 38–39.

99. Christiane Hintermann, "'Beneficial', 'Problematic' and 'Different': Representations of Immigration and Immigrants in Austrian textbooks," in Hintermann et al., *Migration and Memory*, 61–78. This finding also applies to French textbooks, with the exception that the newest editions, according to Benoit Falaize, are increasingly focusing on migrant "success stories"; Falaize, "Labor migration and Immigration History in French Schools," in Hintermann et al., *Migration and Memory* (2010), 94–109.

100. Austria, France, England, Germany, and Sweden.

101. Christiane Hintermann and Vanja Lozic, "Texbooks, Migration and National Narratives: An Introduction," in *Migration and Memory: Representations of Migration in Europe since 1960*, ed. Christiane Hintermann (Innsbruck: Studien Verlag, 2010), 38–39.

102. See also Júlia Szalai, ed., *Contested Issues of Social Inclusion through Education in Multiethnic Communities across Europe* (Budapest: Edumigrom, 2011).

103. Daniel Faas, "The Nation, Europe and Migration," *Journal of Curriculum Studies (JCS)* 43 (2011): 471–92.

104. Hintermann and Lozic, "Texbooks, Migration and National Narratives," 9; Simona Sakács and Yasemin N. Soysal, "Projections of 'Diversity' in Citizenship Education," in *Migration and Memory: Representations of Migration in Europe since 1960*, ed. Christiane Hintermann (Innsbruck: Studien Verlag, 2010), 79–93.

105. When history textbooks from various countries are directly compared, those from England show the highest rate of "multicultural topics" (26.1 percent, as compared to 13.6 percent in German textbooks and 5.9 percent in their Greek counterparts), while German textbooks devote the most significant space to "European" topics (36.4 percent; the comparative figures are 17.4 percent for England and 26.5 percent for Greece). The findings do not differ significantly for civic studies and geography textbooks. Faas, "The Nation, Europe, and Migration," 480.

106. As Benoit Falaize concluded from an analysis of 240 post1990s textbooks, the new concept of "education about immigration" boosts a tendency toward an unhistorical, rather moralizing instead of analytical manner of teaching history. Falaize, "Labor Migration and Immigration History in French Schools."

107. Hannah Schissler and Yasemin Nuhoglu Soysal, eds., *The Nation, Europe and the World: Textbooks and Curricula in Transition* (New York: Berghahn Books, 2005), 3.

108. Hintermann, "'Beneficial', 'Problematic' and 'Different;'" see also the comparative study GEI, ed., *Keine Chance auf Zugehörigkeit?* (2011).

109. Jenny Hestermann, *Analyse fremdsprachiger Schulbücher zur Darstellung Jüdischer Geschichte*, working paper, Georg-Eckert Institute for International Textbook Research. Working paper (Braunschweig: Limbach, 2011), 51.

110. "Recommendation Concerning Education for International Understanding, Cooperation, and Peace and Education Relating to Human Rights and Fundamental Freedoms," adopted by the General Conference at its eighteenth session (Paris, 19 November 1974); Pingel, *UNESCO Guidebook*.

111. United Nations General Assembly. 2013. *A/68/296, Sixty-eight session. Cultural rights. Report of the Special Rapporteur in the field of cultural rights, Farida Shaheed,* 9 August: 10, retrieved 12 May 2016 from https://documents-dds-ny.un.org/doc/UNDOC/GEN/ N13/422/91/pdf/N1342291.pdf?OpenElement. The report points to the fact that a significant number of countries continue to promote overly nationalistic political agendas and monolithic views of dominant powers as well as ignore cultural diversity in their official historical narratives.

112. Thus it seems difficult to identify and describe a discourse on diversity that could be labeled as hegemonic. The history curriculum currently in force in Lower Saxony is representative: On the one hand, they recommend that history teachers avoid a "single self-contained view of the world" and call for approaches that recognize a range of perspectives. On the other hand, however, they stipulate that history classes should help students develop "a well-considered awareness of the connection between German and European identity and of these identities' common basis in *Christianity* and in *European* humanist ideas" (emphasis added). Niedersächsiches Kultusministerium, ed., *Kerncurriculum Geschichte für das Gymnasium – gymnasiale Oberstufe, die Gesamtschule – gymnasiale Oberstufe, das Berufliche Gymnasium, das Abendgymnasium das Kolleg* (Hannover: Druckerei Schwitalla 2008/11), 7–8, retrieved 12 May 2016 from http://db2. nibis.de/1db/cuvo/datei/kc_geschichte_go_i_03-11.pdf.

113. Johanna Ahlrichs, "Migrationsbedingte Vielfalt im Unterricht: Lehrerhandeln zwischen theoretischen Ansprüchen und praktischen Herausforderungen" (unpublished pilot study by the Georg Eckert Institute for International Textbook Research in Braunschweig, 2013).

# Works Cited

Adams, Xavier, and Leon Cuppes. *ANNO 4*. Lier: Uitgeverij Van In, 2000.

Ahlrichs, Johanna. "Migrationsbedingte Vielfalt im Unterricht: Lehrerhandeln zwischen theoretischen Ansprüchen und praktischen Herausforderungen." Unpublished pilot study by the Georg Eckert Institute for International Textbook Research in Braunschweig, 2013.

Ahonen, Pertti, ed. *After the Expulsion. West Germany and Eastern Europe 1945–1990*. Oxford: Oxford University Press, 2003.

Ahonen, Pertti, et al., eds. *People on the Move: Forced Population Movements in Europe in the Second World War and its Aftermath*. Oxford: Bloomsbury Academic, 2008.

Albrecht, Manfred. *Expedition Geschichte. Von der Nachkriegszeit bis zur Gegenwart*. No. 5/6. Braunschweig: Diesterweg, 2008.

Alter, Peter. *Erinnern und Urteilen: Unterrichtseinheiten Geschichte 4*. Stuttgart: Klett, 1981.

Apple, Michael, ed. *Ideology and Curriculum*. 3rd ed. New York: Taylor & Francis, 2004.

"Behandlung des Nationalsozialismus im Unterricht." Beschluss der Kultusminister-Konferenz vom 20.04.1978, Nr. 553; und "Empfehlungen zur Behandlung des Widerstandes in der NS Zeit im Unterricht." Beschluss der Kultusminister-Konferenz vom 04.12.1980., Nr. 561. In *Sammlung der Beschlüsse der Ständigen Konferenz der Kultusminister der Länder in der Bundesrepublik Deutschland*, edited by Kultusministerkonferenz der Länder. Darmstadt/Neuwied: Luchterhand, 1964.

Borries, Bodo von. "The Third Reich in German History Textbooks since 1945." *Journal of Contemporary History* 38 (2003): 45–62.

Brenner, Michael. *After the Holocaust: Rebuilding Jewish Lives in Postwar Germany.* Princeton: Princeton University Press, 1997.

Bruch, Rüdiger vom. *BSV Geschichte 4. Vom Zeitalter des Imperialismus bis zur Gegenwart.* Munich: Oldenbourg Schulbuchverlag, 1988/1993.

Brückner, Dieter, Harald Focke, and Lorenz Maier, eds. *Buchners Kolleg Geschichte.* Bamberg: C.C. Buchner, 2010.

Bungenstab, Karl-Ernst. "Die Schulbuchrevision in der US-Zone nach 1945 im Zusammenhang mit der amerikanischen Umerziehungspolitik." *Internationales Jahrbuch für Geschichtsunterricht* 11 (1968/69): 96–140.

Cesarani, David, ed. *Survivors of Nazi Persecution in Europe after the Second World War.* London: Vallentine Mitchell, 2010.

Christian-Smith, Linda, and Michael Apple, eds. *The Politics of the Textbook.* New York: Routledge, 1991.

Christophe, Barbara. "Migration in German Textbooks: Is Multiperspectivity an Adequate Response?" *The Journal of Educational Media, Memory, and Society (JEMMS)* 1 (2009): 190–202.

Cornelissen, Joachim. *BSV Geschichte 4. Das 20. Jahrhundert.* Munich: Oldenbourg Schulbuchverlag, 1993.

"Deutsch französische Vereinbarung über strittige Fragen europäischer Geschichte." Special issue, *Internationalen Jahrbuch für Geschichtsunterricht* 2 (1953).

Demshuk, Andrew, ed. *The Lost German East: Forced Migration and the Politics of Memory, 1945–1970.* Cambridge: Cambridge University Press, 2012.

Dierkes, Julian, ed. *Postwar History Education in Japan and the Germanys: Guilty Lessons.* London: Routledge, 2010.

Doering-Manteuffel, Anselm, and Lutz Raphael, eds. *Nach dem Boom. Perspektiven auf die Zeitgeschichte seit 1970.* Göttingen: Vandenhoeck & Ruprecht, 2008.

Ebeling, Hans. *Die Reise in die Vergangenheit: Ein geschichtliches Arbeitsbuch.* Braunschweig: Westermann, 1972.

Ebeling, Hans. *Die Reise in die Vergangenheit.* No. 3. Braunschweig: Westermann, 1972/1981.

Ebeling, Hans. *Die Reise in die Vergangenheit.* No. 4. Baden-Württemberg. Braunschweig: Westermann, 1961/1986.

Ebeling, Hans, and Gustav Rüggeberg. *Deutsche Geschichte.* Vol. A. No. 5. Braunschweig: Westermann, 1955.

Eckhardt, Hans-Wilhelm. *Zeit für Geschichte 5/6.* Niedersachsen. Braunschweig: Schroedel, 2009.

Faas, Daniel. "The Nation, Europe and Migration." *Journal of Curriculum Studies (JCS)* 43 (2011): 471–92.

Falaize, Benoit. "Labor Migration and Immigration History in French Schools." In *Migration and Memory: Representations of Migration in Europe since 1960*, edited by Christiane Hintermann, 94–109. Innsbruck: Studien Verlag, 2010.

Frei, Norbert, and Volkhard Knigge, eds. *Verbrechen erinnern. Die Auseinandersetzung mit Holocaust und Völkermord.* Munich: C.H. Beck, 2002.

Gardner Feldman, Lily, ed. *Germany's Foreign Policy of Reconciliation: From Enmity to Amity.* Lanham: Rowman & Littlefield, 2012.

Gemeinsame Deutsch-Polnische Schulbuchkommission. "Empfehlungen für Schulbücher der Geschichte und Geographie in der Bundesrepublik Deutschland und in der Volksrepublik Polen." *Internationales Jahrbuch für Geschichts- und Geographieunterricht* XVII (1976): 158–84.

Georg Eckert Institut für Internationale Schulbuchforschung (GEI), ed. *Keine Chance auf Zugehörigkeit? Schulbücher europäischer Länder halten Islam und modernes Europa getrennt.* Braunschweig: roco druck, 2011. Retrieved 12 May 2016 from http://www.gei.de/ fileadmin/gei.de/pdf/presse/Islamstudie_2011.pdf.

Giesen, Bernhard. "Europäische Identität und transnationale Öffentlichkeit. Eine historische Perspektive." In *Transnationale Öffentlichkeiten und Identitäten im 20. Jahrhundert*, edited by Alexander Schmidt-Gernig, Hartmut Kaelble, and Martin Kirsch, 67–84. Frankfurt a.M.: Campus Verlag, 2002.

Grass, Günther. *Im Krebsgang. Eine Novelle.* Göttingen: Steidl Verlag, 2002.

Grindel, Susanne. "Das Bild von MigrantInnen im Schulbuch". In *Wirtschaften mit Migrationshintergrund: Zur soziokulturellen Bedeutung "ethnischer Ökonomien in urbanen Räumen,"* edited by Alexander Trupp and Maria Dabringer, 120–29. Innsbruck: Studien Verlag, 2008.

Grossman, Atina. *Jews, Germans and Allies: Close Encounters in Occupied Germany.* Princeton: Princeton University Press, 2009.

Hahn, Eva, and Hans Henning Hahn, eds. *Die Vertreibung im deutschen Erinnern. Legenden, Mythos, Geschichte.* Paderborn: Schöningh, 2010.

Herbert, Ulrich, ed. *Fremdarbeiter: Politik und Praxis des "Ausländer-Einsatzes" in der Kriegswirtschaft des Dritten Reiches.* Berlin/Bonn: J.H.W. Dietz Nachf., 1985.

Hestermann, Jenny. *Analyse fremdsprachiger Schulbücher zur Darstellung Jüdischer Geschichte.* Braunschweig: Limbach, 2011.

Hilke, GüntherArndt, ed. *Geschichtsbuch. Die Menschen und ihre Geschichte in Darstellungen und Dokumenten.* No. 4. Berlin: Cornelsen, 1986–88.

Hinrichs, Ernst, ed. *Deutsch-israelische Schulbuchempfehlungen: Zur Darstellung der jüdischen Geschichte sowie der Geschichte und Geographie Israels in Schulbüchern der Bundesrepublik Deutschland.* Studien zur internationalen Schulbuchforschung: Schriftreihe des Georg-Eckert-Instituts für Internationale Schulbuchforschung. Braunschweig/Hannover: Hahn, 1985.

Hintermann, Christiane. "'Beneficial,' 'Problematic' and 'Different': Representations of Immigration and Immigrants in Austrian Textbooks." In *Migration and Memory: Representations of Migration in Europe since 1960*, edited by Christiane Hintermann, 61–78. Innsbruck: Studien Verlag, 2010.

Hintermann, Christiane, and Vanja Lozic. "Texbooks, Migration and National Narratives: An Introduction." In *Migration and Memory: Representations of Migration in Europe since 1960*, edited by Christiane Hintermann, 38–39. Innsbruck: Studien Verlag, 2010.

Hintermann, Christiane, et al. "Debating Migration in Textbooks and Classrooms in Austria." *The Journal of Educational Media, Memory, and Society (JEMMS)* 1 (2014): 79–106.

Hofmeister, Franz. *Forum Geschichte.* No. 4. Berlin: Cornelsen, 2011.

Hug, Wolfgang. *Unsere Geschichte.* No. 4. Baden-Württemberg. Frankfurt a.M.: Diesterweg, 1988.

Hug, Wolfgang, Joachim Hoffmann, and Elmar Krautkrämer. *Geschichtliche Weltkunde.* No. 3. Braunschweig: Diesterweg, 1976/1997.

Huneke, Dorte, and Johanna Ahlrichs. "Sind unsere Schulbücher noch zeitgemäß?" In *Ziemlich deutsch: Betrachtungen aus dem Einwanderungsland Deutschland*, edited by Dorte Huneke, 66–76. Bonn: Bundeszentrale für politische Bildung, 2013.

Immisch, Joachim. *Zeiten und Menschen.* Vol. B. No. 4. Paderborn/Hannover: Schoeningh/ Schroedel, 1967/1974/1980.

Jonker, Gerdien. "Caught in a Nutshell: 'Islam' and the Rise of History Textbooks in Germany (1700–2005)." *The Journal of Educational Media, Memory, and Society (JEMMS)* 3 (2011): 61–80.

Kansteiner, Wulf, ed. *In Pursuit of German Memory: History, Television, and Politics after Auschwitz.* Athens: Ohio University Press, 2006.

Kauders, Anthony D. *Democratization and the Jews. Munich 1945–1965.* Nebraska/London: University of Nebraska Press, 2004.

Kauders, Anthony. *Unmögliche Heimat: Eine deutsch-jüdische Geschichte der Bundesrepublik.* Munich: Deutsche Verlags-Anstalt, 2007.

Kochanowska-Nieborak, Anna, Hans Henning Hahn, and Heidi Hein-Kircher, eds. *Erinnerungskultur und Versöhnungskitsch.* Marburg: Herder-Institut Verlag, 2008.

Kochanowski, Jerzy. "Gathering Poles into Poland. Forced Migration from Poland's Former Eastern Territories." In *Redrawing Nations. Ethnic Cleansing in East-Central Europe 1944– 1948,* edited by Ana Siljak and Philipp Ther, 135–54. Lanham, Boulder, New York and Oxford: Rowman & Littlefield, 2001.

Kogon, Eugen. *Der SS-Staat. Das System der deutschen Konzentrationslager.* Munich: Heyne, 1946.

Korostelina, Karina, and Simone Lässig, eds. *History Education and Post-Conflict Reconciliation. Reconsidering Joint Textbook Projects.* London: Routledge, 2013.

Lange, Dirk. "Fremdheit und Akkulturation im historisch-politischen Schulbuch." In *Interkulturelles Verstehen und kulturelle Integration durch das Schulbuch?,* edited by Carsten Heinze and Eva Matthes, 321–37. Bad Heilbrunn: Verlag Julius Klinkhardt KG, 2004.

Lässig, Simone. "Textbooks and Beyond. Educational Media in Context(s)." *The Journal of Educational Media, Memory, and Society (JEMMS)* 1 (2009): 1–20.

LBI-Kommission für die Verbreitung deutsch-jüdischer Geschichte, ed. *Deutsch-jüdische Geschichte im Unterricht. Eine Orientierungshilfe für Schule und Erwachsenenbildung.* Bad Homburg: VAS-Verlag, 2011. Retrieved 12 May 2016 from http://www.stiftung-evz.de/ fileadmin/user_upload/EVZ_Uploads/Handlungsfelder/Auseinandersetzung_mit_der_ Geschichte_01/Leo_Back_Programm/orientierungshilfe-korrigiert.pdf.

Logemann, Jan. "Europe – Migration – Identity: Connections between Migration Experiences and Europeanness." *National Identities* 1 (2013): 1–8.

Lucas, Friedrich J., and Heinrich Bodensieck. *Menschen in ihrer Zeit.* No. 4. Stuttgart: Klett, 1969.

Margalit, Gilad. *Guilt, Suffering, and Memory. Germany Remembers Its Dead of World War II.* Bloomington: Indiana University Press, 2010.

Menzel, Karl-Heinz, and Fritz Textor. *Geschichte und Geschehen. Kletts Geschichtliches Unterrichtswerk für die Mittelklassen.* Stuttgart: Klett, 1968/1983/1997.

Meyer, Hermann, and Wilhelm Langenbeck. *Grundzüge der Geschichte, Mittelstufe.* Frankfurt a.M.: Diesterweg, 1970.

Moeller, Robert G. "Germans as Victims? Thoughts on a Post–Cold War History of World War II's Legacies." *History & Memory* 17 (2005): 147–94.

Möhring, Maren, ed. *Fremdes Essen. Die Geschichte der ausländischen Gastronomie in der Bundesrepublik Deutschland.* Munich: Oldenbourg Wissenschaftsverlag, 2012.

Motte, Jan, and Rainer Ohliger, eds. *Geschichte und Gedächtnis in der Einwanderungsgesellschaft.* Essen: Klartext Verlag, 2004.

Niedersächsiches Kultusministerium, ed.. *Kerncurriculum Geschichte für das Gymnasium – gymnasiale Oberstufe, die Gesamtschule – gymnasiale Oberstufe, das Berufliche Gymnasium, das Abendgymnasium, das Kolleg.* Hannover: Druckerei Schwitalla, 2011. Retrieved 12 May 2016 from http://db2.nibis.de/1db/cuvo/datei/kc_geschichte_go_i_03-11.pdf.

Niven, Bill, ed. *Germans as Victims: Remembering the Past in Contemporary Germany.* Basingstoke: Palgrave, 2006.

Olick, Jeffrey K., ed. *The Politics of Regret. On Collective Memory and Historical Responsibility.* New York: Routledge, 2007.

Paul, Gerhard. "Der Flüchtlingstreck. Bilder von Flucht und Vertreibung als europäische *lieux de mémoire.*" In *Das Jahrhundert der Bilder*, edited by Gerhard Paul, 666–73. Bonn: Vandenhoeck & Ruprecht, 2009.

Paul, Gerhard. "Leerstelle im kulturellen Gedächtnis. Emigration, Exil und Remigration in deutschsprachigen Schulgeschichtsbüchern 1955–2007." In *Gedächtnis des Exils: Formen der Erinnerung*, edited by Claus-Dieter Krohn and Lutz Winckler, 1–23. Munich: edition text + kritik, 2010.

Pingel, Falk. "From Evasion to a Crucial Tool of Moral and Political Education." In *What Shall We Tell the Children? International Perspectives on School History Textbooks*, edited by Keith A. Crawford and Stuart J. Foster, 131–54. Greenwich: Information Age Publishing, 2006.

Pingel, Falk. *UNESCO Guidebook in Textbook Research and Textbook Revision.* 2nd rev. ed., Paris/Braunschweig: UNESCO/Georg Eckert Institute for International Textbook Research, 2010.

Pingel, Falk. "Geschichtslehrbücher zwischen Kaiserreich und Gegenwart." In *Grenzgänger. Aufsätze von Falk Pingel*, edited by Falk Pingel, 403–24. Göttingen: V&R Unipress, 2009.

Puaca, Brian, ed. *Learning Democracy. Education Reform in West Germany, 1945–1965.* Oxford/New York: Berghahn Books, 2009.

Radkau, Verena. "Vom Umgang mit Verschiedenheit und Vielfalt. Befunde aus deutschen und US-amerikanischen Schulbüchern." In *Interkulturelles Verstehen und kulturelle Integration durch das Schulbuch?*, edited by Carsten Heinze and Eva Matthes, 301–20. Bad Heilbrunn: Verlag Julius Klinkhardt KG, 2004.

Ramirez, Francisco, Patricia Bromley, and Susan Garnett Russell. "The Valorization of Humanity and Diversity." *Multicultural Education Review (MER)* 1.1 (2009): 29–54.

Regenhardt, Hans-Otto, ed. *Forum Geschichte kompakt. Von der Nachkriegszeit bis zur Gegenwart.* No. 2/2. Nordrhein-Westfalen. Berlin: Cornelsen, 2008.

Regenhardt, Hans-Otto, and Claudi Tatsch, eds. *Forum Geschichte. Vom Ende des Weltkriegs bis zur Gegenwart.* No. 4. Berlin: Cornelsen, 2003.

Röger, Maren. "Bilder der Vertreibung: Propagandistischer Kontext und Funktionalisierung in erinnerungskulturellen Diskursen seit dem Ende des Zweiten Weltkrieges." In *Bilder in historischen Diskursen*, edited by Franz X. Eder, et al., 261–82. Wiesbaden: Springer Verlag, 2014.

Rosenzweig, Beate, ed.. *Erziehung zur Demokratie? Amerikanische Besatzungs- und Schulreformpolitik in Deutschland und Japan.* Stuttgart: Franz Steiner Verlag, 1998.

Sadowski, Dirk, and Martin Liepach, eds. *Jüdische Geschichte im Schulbuch.* Göttingen: V&R Unipress, 2014.

Sakács, Simona, and Yasemin N. Soysal. "Projections of 'Diversity' in Citizenship Education." In *Migration and Memory: Representations of Migration in Europe since 1960*, edited by Christiane Hintermann, 79–93. Innsbruck: Studien Verlag, 2010.

Schissler, Hannah, and Yasemin Nuhoglu Soysal, eds. *The Nation, Europe and the World: Textbooks and Curricula in Transition.* New York: Berghahn Books, 2005.

Schmid, Heinz Dieter, ed. *Fragen an die Geschichte.* Frankfurt a.M.: Hirschgraben-Verlag, 1974–78.

Schneider, Christian, and Ulrike Jureit, eds. *Gefühlte Opfer. Illusionen der Vergangenheitsbewältigung.* Stuttgart: Klett-Cotta, 2010.

Schönwälder, Karen. "Integration from Below? Migration and European Contemporary History." In *Conflicted Memories: Europeanizing Contemporary Histories*, edited by Konrad Jarausch, 154–63. New York: Berghahn Books, 2007.

Schüddekopf, Otto-Ernst, ed. *History Teaching and History Textbook Revision*. Strasbourg: Council for Cultural Co-operation of the Council of Europe, 1967.

Shibata, Masako. *Japan and Germany under the U.S. Occupation. A Comparative Analysis of Postwar Education Reform*. Lanham. Lexington Books, 2005.

Ständige Konferenz der Kultusminister der Länder, ed. *"Interkulturelle Bildung und Erziehung in der Schule," Sammlung der Beschlüsse der Ständigen Konferenz der Kultusminister der Länder in der Bundesrepublik Deutschland*, 59–70. Neuwied: Luchterhand, 1996.

Stehling, Jutta, and Michael Guse. *Wir machen Geschichte*. Frankfurt a.M.: Diesterweg, 1998.

Stellman, Martin. *Spiegel der Zeiten. Geschichtsbuch für deutsche Schulen*. No. 4. Frankfurt a.M.: Diesterweg, 1971.

Szalai, Júlia, ed. *Contested Issues of Social Inclusion through Education in Multiethnic Communities across Europe*. Budapest: Edumigrom, 2011.

*Teaching about Islam and the Muslim World. Textbooks and Real Curriculum*. Special issue, *JEMMS* 3 (2011).

United Nations General Assembly. 2013. *A/68/296, Sixty-eight session. Cultural rights. Note by the Secretary-General*, 9 August: 10. Retrieved 12 May 2016 from https://documents-dds-ny.un.org/doc/UNDOC/GEN/N13/422/91/PDF/N1342291.pdf?OpenElement.

Welzer, Harald, ed. *Der Krieg der Erinnerung. Holocaust, Kollaboration und Widerstand im europäischen Gedächtnis*. Frankfurt a.M.: Fischer Taschenbuch Verlag, 2007.

Wuessing, Fritz. *Geschichtsbuch für deutsche Schulen. Wege der Völker*. Vol. D. No. 5. Berlin. Frankfurt a.M.: Pädagogischer Verlag Schulz, 1948.

**Simone Lässig** has been director of the German Historical Institute (GHI) in Washington, DC, since October 2015. For the duration of her tenure at the GHI, she is on leave from her professorship in modern history at the Technical University of Braunschweig, as well as from her post as director of the Georg Eckert Institute for International Textbook Research, which she has held since 2006. During the academic year 2009/10 she was a visiting professor at St Antony's College, Oxford. She has served as the editor of the *Journal for Educational Media, Memory, and Society* (JEMMS) and the series *Eckert: Die Schriftenreihe*, and is also a co-editor of *Geschichte und Gesellschaft*. Among her numerous publications, her book on the embourgeoisement of German Jews in the nineteenth century, *Jüdische Wege ins Bürgertum* (2004), was honored with a prize for best second book (habilitation) by the German Historical Association. Her main fields of research are Jewish history during the nineteenth and twentieth centuries, educational media research, and the history of knowledge.

*Chapter 6*

# REPRESENTATIONS OF IMMIGRATION AND EMIGRATION IN GERMANY'S HISTORIC MUSEUMS

*Dietmar Osses and Katarzyna Nogueira*

Throughout its history, Germany has been significantly shaped by migration. Due to Germany's geographical position in the very middle of Europe without fixed natural borders, migration has always been a central factor in the development of its population. This was even true for the period during which Germany was transitioning from a collection of territories, kingdoms, and principalities into the modern German nation state.

During and after World War II, migration affected Germany in an extraordinary way. Never before were so many people in just one decade compelled to leave their homes and emigrate from, or immigrate to, Germany. Approximately one million left Germany due to persecution by the Nazis. By the end of the war, about eight million people had been brought to Germany by force as civil workers, slave workers, or prisoners of war. Another 12.5 million people came as refugees and expellees from former eastern German territories in the 1940s.[1]

In the 1950s, West Germany focused on the integration of the refugees and expellees on the one hand and, after the beginning of the Cold War, on the integration of West Germany into the Western World, western Europe, and NATO on the other. After the Iron Curtain between Eastern and western Europe became a reality and the wall between the two German states had been built, the routes of immigration to West Germany from the east were cut off. As a result of the labor shortage caused by this restriction of migrant labor, the German government introduced several recruitment agreements with governments in southern and southeastern Europe, beginning with Italy in 1955 and ending with Yugoslavia in 1968. Until the recruitment stoppage during the worldwide economic crisis in 1973, some fourteen million people came to the Federal Republic of Germany as "guest workers". About eleven million returned to their home countries, but three million—mainly workers from Turkey—decided to stay in Germany and many of them brought their families to Germany during the following years.[2] During the 1970s, family members of the "guest workers" made up the vast majority of immigrants in Germany, followed by some 50,000 Vietnamese refugees of war, who received residence permits according to a fixed quota.

During this period of enormous movement and migration to West Germany, the federal government strictly maintained its policy that Germany was not a country of immigration.[3] German refugees and expellees had German citizenship and thus, based on their legal status, were not seen as immigrants. Migrant workers received only temporary residence permits and were seen as a variable buffer workforce for industry, as "guest workers" who would work in Germany for some years and then go back to their countries of origin. Consequently, in 1982, a time of economic and social crisis, the government set up a repatriation program for the purpose of motivating immigrants—especially Turkish "guest workers" and their families—to leave Germany and remigrate.

At the same time, the first Polish migrants arrived in West Germany as political refugees. After the Polish government attempted to extinguish the Solidarność movement and consequently imposed martial law in 1981, nearly 100,000 Poles immigrated to Germany. Only a marginal number of them claimed the right of political asylum and went through the long process of recognition.

Only a few months later—faced with the increasing problems of political and economic crises in Poland—thousands of Poles decided to leave their home country. By 1990, more than one million people had emigrated from Poland to Germany. The vast majority benefited from the possibility of attaining legal status as ethnic German immigrants—a status granted to people of German origin who still lived in territories that had been part of Germany prior to 1937, but which had fallen under Polish administration after 1945, and to ethnic Germans in communist-controlled Eastern Europe who had decided to "remigrate" to the Federal Republic of Germany. In contrast to the strict policy of "non-immigration," in those days it was easy to convince the authorities that one had German roots—in most cases, claiming to have had ancestors who lived in the former German areas, to be of German ancestry, or to declare that one practiced or had practiced German culture was sufficient.[4]

After the fall of the Soviet Union the number of political asylum seekers skyrocketed again. From 1989 to 1993, 1.3 million people applied for political asylum. In 1993, maintaining the policy of "non-immigration," the government tightened the regulations dealing with political asylum seekers. After that point, asylum seekers who entered Germany from another country in the European Union no longer qualified for political asylum. This, of course, led to a sharp drop in application rates.

In addition to the emigrants from Poland, more and more emigrants from the former Soviet Union and Romania claimed legal status as ethnic Germans. All in all, from 1981 to 2000 about four million people from Eastern Europe immigrated to Germany; most of them were accepted as ethnic Germans and were granted German citizenship.

The sharply increasing number of asylum seekers and ethnic German immigrants caused both an increase of xenophobia within German society and a public and political debate over citizenship and immigration. Politicians and the media drew a picture of Germany as a lifeboat in the ocean that was too full to receive any more immigrants: *"Das Boot ist voll"* ("the boat is full").

During the rapid and intense process of German reunification, debates about nation, democracy, and power arose that were often overrun by the extreme dynamic of events. But the xenophobic attacks and assaults on the living quarters of immigrants and asylum seekers in both East and West Germany, which occurred just a few years after the German reunification, sparked a vast and controversial debate on the topic of immigration to Germany.[5]

What role did museums play in the public debate about migration and the nation? During the mid-1980s, historians and museum experts had a long and controversial debate about ideas for two museums of national history in Germany. Based on plans described by German chancellor Helmut Kohl in an official statement after the change of administration in 1982, the Deutsches Historisches Museum (German Historical Museum, DHM), which presented German history in an international context, reflecting the influence of the globalization of economics and work, as well as the internationalization of everyday life, was finally established in 1987 in Berlin.

In 1986, in preparation for the second national historical museum, the government began building a collection dedicated to German history—particularly West German history—from the time of the German division in 1945, and made plans for a new institution, the Haus der Geschichte der Bundesrepublik Deutschland (HdG, House for the History of the Federal Republic of Germany) to be located in the German capital, Bonn.

The debates and public hearings on both projects revealed the thread of a new nationalism. Most of the historians cautioned that the power of objects and emotions in exhibitions could not be controlled. All in all, the debate focused on the political history and questions about the German *Sonderweg*, the unique route taken by Germany to National Socialism and fascism, and the way back to democracy in West Germany.[6] Issues of migration did not play a significant role in those concepts.

Both projects were hampered by German reunification. In the end, after merging with the former East German Museum für Deutsche Geschichte (Museum for German History), the DHM, now presenting German history including the reunification, emerged in 1994. The concept of the HdG in Bonn was approved by the government in 1989 and opened with its permanent exhibition in 1994.

Corresponding to the official policy claiming that Germany was not a country of immigration, the concept of migration had no representation in national historical museums. In contrast to this, a handful of local and regional museums mounted temporary exhibitions dealing with the history and current presence of migrants—in most cases migrant workers. One of the first papers dealing with the question of a museum of migration was presented by Michael Fehr, curator of the art museum in Bochum and organizer of one of the first intercultural festivals in Germany, Kemnade International, but it remained without significant consequences.[7]

By the end of the 1990s, the increasing volume of historical research about migration in Germany and a bottom-up initiative led to two important exhibition projects that developed into milestones for the musealization of migration.

The anthology *Deutsche im Ausland, Fremde in Deutschland* (*Germans Abroad, Foreigners in Germany*),[8] edited by migration expert Klaus Bade, provided the impetus for a cooperative project: a traveling exhibition by five regional museums in East and West Germany. Varying the title of the anthology and following its main steps in migration history, the exhibition "Fremde in Deutschland, Deutsche in der Fremde" ("Foreigners in Germany, Germans Abroad") presented immigration to and emigration from Germany from the late Middle Ages onward, to show migration not as the exception, but as the norm in history. Facing the current xenophobic tendencies in Germany, the exhibition highlighted the nature of Germany as a central place for migration due to its position in the middle of Europe.

With the display of emigration and immigration history in conjunction with the history of flight and expulsion of Germans, as well as the history of "guest workers" and asylum seekers, the exhibition brought together three separate but related discourses, which were extremely affected by controversial political debates. With changing attitudes toward migration, immigration, and emigration and the strange and familiar aspects of migration on display, the curators of the exhibition hoped to foster a collective sensitization to personal experiences of familiarity and otherness on both sides of the border and appreciation of the long history of migration.[9] The exhibition aimed to show that culture in Germany is not and never has been the culture of the Germans alone. Furthermore, the project was explicitly set up as a combined project of museums in both parts of the formerly divided Germany to show that migration was essential for the whole nation.[10]

In contrast to this inventory of different kinds of migration in history, the exhibition "Fremde Heimat" ("Foreign Home"), shown in the Ruhrlandmuseum Essen, focused on the recent history of a single migration route to Germany: the immigration to Germany from Turkey in the 1960s and 1970s—especially to the Ruhr, the industrial powerhouse of Germany.

As a bottom-up initiative, the exhibition was developed as a cooperative project between the NGO DOMIT (Documentation Center for Migration from Turkey) and the municipal museum of the city of Essen, which is located in the center of the biggest industrial region in Europe and is thus very familiar with labor migration.

For the first time in Germany, a migrant organization and a municipal historical museum worked together as equal partners to produce an exhibition. Focusing on two decades of migration history and based on a set of a hundred life-story interviews, the project featured outstanding depth and quality of research. Putting together and discussing different views on issues of migration and everyday life experiences, the team of migrant and non-migrant curators offered different views and approaches to the exhibition. Curator Mathilde Jamin claimed the reversal of fixed images and stereotypes of Germans and even migrants themselves as the most important result of the constantly changing perspectives.[11] Furthermore, the exhibition was seen as an important act of recognition and representation of Turkish migrants. With their own migrant history shown in the museum as part of regional history, many Turkish migrants felt accepted for the first time as an equal part of society.[12] DOMIT emphasized the aspect of "shared memory" as an essential approach to migration history in exhibitions.[13]

The migrant organization DOMIT followed the methods of grassroots movements in public history in dealing with the history of workers, the history of everyday life, and gender studies, and encouraged migrants to research their own history and tell their stories in their own voices. This movement was widespread, especially in the Ruhr area during the 1980s. In addition, the participatory process was not only valued as a moment of recognition, but also as a process of self-empowerment for the migrants. Following this principle, the exhibition "Fremde Heimat" can be seen as a pioneer project of participatory exhibitions dealing with the history of migration.

In 2002, with the help of the Federal Agency for Civic Education, DOMIT started a public debate about a migration museum for Germany. The first conference, "Saving the Heritage of Immigrants – Germany needs a Museum for Migration,"[14] aimed to highlight the cultures and histories of different groups of migrants and to discuss the concept of a national museum of migration. The conference looked at examples of existing migration museums and planned projects; different models and concepts for the museum were discussed.[15] In the end, DOMIT favored a museum with archives, library, and permanent exhibition space to acquire, conserve, research, and show migration history. Furthermore, the museum was meant as a place for discussion and production of culture and art. As a first step, the museum was dedicated to the history of work migration from the 1950s to the 1980s. The main goal was the inclusion of migration history in the national narrative as an act of equality in cultural representation.[16]

The follow-up conference, "A Migration Museum in Germany,"[17] aimed to gather support for the project from a broader public and initiated the work on a concept for the museum. Facing the fact that the first generation of migrant workers was no longer living, DOMIT declared the collection of objects from this generation to be the most prominent task, and saw the museum as a place for cultural recognition and participation. The debate pointed to the lack of concepts for a collective memory with multiple perspectives and showed the demand for a revision and retelling of the national narrative.

The association Migrationsmuseum in Deutschland (Migration Museum in Germany) was founded in 2003 as an additional stepping stone on the way to a migration museum. The first task of the new association was to build up a network of immigrant organizations and activists within the greater society.[18]

The third conference, "Strategies for Cultural Policies in the Immigration Society," exposed the diversity of expectations and contradictory demands for such a museum. Several ethnic groups demanded that their migration history and (ethnic) identity be shown as an act of recognition and representation. Others declined to collaborate or to be shown together with particular groups due to national or ethnic conflicts. The demand for the cultural self-assurance and folklore of particular groups clashed with concepts of hybridism and transculturalism.

But after three years of intensive debates, discussion about a national museum of migration in Germany faded. The reasons were manifold: the discussions of experts had shown the high degree of complexity that a national museum of emigration and immigration would have to deal with. Due to the autonomy of the federal states in cultural and educational affairs, it turned out that the idea of building a new historical museum on a national level lacked enough powerful stakeholders. DOMIT, as one of the activists in the debate, was involved in a new exhibition project on a national level and was focused more and more on this work.[19] Furthermore, public debate about migration, nation, citizenship, and belonging in politics and society declined after the first national immigration act was approved by the German parliament in August 2004.

While public debate about a national migration museum waned, during the past few years, more and more museums in Germany have seen migration as a topic for temporary exhibitions. The new policy of integration, as well as the upcoming anniversaries of the recruitment agreements for migrant workers, have given a strong impetus to all kinds of museums in Germany to deal with issues of migration, integration, and cultural diversity.

With temporary exhibitions, special educational programs, and sometimes changes in permanent exhibitions, historical museums, as well as some ethnographical museums, museums of natural history, and museums of art have showed aspects of migration or have tended to be more appealing to migrant visitors. The variety of concepts and intensity of self-reflection regarding the process of change is widespread.[20]

The new boom of migration exhibits in museums has been accompanied by increased networking and professional discussions. In the late 2000s, several congresses provided platforms for professional reviews of exhibition projects as well as scientific and theoretical discussions, beginning with the international congress "Migration in Museums: Narratives of Diversity in Europe," organized by the International Council of Museums (ICOM) Europe and the Network Migration in Europe. Networks and working groups were established, and in 2010 the German Museum Association decided to set up a migration working group as a platform for professional exchange.[21] In collaboration with associations and experts who themselves were migrants, the group developed a manual for the work of museum professionals on immigration and cultural diversity. The guiding principles as stated in the manual are dialogue, participation, and a multidimensional and multiperspective approach. People with an immigration background, their past and their present, are still strongly underrepresented in museums in Germany—even though their artifacts, stories, and interpretations are an important part of the cultural heritage. The manual promotes a change in all fields of a museum's work: collections, permanent and temporary exhibitions, educational programs, communication, and staff. A far-reaching process of change is necessary if a long-lasting and sustainable contribution to the debate on social cohesion is to be made.

Two projects funded by the federal government provided the opportunity for the German Museum Association to promote the opening of museums for migration issues. The project "The Whole World in a Museum? Museums in the Plural Society," funded by the Federal Office for Migration and Refugees, was aimed at improving access to museums for special target groups with migration backgrounds: adolescents and mothers with their children. The project "Cultural Diversity in Museums," funded by the Federal Commissioner for Culture and Media, focused on new intercultural perspectives of museum collections and on further educational programs for museum experts on the issues of migration, diversity, and intercultural dialogue.

With the help of these projects, the Museum Association increased the presentation of the topic of migration in museums of all sizes and types all over Germany. But how did the national historical museums tackle the issue of migration?

In 2005, both national historical museums in Germany mounted temporary exhibitions dealing with migration. The exhibition "Migrations 1500–2005: Germany, Country of Immigration" shown by the DHM in Berlin, clearly called for a paradigm shift in policy. Very similar to the exhibition "Germans Abroad, Foreigners in Germany," the exhibition offered insights into the different phases and types of immigration in Germany on a national level. Following Klaus Bade's concept of migration as the norm in history, the exhibition targeted building "a consciousness of migration as an essential dimension in German history."[22]

In anticipation of the sixtieth anniversary of the end of World War II, the HdG in Bonn presented "Flight, Expulsion, Integration," which dealt with the history of ethnic Germans who came to West Germany as refugees and expellees from the former east German territories in the 1940s and integrated into the differently developing societies of the Federal Republic of Germany and the German Democratic Republic. The exhibition included video clips from oral history interviews conducted with 350 contemporary witnesses. Whereas the Berlin exhibition highlighted that Germany has been a country of immigration for centuries, the exhibition in Bonn departed from the usual hierarchical top-down approach toward immigration and presented the topic through an innovative combination of perspectives as part of national histories, autobiographical recollections, and individual narratives. The museum's director Herman Schäfer emphasized not only the possibilities and advantages of a multiperspective approach, but the impact of emotions that would arise from encountering the personal stories of the refugees and expellees.[23] The image of the migrants as victims was predominant in the exhibition.

This is even true for the exhibition "Forced Routes: Flight and Expulsion in Europe in the Twentieth Century," curated by the heatedly disputed Center Against Expulsion in Berlin. The exhibition showed one hundred years of ethnic persecution and expulsion in Europe, from the Armenian Genocide in 1915 through to the Yugoslav Wars in 1991–95. Instead of exposing an expected revanchist tendency, the exhibition focused on ethnic belonging and national relations, and highlighted topics like "home" and "camps."

Another exhibition presented new approaches to and perspectives on migration to Germany. A result of an interdisciplinary cooperation between the Cologne Art Association, DOMIT, the Institute of Cultural Anthropology, the European Ethnology department of the Goethe University of Frankfurt am Main, and the Institute for Theory of Design and Art in Zürich, the special exhibition "Project Migration" was shown in five different venues in Cologne. The exhibition claimed to shift the national perspective to a view of migration as a force for change in society. The display focused on "potentials for the future, on moments of utopia and visions drawn by migration."[24] With its experimental combination of scientific and artistic displays, the exhibition tackled questions of power, borders, and justice, and often rejected traditional views and autobiographical approaches.

Contrary to expectations, "Project Migration," as well as the other exhibitions mentioned above, did not provide decisive impetus for further debate on the issue of a national migration museum in Germany. Apart from the debate of the early 2000s, two museums for emigration history were built: the German Emigration Center (Deutsches Auswandererhaus, DAH) in Bremerhaven and the BallinStadt in Hamburg. Both are located at former sites of emigration: the DAH at the former harbor of Bremerhaven where the emigrants left for overseas, and the BallinStadt at the site of the former emigration halls of Hamburg. With extensive use of scenographic installations, both museums tell the story of leaving the country for a better life in the United States. Both museums offer autobiographical approaches as well as research on passenger lists. With an additional permanent exhibition about immigration to Germany in the 1970s, the DAH now presents itself as "the first migration museum in Germany."[25] Has the migration museum now come into Germany through the back door? To widen the perspective, the German situation should be compared with that of France.

## The National Migration Museum in France: From Cité to Musée Nationale de l'Histoire de l'Immigration

In 2007, the first French national museum of immigration, the Cité Nationale de l'Histoire de l'Immigration opened its doors to the public.

The opening was preceded by controversial social and political debates that still reverberate today.

Both Germany and France have long histories of immigration, beginning with the admission of foreign workers during the industrial revolution in the eighteenth and nineteenth centuries.[26] Active recruitment by the French government in the wake of the economic boom of the 1950s and 1960s led to an increase in immigration.[27] Since the mid-1950s more and more immigrants have moved from the former French colonies, especially from Algeria.[28] Due to the economic crisis of the 1970s, French recruitment of foreign workers ended in 1974.[29] As in Germany, the end of French labor recruitment led neither to significant emigration nor to a significant end to immigration. Many workers remained in France and family reunions became a major reason for a new wave of immigration.

During the 1980s and 1990s French immigration policy changed and became more restrictive. Immigration was no longer perceived as a factor in economic success, but as a major reason for social tensions and problems. Riots and demonstrations in the French suburbs,[30] along with the growing popularity of right-wing parties, led to controversial debates about the political and social handling of immigration and cultural diversity in France.

During this period French historians complained about a lack of awareness of the contributions of immigrants in French history.[31] Consequently, they began to try to fill that gap by researching a common French history of immigrant and non-immigrant French citizens. In 1990, immigrants including Pierre Milza, Patrick Weil, and Gérard Noiriel,[32] founded the Association pour un Musée de L'immigration (l'AMI), a committee working toward an immigration museum in France. It was hoped that the museum would be a place of symbolic national recognition situated on the Parisian island Île Seguin. The island, located between Sèvres and Boulogne-Billancourt, is the home of a Renault factory that employed migrants.[33] But the project was discontinued due to a lack of political interest and will.

Although the first attempt at a national immigration museum failed, a new discussion started in subsequent years. Associations, initiatives, and museums began to integrate the history of French immigrants into local and regional history. The idea was also followed by projects on a national level.[34]

With the change of the government in 1997 in favor of the political left, a less restrictive policy began.[35] A positive change in the social debate about French cultural diversity became apparent for the first time. One important example is the soccer World Cup, held in France in 1998, that coined the term "black-blanc-beur"[36] and led to a new and positive understanding of a multicultural French identity. In this context French journalist Phillipe Bernard and Patrick Weil, former director of the Centre National de la Recherche Scientifique (CNRS), tried to revive the national immigration museum project. A new committee was commissioned to prepare a feasibility study that, in the end, recommended the establishment of such a museum. Nevertheless, there were no further actions in the following years.

Shortly after the election of Jacques Chirac in 2002, the government again took on the project. Jacques Toubon, the former culture minister, was commissioned to write another report and to lead a *"mission de préfiguration d'un centre de ressource et de mémoire de l'immigration."*[37] The second report recommended the establishment of a national immigration museum by enlisting the cooperation of existing associations that were dealing with immigration and cultural diversity. The Groupement d'interet privé (GIP), founded in 1998, was meant to be the connection between all of these associations; a new national network was built.

Five years later several problems confronted the plans. One of the primary obstacles was a new political alignment by Nicholas Sarkozy and the establishment of the ministère de l'Immigration, de l'Intégration, de l'Identité nationale et du Développement solidaire (Ministry of Immigration, National Identity, and Solidary Development).

In May 2007, eight academics and historians[38] left the preparatory committee because of the newly established ministry that contradicted the idea of a new common French identity by stigmatizing French immigrants. In addition, there were many concerns about an exertion of influence by the predominantly conservative government. Nevertheless, the project continued, but the controversial debates that started at the very beginning of the museum's history still have an effect today.

In October 2007, the Cité Nationale de l'Histoire de l'Immigration, situated in the Palais de la Porte Dorée in Paris, which was originally built as a museum of the colonies in 1931, opened its doors.[39] The choice of Paris as the location for a French national museum of immigration is hardly surprising; however, the choice of a former colonial museum on the outskirts of Paris did surprise the public. This choice provided the opportunity to deal with the colonial history of France without making it a central topic. The Palais de la Porte Dorée, a building symbolically filled with a part of French history with negative associations, was "filled" with a new and positive one—with a history of cultural diversity and acceptance in France.[40] This was a symbolic act at the very beginning and was even reinforced on a political level.

Considering all of this, it is no longer surprising that the absence of Nicolas Sarkozy and the former minister for immigration and national identity Brice Hortefeux during the opening ceremony raised considerable doubts about political support. These absences were severely criticized in the media, mainly interpreted as a lack of political appreciation and recognition. These conflicts and debates still reverberate today. Finally, in December 2014, more than seven years after its opening, François Hollande officially inaugurated the national immigration museum.

From the very beginning, the museum was positioned between the interests and needs of the state, the immigrants, and the wider society. But although it was designed as a national museum, representing the government, it has become more and more of an open forum for discussion, also for criticism of the government.[41] The museum's goals are extremely meaningful: to change society's perspective in looking at the present and past of French immigration by telling a common history of all people living in France, and to contribute to integration policy.[42] This would not be possible on a regional level. Against this background, the concept of the museum as a national museum, as well as the concept of its permanent exhibitions, gain a new symbolic power. The story told by the museum is a common history without any separation between "real" French citizens and those who have immigrated. Unlike in politics and demographics, where a strict separation between "French," "immigrant," and "foreigner" prevails,[43] the museum's goal corresponds to the demands of French historians in the 1980s, according to a common narrative.

This symbolic power becomes even more apparent by taking a look at the permanent exhibition, "Galerie des Dons." Unlike the central permanent exhibition "Repères," which focuses on the last 120 years of national immigration history from a multidisciplinary point of view, the "Galerie des Dons" puts individual biographies at the center of attention. The cooperation between the institution and the "immigrant Frenchmen" is called a symbolic act of dialogue and recognition. Normally, the objects of every French national museum automatically become part of the national heritage. But the objects acquired from immigrants or their descendants were initially seen as being on permanent loan. By making them part of the collection and consequently part of the national heritage of France today,[44] the symbolism could hardly be stronger.

Both in its permanent and in its temporary exhibitions, the museum gives the immigrants their own voice. There they have the opportunity to present their own perspectives and history as part of a common history. The director general, Luc Gruson, emphasized the importance of this kind of presentation because an "invisibility of the French immigrants" still exists.[45] It is a double invisibility in that first it is an invisibility of the common history, and second because there is—especially in the media—a predominantly one-sided presentation. Even though migration and cultural diversity are common topics in the media, there still is an "invisibility" of the immigrant's voice. One of the museum's central goals is to disrupt this double invisibility. This is why the museum continues to actively collect personal histories and objects of immigration—as well as to continuously expand the permanent exhibitions and the collection. Both permanent exhibitions were modified, supplemented, or even extended in the spring and summer of 2014. Today the "new" "Galerie des Dons" includes forty biographical stories and approximately 120 objects. The exhibition space has been restructured in close dialogue and cooperation with the lenders.[46] But in 2010 the French newspaper *Le Monde* called the museum a "Musée fantôme"[47] and made clear that, just a few years after its opening, neither the museum's prominence nor its visitor numbers were very high. The tropical aquarium, also located in the Palais de la Porte Dorée, was better known by the public and more closely associated with the Palais than the museum itself.

In 2013, the former Cité Nationale de l'Histoire de l'Immigration was renamed Musée Nationale de l'Histoire de l'Immigration. Its new logo shows the Palais de la Porte Dorée, to create a stronger connection between the building and the museum.[48] A further argument for the change of name was seen in the word *Cité*. On the one hand, *Cité* stands for the basic idea of being a forum and more than "just" a museum. On the other hand, it also suggests the socially weak neighborhoods and outlying areas that are, in many cases, characterized by a high number of immigrants. Consequently, the change of name should avoid future misunderstandings and false allusions.

While the National Museum of Migration in France has been in operation for several years, in Germany the erection of a migration museum on a national level is not currently on the agenda. But the boom of migration exhibitions on all levels, increasing scientific debate and reflection about the impact of musealizing migration history, as well as changes in collection concepts and educational strategies show that issues of migration, and as a consequence, of cultural diversity have become essential for the work of German museums.[49]

The symbolic gesture of devoting an entire national institution to migration, dedicating it, and locating it in a single, representative, and meaningful building, is still lacking in Germany. But according to the principles of a multiperspective view of history and a polyphonic narrative, work on migration history is widespread in Germany and at the same time present overall.

Corresponding to this development, museum experts such as Gottfried Korff, Michael Fehr, and Joachim Baur agree that there is doubt about the need for a single national migration museum in Germany. At the peak of the German debate about a migration museum, Korff argued not for a migration museum as a new type of museum, but for migration as an essential issue, especially for local, municipal, and regional museums: migration not as type, but as a topic of museums.[50] Along with Michel Fehr, he pointed out the challenge for museums as institutions that traditionally reduce complexity and give homogeneous meaning, and the issues of mobility and migration with their ambiguity and fluidity. Fehr still doubts whether attempts to create a migration museum as a new type of museum will be useful and successful. He threatens that a national migration museum will homogenize diverse narratives and incorporate them into a single national(istic) one. Fehr insists on the need for change in all museums and argues for a "migration mainstream" and participatory concept for museums.[51] Joachim Baur goes a step further, arguing for migration mainstreaming. He argues for migration as a method, for using the perspective of migration to focus on society as a whole. Furthermore, he tries to neutralize the national migration museum's threat of the homogenization and nationalization of the topic by arguing for multiple migration museums: let's create one, two, multiple migration museums—why not?[52]

From this point of view, it appears that museums in Germany are on the right path. Migration mainstreaming in museums offers the possibility of experiencing the effects of migration, mobility, transnational and even global connections and their consequences for everyday life in the precise areas where people live. Looking at migration history from diverse perspectives and questioning traditional points of view, museums dealing with the issues of migration and cultural diversity not only work within a new polyphonic narrative but make transnational, transcultural, European, and global relations evident. As a side effect, taking into account the range from local to global relations will even shape the image of Europe.

## Notes

1. Data taken from Klaus J. Bade, Pieter C. Emmer, Leo Lucassen, Jochen Oltmer, eds., *Enzyklopädie Migration in Europa. Vom 17. Jahrhundert bis zur Gegenwart* (Munich: Ferdinand Schöningh, 2008); Jochen Oltmer, *Migration im 19. und 20. Jahrhundert* (Munich: Oldenbourg Verlag, 2010), 43–52; Detlef Brandes, Holm Sundhaussen, Stefan Troebst, eds., *Lexikon der Vertreibungen. Deportation, Zwangsaussiedlung und ethnische Säuberungen im Europa des 20. Jahrhunderts* (Vienna/Cologne/Weimar: Böhlau-Verlag, 2010).
2. Oltmer, *Migration im 19. und 20. Jahrhundert*, 52 et seq.

3. Federal Ministry of the Interior, ed., *Immigration Law and Policy* (Berlin: n.p., 2005), accessed 13 October 2014, http://www.bmi.bund.de/SharedDocs/Downloads/EN/Broschueren/ Zuwanderungspolitik_und_Zuwanderungsrecht_en.pdf?__blob=publicationFile. See also: Dietmar Osses, "Beyond Integration Courses. Ways to Face the Challenge of Intercultural Dialogue in Museums in Germany," in *Museums and Intercultural Dialogue. The Learning Museum Network Project Report Nr. 4*, ed. Ineta Zelča Sīmansone (Riga: Mantoprint, 2013), 34–47, accessed 13 January 2015, http://online.ibc.regione.emilia-romagna.it/I/libri/pdf/LEM4rd-report-museums-and-intercultural-dialogue.pdf.
4. Andrzej Stach, "Auswanderer und Rückkehrer, Patrioten und Verräter," *Inter Finitimos* 6 (2008): 29–49; Christoph Pallaske, "Langfristige Zuwanderungen aus Polen in die Bundesrepublik Deutschland in den 1980er Jahren," *Inter Finitimos* 6 (2008): 246–56.
5. Rainer Münz, Wolfgang Seifert, and Ralf Ulrich, eds., *Zuwanderung nach Deutschland. Strukturen, Wirkungen, Perspektiven* (Frankfurt a.M./New York: Campus Verlag, 1999); Hans-Martin Hinz, ed., *Zuwanderungen - Auswanderungen. Integration und Desintegration nach 1945* (Berlin: Minerva, 1999); for a view on the policy of remembrance and social memory, see Jan Motte and Rainer Ohliger, eds., *Geschichte und Gedächtnis in der Einwanderungsgesellschaft. Migration zwischen historischer Rekonstruktion und Erinnerungspolitik* (Essen: Klartext-Verlag, 2004).
6. The main documents of the debate are edited in Christoph Stölzl, ed., *Deutsches Historisches Museum. Ideen – Kontroversen – Perspektiven* (Frankfurt a.M.: Propyläen, 1988).
7. Michael Fehr, "Museum für die Geschichte und Kultur der Arbeitsmigranten," in *Kulturelles Wirken in einem anderen Land. Loccumer Protokolle 03/87*, ed. Evangelische Akademie Loccum (Loccum/Hagen: Kulturpolitische Gesellschaft e.V., 1987), 118–21.
8. Klaus J. Bade, ed., *Deutsche im Ausland – Fremde in Deutschland* (Munich: C.H. Beck, 1992).
9. Christoph Reinders-Düselder, "Einführung," in *Fremde in Deutschland – Deutsche in der Fremde. Epochale Schlaglichter von der Frühen Neuzeit bis in die Gegenwart*, eds. Uwe Meiners and Christoph Reinders-Düselder (Cloppenburg: Museumsdorf Cloppenburg, 1999), 16.
10. Ibid., 18.
11. Mathilde Jamin, "Einführung," in *Fremde Heimat. Eine Geschichte der Einwanderung aus der Türkei*, eds. Aytac Eryilmaz and Mathilde Jamin (Essen: Klartext Verlag, 1998), 23–5.
12. Mathilde Jamin, "Migrationsgeschichte im Museum. Erinnerungsorte von Arbeitsmigration – kein Ort der Erinnerung?" in *Geschichte und Gedächtnis in der Einwanderungsgesellschaft. Migration zwischen historischer Rekonstruktion und Erinnerungspolitik*, eds. Jan Motte and Rainer Ohliger (Essen: Klartext-Verlag, 2004), 145–57.
13. Aytac Eryilmaz and Martin Rapp, "Wer spricht? Geteilte Erinnerungen in der Migrationsgesellschaft," in *Jahrbuch Kulturpolitik* (Essen: Klartext-Verlag, 2009), 271–9.
14. "Rainer Ohliger, Tagungsbericht: Das historische Erbe der Einwanderer sichern. Die Bundesrepublik braucht ein Migrationsmuseum," H-Soz-Kult, accessed 13 October 2014, http://hsozkult.geschichte.hu-berlin.de/tagungsberichte/id=92.
15. Rainer Ohliger, "Die Bundesrepublik braucht ein Migrationsmuseum: Braucht die Bundesrepublik ein Migrationsmuseum? Oder vom Nutzen und Nachteil eines Migrationsmuseums für die Gesellschaft" (Report on conference "Das historische Erbe der Einwanderer sichern. Die Bundesrepublik Deutschland braucht ein Einwanderungsmuseum," organized by DOMIT and BPB, Brühl, 4–6 October 2002, accessed 13 October 2014, http://www.network-migration.org/MigMuseum/Migration smuseum_DoMiT.pdf.
16. Mathilde Jamin, "Migrationsgeschichte im Museum. Erinnerungsorte von Arbeitsmigration – kein Ort der Erinnerung?" in *Geschichte und Gedächtnis in*

der Einwanderungsgesellschaft. *Migration zwischen historischer Rekonstruktion und Erinnerungspolitik,* eds. Jan Motte and Rainer Ohliger (Essen: Klartext Verlag, 2004), 145–57, 157.

17. "Ulrich Raiser, Tagungsbericht: Ein Migrationsmuseum in Deutschland. Thesen, Entwürfe und Erfahrungen, Zweite Internationale Tagung Kölnischer Kunstverein, Köln, 17–19 October 2003," H-Soz-Kult, accessed 13 October 2014, http://hsozkult.geschichte. hu-berlin.de/tagungsberichte/id=317.

18. Aytac Eryilmaz, "Deutschland braucht ein Migrationsmuseum. Plädoyer für einen Paradigmenwechsel in der Kulturpolitik," in *Geschichte und Gedächtnis in der Einwanderungsgesellschaft. Migration zwischen historischer Rekonstruktion und Erinnerungspolitik,* eds. Jan Motte and Rainer Ohliger (Essen: Klartext Verlag 2004), 305–19.

19. In 2007 DOMIT merged with the association for a migration museum in Germany and changed its name and focus to DOMID—Dokumentationszentrum und Museum über die Migration in Deutschland (Documentation Center and Museum about Migration in Germany). With a broader perspective including all types of migration to Germany from the 1950s on, DOMID continues to appeal for a national museum of migration.

20. Dietmar Osses, "Perspektiven der Migrationsgeschichte in deutschen Ausstellungen und Museen," in *Museum und Migration. Konzepte – Kontexte – Kontroversen,* eds. Regina Wonisch and Thomas Hübel (Bielefeld: transcript-Verlag, 2012), 69–88.

21. Dietmar Osses, "Migration und kulturelle Vielfalt: Eine Herausforderung für die Museen," *Museumskunde* 75 (2010): 36–45.

22. Rosemarie Beier-de Haan, "Zuwanderungsland Deutschland. Migration 1500–2005. Einführung," in *Zuwanderungsland Deutschland. Migration 1500–2005,* ed. Rosemarie Beier-de Haan (Berlin: Minerva, 2005), 9–17, 12.

23. Hermann Schäfer, "Zur Ausstellung 'Flucht, Vertreibung, Integration'," in *Flucht, Vertreibung, Integration,* ed. Stiftung Haus der Geschichte der Bundesrepublik Deutschland (Bonn/Bielefeld: Christof Kerber Verlag, 2005), 7.

24. Marion von Osten, "Auf der Suche nach einer neuen Erzählung. Reflektionen des Ausstellungsprojekts 'Projekt Migration'," in *Crossing Munich. Beiträge zur Migration aus Kunst, Wissenschaft und Aktivismus,* eds. Natalie Bayer, Andrea Engl, Sabine Hess, and Johannes Moser (Munich: Schreiber, 2009), 90–3, 93; See also: Kerstin Poehls, "Zum Stand der Dinge: Migration im Museum. Überlegungen zur auratischen Praxis in Ausstellungen," in Bayer, Engl, Hess, and Moser, *Crossing Munich,* 94–8.

25. Deutsches Auswandererhaus Bremerhaven – History and Concept, accessed 13 October 2014, http://www.dah-bremerhaven.de/ENG/en.museum.php.

26. The reasons for the shortage of workers were, for example, a declining birth rate, as well as a declining population in the wake of the Franco-German War (1970/71), and the First World War. See "Engler, Marcus, IMIS Länderprofile: Frankreich," Bundeszentrale für Politische Bildung, accessed 19 July 2014, http://www.bpb.de/gesellschaft/migration/laenderprofile/135107/frankreich.

27. Bilateral recruitment agreements were, for instance, concluded with: Italy (1946), Greece (1960), Spain (1963), Portugal (1964), Morocco (1964), Tunisia (1964), Algeria (1964), Turkey (1965), and Yugoslavia (1968).

28. One of the main reasons for this can be found in the Algerian War (1954–62) that culminated in the independence of Algeria in 1962. As a result, French settlers, especially pro-French Algerians, immigrated to France. See "Engler, Marcus, IMIS Länderprofile: Frankreich," Bundeszentrale für Politische Bildung, accessed 19 July 2014, http://www. bpb.de/gesellschaft/migration/laenderprofile/135107/frankreich.

29. When the labor recruitment ended, 3.5 million immigrants lived in France, most of them Algerians and Portuguese. "Recensement 2008 Exploitation Principale," INSEE, accessed 20 July 2014, www.insee.fr.

30. The last riots took place in the fall of 2005 and 2007, and in the summer of 2010.

31. One of the most important public statements: Gérard Noiriel, "L'immigration enjeu de mémoire," *Le Monde*, 20 October 1989; Marie-Claude Blanc-Chaléard, "Du non-lieu de mémoire à la CNHI," *Diasporas – Histoire et Société* 6 (2004): 11–22.

32. The historian Gérard Noiriel is one of the pioneers of French migration research. He coined the designation of France as a cultural "melting pot" (*creuset français*) and named the problem of a gap in the collective memory in France in terms of its immigration history. See Gérard Noiriel, *Le creuset français. Histoire de l'immigration XIXe – XXe siècle* (Paris: Seuil, 1988).

33. The factory was opened in 1929 and ceased production in 1992. The factory buildings were torn down in 2005. See Alain Michel et Laure Pitti, "Renault à Billancourt: des usines au(x) patrimoine(s), histoire d'une conquête et d'un effacement." In *La mémoire de l'industrie: de l'usine au patrimoine*, ed., Jean-Claude Daumas (Paris: Presses Universitaires de Franche-Comté, 2006), 377–400; Blanc-Chaléard, "Du non-lieu de mémoire à la CNHI," 14.

34. For example, the series *Français d'ailleurs, peuple d'ici* (1995) and the exposition *Toute la France* (1999).

35. For example, the establishment of a special status for highly qualified immigrants, or a legalization program for illegal immigrants in France.

36. The name is a reference to the French national flag (*bleu, blanc, rouge*) and alludes to a new French identity, that is characterized by cultural diversity—just like the former national team. *Beur* is a French expression for "Arab" in the so-called "*verlan*," argot in the French language.

37. This reads in English "preliminary organization for a center of sources and memory of immigration" (translated by the author). See Blanc-Chaléard, "Du non-lieu de mémoire à la CNHI," 15.

38. For example Patrick Weil, Gérard Noiriel, Nancy Green, Patrick Simon, Vincent Viet, Marie-Christine Volovitch Tavarès, Marie-Claude Blanc-Chaléard, Geneviève Dreyfus-Armand.

39. The Palais was built for the Colonial Exposition (Exposition Coloniale Internationale) in 1931. In the following years it hosted the Musée des Colonies as well as the Musée de la France d'outre-mer (1935–1950s). Beginning in 1961 it became the Musée des Arts africains et océaniens and in 1990 the Musée Nationale des Art d'Afrique et d'Océanie (MAAO), which was closed in 2003. See Maureen Murphy, *Un palais pour une Cité. Du Musée des Colonies à la Cité Nationale de l'Histoire de l'Immigration* (Paris: RMN, 2007).

40. Nancy L. Green, "A French Ellis Island? Museums, Memory and History in France and the United States," *History Workshop Journal* 63 (2007): 244.

41. Mary Stevens, "Immigrants into Citizens. Ideology and Nation-Building in the Cité Nationale de l'Histoire de l'Immigration," *Museological Review* 13 (2008): 64.

42. Jacques Toubon, "Préface," in *Guide de l'exposition permanente*, ed. Cité Nationale de l'Histoire de l'Immigration (Paris: CNHI, 2007), 2–3.

43. "Engler, Marcus, IMIS Länderprofile: Frankreich," Bundeszentrale für Politische Bildung.

44. Musée de l'Histoire de l'Immigration, ed., *Guide de la Galerie des Dons* (Paris: Musée de l'Histoire de l'Immigration, 2014).

45. Luc Gruson, "Changer les représentations sur l'immigrations? Retour sur les enjeux de la Cité nationale de l'histoire de l'immigration et sur son occupation par les sans-papier," *Hommes & Migrations, l'immigration dans les musées. Une comparaison internationale* 1293 (2011): 12–21, 13.

46. The new structure includes the following points: *hériter* (inherit), *partager* (share), *contribuer* (contribute) and *accepter* (accept).

47. Michel Guerin, "Le musée fantôme," *Le Monde*, 19 March 2010.

48. A newly opened permanent exhibition, the *"Parcours historique,"* deals with the history of the Palais.

49. For the ongoing debates compare: Henrike Hampe, ed., *Migration und Museum. Neue Ansätze in der Museumspraxis* (Münster: LIT-Verlag, 2005). Christiane Hintermann and Christina Johansson, eds., *Migration and Memory. Representations of Migration in Europe since 1960* (Innsbruck/Vienna/Bozen: Studien-Verlag, 2010). Martin Schlutow, *Das Migrationsmuseum. Geschichtskulturelle Analyse eines neuen Museumstyps* (Berlin: LIT-Verlag, 2012). Regina Wonisch and Thomas Hübel, eds., *Museum und Migration. Konzepte – Kontexte – Kontroversen* (Bielefeld: transcript-Verlag, 2012). *Museumskunde* 75 (Berlin 2010), *Museumskunde* 77 (Berlin 2012), *Museumskunde* 78 (Berlin 2013); Patricia Deuser. "Migration im Museum – Zum aktuellen Stand der Auseinandersetzung mit den Themen Migration und kulturelle Vielfalt in deutschen Museen," *Museumskunde* 78 (2013): 65–69.

50. Gottfried Korff, "Fragen zur Migrationsmusealisierung. Versuch einer Einleitung," in *Migration und Museum. Neue Ansätze in der Museumspraxis*, ed. Henrike Hampe (Münster: LIT Verlag, 2005), 5–15, 11; Joachim Baur, *Die Musealisierung der Migration. Einwanderungsmuseen und die Inszenierung der multikulturellen Nation* (Bielefeld: Transcript-Verlag 2009).

51. Michael Fehr, "Überlegungen zu einem 'Migrationsmuseum' in der Bundesrepublik," *Museumskunde* 75 (2010): 67–70.

52. Joachim Baur, "Moving On – oder: Die letzte Migrationsausstellung. Versuch einer Bestandsaufnahme," *Museumskunde* 77 (2012): 7–12.

# Works Cited

Bade, Klaus J., ed. *Deutsche im Ausland – Fremde in Deutschland*. Munich: C.H. Beck, 1992.

Bade, Klaus J., Pieter C. Emmer, Leo Lucassen, and Jochen Oltmer, eds. *Enzyklopädie Migration in Europa. Vom 17. Jahrhundert bis zur Gegenwart*. Munich: Ferdinand Schöningh, 2008.

Baur, Joachim. *Die Musealisierung der Migration. Einwanderungsmuseen und die Inszenierung der multikulturellen Nation*. Bielefeld: Transcript-Verlag, 2009.

Baur, Joachim. "Moving On – oder: Die letzte Migrationsausstellung. Versuch einer Bestandsaufnahme." *Museumskunde* 77 (2012): 7–12.

Beier-de Haan, Rosemarie. "Zuwanderungsland Deutschland. Migration 1500–2005. Einführung." In *Zuwanderungsland Deutschland. Migration 1500–2005*, edited by Rosemarie Beier-de Haan, 9–17. Berlin: Minerva, 2005.

Blanc-Chaléard, Marie-Claude. "Du non-lieu de mémoire à la CNHI." *Diasporas – Histoire et Société* 6 (2004): 11–22.

Brandes, Detlef, Holm Sundhaussen, and Stefan Troebst, eds. *Lexikon der Vertreibungen. Deportation, Zwangsaussiedlung und ethnische Säuberungen im Europa des 20. Jahrhunderts.* Vienna/Cologne/Weimar: Böhlau-Verlag, 2010.

Bundeszentrale für Politische Bildung. "Engler, Marcus, IMIS Länderprofile: Frankreich." Accessed 19 July 2014. http://www.bpb.de/gesellschaft/migration/laenderprofile/135107/frankreich.

Cité Nationale de l'Histoire de l'Immigration, ed. *Guide de l'exposition permanente.* Paris: CNHI, 2007.

Cité Nationale de l'Histoire de l'Immigration, ed. *La collection d'art contemporain.* Paris: CNHI, 2011.

Deuser, Patricia. "Migration im Museum – Zum aktuellen Stand der Auseinandersetzung mit den Themen Migration und kulturelle Vielfalt in deutschen Museen." *Museumskunde* 78 (2013): 65–69.

Eryilmaz, Aytac. "Deutschland braucht ein Migrationsmuseum. Plädoyer für einen Paradigmenwechsel in der Kulturpolitik." In *Geschichte und Gedächtnis in der Einwanderungsgesellschaft. Migration zwischen historischer Rekonstruktion und Erinnerungspolitik,* edited by Jan Motte and Rainer Ohliger, 305–19. Essen: Klartext Verlag, 2004.

Eryilmaz, Aytac, and Martin Rapp. "Wer spricht? Geteilte Erinnerungen in der Migrationsgesellschaft." *Jahrbuch Kulturpolitik,* 271–79. Essen: Klartext-Verlag, 2009.

Federal Ministry of the Interior, ed. *Immigration Law and Policy.* Berlin: n.p., 2005. Accessed 13 October 2014. http://www.bmi.bund.de/SharedDocs/Downloads/EN/Broschueren/Zuwanderungspolitik_und_Zuwanderungsrecht_en.pdf?__blob=publicationFile.

Fehr, Michael. "Museum für die Geschichte und Kultur der Arbeitsmigranten." In *Kulturelles Wirken in einem anderen Land. Loccumer Protokolle 03/87,* edited by Evangelische Akademie Loccum, 118–21. Loccum/Hagen: Kulturpolische Gesellschaft e.V., 1987.

Fehr, Michael. "Überlegungen zu einem 'Migrationsmuseum' in der Bundesrepublik." *Museumskunde* 75 (2010): 67–70.

Green, Nancy L. "A French Ellis Island? Museums, Memory and History in France and the United States." *History Workshop Journal* 63 (2007): 239–53.

Gruson, Luc. "Changer les représentations sur l'immigrations? Retour sur les enjeux de la Cité nationale de l'histoire de l'immigration et sur son occupation par les sans-papier." *Hommes & Migrations, l'immigration dans les musées. Une comparaison international* 1293 (2011): 12–21.

Guerin, Michel. "Le musée fantôme." *Le Monde,* 19 March 2010.

Hampe, Henrike, ed. *Migration und Museum. Neue Ansätze in der Museumspraxis.* Münster: LIT Verlag, 2005.

Hintermann, Christiane, and Christina Johansson, eds. *Migration and Memory. Representations of Migration in Europe since 1960.* Innsbruck/Vienna/Bozen: Studien Verlag, 2010.

Hinz, Hans-Martin, ed. *Zuwanderungen - Auswanderungen. Integration und Desintegration nach 1945.* Berlin: Minerva, 1999.

H-Soz-Kult. "Rainer Ohliger, Tagungsbericht: Das historische Erbe der Einwanderer sichern. Die Bundesrepublik braucht ein Migrationsmuseum." Accessed 13 October 2014. http://hsozkult.geschichte.hu-berlin.de/tagungsberichte/id=92.

H-Soz-Kult. "Ulrich Raiser, Tagungsbericht: Ein Migrationsmuseum in Deutschland. Thesen, Entwürfe und Erfahrungen, Zweite Internationale Tagung Kölnischer Kunstverein, Köln, 17–19 October 2003." Accessed 13 October 2014. http://hsozkult.geschichte.hu-berlin.de/tagungsberichte/id=317.

INSEE – Institut national de la statistique et des études économiques. "Recensement 2008 Exploitation Principale." Accessed 20 July 2014. http://www.insee.fr.

Jamin, Mathilde. *"Einführung."* In *Fremde Heimat. Eine Geschichte der Einwanderung aus der Türkei*, edited by Aytac Erilmaz and Mathilde Jamin, 23–6. Essen: Klartext-Verlag, 1998.

Jamin, Mathilde. "Migrationsgeschichte im Museum. Erinnerungsorte von Arbeitsmigration – kein Ort der Erinnerung?" In *Geschichte und Gedächtnis in der Einwanderungsgesellschaft. Migration zwischen historischer Rekonstruktion und Erinnerungspolitik*, edited by Jan Motte and Rainer Ohliger, 145–57. Essen: Klartext-Verlag, 2004.

Johansson, Christina, and Christiane Hintermann. "Museums, Migration and Diversity – An Introduction." In *Migration and Memory. Representations of Migration in Europe since 1960* (Studies in European History and Public Spheres; vol. 3), 135–144. Innsbruck/Bozen/Wien: StudienVerlag und Brunswick, NJ, 2010.

Korff, Gottfried. "Fragen zur Migrationsmusealisierung. Versuch einer Einleitung." In *Migration und Museum. Neue Ansätze in der Museumspraxis*, edited by Henrike Hampe, 5–15. Münster: LIT-Verlag, 2005.

Michel, Alain, and Laure Pitti. "Renault à Billancourt: des usines au(x) patrimoine(s), histoire d'une conquête et d'un effacement." In *La mémoire de l'industrie: de l'usine au patrimoine*, edited by Jean-Claude Daumas, 377–400. Paris: Presses Universitaires de Franche-Comté, 2006.

Motte, Jan, and Rainer Ohliger, eds. *Geschichte und Gedächtnis in der Einwanderungsgesellschaft. Migration zwischen historischer Rekonstruktion und Erinnerungspolitik.* Essen: Klartext-Verlag, 2004.

Münz, Rainer, Wolfgang Seifert, and Ralf Ulrich, eds. *Zuwanderung nach Deutschland. Strukturen, Wirkungen, Perspektiven.* Frankfurt a.M./New York: Campus-Verlag, 1999.

Murphy, Maureen. *Un palais pour une Cité. Du Musée des Colonies à la Cité Nationale de l'Histoire de l'Immigration.* Paris: RMN, 2007.

Musée de l'Histoire de l'Immigration, ed. *Guide de la Galerie des Dons.* Paris: Musée de l'Histoire de l'Immigration, 2014.

Noiriel, Gérard. *Le creuset français. Histoire de l'immigration XIXe – Xxe siècle.* Paris: Seuil, 1988.

Noiriel, Gérard. "L'immigration enjeu de mémoire." *Le Monde*, 20 October 1989.

Ohliger, Rainer. "Die Bundesrepublik braucht ein Migrationsmuseum: Braucht die Bundes-republik ein Migrationsmuseum? Oder vom Nutzen und Nachteil eines Migrations-museums für die Gesellschaft." Report on conference "Das historische Erbe der Einwanderer sichern. Die Bundesrepublik Deutschland braucht ein Einwanderungsmuseum," organized by DOMIT and BPB, Brühl, 4–6 October 2002. Accessed 13 October 2014. http://www.network-migration.org/MigMuseum/Migrationsmuseum_DoMiT.pdf.

Oltmer, Jochen. *Migration im 19. und 20. Jahrhundert.* Munich: Oldenbourg Verlag, 2010.

Osses, Dietmar. "Migration und kulturelle Vielfalt: Eine Herausforderung für die Museen." *Museumskunde* 75 (2010): 36–45.

Osses, Dietmar. "Perspektiven der Migrationsgeschichte in deutschen Ausstellungen und Museen." In *Museum und Migration. Konzepte - Kontexte - Kontroversen*, edited by Regina Wonisch and Thomas Hübel, 69–88. Bielefeld: transcript-Verlag, 2012.

Osses, Dietmar. "Beyond Integration Courses. Ways to Face the Challenge of Intercultural Dialogue in Museums in Germany." In *Museums and Intercultural Dialogue. The Learning Museum Network Project Report Nr. 4*, edited by Ineta Zelča Sīmansone, 34–47. Riga: Mantoprint, 2013. Accessed 13 January 2015. http://www.lemproject.eu/WORKING-GROUPS/Intercultural-dialogue/4rd-report-museums-and-intercultural-dialogue/at_download/file/LEM_Report4_EDcover.pdf.

Osten, Marion von. "Auf der Suche nach einer neuen Erzählung. Reflektionen des Ausstellungsprojekts 'Projekt Migration'." In *Crossing Munich. Beiträge zur Migration aus Kunst, Wissenschaft und Aktivismus*, edited by Natalie Bayer, Andrea Engl, Sabine Hess, and Johannes Moser, 90–3. Munich: Schreiber, 2009.

Pallaske, Christoph. "Langfristige Zuwanderungen aus Polen in die Bundesrepublik Deutschland in den 1980er Jahren," *Inter Finitimos* 6 (2008): 246–56.

Poehls, Kerstin. "Zum Stand der Dinge: Migration im Museum. Überlegungen zur auratischen Praxis in Ausstellungen." In *Crossing Munich. Beiträge zur Migration aus Kunst, Wissenschaft und Aktivismus*, edited by Natalie Bayer, Andrea Engl, Sabine Hess, and Johannes Moser, 94–8. Munich: Schreiber, 2009.

Reinders-Düselder, Christoph. "Einführung." In *Fremde in Deutschland – Deutsche in der Fremde. Epochale Schlaglichter von der Frühen Neuzeit bis in die Gegenwart*, edited by Uwe Meiners and Christoph Reinders-Düselder, 16–19. Cloppenburg: Museumsdorf Cloppenburg, 1999.

Schäfer, Hermann. "Zur Ausstellung 'Flucht, Vertreibung, Integration'." In *Flucht, Vertreibung, Integration*, edited by Stiftung Haus der Geschichte der Bundesrepublik Deutschland, 7–13. Bonn/Bielefeld: Christof Kerber Verlag, 2005.

Schlutow, Martin. *Das Migrationsmuseum. Geschichtskulturelle Analyse eines neuen Museumstyps.* Berlin: LIT-Verlag, 2012.

Stach, Andrzej. "Auswanderer und Rückkehrer, Patrioten und Verräter." *Inter Finitimos* 6 (2008): 29–49.

Stevens, Mary. "Immigrants into Citizens. Ideology and Nation-Building in the Cité Nationale de l'Histoire de l'Immigration." *Museological Review* 13 (2008): 57–73.

Stölzl, Christoph, ed. *Deutsches Historisches Museum. Ideen – Kontroversen – Perspektiven.* Frankfurt a.M.: Propyläen, 1988.

Wonisch, Regina. "Museum und Migration. Einleitung." In *Museum und Migration. Konzepte-Kontexte -Kontroversen.* Edited by Regina Wonisch and Thomas Hübel, 9–31. Bielefeld: transcript-Verlag, 2012.

Wonisch, Regina, and Thomas Hübel, eds. *Museum und Migration. Konzepte – Kontexte – Kontroversen.* Bielefeld: transcript-Verlag, 2012.

**Dietmar Osses** is director of the LWL Industriemuseum Zeche Hannover in Bochum, Westfälisches Landesmuseum für Industriekultur (LWL Industrial Museum Hannover Colliery, Bochum, Westphalian State Museum of Industrial Heritage and Culture). Osses is also an adjunct professor at Ruhr University, Bochum. He has curated several exhibitions dealing with migration history, cultural diversity, and social history in Westphalia and the Ruhr. Since 2010, he has headed the Migration Working Group of the German Museum Association.

**Katarzyna Nogueira** is currently a research fellow at the History of the Ruhr Foundation in Bochum. After studying cultural anthropology, she curated exhibitions on regional history, immigration, and cultural diversity for the Westphalian Museum of Industrial Heritage in Bochum. In 2013, she was a fellow at the Musée National de l'Histoire de l'Immigration in Paris and is a member of the German Museums Association's Migration and Museum Working Group. Her research focuses on oral history, labour history and migration studies.

*Chapter 7*

# ARCHIVAL COLLECTIONS AND THE STUDY OF MIGRATION

*Klaus A. Lankheit*

## Contemporary History and Migration

The study of population shifts from the beginning of World War II to the present is currently experiencing increasing interest among German and international historians.[1] The historical study of recent migration has largely been shaped by the limited availability and accessibility of public records pertaining to migration and its public discourse. Published sources like newspapers and public records such as speeches, political statements, and autobiographies are often insufficient as sources when attempting to analyze the multifaceted transnational circumstances, challenges, and experiences that migrants meet as people on the move, and as subjects and objects in a process of transformation and communication with a new society.

Given the subject of this chapter, it is the author's intent that it be used as a practical guide to archival sources. In Germany alone there are over three thousand archives, and this number multiplies accordingly when looking at the European Community as a whole. Therefore, an overview will be provided on the variety of records that are kept in state and municipal archives, as well as the archives of different non-governmental organizations.[2] This chapter will therefore address how non-official records—primarily in Germany, but increasingly in Europe in general—have been made available to researchers as a reaction to a scholarly attempt to understand migration as a central experience of European societies. This trend in archival preservation did not emerge coherently, but varied regarding diverse migration movements. The combined use of public records and new source materials highlighting the subjective

Notes for this chapter begin on page 192.

experience of the migrant or an ethnic group allowed scholars to develop brand new insights into the subject matter.[3] Thus, I intend to explore the policies of archiving records documenting the major postwar immigration movements. While the chapter will focus on Germany, it will also discuss the issue in a larger comparative European setting, where immigration often resulted from decolonization. Since the European Union has created a framework of legal, economic, and social activity regarding internal as well as external migration that is increasingly relevant, the chapter will also present an overview of sources pertaining to archives of the different European Union institutions.

## Displaced Persons

Most of the movement of people that followed World War II was not voluntary. At the war's end, more than eight million displaced persons remained in Germany alone, among them some six million foreign workers, two million prisoners of war, and 700,000 survivors of concentration camps. By the end of September 1945, most of these people were able to return to their home countries. It was more difficult to find a solution for the remaining 1.2 million persons.[4] The United Nations Relief and Rehabilitation Administration (UNRRA)[5] and the U.S. Office of Military Government for Germany (OMGUS) were responsible for repatriating the liberated forced laborers and concentration camp prisoners. By 1951, their efforts had reduced the official number of recorded displaced persons to about 38,000 stateless residents in West German camps.[6] In the immediate postwar period, German authorities were more than happy for the Allies to relieve them of the responsibility of dealing with this humanitarian crisis. Indeed, the tendency among German officials, as well as the German public, was to regard the displaced persons as a source of irritation and disruption.[7] Moreover, potential confrontation between displaced persons and the German public threatened to reactivate anti-Semitism and racism.[8]

Due to the fact that during the postwar era the American military government, the United Nations, and other non-governmental organizations based in the United States assumed direct responsibility for organizing and repatriating displaced persons, many important archival collections from this period are today located in the United States. The UNRRA files are kept in the United Nations Archives and Records Management Section (ARMS),[9] and the original OMGUS files can be found in the National Archives.[10] Records pertaining to failed attempts by displaced persons to return to their home countries are documented in these archives, as are forced repatriations to Eastern Europe. Papers concerning many of the displaced persons camps in Germany, Austria, and Italy from 1945 to 1952, are held by the archives of the Institute for Jewish Research, YIVO,[11] which also keeps records of the American Jewish Joint Distribution Committee up to 1950, which moreover runs its own archives.[12] Testimonials by contemporary witnesses are held in, among other archives, the archives of the United States Holocaust Memorial Museum, where they complement the official records.[13]

In Germany, the archives of the International Tracing Service in Bad Arolsen also hold records pertaining to countless individual cases of violence and forced migration.[14] Conflicts with German authorities and the population are documented in regional and local German archives. Even though German and international historians have been exploring the issue for some time,[15] understanding these particular population movements as a form of migration holds potential for further study.

## Expellees

At the end of World War II, ethnic Germans from different parts of Europe poured into Germany. These were people who, in spite of Hitler's orders to fight the approaching Soviet army to the death, had chosen to seek refuge in the western parts of Germany in the face of the advance of the Red Army. Among the expellees were also people who had been forced to leave their ancestral homes after the end of the war—a practice initially condoned by the Allies and later legally sanctified by the Potsdam Agreement.[16]

In 1951, there were eight million expellees in the western occupation zones,[17] and four million in the Soviet occupation zone,[18] a number that amounted to almost a fifth of Germany's total population. The integration of expellees was particularly difficult in areas with a previously homogeneous religious denomination. Areas which had been dominated for hundreds of years by Roman Catholics, for example, saw indigenous populations reacting with considerable hostility toward the flood of mostly Lutheran refugees.

What appeared as preferential provisioning for the expellees also caused resentment among locals. In hindsight, the differences between these groups were probably negligible. However, in spite of official calls for solidarity, indigenous residents often felt threatened and reacted defensively.[19]

Together, the records of the Bundesministerium für Vertriebene, Flüchtlinge und Kriegsgeschädigte (Federal Ministry for Expellees,

Refugees, and War Victims) held by the Bundesarchiv (German Federal Archives) and those records belonging to the corresponding ministries of the federal states (held by the respective state archives) contain valuable information on how the public administration in West Germany dealt with the challenge of accommodating, provisioning, and finally integrating expellees. Still, the story behind the population shifts and how they unfolded can only be partially reconstructed through these records. This problem was recognized early on; accordingly, the Bundesministerium für Vertriebene, Flüchtlinge und Kriegsgeschädigte was charged with conducting oral history interviews for a publication project.[20] The project was conducted on a strictly scholarly basis. At the time, this collection was, however, also designed to serve as a source of propaganda for the Cold War. Today, researchers can access this collection of 18,132 eyewitness reports in the Lastenausgleichsarchiv in Bayreuth.[21] The collection, provided by expellees from the territories east of the rivers Oder and Neiße, is organized by region. The so-called "equalization of the economic and social situation by shared burden" (those who had lost their property because of war-related damages or because of displacement were compensated by those who had lost less or nothing at all)[22] is also documented in the Lastenausgleichsarchiv (War Indemnity Archives).[23] In addition to these collections, numerous private archival collections gathered and administered by Landsmannschaften (representations of groups of refugees by their regions of origin in West Germany) can be found throughout Germany, each representing a former province or settlement area of ethnic Germans. In order to preserve their cultural identities, groups of expellees often founded organizations and associations corresponding with their regional origins. Since the records of these organizations are privately owned, access to their collections will vary.[24] The older records of the Bund der Vertriebenen – Vereinigte Landsmannschaften und Landesverbände e.V. (Federation of Expellees) — the umbrella organization for the private associations of expellees — were acquisitioned in 1979 by the Bundesarchiv and are, of course, open to the general public.[25] Indeed, it should be pointed out that the history of the Federation of Expellees makes clear that certain historical processes can only be made transparent by analyzing archival sources. As a recent in-depth study initiated by the Institut für Zeitgeschichte has shown, published records, as well as archival sources, allow historians to evaluate the political standpoint and activism of leading representatives from the Federation of Expellees during and after National Socialism in more detail, thus allowing us to understand this group's historic role in Germany's postwar lobbying in a different way.[26] In this case, historians have highlighted the behind-the-scenes conflict that took place within the leadership of the organization in the early years of the Federal Republic. Indeed, until 1989, the successful integration of expellees was seen by the West German government as an important measure of the young democracy's success. The story of the Federation of Expellees sheds light on the difficult balance of integration and representation of thousands of expellees with a difficult past and their political integration into the new German democracy.

In former East Germany the experience of expellees was quite different. Given that most of the expellees blamed Soviet politics for their displacement, the East German government regarded them, on the one hand, as a potential source of social and political unrest, while on the other hand, welcoming them as additional workers. Problems of accommodation, provisioning, and integration could never be adequately concealed. However, starting at the end of 1947, the regime enacted an assimilation policy that prohibited the naming of residential areas or companies after places or areas of origin, and the fostering of traditions. Likewise, efforts toward self-organization were also hampered. Therefore, non-governmental sources are largely non-existent for East Germany; this is, however, compensated by the fact that the number of reports and surveillance accounts produced by government agencies is much higher than in West Germany.[27]

## Fuel for the Economic Miracle: Labor Immigration

### Germany

In 1933, the year Hitler took power, fewer than 760,000 foreign nationals lived within the borders of Germany, then inhabited by nearly seventy million Germans.[28] Today, a completely different situation presents itself: at the end of 2012, the Statistisches Bundesamt (German Federal Statistical Office) announced that 10.7 million migrants from 194 countries live in Germany, while the total population numbers about eighty million.[29] It is largely the immigration of workers (and their families) over the last fifty years that has contributed to this development. Initially recruited as "guest workers," millions of workers—both men and women—left their home countries and moved to Germany, primarily between the 1950s and 1970s. While their integration into German society caused numerous economic and social challenges, their presence in Germany also produced a fundamental change in German society. Relevant statistical figures can be acquired from the German Federal Statistical Office, either from its website or from its publications, most of them now digitized.[30]

Strategic planning for bringing "guest workers" to West Germany took place within the Bundesministerium für Arbeit und Sozialordnung

(Ministry of Labor and Social Affairs); subsequently, records pertaining to the start of this immigration wave during the 1950s and its peak in the 1960s are held by the Federal Archives in Koblenz. Finding aids are accessible online.[31] The minutes of the routine meetings of the Arbeitskreis für Fragen der Beschäftigung ausländischer Arbeitnehmer (Working Group for Questions Concerning the Employment of Foreign Workers) are available beginning with the year 1962. Many different aspects of this immigrant wave are covered by the records, from general labor demand, planning for medical examination procedures and family benefits, and even, as the title of one record puts it, the "Basic Assumptions for Military and Civil Defense. Foreign Workers in Crisis, Tension and the Case of Defense."[32] Beginning in 1960, the Ständige Konferenz der Kultusminister der Länder der Bundesrepublik Deutschland (Standing Conference of the West German *Länder*'s Education Ministers, KMK) discussed the school attendance of the children of foreign workers.[33] More administrative facts can be drawn from the files of the Bundesanstalt für Arbeit (Federal Institute for Labor), which was the central agency for recruitment agreements. Overall, these files provide insight into the actions and challenges of dealing with foreign workers from the perspective of the government including the bureaucratic procedures behind recruiting, initially unforeseen unemployment, exceptional single cases, reports about the recruitment of residents in foreign countries, and the care and control of commissions from the countries of origin. Relevant finding aids are available online.[34]

Conflicts between the resident population and newcomers are reflected in the files of the police and security authorities in regional and local archives. Record titles such as "Complaint by the Prussian Electrical Corporation for Alleged Pollution and Disorderly Conduct by Foreign Laborers and Their Families in Working-class Quarters in Großkrotzenburg," located in the Hessisches Hauptstaatsarchiv (Hessian Main State Archives) show that the authorities were concerned with small problems related to immigrants.[35] However, personal data protection laws might complicate access to these files. On the local level, early attempts to improve the living conditions for foreign workers and to more successfully integrate them into German society can be detected. These activities ranged from providing sporting facilities to building residential projects to making additional educational opportunities available.[36] However, because German citizenship laws did not aim to foster integration but rather exclusion, immigrants were also commonly denied many legal rights.[37] Because of this, increasing problems with immigrant laborers were discussed at the international level. In August 2013, this became evident when declassified British documents made the headlines in German newspapers and magazines.[38] In his first conversation with Prime Minister Margaret Thatcher in

1982, newly elected Chancellor Helmut Kohl announced that he wanted to get rid of half of the Turkish residents in Germany. Given that Turkish residents represented the largest group of non-nationals in Germany, this seemed to be a convenient approach to reducing unemployment during an economic recession.[39] Indeed, the Islamic tradition practiced by the Turkish immigrants was considered to be a major obstacle to integration.[40] Eventually, the German government tried to encourage "guest workers" to return to their home countries by offering them financial incentives. Politicians did not yet see that the influx of foreign laborers was in fact an immigration process. That realization would take another twenty years.[41]

In comparison to that of West Germany, the government in East Germany tried to reduce its growing labor deficit by recruiting contract workers, mostly in Vietnam, but also in Cuba, Mozambique, Angola, and even China. While the search for foreign workers was initiated later than in West Germany, the approach to the issue was similar. The government, in this case, the Ministerrat der DDR (Council of Ministers of the GDR) and the Zentralkommitee der SED (Central Committee of the Socialist Unity Party of Germany), made the fundamental decisions, while several subordinate agencies, such as the Staatliche Plankommission (State Planning Commission, SPK) and the Staatssekretariat für Arbeit und Löhne (State Secretariat of Labor and Wages), implemented the Council's directives. These documents are kept at the Federal Archives and the Stiftung Archiv der Parteien und Massenorganisationen der DDR im Bundesarchiv (SAPMO, Foundation Archives of Parties and Mass Organizations of the GDR in the Federal Archives).[42] One should bear in mind that the Staatssicherheitsdienst ("Stasi," the East German Secret Police) also closely observed any ongoing developments within the GDR, and for this reason, researchers should always check for relevant files with the Archiv des Bundesbeauftragten für die Unterlagen des Staatssicherheitsdienstes der ehemaligen Deutschen Demokratischen Republik (Archive of the Federal Commissioner for State Security Service of the former German Democratic Republic). Contacts beyond the labor sphere were systematically prevented.[43]

Although there was little friendly interaction in West Germany between ethnic German residents and foreign immigrants, public opinion today often compares the experience of immigrants in pre-unification Germany with the xenophobic riots that later took place in former East Germany. What is often forgotten though, is that in 1980 and 1981, West Germany also experienced its share of violent outbursts aimed at foreigners.[44]

Since the fifty-year anniversary of the recruitment agreements with Italy, Spain, Greece, Turkey, Portugal, and former Yugoslavia coincided

with the political debates surrounding the 2004 reform of German immigration laws, several exhibitions on the history of immigration into
Germany were initiated around the same time, such as those at the Munich
central railway station in 2000,[45] at the Deutsches Historisches Museum
(German Historical Museum) in Berlin in 2006,[46] or at the Munich city
hall in 2009.[47] In 2010, nine cities of the Ruhr area coordinated exhibitions
identifying diversity and assimilation as central themes.[48] Developing
concepts for these exhibitions, curators and historians not only looked
for objects, photos, or films, but also for documents. At first glance, there
seems to be a dearth of records and documents pertaining to the everyday
life of immigrants, including such issues as housing, working conditions,
social life, recreational activities, or political and union participation. But a
closer look at the holdings of countless archives and archival collections in
Germany indicates that immigrants certainly left their mark. In this light,
one German-wide source for locating archival material is "Archivportal D",
an online portal that provides access to information on archival material
from numerous German archives.[49] Some of the individual German states
already have similar portals, making it possible to search the archives in
these states for documents pertaining to immigration. For example, in
the archival portals of Nordrhein-Westfalen (North Rhine-Westphalia),[50]
Niedersachsen (Lower Saxony),[51] and Hessen (Hesse),[52] a search for
terms such as *"Gastarbeiter"* (guest worker) or *"ausländische Arbeitnehmer"*
(foreign laborers) provides an assortment of related topics as well as
information on a variety of archival source material.

Many institutions that came into contact with migrant laborers also
have their own archives, a few of which bear mentioning. Catholic foreign workers, for instance, often found support from the Roman Catholic
Church, and the church subsequently documented social and pastoral care
in the archives of their dioceses in industrial hotspots. This leads mainly
to migrants from Italy, Spain, Portugal, and parts of former Yugoslavia.
Among these dioceses, the archives of the archdiocese of Munich are
particularly promising given that the Munich central railway station was
the final destination for the chartered trains that carried foreign workers from their countries of origin, and thus served as a central collecting point.[53] Trade unions, whose records are kept at the archives of the
Friedrich-Ebert-Stiftung (Friedrich Ebert Foundation), also frequently
contacted foreign workers as they entered the country. The Deutscher
Gewerkschaftsbund (German Trade Union Confederation), for instance,
even created a special section dedicated to the needs of foreign workers.[54]
The central motives and aims of these activities, the extent of participation of the immigrants themselves, and the effect that immigrants had on
politics prove to be an interesting field of study.[55]

In addition to these two groups, there are also a few noteworthy business archives worth consulting. In most cases, business archives represent either a single corporation or are organized as regional collaborative institutions such as the Bergbau-Archiv Bochum (Mining Archive in Bochum),[56] the Rheinisch Westfälisches Wirtschaftsarchiv (Business Archive for Rhineland-Westphalia),[57] or the Bayerisches Wirtschaftsarchiv (Bavarian Business Archive).[58] However, it is usually only those businesses with a distinct awareness of history and tradition that keep and maintain their records. Businesses that have, since the 1960s, employed a large number of foreign workers include, for example, Daimler AG,[59] BMW,[60] Siemens AG,[61] or ThyssenKrupp AG.[62] First and foremost, these archives serve the purposes and interests of their corporate patrons, so be prepared to face restrictions. Depending on what has been preserved, these archives can provide a comprehensive perspective into the living and working conditions of foreign workers. Lastly, material in the archives of the established political parties will shed some light on the topic of immigration and how it has changed among politicians, while also providing information on immigrants and their interaction with the political process.[63]

Notwithstanding this comprehensive survey, it is obvious that no systematic archival collecting activity was ever set up to record the cultural heritage of labor immigration and the perspectives of those directly affected by immigration. Apparently, neither the Germans nor the immigrants saw the need to record the experiences of the people who were directly affected. Mehmet Gürcan Daimagüler, a Berlin attorney at law with Turkish roots in Siegen, Germany, and author of a critical homage to the country of his birth, offers one plausible explanation as to why: because no one expected Turkish workers to remain in Germany permanently, making them a part of German society was never seriously considered. Accordingly making these immigrants' stories part of the larger German historic narrative did not seem necessary. The adult members of Daimagüler's family also talked about finally returning to Turkey in one or two more years at the latest. They never made a serious attempt, but for better or worse, subsequent generations were effectively born into conflicted identities. The first generation of immigrants themselves saw life in Germany as temporary. For their children though, having been born in Germany, there was no motivation to return to some mythical homeland. Germany, in many ways, was their home, and for them, living in Germany was real and present.[64]

Ultimately, this gap in archival collections was addressed by the immigrants themselves. In 1990, in an effort to reduce the deficit in historical sources related to immigration, Turkish immigrants founded the predecessor of today's Dokumentationszentrum und Museum über die Migration in

Deutschland (DOMID) (Documentation Center and Museum of Migration in Germany) in Cologne. Since its founding, this association has become a multinational effort, documenting the experience of immigrants from all countries. Their acquisitional activities are nationwide. Indeed, after twenty years of collecting, DOMID has brought together an impressive number of objects and archival holdings. Furthermore, it is open to the public.[65] To expand its collections, DOMID even recruited members from immigrant communities (who are familiar with the concerns of different cultures) to approach potential donors. As a result of their efforts, second- and third-generation immigrants are now much more aware that they are an important part of German postwar history. It is a good sign for the future that among these immigrants there are trained historians and other scholars—increasingly without immigration backgrounds themselves—who are developing an interest in the topic of immigration and ethnic groups in Germany, because it reflects the growing integration of migration into the larger German historic narrative. Meanwhile, DOMID is funded by federal authorities. An interesting attempt at preserving memory is an oral history archive migration-audio-archiv (Migration Audio Archives) in Cologne that holds more than 150 recordings of migrants collected in the last twelve years.[66]

## *Other Receiving Countries*

In the immediate aftermath of World War II, the industrialized countries of western Europe all suffered from an acute scarcity of labor. This shortage was especially noticeable in the mining industry. Even though the demand for coal had to be met (it was still the most important energy source at that time), iron ore for steelmaking was needed for reconstruction. In Belgium and France, there was an attempt to recruit indigenous workers for the mining industry through a combination of incentives and sanctions. However, this policy failed because—among other reasons—of the strong resistance of the labor unions. Therefore, France, Belgium, Great Britain, and the Netherlands began to recruit workers from abroad.

In 1946, some 700,000 German prisoners of war in France, and roughly 50,000 in Belgium worked in mines and other industries. Attempts to employ them further on a voluntary basis after their release were largely unsuccessful. Meanwhile, in occupied Germany, there were still many displaced persons who had no chance of employment there. Given the acute need for labor in most western European countries, this reservoir of workers was soon exhausted. As a result, Great Britain absorbed 90,000 displaced persons, France 35,000, Belgium 22,000, and the Netherlands 4,000.

Between 1947 and 1949 some 260,000 Algerian workers immigrated to France; they took this as an easy opportunity to leave Algeria after Algerian Muslims were granted French citizenship in 1947. Until Algeria was granted independence in 1964, the French government was hardly able to control or regulate this steady stream of migrants. In 1947, Belgium temporarily ceased to employ North Africans because of strong resentment of their work performance, discipline, and ability to adapt.[67]

At this point, there were only a few countries left in Europe where it seemed possible to recruit workers. For political reasons, recruitment in Eastern Europe, Spain, or Portugal was not possible. France and Belgium therefore agreed to recruitment agreements with Italy. Before 1948, 100,000 Italians immigrated to France and another 80,000 to Belgium. Because of the common border shared by France and Italy—and also because of the abolition of travel restrictions—a completely independent and unregulated (though tolerated) migration of labor gradually developed between these two countries.

In 1951, Great Britain also tried to come to an agreement with Italy, but failed to do so because of the overwhelming opposition from British labor unions. In the meantime, it had also become clear that the unregulated arrival of workers from Ireland, the Caribbean, India, and Pakistan was actually enough to satisfy labor needs in Britain at the time and reflected Britain's commitment to the Commonwealth of Nations (an organization primarily composed of former British colonies). In addition, the liberalization of citizenship laws in 1948 had helped to make this possible.[68]

By the beginning of the 1950s, Italy, which possessed the largest pool of available workers in Europe, began to press for better terms and conditions for its citizens working abroad. In reaction to this, France and Belgium began to negotiate recruitment contracts with other countries. In Europe, the remaining authoritarian dictatorships of Portugal and Spain, as well as the communist but non-aligned Yugoslavia opened up as possible countries for the recruitment of labor. Between 1954 and 1970, France, Belgium, and the Netherlands signed bilateral recruitment contracts with Greece, Yugoslavia, Morocco, Portugal, Spain, Turkey, and Tunisia.[69]

Aside from Germany, where developments have already been described, Switzerland and the Scandinavian countries also joined in the search for workers. Like Germany and the Netherlands, these countries were afforded a distinct advantage in the search for labor because of their stable currencies. However, this chapter focuses on the members of the European Economic Community (EEC) until the middle of the 1970s. Therefore the situation in the states mentioned above will not be analyzed.

The leading European industrial nations were anxious to keep their domestic job markets flexible and only agreed to temporary contracts with foreign workers. In reality though, the recruitment of temporary workers developed into permanent immigration.[70]

Source material for research into labor migration in a larger European context is available. Raw statistical data can be easily found.[71] State archives throughout Europe are organized in a similar fashion as in Germany. There is the national level, the regional level, and the municipal level. However, the regional level, the *départements* in France, the Dutch provinces or, to name a country that generally provided labor, the Italian provinces, have different responsibilities and positions within their respective state systems. Access to public archives is regulated by law in all European Union member states. In France, which has an excellent, well-organized system of state archives,[72] many non-governmental and private collections are also preserved by the state. Of note are the Archives nationales du monde du travail (National Archives of the Labor Sphere)[73] and the collections belonging to the Musée de l'histoire de l'immigration (Museum of Immigration History).[74] The National Archives of Great Britain provide, among other things, insight into dealing with postcolonial migration.[75] Aside from the Belgian state archives,[76] the collections of the Miners' Union held by the Institut Emile Vandervelde in Brussels bears mentioning.[77] In the Netherlands, the Internationaal Instituut voor Sociale Geschiedenis (International Institute of Social History) is, aside from the state archives,[78] especially important. Its archives hold the records of the Dutch Recruitment Bureau in Ankara and of De Werkgroep Buitenlands Arbeiders (Foreign Workers Study Group) in Leiden.[79] In addition, it offers other services, such as a database on immigrant organizations in the Netherlands.[80] The Dutch municipal archives have also collected testimonies of labor immigrants.[81] This international overview of selected municipalities and their archival materials promises a fruitful field of study.[82]

## Sending Countries

In order to obtain a comprehensive picture of the history of labor migrations in postwar Europe, it is also necessary to study the situation in the sending countries and the motives of their governments. For populous countries with few natural resources, labor was an export item that secured a source of much-needed foreign currency. The fate of those for whom employment abroad was only temporary and who later returned to their home countries can best be understood by conducting research in the sending countries.

Turkey, one of the most important sending countries, has been the subject of a baseline study designed with a multifaceted approach,[83] and could inspire further research. In Spain[84] and Italy,[85] archival sources have in fact already produced quantifiable results. In the case of the Centro di Emigrazione (the Italian Center for Emigration) in Verona, it is largely thanks to an Italian historian that all the records were preserved. Meanwhile, although the former Yugoslavia was not aligned with the communist bloc during the Cold War, labor migration brought foreign currency and contact with the Western lifestyle became infectious.[86]

The archival situation in those sending countries that are not part of the European Union can be difficult to assess. As a glance into the literature shows, difficulties arise either in regard to access,[87] or in regard to the acquisition of records.[88] This should be taken into account when planning for research projects. For individual researchers, language problems also arise more frequently in the sending countries than in those receiving immigrant workers. One solution to this problem could be the national centers for migration studies that can be found in these countries, as well as their international networks.[89] Moreover, it is evident that this field of study is particularly open to the growing number of scholars who are themselves second- or third-generation descendants of immigrants, insofar as they understand the language of their parents or grandparents.

## The European Level

Within the growing framework of the European Community records are far easier to trace. The intergovernmental contracts for the recruitment of workers were based on conventions and patterns that the International Labor Organization (ILO; founded in 1919) in Geneva had already established in the first half of the twentieth century. Even though the ILO operates around the world, its bilateral model contracts served as a basis for negotiating the codification of European labor migration in the second half of the last century.[90] The ILO keeps its own, publicly accessible archive.[91]

Driven primarily by Italy, labor mobility was established within the European Economic Community when it was founded in 1958. Since 1961, this principle had applied to all citizens of the EEC, even though it only went into full effect after 1968, when the provision to first fill job openings with indigenous workers fell away.

The slowdown of the postwar economy and the economic crises of the late 1960s led to the closing of job markets. In early 1973, Great Britain was the first country to limit immigration, which primarily affected people from the Commonwealth. In that same year, Belgium and the Netherlands, and then finally Germany, brought an end to the recruitment of foreign labor. France followed with restrictions in July of 1975. At first, these measures did not reduce the number of immigrants. Even though the organized immigration of labor ceased, immigrants already within the country were still allowed to have their families follow them. This changed the social structure of the respective immigrant communities.

Still, in contrast to appearances, the end of foreign labor recruitment within the European Union was not a coordinated campaign, but rather the result of similar problems. The European Commission, the highest executive body of the newly founded European Economic Community, tried to take charge of the regulation and coordination of labor immigration from very early on. As it was, the European states had developed different approaches to dealing with the foreign workers they had brought in—people whom they now increasingly perceived as a problem. Governments exchanged ideas and concepts bilaterally, as well as on the level of the EEC. However, a transfer of responsibilities to European-wide institutions did not happen until 1999.[92]

Because the end of organized labor recruitment within individual nations also marks the point at which the European Union began to gradually develop a common immigration policy, scholars with supranational research interests should consult the archives of the European Union. Ever since English became one of the official languages of the EEC in 1973, all documents are also available in this language. The following institutions of the European Union support their own archives. The Council of the European Union, also known as the Council of Ministers,[93] represents the governments of the member states and, together with the European Parliament,[94] develops legislation. The European Commission is a supranational executive body.[95] In addition, there is a common historical archive of the European Union.[96] The Archives of the Bank for International Settlements, which is not a purely European organization, also holds interesting material for certain research questions.[97]

## Dreaming of Lands of Milk and Honey

### Germany

The *Grundgesetz* ("basic law"; constitution) of the West German republic, which went into effect in 1949, guaranteed an unrestricted right of asylum to international victims of political persecution. During the Cold War, asylum seekers from Eastern Europe especially were accepted into West Germany without much issue. These immigrants were hardly considered a social problem.[98]

By the end of the twentieth century however, the rising number of people seeking asylum in Germany began to be seen as a problem. At the end of the 1970s, asylum seekers in Germany did not number more than about a thousand per year. By 1980, that number had grown to about 100,000, and then to 400,000 by the mid-1990s. At the same time, the ethnic makeup and cultural background of asylum seekers had also changed. It was commonly argued in public discourse that the vast majority of people who sought asylum in Germany did so for economic reasons, that is, to take advantage of Germany's comparatively generous social welfare system. It was in this climate of political debate that the term *Scheinasylanten* (bogus asylum seekers) began to appear frequently. Indeed, the question of asylum seekers became a constant theme in domestic politics, playing upon voters' fears of social decline and cultural marginalization.[99] After heavy political debate, the right of asylum seekers was seriously curtailed in 1993. Among those who lost the right to seek asylum in Germany were those who had petitioned for asylum in another member state of the European Union.[100]

Even though Germany had taken in the majority of people seeking asylum in Europe, other countries in the European Union had faced similar problems.[101] This was especially so because, like Germany, other western European states had generally ended their support for the institutionalized immigration of labor after the mid-1970s. As a consequence, the number of people seeking asylum only rose.[102] In France—a nation with a strong tradition of providing refuge to asylum seekers—the government gradually moved to curtail this right. In 1981, eighty percent of all petitions for asylum in France were granted. By 2009 that number had shrunk to less than thirty percent.[103] During the same period, all of the other member states of the European Union restricted their rights of asylum as well, including Italy, Spain, and Portugal.[104] These three countries are singled out because they form the southern border of the European Union, and have therefore experienced the most pressure from asylum seekers. For many European states, the issue of asylum seekers today serves as a battleground for domestic and, increasingly, European politics. Every time immigration comes up for debate in western European countries, a boost in populist-nationalist sentiment follows.[105] More restrictive laws are often called for with the pretense of harmonizing them with existing policies across the European Union.[106]

## The Europeanization of a Problem

Since the 1970s, immigration from outside of the European Economic Community has been primarily discussed as a question of security. In 1975, this problem was initially addressed on an intergovernmental level by a conference of interior and justice ministers known as TREVI (Terrorisme, Radicalisme, Extrémisme et Violence Internationale). Still, the effort toward lifting border controls between member states, as laid out in the 1985 Schengen Agreement, encountered difficulties upon confronting the details. In 1999, when it was agreed that the European Economic Community should aim to be an "area of freedom, security, and justice" (AFSJ), this, too, was done with the purpose of developing a more common policy on matters related to asylum and immigration. At the 2002 summit in Seville, numerous measures were adopted in an attempt to deal with illegal immigration.[107]

As long as the European Community, along with North America, stands as one of the few regions in the world that offers individuals adequate economic opportunity, legal protections, and material security, its pull on immigrants will only continue to grow. Despite the increasingly restrictive management of political asylum, the countries of the European Union continue to respect the principle of *non-refoulement*, that is, no person is rendered back into a country where he or she is suffering from persecution or violations of human rights. In this respect, the growth of restrictive regulations has only had a limited impact.[108] Whether or not the European Union can develop a policy strategy that is both open-minded and mindful of traditions and accepted values, or if it will transform itself into a "Golden Cage," such as a gated community, remains to be seen.[109]

Meanwhile, the movement of asylum seekers continues unabated. Refused applicants appeal to courts,[110] and eventually, the files of their cases, too, land in archives. This holds true for the documents of states as well as of supranational administrations whose records have not yet made their way to archives, but will hopefully be available once their access restrictions are lifted. Naturally, contemporary historians should not be intimidated by these circumstances; rather, they should rely on published resources and, when available, interviews of contemporary witnesses. After all, archivists also face limitations. They can only collect material that is not currently in use. A historical process has to be completed or have reached another stage before associated documents can be historicized and thus filed in an archive. It is therefore important, when taking those first steps into the study of European immigration policies, to be aware of the access restrictions on archival material.

## The Challenge of Collecting Sources

In respect to the many different waves of migrations discussed above, there are sources that have been assembled and that are available for historical research in archives open to the public. This does not mean, however, that the work of the archivist is complete.

A new sensitivity among professional archivists inspired a discussion on how to preserve the cultural heritage of new groups of immigrants, such as asylum seekers and immigrants from the former Soviet Union with Jewish or German roots. However, recognizing the challenge of detecting and collecting sources on migration by professional archivists was a phenomenon of the last decade.

In 2006, the Nuremberg municipal archives began an oral history project on immigration, which was later extended in order to contact cultural associations of migrants and encourage them to file their written records.[111] In 2007, the Verband deutscher Archivarinnen und Archivare (VdA) (Professional Organization of German Archivists) invited DOMID[112] and the Migration Audio Archives[113] to present their projects at their annual meeting. An initial survey conference about the problems related to documenting immigration from a multitude of perspectives took place in Munich in 2010.[114] In May 2013, the municipal council of Munich charged the municipal museum and the archives to collect documents and objects on immigration. Finally, the regional meeting of southwest Germany's archivists, which took place in June 2013, convened under the motto "Archive und Migration" (Archives and Migration).

These are examples of a development that has just begun and continues to steadily accelerate. Specifically, it is important to get in touch with German non-governmental organizations concerned with refugees and asylum seekers and to bring to their attention that the documentation of their activities should be kept for historical research and future generations.

To all historians who work in this area of study, a plea goes out to put public access archives in touch with any private collectors holding documents of interest that surface during research. The same is true of interviews with contemporary witnesses, which should be treated as raw research data and made available to other researchers through public access archives. In accordance with the principle of *Sammeln im Verbund* (collecting in association), every archivist in Germany will direct you to the appropriate institution.

## Notes

1. An overview of current research is provided in Victoria Harris, Barbara Könczöl, and David Motadel, "Introduction," in "Migration in Germany's Age of Globalization," eds. Victoria Harris, Barbara Könczöl, and David Motadel, special issue, *Journal of Contemporary History* 49 (2014): 3–8.

2. Individual examples will be pointed out in the text from time to time to provide an impression of how versatile and different the sources for this area of study can be. The scholarly literature on sources is particularly significant.

3. This is pointed out by Karin Hunn, Jochen Oltmer, and Johannes-Dieter Steinert. Steinert believes that his argument, which was still controversial in the mid-1990s, has been confirmed by archival material that has been released since then. Karin Hunn, *"Nächstes Jahr kehren wir zurück…" Die Geschichte der türkischen "Gastarbeiter" in der Bundesrepublik*, Moderne Zeit 11 (Göttingen: Wallstein, 2005), 13–14; Jochen Oltmer, Axel Kreienbrink, and Carlos Sanz Díaz, eds. *Das "Gastarbeiter"-System: Arbeitsmigration und ihre Folgen in der Bundesrepublik Deutschland und Westeuropa* (Munich: Oldenbourg, 2012), 13, 15; Johannes-Dieter Steinert, "Migration and Migration Policy: West Germany and the Recruitment of Foreign Labour, 1945–61," in Harris, Könczöl, and Motadel, "Migration in Germany's Age of Globalization," 12–13.

4. Figures provided by Anna M. Holian, *Between National Socialism and Soviet Communism: Social History, Popular Culture, and Politics in Germany* (Ann Arbor: University of Michigan Press, 2011), 3.

5. For more on the history of refugee relief organizations, see Sharif Gemie, *Outcast Europe: Refugees and Relief Workers in an Era of Total War 1936–48* (London: Continuum, 2012).

6. Statistisches Bundesamt, *Statistisches Jahrbuch für die Bundesrepublik Deutschland 1953* (Stuttgart/Cologne: W. Kohlhammer, 1953), 53. For full particulars interpreting the official figures see the chapter by Anna Holian in this anthology.

7. See, for example, Institut für Besatzungsfragen, *Das DP-Problem: Eine Studie über die ausländischen Flüchtlinge in Deutschland* (Tübingen: Mohr, 1950), which expresses these sentiments exactly. For more recent research into this matter based on sources from German state archives, see Holian, *Between National Socialism and Soviet Communism*, 327–28; Jan-Hinnerk Antons, "Displaced Persons in Postwar Germany," in Harris, Könczöl, and Motadel, "Migration in Germany's Age of Globalization," 92–114.

8. Atina Grossmann, "From Victims to 'Homeless Foreigners': Jewish Survivors in Postwar Germany," in *After the Nazi Racial State: Difference and Democracy in Germany and Europe, Social History, Popular Culture, and Politics in Germany*, eds. Rita Chin et al. (Ann Arbor: University of Michigan Press, 2009), 66–8.

9. United Nations Archives and Records Management, "Archival Fonds," accessed 4 September 2014, https://archives.un.org/content/archival-fonds.

10. United States National Archives and Records Administration, "Records of U.S. Occupation Headquarters, World War II," accessed 4 September 2014, http://www.archives.gov/research/guide-fed-records/groups/260.html.

11. YIVO Institute for Jewish Research, "Major Collections," accessed 4 September 2014, http://www.yivo.org/library/index.php?tid=45&aid=102.

12. American Jewish Joint Distribution Committee, "JDC Archives," accessed 4 September 2014, http://archives.jdc.org/.

13. The collections held by the USHMM include many autobiographical reports that also provide further details on the experiences of displaced persons. For example: United States Holocaust Memorial Museum, "Illinois Institute of Technology Psychology Laboratory Project MH 156: David P. Boder oral history interviews with displaced persons, 1946," accessed 4 September 2014, http://collections.ushmm.org/search/catalog/irn502045.

14. International Tracing Service, "Archives," accessed 4 September 2014, https://www.its-arolsen.org/en/archives/.

15. Initially, for example, Wolfgang Jacobmeyer published an article on the topic, and a monograph followed later: Wolfgang Jacobmeyer, "Polnische Juden in der amerikanischen Besatzungszone Deutschlands 1946/47," *Vierteljahrshefte für Zeitgeschichte* 25 (1977): 120–35; and Wolfgang Jacobmeyer, *Vom Zwangsarbeiter zum heimatlosen Ausländer: Die Displaced Persons in Westdeutschland, 1945–1951* (Göttingen: Vandenhoeck & Ruprecht, 1985); furthermore Ulrich Herbert, *Fremdarbeiter* (Bonn: Dietz, 1985).

16. Mathias Beer, *Flüchtlinge und Vertriebene im deutschen Südwesten nach 1945: Eine Übersicht der Archivalien in den staatlichen und kommunalen Archiven des Landes Baden-Württemberg.* (Sigmaringen: Thorbecke, 1994), 13.

17. Statistisches Bundesamt, *Statistisches Jahrbuch für die Bundesrepublik Deutschland 1953*, 50.

18. Michael Schwartz, "'Vom Umsiedler zum Staatsbürger': Totalitäres und Subversives in der Sprachpolitik der DDR," in *Vertriebene in Deutschland: Interdisziplinäre Ergebnisse und Forschungsperspektiven*, eds. Dierk Hoffmann, Marita Krauss, and Michael Schwartz (Munich: Oldenbourg Verlag, 2000), 135–66, here 140.

19. An overview of this can be found in Marita Krauss, "Das 'Wir' und das 'Ihr': Ausgrenzung, Abgrenzung, Identitätsstiftung bei Einheimischen und Flüchtlingen nach 1945," in Hoffmann et al., *Vertriebene in Deutschland*, 27–39.

20. For more on this project and how it began, see Mathias Beer, "Die Dokumentation der Vertreibung der Deutschen aus Ost-Mitteleuropa," *Geschichte in Wissenschaft und Unterricht* 50 (1999): 99–117. A selection of documents was also translated and published in English under Theodor Schieder, *Documents on the Expulsion of the Germans from Eastern-Central-Europe* (Göttingen: Schwarz, 1956–61).

21. Bundesarchiv, "Bestände des Lastenausgleichsarchivs in Bayreuth," accessed 4 September 2014, http://www.bundesarchiv.de/benutzung/zeitbezug/nationalsozialismus/02655/index.html.de.

22. The Lastenausgleichsgesetz (Equalization of Burdens Act) determined that those who had lost their property were compensated by those who had lost less or nothing at all. For large fortunes, the amount owed could be as high as fifty percent of a person's estimated financial worth. This enabled the destitute to rebuild their economic existence. Michael L. Hughes, *Shouldering the Burdens of Defeat* (Chapel Hill: University of North Carolina Press, 1999).

23. Historians owe it to the dedication of the archivist Hugo Stehkämper that these records were secured at all, records which are incredibly valuable for research into the history of West Germany's economic and social policies: Ulrich Ringsdorf, "Die Bestände des Lastenausgleichsarchivs," in Hoffmann et al., *Vertriebene in Deutschland*, 421–6. Stehkämper publicly declared that these records should not be destroyed in Hugo Stehkämper, "Akten der Lastenausgleichsverwaltung," *Der Archivar. Mitteilungsblatt für deutsches Archivwesen* 22 (1969): 177–92.

24. Further information on archival sources for expellees in West Germany can be found in Albert A. Feiber, "Die archivalischen Bestände der deutschen Vertriebenengruppen und anderer 'nichtöffentlicher' Institutionen," in Hoffmann et al., *Vertriebene in Deutschland*, 427–36; Johannes Grützmacher, "Staatliche und nichtstaatliche Überlieferung zum Thema 'Vertriebene' — Überlieferungsbildung im Verbund?" in *Lebendige Erinnerungskultur für die Zukunft*, ed. Heiner Schmitt, vol. 12 of Tagungsdokumentationen zum Deutschen Archivtag (Fulda: Selbstverlag des VdA, 2008), 157–65. For a more regional compilation of archival sources, see Beer, *Flüchtlinge und Vertriebene im deutschen Südwesten nach 1945*.

25. Bundesarchiv, "Bund der Vertriebenen – Vereinigte Landsmannschaften und Landesverbände," call number B 234.

26. Michael Schwartz, *Funktionäre mit Vergangenheit* (Munich: Oldenbourg, 2013), 3–82.
27. Manfred Wille, "Die Vertriebenen und das politisch-staaliche System der SBZ/ DDR," in Hoffmann et al., *Vertriebene in Deutschland*, 203–17; Michael Schwartz, "Integration und Transformation: 'Umsiedler'-Politik und regionaler Strukturwandel in Mecklenburg-Vorpommern von 1945 bis 1953," in *Sozialismus auf dem platten Lande: Tradition und Transformation in Mecklenburg-Vorpommern von 1945 bis 1952*, ed. Damian van Melis (Schwerin: Helms, 1999), 135–94. On the state of sources, see Margret Fruth, "Die Bestände des Bundesarchivs Berlin und der SAPMO zur Integration von Flüchtlingen und Vertriebenen nach 1945," in Hoffmann et al., *Vertriebene in Deutschland*, 409–16.
28. Statistisches Reichsamt, *Statistisches Jahrbuch für das Deutsche Reich 1935* (Berlin: Verlag für Sozialpolitik, Wirtschaft und Statistik, 1935), 16.
29. "Press Releases – Migration: A Long-Standing Tradition in Germany – Federal Statistical Office (Destatis)," accessed 1 June 2014, https://www.destatis.de/EN/ PressServices/Press/pr/2013/12/PE13_430_122.html. The German version is more detailed: "Pressemitteilungen - Migration hat eine lange Tradition in Deutschland – Statistisches Bundesamt (Destatis)," accessed 1 June 2014, https://www.destatis.de/DE/ Startseite.html;jsessionid=9AFCDA335A61ED72BFA250F8D1E345C4.cae3.
30. DigiZeitschriften e.V. "Statistisches Jahrbuch für die Bundesrepublik Deutschland," accessed 9 July 2014, http://www.digizeitschriften.de/de/dms/toc/?PPN=PPN514402342.
31. Bundesarchiv, "Bundesministerium für Arbeit und Sozialordnung, Teil 1 – Arbeitsmarktpolitk, Arbeitsvermittlung, Arbeitslosenversicherung, Berufsberatung," accessed 16 May 2014, http://startext.net-build.de:8080/barch/MidosaSEARCH/B149-20995/index.htm.
32. Bundesarchiv, "Grundannahmen zur militärischen und zivilen Verteidigung. Ausländische Arbeitnehmer im Krisen, Spannungs und Verteidigungsfalle," call number: B 149/121837.
33. Bundesarchiv, Ständige Konferenz der Kultusminister der Länder der Bundesrepublik Deutschland, "Schulische Betreuung von Kindern ausländischer Arbeitnehmer," call number B 304/3733.
34. Bundesarchiv, Bundesanstalt für Arbeit, accessed 16 May 2014, http://startext.net-build. de:8080/barch/MidosaSEARCH/B119-17967/index.htm.
35. Hessisches Hauptstaatsarchiv Wiesbaden, Landratsamt Hanau, call number 2335.
36. For a comparison, see Sarah Hackett, "Integration im kommunalen Raum: Bremen und Newcastle-upon-Tyne im Vergleich," in Oltmer et al., *Das "Gastarbeiter"-System*, 247–59
37. Rita Chin and Heide Fehrenbach, "German Democracy and the Question of Difference, 1945–1995," in Chin et al., *After the Nazi Racial State*, 107–8.
38. For example, see "Britische Geheimprotokolle: Kohl wollte offenbar jeden zweiten Türken loswerden" *Spiegel Online*, 1 August 2013, accessed 17 May 2014, http://www. spiegel.de/politik/deutschland/kohl-wollte-jeden-zweiten-tuerken-in-deutschland-loswerden-a-914318.html.
39. Rita Chin, *The Guest Worker Question in Postwar Germany* (Cambridge: Cambridge University Press, 2007), 144–5; and Hunn, *"Nächstes Jahr kehren wir zurück…,"* 343–4, 446.
40. Hunn, *"Nächstes Jahr kehren wir zurück…,"* 423–46; Rita Chin, "Guest Worker Migration and the Unexpected Return of Race," in Chin et al., *After the Nazi Racial State*, 95–8.
41. Helen Williams, "Changing the National Narrative: Evolution in Citizenship and Integration in Germany 2000–2010," in Harris, Könczöl, and Motadel, "Migration in Germany's Age of Globalization," 54–74.

42. Hans-Christian Herrmann, "Gab's das wirklich? – Migration in die DDR," in Schmitt, *Lebendige Erinnerungskultur für die Zukunft*, 115–35. For additional guidance, see Bundesarchiv, Archivgut der SED und des FDGB, accessed 9 July 2014, http://www.bundesarchiv.de/sed-fdgb-netzwerk/.

43. For a general overview, see Jochen Hecht, "Das Archiv des Bundesbeauftragten für die Unterlagen des Staatssicherheitsdienstes der ehemaligen Deutschen Demokratischen Republik (BStU) – ein Spezialarchiv auf Zeit?" in Schmitt, *Lebendige Erinnerungskultur für die Zukunft*, 235–48.

44. Chin, *The Guest Worker Question in Postwar Germany*, 147.

45. Franziska Dunkel and Gabriella Stramaglia-Faggion, *Zur Geschichte der Gastarbeiter in München: "für 50 Mark einen Italiener"* (Munich: Buchendorfer, 2000).

46. Rosmarie Beier-de Haan, *Zuwanderungsland Deutschland: Migrationen 1500–2005* (Wolfratshausen/Berlin: Minerva and DHM, 2005).

47. Sabine Hess, "Migration als Teil der Stadtgeschichte: Lehren aus einem Ausstellungsprojekt zur Geschichte der Migration in München," in *Migranten in München, Archivische Überlieferung und Dokumentation: Dokumentation zum Kolloquium vom 20. Juli 2010 im Stadtarchiv München*, ed. Brigitte Huber (Munich: Stadtarchiv, 2010), 9–19.

48. Klaus Wisotzky, ed. *Fremd(e) im Revier!? Zuwanderung und Fremdsein im Ruhrgebiet; ein Projekt der Kulturhauptstadt Europas Ruhr, 2010* (Essen: Klartext, 2010).

49. Archivportal-D," accessed 23 May 2016, https://www.archivportal-d.de/?lang=en.

50. Landesarchiv Nordrhein-Westfalen, "Portal der Archive in NRW," accessed 9 July 2014, http://www.archive.nrw.de/LAV_NRW/jsp/erweitertSuche.jsp.

51. Niedersächsisches Landesarchiv – Zentrale Archivverwaltung, "Archivportal Niedersachsen," accessed 9 July 2014, http://archivportal.niedersachsen.de/.

52. Hessisches Hauptstaatsarchiv, "Hessisches Archiv-Dokumentations und Informationsystem," accessed 9 July 2014, http://www.hauptstaatsarchiv.hessen.de.

53. Peter Pfister, "Migration und Katholische Kirche: Quellen und Forschungsmöglichkeiten in katholischen Archiven," in Huber, *Migranten in München*, 45–51.

54. Friedrich-Ebert-Stiftung: Archiv der sozialen Demokratie, "Deutscher Gewerkschaftsbund, Bundesvorstand. Abteilung Ausländische Arbeitnehmer; Laufzeit: 1949–1983," accessed 16 May 2014, http://www.fes.de/archiv/adsd_neu/inhalt/gewerkschaften/abteilungen/auslaendische_arbeitnehmer.htm.

55. Simon Goeke, "The Multinational Working Class? Political Activism and Labour Migration in West Germany during the 1960s and 1970s," in Harris, Könczöl, and Motadel, "Migration in Germany's Age of Globalization," 160–82.

56. Deutsches Bergbau-Museum, "Bergbau-Archiv Bochum," accessed 13 July 2014, http://www.archive.nrw.de/wirtschaftsarchive/Bergbau-ArchivBochum/bestaende/index.php.

57. Industrie- und Handelskammer zu Köln, "Rheinisch Westfaelisches Wirtschaftsarchiv," accessed 13 July, http://www.ihk-koeln.de/Rheinisch_Westfaelisches_Wirtschaftsarchiv. AxCMS?ActiveID=1223.

58. Eva Moser, "'Gastarbeiter-Bilderbogen': Quellen zu ausländischen Arbeitskräften im Bayerischen Wirtschaftsarchiv," in Huber, *Migranten in München*, 53–6.

59. Daimler AG, "Mercedes-Benz Classic Home – Archives & Collection – Corporate Archives," accessed 13 July 2014, http://www.mercedes-benz-classic.com/content/classic/mpc/mpc_classic_website/en/mpc_home/mbc/home/history/archives_and_collection/company_archive.html.

60. Nicole Bergmann, "'Gastarbeit' bei BMW in den 1960er und 1970er Jahren: Zur historischen Entwicklung und Quellenlage im BMW Group Archiv," in Huber, *Migranten in München*, 57–68.

61. Siemens AG., "Siemens History Site – Corporate Archives," accessed 13 July 2014, http://www.siemens.com/history/en/siemens_historical_institute/corporate_ archives/.

62. ThyssenKrupp AG, "Archive," accessed 13 July 2014, http://www.thyssenkrupp.com/ de/konzern/geschichte_archive.html.

63. The parties that were the most significant from the 1960s to the 1990s all have their own archives: for the SPD, the Friedrich-Ebert-Stiftung, "Archiv der sozialen Demokratie," accessed 13 July 2014, http://www.fes.de/archiv/adsd_neu/index.htm; for the CDU, the Konrad-Adenauer-Stiftung, "Archiv für Christlich-Demokratische Politik," accessed 13 July 2014, http://www.kas.de/wf/de/42.7; for the CSU, the Hanns-Seidel-Stiftung, "Archiv für Christlich-Soziale Politik," accessed 13 July 2014, http://www.hss.de/mediathek/ archiv-fuer-christlich-soziale-politik.html; for the FDP the Friedrich-Naumann-Stiftung für die Freiheit, "Archiv des Liberalismus," accessed 13 July 2014, http://www.frei-heit.org/webcom/show_uebersicht.php/_c-716/_lkm-318/i.html; and for the Greens, the Heinrich-Böll-Stiftung, "Archiv Grünes Gedächtnis," accessed 13 July 2014, www.boell. de/de/navigation/archiv-588.html.

64. Mehmet G. Daimagüler, *Kein schönes Land in dieser Zeit: Das Märchen von der gescheiterten Integration* (Gütersloh/Munich: Gütersloher Verlagshaus; Random House, 2011), 28–9. The title that Karin Hunn chose for her monograph indicates that this was not a perception isolated to a few people. The full title again: Karin Hunn, *"Nächstes Jahr kehren wir zurück..." Die Geschichte der türkischen "Gastarbeiter" in der Bundesrepublik*, Moderne Zeit 11 (Göttingen: Wallstein, 2005).

65. Nina Matuszewski, "DOMiD Dokumentationszentrum und Museum über die Migration in Deutschland e.V.," in Schmitt, *Lebendige Erinnerungskultur für die Zukunft*, 151–5; and Aytac Eryilmaz, "20 Jahre Sammeln, Bewahren und Darstellen der Migrationsgeschichte," in Huber, *Migranten in München*, 21–5.

66. Seva I. Suvak, "Die Geschichte der Migration ist vielstimmig. Das migration-audio-archiv sammelt Biografien von Einwanderern," in Schmitt, *Lebendige Erinnerungskultur für die Zukunft*, 148–50.

67. Frank Caestecker and Eric Vanhaute, "Zuwanderung von Arbeitskräften in die Industriestaaten Westeuropas: Eine vergleichende Analyse der Muster von Arbeitsmarktmigration und Rückkehr 1945–1960," in Oltmer et al., *Das "Gastarbeiter"-System*, 48 n. 39.

68. Caestecker and Vanhaute, "Zuwanderung von Arbeitskräften in die Industriestaaten Westeuropas," 39–44.

69. Ahmet Akgündüz, *Labour Migration from Turkey to Western Europe, 1960–1974: A Multidisciplinary Analysis*, Research in Migration and Ethnic Relations Series (Aldershot, England/Burlington, VT: Ashgate, 2008), 105–10.

70. Caestecker and Vanhaute, "Zuwanderung von Arbeitskräften in die Industriestaaten Westeuropas," 44.

71. For France, see INSEE (National Institute for Statistics and Economic Studies), accessed 28 July 2014, "Foreigners – Immigrants," http://www.insee.fr/en/themes/theme. asp?theme=2&sous_theme=5.

72. Ministère de la Culture et de la Communication, "Archives nationales (France)," accessed 28 July 2014, http://www.archives-nationales.culture.gouv.fr/sia/web/guest/ home.

73. Ministère de la Culture et de la Communication, "Archives nationales du monde du travail," accessed 28 July 2014, http://www.archivesnationales.culture.gouv.fr/camt/index. html.

74. Musée de l'histoire de l'immigration, "Collections," accessed 28 July 2014, http://www. histoire-immigration.fr/musee/collections/document d-archive.
75. For example, see: The National Archives, "Dominions Office and Commonwealth Relations Office. Migration and General Department: Migration Council," accessed 4 September 2014, http://discovery.nationalarchives.gov.uk/details/r/C4719384 and "Ministry of Labour and successors. Employment Policy: Impact of migration on manpower resources," accessed 4 September 2014, http://discovery.nationalarchives.gov.uk/ details/r/C2692726.
76. State Archives in Belgium, "Introduction," accessed 20 July 2014, http://arch.arch.be/ index.php?lang=en_GB.
77. Institut Emile Vandervelde (I.E.V.), "Bibliothèque et archives," accessed 28 July 2014, http://www.iev.be/Bibliotheque/Fonds.aspx.
78. Ministerie van Onderwijs Cultuur en Wetenschap, "Nationaal Archief Het nationaal geheugen van de overheid," accessed 28 July 2014, http://www.nationaalarchief.nl/.
79. International Institute of Social History, "Archives," accessed 20 July 2014, http:// socialhistory.org/en/archives.
80. International Institute of Social History, "Migranten organisaties in Nederland," accessed 3 August 2014, http://socialhistory.org/en/projects/migrantenorganisaties-nederland.
81. Horst-Dieter Beyerstedt, "Migrationsforschung und Kommunalarchive: Bericht über den thematischen Teil der Sitzung der Fachgruppe 2," in Schmitt, *Lebendige Erinnerungskultur für die Zukunft*, 203–99.
82. For example, see Bettina Severin-Barboutie, "Stadt – Migration – Transformation: Stuttgart und Lyon im Vergleich," in Oltmer et al., *Das "Gastarbeiter"-System*, 233–45; and Hackett, "Integration im kommunalen Raum," 247–59.
83. Akgündüz, *Labour Migration from Turkey to Western Europe, 1960–1974*.
84. For example, see Axel Kreienbrink, "Auswanderungslenkung und 'asistencia al emigrante': das Instituto Español de Emigración im franquistischen Spanien," in Oltmer et al., *Das "Gastarbeiter"-System*, 103–17. Also see Ministerio de Educación, Cultura y. D. "Archivo General de la Administración," accessed 3 August 2014, www.mecd.gob.es/cultura-mecd/areas-cultura/archivos/mc/archivos/aga/portada.html.
85. For example, see Grazia Prontera, "Das Emigrationszentrum in Verona: Anwerbung und Vermittling italienischer Arbeitskräfte in die Bundesrepublik Deutschland 1955–1975," in Oltmer et al., *Das "Gastarbeiter"-System*, 89–102. For more on archival sources see Ministero dei beni e delle attività culturali e del turismo, "Archivio Di Stato Di Verona," accessed 3 August 2014, http://www.archiviodistatoverona.beniculturali.it/.
86. Karolina Novinšćak, "Auf den Spuren von Brandts Ostpolitik und Titos Sonderweg: deutsch-jugoslawische Migrationsbeziehungen in den 1960er und 1970er Jahren," in Oltmer et al., *Das "Gastarbeiter"-System*, 133–48.
87. Hunn, *"Nächstes Jahr kehren wir zurück...,"* 15, n. 21.
88. Supposedly, the records of the İş ve İşçi Bulma Kurumu (Turkish labor administration) were destroyed in the early 1980s. See Akgündüz, *Labour Migration from Turkey to Western Europe, 1960–1974*, 4, n. 11.
89. For example, see IMIS, "Institut für Migrationsforschung und Interkulturelle Studien," accessed 3 August 2014, http://www.imis.uni-osnabrueck.de/startseite.html; MIGRINTER, "Migrations Internationales," http://mshs.univ-poitiers.fr/migrinter/; and IMISCOE, "International Migration, Integration and Social Cohesion in Europe," accessed 3 August 2014, http://www.imiscoeconferences.org/.

90. Christoph A. Rass, "Die Anwerbeabkommen der Bundesrepublik Deutschland mit Griechenland und Spanien im Kontext eines europäischen Migrationssystems," in Oltmer et al., *Das "Gastarbeiter"-System*, 53–69, 58–9.

91. International Labour Organization, "ILO Archives," accessed 20 July 2014, http://www. ilo.org/century/research/archives/lang--en/index.htm.

92. Marcel Berlinghoff, "Der europäisierte Anwerbestopp," in Oltmer et al., *Das "Gastarbeiter"-System*, 149–64.

93. Council of the European Union, "Consilium – Archives of the Council of the EU," accessed 20 July 2014, http://www.consilium.europa.eu/documents/archives?lang=en.

94. European Parliament, "Historical Archives," accessed 20 July 2014, http://www. europarl.europa.eu/aboutparliament/en/0097d628af/Introduction.html.

95. European Commission, "Historical Archives," accessed 20 July 2014, http://ec.europa. eu/historical_archives/index_en.htm.

96. European University Institute, "Historical Archives of the European Union," accessed 3 August 2014, http://www.eui.eu/Research/HistoricalArchivesOfEU/Index.aspx.

97. Bank for International Settlements, "The Archive Collections of the BIS," accessed 3 August 2014, http://www.bis.org/about/archive.htm.

98. Patrice P. Poutrus, "Asylum in Postwar Germany: Refugee Admission Policies and Their Practical Implementation in the Federal Republic and the GDR Between the Late 1940s and the Mid-1970s," in Harris, Könczöl, and Motadel, "Migration in Germany's Age of Globalization," 115–33.

99. Chin, *The Guest Worker Question in Postwar Germany*, 146.

100. Chin and Fehrenbach, "German Democracy and the Question of Difference, 1945–1995," 119.

101. Virginie Guiraudon, "L'européanisation des politiques publiques de migration," in *L'Europe face à l'autre: Politiques migratoires et intégration européenne*, eds. Maximos Aligisakis and Matteo Gianni, Europa 21 (Geneva: Institut Européen de l'Université de Genève, 2003), 51.

102. Berlinghoff, "Der europäisierte Anwerbestopp," 150; Catherine Withol De Wenden, "L'Europe migratoire," in Aligisakis and Gianni, *L'Europe face à l'autre: Politiques migratoires et intégration européenne*, 56–8.

103. Silvia-Maria Wieser, "Asylpolitik in Frankreich." PhD diss., University of Vienna, 2010; accessed 4 September 2014, http://othes.univie.ac.at/10990/1/2010-08-17_0516265. pdf.

104. Withol De Wenden, "L'Europe migratoire," 69–70.

105. Geoff Eley, "The Trouble with 'Race:' Migrancy, Cultural Difference, and the Remaking of Europe," in Chin et al., *After the Nazi Racial State*, 179–80.

106. Wieser, "Asylpolitik in Frankreich," 131.

107. Guiraudon, "L'européanisation des politiques publiques de migration," 34.

108. Wieser, "Asylpolitik in Frankreich," 128–9.

109. Maurice Blanc, "Les trois âges des migrations en Europe: comparaison Allemagne, France et Grand-Bretagne," in *Migrations et Identité: L'exemple de l'Allemagne aux XIXe et XXe siècles*, eds. Jean-Paul Cahn and Bernard Poloni, Mondes germaniques (Villeneuve-d'Asq: Presses universitaires du Septentrion, 2009), 223.

110. Cécile Prat-Erkert, "Une identité impossible? Le cas des demandeurs d'asile politique déboutés," in Cahn and Poloni, *Migrations et Identité*, 83–90.

111. Michael Diefenbacher, "Das Forschungsprojekt 'Migration' im Stadtarchiv Nürnberg: 'Zuwanderung nach Nürnberg nach 1945 bis heute'," in Huber, *Migranten in München*, 27–36.

112. Matuszewski, "DOMiD Dokumentationszentrum und Museum über die Migration in Deutschland e.V.," 151–5.
113. Suvak, "Die Geschichte der Migration ist vielstimmig," 148–50.
114. Huber, *Migranten in München*.

# Works Cited

Akgündüz, Ahmet. *Labour Migration from Turkey to Western Europe, 1960–1974: A Multidisciplinary Analysis*. Research in Migration and Ethnic Relations Series. Aldershot, England/Burlington, VT: Ashgate, 2008.

Aligisakis, Maximos, and Matteo Gianni, eds. *L'Europe face à l'autre: Politiques migratoires et intégration européenne*. Europa 21. Geneva: Institut Européen de l'Université de Genève, 2003.

Antons, Jan-Hinnerk. "Displaced Persons in Postwar Germany." In "Migration in Germany's Age of Globalization," edited by Victoria Harris, Barbara Könczöl, and David Motadel. Special issue, *Journal of Contemporary History* 49 (2014): 92–114.

Beer, Mathias. *Flüchtlinge und Vertriebene im deutschen Südwesten nach 1945: Eine Übersicht der Archivalien in den staatlichen und kommunalen Archiven des Landes Baden-Württemberg*. Sigmaringen: Thorbecke, 1994.

Beer, Mathias. "Die Dokumentation der Vertreibung der Deutschen aus Ost-Mitteleuropa." *Geschichte in Wissenschaft und Unterricht* 50 (1999): 99–117.

Beier-de Haan, Rosmarie. *Zuwanderungsland Deutschland: Migrationen 1500–2005*. Wolfratshausen/Berlin: Minerva and DHM, 2005.

Bergmann, Nicole. "'Gastarbeit' bei BMW in den 1960er und 1970er Jahren: Zur historischen Entwicklung und Quellenlage im BMW Group Archiv." In *Migranten in München, Archivische Überlieferung und Dokumentation: Dokumentation zum Kolloquium vom 20. Juli 2010 im Stadtarchiv München*, edited by Brigitte Huber, 57–68. Munich: Stadtarchiv, 2010.

Berlinghoff, Marcel. "Der europäisierte Anwerbestopp." In *Das "Gastarbeiter"-System: Arbeitsmigration und ihre Folgen in der Bundesrepublik Deutschland und Westeuropa*, edited by Jochen Oltmer, Axel Kreienbrink, and Carlos Sanz Díaz, 149–64. Schriftenreihe der Vierteljahrshefte für Zeitgeschichte 104. Munich: Oldenbourg, 2012.

Beyerstedt, Horst-Dieter. "Migrationsforschung und Kommunalarchive: Bericht über den thematischen Teil der Sitzung der Fachgruppe 2." In *Lebendige Erinnerungskultur für die Zukunft*, edited by Heiner Schmitt, 203–99. Tagungsdokumentationen zum Deutschen Archivtag 12. Fulda: Selbstverlag des VdA, 2008.

Blanc, Maurice. "Les trois âges des migrations en Europe: comparaison Allemagne, France et Grand-Bretagne." In *Migrations et Identité: L'exemple de l'Allemagne aux XIXe et XXe siècles*, edited by Jean-Paul Cahn and Bernard Poloni, 211–23. Mondes germaniques. Villeneuve-d'Asq: Presses universitaires du Septentrion, impr. 2009.

Caestecker, Frank, and Eric Vanhaute. "Zuwanderung von Arbeitskräften in die Industriestaaten Westeuropas: Eine vergleichende Analyse der Muster von Arbeitsmarktmigration und Rückkehr 1945–1960. In *Das "Gastarbeiter"-System: Arbeitsmigration und ihre Folgen in der Bundesrepublik Deutschland und Westeuropa*, edited by Jochen Oltmer, Axel Kreienbrink, and Carlos Sanz Díaz, 39–52. Schriftenreihe der Vierteljahrshefte für Zeitgeschichte 104. Munich: Oldenbourg, 2012.

Cahn, Jean-Paul, and Bernard Poloni, eds. *Migrations et Identité: L'exemple de l'Allemagne aux XIXe et XXe siècles*. Mondes germaniques. Villeneuve-d'Asq: Presses universitaires du Septentrion, impr. 2009.

Chin, Rita. *The Guest Worker Question in Postwar Germany*. Cambridge: Cambridge University Press, 2007.

Chin, Rita. "Guest Worker Migration and the Unexpected Return of Race." In *After the Nazi Racial State: Difference and Democracy in Germany and Europe*, edited by Rita Chin et al., 80–101. Ann Arbor: University of Michigan Press, 2009.

Chin, Rita, and Heide Fehrenbach. "German Democracy and the Question of Difference, 1945–1995." In *After the Nazi Racial State*, edited by Rita Chin et al., 102–36. Ann Arbor: University of Michigan Press, 2009.

Chin, Rita, Heide Fehrenbach, and Geoff Ely, eds. *After the Nazi Racial State: Difference and Democracy in Germany and Europe*. Ann Arbor: University of Michigan Press, 2009.

Daimagüler, Mehmet G. *Kein schönes Land in dieser Zeit: Das Märchen von der gescheiterten Integration*. Gütersloh/Munich: Gütersloher Verlagshaus; Random House, 2011.

Diefenbacher, Michael. "Das Forschungsprojekt 'Migration' im Stadtarchiv Nürnberg: 'Zuwanderung nach Nürnberg nach 1945 bis heute'." In *Migranten in München, Archivische Überlieferung und Dokumentation: Dokumentation zum Kolloquium vom 20. Juli 2010 im Stadtarchiv München*, edited by Brigitte Huber, 27–36. Munich: Stadtarchiv, 2010.

Dunkel, Franziska, and Gabriella Stramaglia-Faggion. *Zur Geschichte der Gastarbeiter in München: "für 50 Mark einen Italiener."* Munich: Buchendorfer, 2000.

Eley, Geoff. "The Trouble with 'Race': Migrancy, Cultural Difference, and the Remaking of Europe." In *After the Nazi Racial State: Difference and Democracy in Germany and Europe*, edited by Rita Chin, 137–81. Ann Arbor: University of Michigan Press, 2009.

Eryilmaz, Aytac. "20 Jahre Sammeln, Bewahren und Darstellen der Migrationsgeschichte." In *Migranten in München, Archivische Überlieferung und Dokumentation: Dokumentation zum Kolloquium vom 20 Juli 2010 im Stadtarchiv München*, edited by Brigitte Huber, 21–5. Munich: Stadtarchiv, 2010.

Feiber, Albert A. "Die archivalischen Bestände der deutschen Vertriebenengruppen und anderer 'nichtöffentlicher' Institutionen." In *Vertriebene in Deutschland: Interdisziplinäre Ergebnisse und Forschungsperspektiven*, edited by Dierk Hoffmann, Marita Krauss, and Michael Schwartz, 427–36. Munich: Oldenbourg Verlag, 2000.

Fruth, Margret. "Die Bestände des Bundesarchivs Berlin und der SAPMO zur Integration von Flüchtlingen und Vertriebenen nach 1945." In *Vertriebene in Deutschland*, edited by Dierk Hoffmann, Marita Krauss, and Michael Schwartz, 409–16. Munich: Oldenbourg Verlag, 2000.

Gemie, Sharif. *Outcast Europe: Refugees and Relief Workers in an Era of Total War 1936–48*. London: Continuum, 2012.

Goeke, Simon. "The Multinational Working Class? Political Activism and Labour Migration in West Germany during the 1960s and 1970s." In "Migration in Germany's Age of Globalization," edited by Victoria Harris, Barbara Könczöl, and David Motadel. Special issue, *Journal of Contemporary History* 49 (2014): 160–82.

Grossmann, Atina. "From Victims to 'Homeless Foreigners': Jewish Survivors in Postwar Germany." In *After the Nazi Racial State: Difference and Democracy in Germany and Europe*, edited by Rita Chin et al., 55–79. Ann Arbor: University of Michigan Press, 2009.

Grützmacher, Johannes. "Staatliche und nichtstaatliche Überlieferung zum Thema 'Vertriebene' – Überlieferungsbildung im Verbund?" In *Lebendige Erinnerungskultur für die Zukunft*, edited by Heiner Schmitt, 157–65. Tagungsdokumentationen zum Deutschen Archivtag 12. Fulda: Selbstverlag des VdA, 2008.

Guiraudon, Virginie. "L'européanisation des politiques publiques de migration." In *L'Europe face à l'autre: Politiques migratoires et intégration européenne*, edited by Maximos Aligisakis, and Matteo Gianni, 31–51. Europa 21. Geneva: Institut européen de l'Université de Genève, 2003.

Hackett, Sarah. "Integration im kommunalen Raum: Bremen und Newcastle-upon-Tyne im Vergleich." In *Das "Gastarbeiter"-System: Arbeitsmigration und ihre Folgen in der Bundesrepublik Deutschland und Westeuropa*, edited by Jochen Oltmer, Axel Kreienbrink, and Carlos Sanz Díaz, 247–59. Schriftenreihe der Vierteljahrshefte für Zeitgeschichte 104. Munich: Oldenbourg, 2012.

Harris, Victoria, Barbara Könczöl, and David Motadel. "Introduction." In "Migration in Germany's Age of Globalization," edited by Victoria Harris, Barbara Könczöl, and David Motadel. Special issue, *Journal of Contemporary History* 49 (2014): 3–8.

Hecht, Jochen. "Das Archiv des Bundesbeauftragten für die Unterlagen des Staatssicherheitsdienstes der ehemaligen Deutschen Demokratischen Republik (BStU): ein Spezialarchiv auf Zeit?" In *Lebendige Erinnerungskultur für die Zukunft*, edited by Heiner Schmitt, 235–48. Tagungsdokumentationen zum Deutschen Archivtag 12. Fulda: Selbstverlag des VdA, 2008.

Herbert, Ulrich. *Fremdarbeiter*. Bonn: Dietz, 1985.

Herrmann, Hans-Christian. "Gab's das wirklich? Migration in die DDR." In *Lebendige Erinnerungskultur für die Zukunft*, edited by Heiner Schmitt, 115–35. Tagungsdokumentationen zum Deutschen Archivtag 12. Fulda: Selbstverlag des VdA, 2008.

Hess, Sabine. "Migration als Teil der Stadtgeschichte: Lehren aus einem Ausstellungsprojekt zur Geschichte der Migration in München." In *Migranten in München, Archivische Überlieferung und Dokumentation: Dokumentation zum Kolloquium vom 20 Juli 2010 im Stadtarchiv München*, edited by Brigitte Huber, 9–19. Munich: Stadtarchiv, 2010.

Hoffmann, Dierk, Marita Krauss, and Michael Schwartz, eds. *Vertriebene in Deutschland: Interdisziplinäre Ergebnisse und Forschungsperspektiven*. Munich: Oldenbourg Verlag, 2000.

Holian, Anna M. *Between National Socialism and Soviet Communism: Social History, Popular Culture, and Politics in Germany*. Ann Arbor: University of Michigan Press, 2011.

Huber, Brigitte, ed. *Migranten in München, Archivische Überlieferung und Dokumentation: Dokumentation zum Kolloquium vom 20 Juli 2010 im Stadtarchiv München*. Munich: Stadtarchiv, 2010. Accessed 9 September 2014. http://www.muenchen.de/rathaus/dms/Home/Stadtverwaltung/Direktorium/Stadtarchiv/pdf/Migr.pdf.

Hughes, Michael L. *Shouldering the Burdens of Defeat*. Chapel Hill: University of North Carolina Press, 1999.

Hunn, Karin. *"Nächstes Jahr kehren wir zurück ..." Die Geschichte der türkischen "Gastarbeiter" in der Bundesrepublik*. Moderne Zeit 11. Göttingen: Wallstein, 2005.

Institut für Besatzungsfragen. *Das DP-Problem: Eine Studie über die ausländischen Flüchtlinge in Deutschland*. Tübingen: Mohr, 1950.

Jacobmeyer, Wolfgang. "Polnische Juden in der amerikanischen Besatzungszone Deutschlands 1946/47." *Vierteljahrshefte für Zeitgeschichte* 25 (1977). http://www.ifz-muenchen.de/heftarchiv/1977_1_4_jacobmeyer.pdf.

Jacobmeyer, Wolfgang. *Vom Zwangsarbeiter zum heimatlosen Ausländer: Die Displaced Persons in Westdeutschland, 1945–1951*. Kritische Studien zur Geschichtswissenschaft 65. Göttingen: Vandenhoeck & Ruprecht, 1985.

Krauss, Marita. "Das 'Wir' und das 'Ihr': Ausgrenzung, Abgrenzung, Identitätsstiftung bei Einheimischen und Flüchtlingen nach 1945." In *Vertriebene in Deutschland: Interdisziplinäre Ergebnisse und Forschungsperspektiven*, edited by Dierk Hoffmann, Marita Krauss, and Michael Schwartz, 27–39. Munich: Oldenbourg Verlag, 2000.

Kreienbrink, Axel. "Auswanderungslenkung und 'asistencia al emigrante': das Instituto Español de Emigración im franquistischen Spanien." In *Das "Gastarbeiter"-System: Arbeitsmigration und ihre Folgen in der Bundesrepublik Deutschland und Westeuropa*, edited by Jochen Oltmer, Axel Kreienbrink, and Carlos Sanz Díaz, 103–17. Schriftenreihe der Vierteljahrshefte für Zeitgeschichte 104. Munich: Oldenbourg, 2012.

Matuszewski, Nina. "DOMiD Dokumentationszentrum und Museum über die Migration in Deutschland e.V." In *Lebendige Erinnerungskultur für die Zukunft*, edited by Heiner Schmitt, 151–5. Tagungsdokumentationen zum Deutschen Archivtag 12. Fulda: Selbstverlag des VdA, 2008.

Moser, Eva. "'Gastarbeiter-Bilderbogen': Quellen zu ausländischen Arbeitskräften im Bayerischen Wirtschaftsarchiv." In *Migranten in München, Archivische Überlieferung und Dokumentation: Dokumentation zum Kolloquium vom 20 Juli 2010 im Stadtarchiv München*, edited by Brigitte Huber, 53–6. Munich: Stadtarchiv, 2010.

Novinšćak, Karolina. "Auf den Spuren von Brandts Ostpolitik und Titos Sonderweg: deutsch-jugoslawische Migrationsbeziehungen in den 1960er und 1970er Jahren." In *Das "Gastarbeiter"-System: Arbeitsmigration und ihre Folgen in der Bundesrepublik Deutschland und Westeuropa*, edited by Jochen Oltmer, Axel Kreienbrink, and Carlos Sanz Díaz, 133–48. Schriftenreihe der Vierteljahrshefte für Zeitgeschichte 104. Munich: Oldenbourg, 2012.

Oltmer, Jochen, Axel Kreienbrink, and Carlos Sanz Díaz, eds. *Das "Gastarbeiter"-System: Arbeitsmigration und ihre Folgen in der Bundesrepublik Deutschland und Westeuropa*. Schriftenreihe der Vierteljahrshefte für Zeitgeschichte 104. Munich: Oldenbourg, 2012.

Pfister, Peter. "Migration und Katholische Kirche: Quellen und Forschungsmöglichkeiten in katholischen Archiven." In *Migranten in München, Archivische Überlieferung und Dokumentation: Dokumentation zum Kolloquium vom 20 Juli 2010 im Stadtarchiv München*, edited by Brigitte Huber, 45–51. Munich: Stadtarchiv, 2010.

Poutrus, Patrice P. "Asylum in Postwar Germany: Refugee Admission Policies and Their Practical Implementation in the Federal Republic and the GDR between the Late 1940s and the Mid-1970s." In "Migration in Germany's Age of Globalization," edited by Victoria Harris, Barbara Könczöl, and David Motadel. Special issue, *Journal of Contemporary History* 49 (2014): 115–33.

Prat-Erkert, Cécile. "Une identité impossible? Le cas des demandeurs d'asile politique déboutés." In *Migrations et Identité: L'exemple de l'Allemagne aux XIXe et XXe siècles*, edited by Jean-Paul Cahn and Bernard Poloni, 83–90. Mondes germaniques. Villeneuve-d'Asq: Presses universitaires du Septentrion, impr. 2009.

Prontera, Grazia. "Das Emigrationszentrum in Verona: Anwerbung und Vermittlung italienischer Arbeitskräfte in die Bundesrepublik Deutschland 1955–1975." In *Das "Gastarbeiter"-System: Arbeitsmigration und ihre Folgen in der Bundesrepublik Deutschland und Westeuropa*, edited by Jochen Oltmer, Axel Kreienbrink, and Carlos Sanz Díaz, 89–102. Schriftenreihe der Vierteljahrshefte für Zeitgeschichte 104. Munich: Oldenbourg, 2012.

Rass, Christoph A. "Die Anwerbeabkommen der Bundesrepublik Deutschland mit Griechenland und Spanien im Kontext eines europäischen Migrationssystems." In *Das "Gastarbeiter"-System: Arbeitsmigration und ihre Folgen in der Bundesrepublik Deutschland und Westeuropa*, edited by Jochen Oltmer, Axel Kreienbrink, and Carlos Sanz Díaz, 53–69. Schriftenreihe der Vierteljahrshefte für Zeitgeschichte 104. Munich: Oldenbourg, 2012.

Ringsdorf, Ulrich. "Die Bestände des Lastenausgleichsarchivs." In *Vertriebene in Deutschland: Interdisziplinäre Ergebnisse und Forschungsperspektiven*, edited by Dierk Hoffmann, Marita Krauss, and Michael Schwartz, 421–6. Munich: Oldenbourg Verlag, 2000.

Schieder, Theodor, ed. *Documents on the Expulsion of the Germans from Eastern-Central-Europe: A Selection and Translation from Dokumentation der Vertreibung der Deutschenaus Ost-Mitteleuropa.* 4 vols. Translated by Vivian Stranders. Göttingen: Schwarz, 1956–61.

Schmitt, Heiner, ed. *Lebendige Erinnerungskultur für die Zukunft.* Tagungsdokumentationen zum Deutschen Archivtag 12. Fulda: Selbstverlag des VdA, 2008.

Schwartz, Michael. "Integration und Transformation: 'Umsiedler'-Politik und regionaler Strukturwandel in Mecklenburg-Vorpommern von 1945 bis 1953." In *Sozialismus auf dem platten Lande: Tradition und Transformation in Mecklenburg-Vorpommern von 1945 bis 1952,* edited by Damian van Melis, 135–94. Schwerin: Helms, 1999.

Schwartz, Michael. "'Vom Umsiedler zum Staatsbürger': Totalitäres und Subversives in der Sprachpolitik der DDR." In *Vertriebene in Deutschland: Interdisziplinäre Ergebnisse und Forschungsperspektiven,* edited by Dierk Hoffmann, Marita Krauss, and Michael Schwartz, 135–66. Munich: Oldenbourg Verlag, 2000.

Schwartz, Michael. *Funktionäre mit Vergangenheit.* Munich: Oldenbourg, 2013.

Severin-Barboutie, Bettina. "Stadt – Migration – Transformation: Stuttgart und Lyon im Vergleich." In *Das "Gastarbeiter"-System: Arbeitsmigration und ihre Folgen in der Bundesrepublik Deutschland und Westeuropa,* edited by Jochen Oltmer, Axel Kreienbrink, and Carlos Sanz Díaz, 233–45. Schriftenreihe der Vierteljahrshefte für Zeitgeschichte 104. Munich: Oldenbourg, 2012.

*Spiegel Online.* "Britische Geheimprotokolle: Kohl wollte offenbar jeden zweiten Türken loswerden." 1 August 2013. Accessed 17 May 2014. http://www.spiegel.de/politik/deutschland/kohl-wollte-jeden-zweiten-tuerken-in-deutschland-loswerden-a-914318.html.

Statistisches Bundesamt. *Statistisches Jahrbuch für die Bundesrepublik Deutschland 1953.* Stuttgart/Cologne: W. Kohlhammer, 1953.

Statistisches Reichsamt. *Statistisches Jahrbuch für das Deutsche Reich 1935.* Berlin: Verlag für Sozialpolitik, Wirtschaft und Statistik, 1935.

Stehkämper, Hugo. "Akten der Lastenausgleichsverwaltung." *Der Archivar. Mitteilungsblatt für deutsches Archivwesen* 22 (1969): 177–92.

Steinert, Johannes-Dieter. "Migration and Migration Policy: West Germany and the Recruitment of Foreign Labour, 1945–61." In "Migration in Germany's Age of Globalization," edited by Victoria Harris, Barbara Könczöl, and David Motadel. Special issue, *Journal of Contemporary History* 49 (2014): 9–27.

Suvak, Seva I. "Die Geschichte der Migration ist vielstimmig: Das migration-audio-archiv sammelt Biografien von Einwanderern." In *Lebendige Erinnerungskultur für die Zukunft,* edited by Heiner Schmitt, 148–50. Tagungsdokumentationen zum Deutschen Archivtag 12 Fulda: Selbstverlag des VdA, 2008.

Van Melis, Damian, ed. *Sozialismus auf dem platten Lande: Tradition und Transformation in Mecklenburg-Vorpommern von 1945 bis 1952.* Schwerin: Helms, 1999.

Wieser, Silvia-Maria. "Asylpolitik in Frankreich." PhD diss., University of Vienna, 2010. Accessed 9 September 2014. http://othes.univie.ac.at/10990/1/2010-08-17_0516265.pdf.

Wille, Manfred. "Die Vertriebenen und das politisch-staatliche System der SBZ/DDR." In *Vertriebene in Deutschland: Interdisziplinäre Ergebnisse und Forschungsperspektiven,* edited by Dierk Hoffmann, Marita Krauss, and Michael Schwartz, 203–17. Munich: Oldenbourg Verlag, 2000.

Williams, Helen. "Changing the National Narrative: Evolution in Citizenship and Integration in Germany 2000–2010." In "Migration in Germany's Age of Globalization," edited by Victoria Harris, Barbara Könczöl, and David Motadel. Special issue, *Journal of Contemporary History* 49 (2014): 54–74.

Wisotzky, Klaus, ed. *Fremd(e) im Revier!? Zuwanderung und Fremdsein im Ruhrgebiet; ein Projekt der Kulturhaupstadt Europas Ruhr. 2010 [eine Ausstellungsreihe der Ruhrgebietsarchive].* Essen: Klartext, 2010.

Withol De Wenden, Catherine. "L'Europe migratoire." In *L'Europe face à l'autre: Politiques migratoires et intégration européenne,* edited by Maximos Aligisakis and Matteo Gianni, 52–105. Europa 21. Geneva: Institut européen de l'Université de Genève, 2003.

**Klaus Lankheit** is currently chief archivist of the Institut für Zeitgeschichte, Munich–Berlin. He is an expert in modern records management and has published broadly on archival repositories and modern German history. He published *Preußen und die Frage der europäischen Abrüstung 1867–1870* (1993) and was co-editor of *Hitler: Reden, Schriften, Anordnungen* (1991–2003).

*Chapter 8*

# THINKING DIFFERENCE IN POSTWAR GERMANY
## Some Epistemological Obstacles around "Race"

*Rita Chin*

In October 2010, German Chancellor Angela Merkel stood before the annual gathering of the Christian Democratic Union's (CDU) youth organization, Junge Union, and declared, "The multicultural concept is a failure, an absolute failure."[1] This pointed statement elicited extended applause from her audience of young Christian Democrats. By the next morning, headlines in the domestic and international press proclaimed, "German multiculturalism has failed."[2] The speech was actually about much more than multiculturalism. Merkel had been invited to outline a vision for the youth wing of the CDU in advance of state elections in the spring. She detailed her views on many pressing issues forcefully: the Eurozone crisis, energy policy, Germany's aging population, unemployment, and the healthcare system. But this provocative assertion was what stuck.

Having written my first book on the emergence of multiculturalism in Germany, Merkel's pronouncement came as something of a surprise. In the late 1980s, after all, multiculturalism was still an open question, with critics and policymakers across the political spectrum actively debating the concept. By 1989, it had become so ubiquitous in mainstream political culture that even the CDU General Secretary at the time, Heiner Geißler, urged his conservative party to incorporate multicultural principles into its foreigner policy.[3] How, then, do we explain Merkel's unqualified dismissal of multiculturalism roughly twenty years later?

First, it is important to consider what exactly Merkel meant here. In terms of her words, what she actually said, she likened multiculturalism to a vague notion that Germans and guest workers would "live happily side by side."[4] She juxtaposed this concept with a demand for "integration."

---

Notes for this chapter begin on page 222.

"Those who want to have a part in our society," Merkel explained, "must not only obey our laws and know the constitution; they must, above all, learn our language." She elaborated further:

> It is correct that a language test be taken in union-governed states. It is important that students who go to school understand their teacher ... And it is, without question, important and correct to say that young girls must attend school field trips and participate in gym classes, and that we do not believe in forced marriages; they are not compatible with our laws.[5]

Multiculturalism, in this view, involved a laissez-faire approach to the coexistence of different cultures, whereas integration—the prerequisite for any successful coexistence—required immigrants to meet concrete demands. On one level, then, Merkel was making a policy statement: she rejected naïve celebrations of coexisting cultures in favor of a seemingly new and tougher approach to dealing with guest workers and their descendants.

On another level, though, Merkel was asserting a particular ideological position: immigrant differences (like language or gender norms) have no place in German society; ethnic and cultural diversity must ultimately give way to a single *Leitkultur* (dominant culture). Merkel's declaration, in a sense, was a repudiation of the very fact of multiculturalism, a rejection of this demographic experiment. And it was precisely this message that media outlets picked up on. It's worth asking again: how was it possible for Merkel to make such a statement in the face of an overwhelming demographic reality that Germany has lived with since the end of World War II?

Part of the answer, no doubt, has to do with the specific political context. Merkel's speech came after a string of public controversies around Turkish immigrants that autumn, touched off by the publication of feminist Alice Schwarzer's *Die große Verschleierung* (The Great Obfuscation) and Thilo Sarrazin's *Deutschland schafft sich ab* (Germany Does Away with Itself).[6] These books, both written by self-identified leftists, argued vociferously for the incompatibility of Muslim Turks with German society, culture, and values. Along with pressure from her own party to adopt a tougher stance on immigrants, these statements by members of the traditionally more open-minded left must have fueled Merkel's resolve.

But another part of the answer has to do with deeply ingrained perspectives on national identity, what it means to be German, and the central place of "difference" in structuring German conceptions of belonging. The fact that a head of state could declare so unequivocally that multiculturalism was an "absolute failure" bespoke a denial of the inevitable social and cultural transformations wrought by immigration. How do we explain this blindness? How do we explain this inability to perceive immigrants—after half a century of living side-by-side—as a recognizable part of the national German imaginary?

My chapter seeks to answer these questions by considering several orders of "epistemological obstacle" that have made it difficult for post-war Germans to apprehend certain kinds of "difference"—especially around guest workers and their descendants. I borrow this concept from French philosopher Gaston Bachelard, who coined the term to identify the unavoidable presence of preconceived and misleading ideas derived from the very nature of language and culture.[7] For Germans in the immediate postwar period, of course, the question of how to deal with groups of people understood as different from themselves was present in all sorts of forms: Holocaust survivors, displaced persons, expellees, occupation forces. Yet public discourse hardly registered the existence of guest work-ers in the first decades after their arrival, and most West Germans were remarkably silent on the place of labor migrants in their society until the late 1970s. Thus, part of what needs to be explained is the relative absence of guest workers in German public debate, how it came about, and what the long-term effects of the initial lack of engagement have been.

This chapter is divided into three sections, each of which deals with a distinct register of epistemological obstacle around immigrant "dif-ference" in German society. First, I unpack the historically constituted, ideological conditions that made "difference" an integral element of West German self-understanding *and*, at the same time, rendered guest workers largely invisible during the first decades of their residence in the Federal Republic. I focus here on three key frameworks: the project of democratization, the terms of the labor migration, and the legacy of Nazism. Next, I examine several psychic patterns that have frequently appeared in the public pronouncements around guest workers. The goal here is not to engage in some sort of collective psychoanalysis, but rather to bring a greater degree of analytical precision to our understanding of how the guest worker question has been discussed. Finally, I explore the cognitive limits created by the rejection of "race" as an acceptable or available category of analysis and understanding in German public discourse.

## Historical Conditions

If we are to grasp the crucial role of "difference" in constituting West German identity and society, it seems important to go back to the foun-dational moments of the Federal Republic. In the aftermath of World War II, the Allies (and the international community more generally) pressed

Germans to make a clean break from the Nazi regime by "disavowing state-sponsored racism" and publicly embracing democratization.[8] Part of this process involved re-education and denazification policies introduced during occupation. Re-education aimed at weaning Germans from undue respect for authority, while denazification sought to eliminate Nazis from public life and civil service. Both programs had significant limitations—above all, they were administered haphazardly from zone to zone. But they did push postwar Germans to reformulate the social and ideological parameters of their national identity. In particular, these policies underscored the fact that the Third Reich's national ideal of an Aryan *Volksgemeinschaft* (Nazi racial community) had been powerfully discredited by the Nazi defeat. Privileging of an Aryan master race, efforts to destroy the Jews, and the belief in biologically based, essential differences between groups of people were now firmly attached to the tarnished notion of *Rasse* (race). The concept itself had to be officially repudiated in order to transform West Germany into a democratic nation.

Beyond these formalized programs, the U.S. occupation greatly influenced how West Germans thought about the relationship between the nation and "difference." For one thing, the multi-ethnic composition of the occupation armies meant that former racial subordinates—whether Jews, Slavs, North Africans, or African-Americans—now held positions of authority over Germans as members of the Allied forces.[9] At the same time, the U.S. Army's practice of racial segregation and anti-black racism taught West Germans that "democratic forms and values" could be, as Heide Fehrenbach has argued, "consistent with racialist, even racist, ideology and social organization."[10] In this way, military occupation reinforced ideas of white supremacy across American and German cultures, thereby encouraging West Germans to reframe their conceptions of difference through a black/white lens. As they rejected the idea of *Rasse* and its associations, then, West Germans gradually absorbed alternative modes of racial distinction.

In grappling with the exigencies of the immediate postwar period, West German society developed a complex, even erratic, position towards race and difference. On the one hand, the category of *Rasse* was irrevocably tainted by the Nazi legacy, linked permanently to discredited forms of racial science, eugenics, and genocide. On the other hand, public leaders and political figures did not espouse a uniform or consistent policy against more immediate forms of racism in the present. Different expressions of racism were treated differently: for example, it became *impossible* to invoke *Rasse* in relation to Jewish Holocaust survivors who remained in Germany. Yet it *was* possible to accommodate the racialist binary of black/white in thinking about the "problem" of Afro-German children.

These two racial taxonomies were always understood as separate and discrete, in no way part of a related set of ideas about difference. While West Germans roundly condemned one taxonomy as racist or racialist, they unself-consciously relied on the other to develop social policy.

The emergence of the Cold War mandate pushed the project of democratization in a distinctly different direction. As divisions hardened between the Allies, the United States and Britain prioritized economic revival and integrating their zones into the western security alliance. The primary tasks of democratization thus shifted away from purging the remnants of Nazi influence and now lay in building a strong capitalist economy, shoring up democratic political institutions, and forging close economic and military relations with the Western powers.[11] For most West Germans, government ministers and ordinary citizens alike, economic prosperity became *the* measure of successful democratization.

The economic miracle, of course, also served as the crucial catalyst for bringing millions of visible foreigners back onto German soil. The economic takeoff that began in the 1950s created an urgent demand for manpower, which the native population was ill-equipped to provide. Facing a massive labor shortage, authorities inaugurated a guest worker program. The German Labor Minister signed a recruitment treaty with Italy in 1955, and concluded agreements with Spain, Portugal, Turkey, Greece, and Yugoslavia throughout the 1960s. By the fall of 1964, the number of foreign workers in West Germany surpassed one million; five years later, the figure had nearly doubled.

The basic parameters of the guest worker program offered a second framework for shaping the way West Germans perceived foreign laborers and the problem of "difference" in their society. The program's central premise was that migrants would come to the Federal Republic to work on a temporary, short-term basis. Political authorities and industrial leaders agreed on a system in which recruited laborers would rotate in and out of the German labor force based on production demands. Accordingly, labor treaties stipulated two-year work and residence permits in order to enforce the expectation of return to the country of origin. Citizenship law, moreover, reserved citizen status for those with German ancestry based on the principle of *jus sanguinis*. By this definition, guest workers were always foreigners. The postwar labor recruitment program presumed that the Federal Republic, at its core, was not an "immigration country." Guest workers were recruited *not* to become permanent additions to German society, but to provide labor for a limited period and then to leave.

Political leaders, furthermore, clung to this view long after shifting economic conditions had undermined the initial logic of short-term rotation.

By the early 1960s, firms employing foreigners realized that it cost more to import new workers every couple of years than to keep the trained ones and absorb the fluctuations in production demands. As rotation proved increasingly unprofitable, authorities ceased to enforce the rule of quick return: that is, they almost always granted extensions, effectively allowing Turks and other labor migrants to remain in Germany indefinitely. Guest workers, in turn, stretched their stays into years and even decades; many sent for their spouses and children, especially after 1973 when the Federal Republic halted further recruitment. By the mid-1970s, moreover, Turks had surpassed Italians and all other nationalities as the largest community of foreigners in West Germany. Yet despite the fact that permanent settlement belied the rhetoric of temporary residence, political leaders regularly intoned the same basic mantra on the question of pluralism: "the Federal Republic is not a country of immigration."

For most West Germans, this approach to labor migration made it difficult to apprehend guest workers as a significant or legitimate part of the social fabric. Everyday slights such as serving fellow Germans first, telling off-color jokes about Italians and Greeks, refusing to rent an apartment to Yugoslavs, or using derogatory phrases such as *Türkenkoffer* to describe the cheap plastic grocery bags favored by Turks seemed like excusable, minor infractions against transient populations, rather than evidence of systematic discrimination or prejudice that indicated an endemic social problem. But even the decision to house guest workers in barracks on the outskirts of town, or city ordinances restricting Turks from living in certain neighborhoods, or the disproportionate number of foreigners concentrated in the dirtiest, harshest, and most unpleasant kinds of work generally did not register as racism, because guest workers were not understood as members of West German society. Racism, in this view, could only be present if prejudice and discrimination were directed against a portion of one's own population. And once ideas about race and difference were redefined around a black/white binary over the course of the 1950s, the possibilities for recognizing racialized or racist attitudes and behaviors beyond this horizon decreased substantially.

But perhaps the most immediate reason for the abiding blindness toward guest workers has to do with the long shadow cast by Nazism. Serious public discussion of the Nazi past began in the late 1950s and gained momentum during the first half of the 1960s.[12] These debates were intensified by young leftists who wanted to purge postwar society of what they saw as the lingering effects of Nazi fascism. As the 1968ers came of age, many became increasingly dissatisfied with the clipped descriptions of the Nazi era in their schoolbooks. They began to pose more pointed questions to their parents, and the most radical among them openly "condemned [the elder] generation both for its complicity with Nazism and its conspicuous silence about the Nazi period."[13]

The critique leveled by young leftists was intimately bound up with the West German version of liberal democracy built and embraced by their parents.[14] According to many 1968ers, this "Auschwitz generation" had blindly pursued capitalist prosperity and embraced anticommunism at the expense of taking responsibility for Nazi crimes. The failure to deal with the past, these New Leftists reasoned, meant that fascism had not been fully rooted out of German society. "Far from viewing the Federal Republic as democratic in any meaningful sense, the students viewed its political institutions as totally corrupt, and as themselves facilitating an imminent reconstitution of fascism in West Germany."[15] The sense of continuity, moreover, was bolstered by young leftists' theoretical understanding of Nazism, which interpreted fascism as a product of the highest stage of capitalism.

The New Left's preoccupation with capitalism and fascism had a number of unintended consequences. For one thing, this theoretical position unwittingly led radical critics to "subsume the singularity" of the Nazi genocide under the "generic category of fascism."[16] The effect was to obscure the distinctiveness of National Socialism as it had developed in Germany, downplaying the anti-Semitic aspects of Nazism and ignoring its Jewish victims.[17] But the fixation on capitalism and fascism also obscured the growing importance of new forms of race and difference for West German society.[18] To be sure, a handful of leftist artists and intellectuals did extend their criticism to the guest worker program.[19] In most cases, though, the exploitation of foreign workers simply offered an extreme example of West Germany's indifference to the human costs of unbridled capitalism. By framing their social critique through capitalism and fascism, New Leftists were highly conscious of the structural continuities between the Nazi regime and the Federal Republic, but surprisingly oblivious to the ways in which social actors and conditions had changed.

In important respects, these three historical frameworks laid the groundwork for an ideological common sense about the place of racial and ethnic "difference" in the Federal Republic. Embracing democracy did not mean that racial distinctions disappeared, but rather they were reformulated in terms of a black/white binary that seemed to have limited relevance for German society. Guest workers (as well as many Holocaust survivors and displaced persons, for that matter) were understood as foreigners, and thus unimaginable as members of the national body. And especially with the maturation of 1968ers, vigilance against any expression of Nazi fascism represented *the* central task of Germany's engagement with difference in the postwar period.

## Psychic Patterns

What is clear from this common sense is that guest workers and their descendants did not figure very prominently in how postwar Germans thought about racial and ethnic difference. And yet, the tendency to downplay their presence and significance for German society has often flown in the face of ground-level reality. I want to turn now to a second register of epistemological obstacle that manifests itself in terms of what I will loosely describe as "psychic patterns." I propose drawing on the Freudian concepts of *Verleugnung* (disavowal) and *Verneinung* (negation), not so much to diagnose some kind of deep-seated German psychosis, but to help illuminate some of the recurring rhetorics and logics in the German public discourse around guest workers and minority groups more generally. Here, I am following the lead of anthropologist Didier Fassin, who has used these concepts to explain the French denial of racial discrimination.[20]

Freud developed the ideas of *Verleugnung* and *Verneinung* in an attempt to understand how people deal with ambivalence and contradiction, and especially traumatic perceptions. He began using *Verleugnung* to refine his theory of the "phallic phase" and explain the attitude of the boy who refuses to recognize the absence of a penis in a girl. In one of his first case studies, he observed that little boys firmly believe "a genital like their own is to be attributed to everyone they know. This conviction is energetically maintained by boys [and] is obstinately defended against the contradictions which soon result from observation."[21] Disavowal, in Freud's view, refers to the mental act of rejecting a perception as inconceivable.[22]

We can see this mechanism at work in the German public discussions of guest workers. Indeed, starting in the late 1970s at precisely the moment when it became impossible to deny labor migrants' long-term residence on any practical level, political leaders—especially from the ruling CDU party—began to insist that "the Federal Republic is not a country of immigration." Chancellor Helmut Kohl repeated this catchphrase throughout his sixteen-year rule virtually every time the question of guest workers and foreigner policy came up. A similar rhetorical strategy is also at work in Merkel's recent pronouncement. "We are a country," she stated, "that brought guest workers to Germany at the beginning of the 1960s. And now they live among us. We kidded ourselves for a while that they wouldn't stay. But that's not the reality." In the next breath, though, Merkel declared "multiculturalism is an absolute failure," effectively denying the social consequences of the demographic experiment.[23] In each case, the growing evidence that guest workers and their descendants have become a permanent part of German society contradicts the dominant conception of German identity. This revelation is too troubling to be accepted, so it is simply disavowed.

*Verneinung*, according to Freud, is the psychic process by which an intolerable thought is rejected at the very moment it is formulated. In his short essay "Negation," he explains that when a patient says,

> "You ask who this person in the dream can be. It's not my mother." ... In our interpretation, we take the liberty of disregarding the negation and of picking out the subject-matter alone of the association. It is as though the patient had said: "It's true that my mother came into my mind as I thought of this person, but I don't feel inclined to let the association count."[24]

Negation, Freud suggests, is a defense mechanism that is more supple than repression because it preserves the thought content that repression would render unconscious. What makes negation defensive is its distancing effect, which allows the patient to avoid accepting the disagreeable implications of a thought that has successfully formed. Negation thus involves acknowledging the troubling idea, but immediately rejecting it because of the discomfort it provokes.[25] Hence, the logic: it is not what you think.

This kind of reflex has manifested itself quite frequently in the political responses to campaigns or violence against guest workers and immigrants. The 1979 coalition of leftists who organized the inaugural "Rock gegen Rechts" (Rock against the Right) event in Frankfurt, for example, enacted a version of negation. Seeking a peaceful and inclusive way to challenge the inroads of the far-right Nationaldemokratische Partei Deutschlands (NPD, National Democratic Party of Germany), planners modeled the concert on the "Rock against Racism" festivals that had begun in Britain three years earlier. By choosing the British "Rock against Racism" event as their template, they seemed to acknowledge that the crucial objection to the NPD was its racist ideology, its explicitly racist position on guest workers and immigrants. Yet in renaming their event "Rock gegen Rechts," organizers effectively dismissed this insight, opting instead to frame the problem in Germany as right-wing extremism. German society did not suffer from systemic racism, they suggested, but rather from the antics of the radical right fringe.

Similarly, the official political response to the spate of violence against guest workers, contract workers, immigrants, and asylum seekers in the early 1990s also followed a pattern of negation. From Hoyerswerda in 1991 to Rostock in 1992 to Mölln and Solingen in 1993, young hooligans, skinheads, and right-wing extremists carried out a series of vicious assaults against foreigners. They attacked hostels housing asylum seekers and the homes of Turkish guest workers, often to the chorus of "Foreigners out!"

and "Germany for the Germans." These incidents prompted widespread public outcry, especially after the fire bombings of Turkish homes. Between December 1992 and January 1993, nearly two million Germans participated in candlelight vigils to condemn racism and demand public action against racial violence. Yet politicians dismissed the problem by shifting the focus to the abuse of Germany's generous asylum law.[26] Instead of formulating policies to prevent attacks against immigrants and foreigners, government leaders debated and passed legislation to curb the "uncontrollable flow" of refugees. "By linking these two issues," Helsinki Watch has argued, "the government failed to acknowledge the severity of the crimes being committed against foreigners by German citizens. Instead it subtly shifted the blame to foreigners themselves."[27]

In contrast to Fassin, who has used *Verleugnung* and *Verneinung* to differentiate two distinct moments in the French denial of racial discrimination, I want to suggest that both mechanisms have been in play simultaneously in German political discourse. In the German case, they offer a reservoir of rhetorical strategies for debating the guest worker question. They routinely appear, moreover, at any hint that German society itself might be required to change as a consequence of its labor recruitment policy and the presence of immigrants. Kohl as well as Merkel disavowed the effects of the guest worker program, refusing the very idea that Germany had become a country of immigration or a multicultural society. And even in 1999, when the socialist-green coalition under Chancellor Gerhard Schröder expected to pass a monumental reform of German citizenship law effectively affirming the country's "irreversible process of immigration," the CDU/CSU launched a populist campaign to oppose the new law and especially the provision of dual citizenship that garnered over five million signatures.[28] Progressive activists as well as conservative political leaders shifted attention away from the prospect of persistent racism in the Federal Republic, minimizing racially motivated campaigns and violence as the actions of a few right-wing extremists and disaffected youth. These reflexive responses, whether in the form of disavowal or negation, transcend individual contexts, single regimes, or even political partisanship. Their very ubiquity suggests just how troubling the social and cultural impacts of immigration on Germany remain.

## Cognitive Limits

If the psychic mechanisms I have just outlined worked to deny or deflect the ground-level effects of guest workers on the Federal Republic, the unavailability of "race" as an analytic category has made the process of coming to terms with immigration and its consequences even more difficult. In the immediate postwar period, the term *Rasse* quickly became taboo, and the language of race was largely expunged from public discourse. Race thus ceased to be an explicit or widely invoked frame of reference for most Germans after 1945. As I have suggested, this repudiation took hold as part of the Federal Republic's democratizing process. And it was further bolstered by the 1968ers' commitment to *Vergangenheitsbewältigung* (coming to terms with the past). A crucial component of overcoming Germany's fascist past was policing any action, attitude, or language that smacked of Nazism. In this respect, there has been symbolic capital attached not just to the term *Rasse*, but also to its *absence*. As Claudia Lohrenscheit, a former consultant to the German Institute for Human Rights has explained, "in not using it, people show where they stand when they don't write down or say the term."[29] This symbolic investment perpetuates a related pair of assumptions. First, any use of the term *Rasse* is tantamount to endorsing a worldview that categorizes and ranks groups of people based on biological differences. But also the converse: namely, avoiding the use of *Rasse* is assumed to eradicate the racialist and racist worldview that the word signifies.

At this point, I want to consider a couple of examples in order to tease out the cognitive limits created by this conception of race and its proscription in German public discourse. One occurred during the run-up to the 2006 World Cup in Germany. I learned about the incident from Heide Fehrenbach, who subsequently analyzed it in our co-authored introduction to *After the Nazi Racial State*.[30] In a match between fourth-division German football teams Halle and Sachsen Leipzig, Halle fans mocked Sachsen Leipzig's midfielder Adebowale Ogungbure from Nigeria, making "monkey noises" every time he touched the ball. At the end of the match, fans spat on him and taunted him with racist epithets.[31] Ogungbure initially ignored the abuse and kept walking. But as he passed the grandstand to a crescendo of jungle sounds, he turned to the crowd, put two fingers above his mouth to simulate a Hitler mustache, and thrust his right arm forward in a Nazi salute. Ogungbure's gestures elicited angry responses from some of the fans, who physically attacked him with a corner flag and put him in a stranglehold. German authorities responded to the incident not by identifying and detaining the spectators who had assaulted Ogungbure. Instead, the Halle police investigated the Nigerian for "unconstitutional behavior" because he had made the Nazi salute.[32]

Juxtapose this case with an incident from December 2010. On the train from Kassel to Frankfurt, two policemen asked a twenty-six-year-old black German architecture student to show his ID. When he refused, claiming that the request was discriminatory and reminiscent of "Nazi methods," they hauled him off the train and held him at the police station. The student was released after surrendering his driver's license, which confirmed his German citizenship. But he was charged with slander for accusing the police of SS behavior. Outraged at his treatment in this particular incident and indignant at having been subjected to random ID checks at least ten times previously on the same train route, the young man (who chose to remain anonymous throughout the process) sued the police for discrimination. During the trial before a Koblenz administrative court, one of the officers admitted that he had singled out the young man based on skin color, explaining that this practice was normal if a person looked like he or she might be in the country illegally. The judge ruled that under German law, on certain train routes believed to be frequented by illegal immigrants, federal police are permitted to ask for identification papers of people who appear to be foreigners even without the suspicion of wrong-doing. The student subsequently appealed the decision to a higher court, which overturned the initial ruling by arguing that skin color could not be the decisive factor in determining whether or not to conduct an identity check. But for about eight months and with relatively little fanfare, the Federal Republic legally sanctioned ID checks based on passengers' physical traits for train routes suspected of being used by illegal immigrants.[33]

In certain respects, these cases were quite similar. Both incidents involved people of African descent, who were subjected to racial stereotyping and harassment. Both victims pointed out the connection between their experiences of contemporary German racism and the Nazi racist past. Both young men initially faced legal charges stemming from their commentary—in essence, for violating the taboo of openly invoking Nazism. And in both cases, authorities studiously avoided addressing the broader questions of racial discrimination and racism in German society that had provoked the comparison in the first place.

Yet, there were also some important differences. One was the legal status of the victims. Ogungbure was from Nigeria, a foreign, journeyman player making a stop in the German football league. The architecture student, by contrast, was born and raised in Germany, a German citizen of African descent. A second difference emerged in terms of the authorities' initial responses. The Halle police treated the confrontation between Ogungbure and the football fans as a violation of the criminal code's article 86a, which prohibits using symbols of unconstitutional organizations such as the Nazi Party. At least for these authorities, miming a "Nazi" gesture registered as a racist act more emphatically than taunting and bodily attacks based on skin color. The Koblenz administrative court, by contrast, endorsed the police decision to target the architecture student for a random ID check. It effectively legalized racial profiling, ignoring the ways in which such a ruling resembled Nazi race-based laws and practices.

What, then, can we glean from these incidents about the absence of "race" and the cognitive limits this lacuna has engendered? At the most basic level, they underscore that the assumptions of *Rasse* have in fact persisted in German public life, in spite of the term's taboo status. Both Ogungbure and the architecture student were singled out and mistreated because of the color of their skin, even if authorities were unwilling to acknowledge the presence of racial thinking. In this way, we see how even concepts that have been repudiated as pernicious ideological fictions can nonetheless have very real, indeed concrete, social and juridical effects. But *Rasse* has continued to operate in public thinking on another level, too. Germany's firm commitment to dealing with its past of racial discrimination, hatred, and genocide, ironically, has meant that race *is* present even in its absence. No other country has confronted its troubled history in such a self-reflective and socially pervasive manner. The task is a paramount responsibility of the Federal Republic and must remain an ongoing obligation. But at this historical moment, at this political conjuncture, it also behooves us to acknowledge that the *presence of a seemingly absent Rasse* has created a number of blind spots around "difference," which have hindered Germany's efforts to deal with the consequences of postwar immigration.

For one thing, the notion of race that continues to be operative is fossilized, even ossified, in its Nazi definitions and associations. On the one hand, merely invoking Nazi signs indicates the presence of racism, regardless of whether such symbols are employed to express approval of Nazism or to condemn its racist logics. Hence, Ogungbure and the architecture student both initially faced legal prosecution for their references to Nazism. On the other hand, any public reference to Nazi signs trumps other articulations of racism operating simultaneously. Thus, German authorities failed to take seriously the anti-black racism directed at both Ogungbure and the architecture student. In the Ogungbure incident, the president of the Halle football club claimed not to have heard any "discriminatory expressions" within his earshot, while his counterpart for Sachsen Leipzig downplayed the harassment as "misguided fervor on the part of the fans." And in the train incident, the arresting officer seemed to have little consciousness that ID checking passengers based on skin color could be construed as a form of racism. Vigilance against Nazi forms of racism, in short, has been both rigidly literal and selective in application. Whereas the literal invocation of a sign or term linked to Nazism triggers immediate recognition of the presence of *Rasse* and often results in criminalization, more oblique reliance on racial logics or racialized assumptions is often not understood as connected to race at all. Because the train case involved ferreting out illegal immigrants, a context completely divorced from Nazi associations for most Germans, it was possible for the Koblenz administrative court to sanction racial profiling and completely miss the policy's recapitulation of Nazi race thinking.

In all of these ways, postwar German ideas about race continue to be informed—indeed, defined—by an older notion of *Rasse*, with its emphasis on biologically based conceptions of difference. Because *Rasse* and "race" are conjoined in this way, it has been somewhat easier to recognize contemporary forms of racism in their most obvious guise: as acts of prejudice or bigotry driven by skin color or other somatic features. This understanding, moreover, was inadvertently reinforced under U.S. occupation, as postwar Germans learned that black/white racial distinctions were fully compatible with democracy. Thus, it is not so surprising that the German media reported the harassment experienced by both Ogungbure and the architecture student as examples of racism, despite the initial distraction with Nazi associations.[34] The category of *Rasse* fit these individuals in its most straightforward form.

Ultimately, though, continuing to see race through the Nazi lens has not just resulted in the repudiation of *Rasse* because of its association with a set of natural, biological differences. This perspective has also made it nearly impossible to grasp the broader, more open-ended ways in which race operates at the level of representation and social experience: race as a mutable and capacious category of discourse, culture, and history that is always in formation, always absorbing and mobilizing different symbols, traits, or vocabularies to mark essential, incommensurable difference. In many ways, German insistence on this epistemological narrowness makes sense. A fluid conception of race, after all, contradicts the idea of *Rasse* as a specifically Nazi way of understanding human difference, a mode of thinking that Germans have spent the last seventy years trying to transcend. But this circumscription has also come with an unexpected price: namely, a certain blindness to the racial assumptions that authorize the increasingly commonsense view of Muslim Turks as fundamentally incompatible with Germans. Within this framework, the oppression of Turkish women, the propensity of Turkish men to violence, and the poor performance of Turkish children in the German educational system all remain uninterrogated "truths" that corroborate an inevitable conclusion—that Muslims simply cannot be integrated.

It also seems important to acknowledge that this pattern has extended to scholarly debate. There has, in fact, been a notable silence on the question of race in the post-1945 period, as if the problem largely disappeared with the collapse of the Third Reich. To the extent that the issue has been taken up, scholars have generally focused on the contexts of U.S. military occupation and Americanization.[35] But even for earlier periods, the tendency has been to limit inquiries on race and difference to highly specific episodes—Germany's colonial projects in Africa and Asia, the experience of Rhineland occupation during the interwar period, or the Nazi state.[36] This inclination to circumscribe the relevance of race as a category of analysis has made it difficult to grasp both the continuities and discontinuities in racial ideologies across modern German history. An important exception here is Wolfgang Benz, former director of the Zentrum für Antisemitismusforschung (Center for Anti-Semitism Research), who stirred up controversy by suggesting that contemporary fears about the Islamization of Europe resemble nineteenth-century anti-Semitism. Certain twenty-first-century critics of Islamic headscarves and minarets, he has argued, employ similar means to those of radical anti-Semites in constructing their images of the enemy.[37] It is worth noting, though, that Benz studiously avoids the terms "race" or "*Rasse*" in drawing these connections.

Most fundamentally perhaps, there has been a conceptual inability to distinguish race as a fixed, almost natural category of difference from what scholars in other fields now refer to as "racial formation" or "racialization," processes that repurpose "race" as a tool of critical analysis. "Race," in the latter framework, is understood as a socially constructed, historically contingent category of essential difference. "The meaning of race," as Michael Omi and Howard Winant first suggested over thirty years ago, "is defined and contested in both collective action and personal practice." In the process, they argue, "racial categories themselves are formed, transformed, destroyed and re-formed."[38] Racial formation, then, refers to the process of investing meaning in racial categories—"the extension of racial meaning to relationships, social practices, or groups" previously understood in non-racial terms.[39] Such a notion of race has been largely unavailable in the German context, foreclosed by the ossified definition of *Rasse*. But precisely because the meaning of *Rasse* has remained trapped in the past, it seems particularly important for historians of postwar Germany to invest this term with critical possibilities so as to better understand the present.

Nevertheless, many historians continue to resist the notion that Anglo-American conceptions of "race" might be usefully applied to Germany because of the country's singular past. In this respect, German scholars have adopted a position similar to that of their French counterparts, who dismiss the English-language notion of race as "un-French."[40] While it is necessary to remain cognizant of the historical specificity of *Rasse* and "race," there has been a lack of clarity about the divergent careers of these two concepts. In postwar Germany, *Rasse* was dismissed as bankrupt and repudiated precisely because of its vexed association with National Socialism. But in the United States, "race" has cycled through many conceptual lives and political projects. Used initially to connote essentializing logics of difference in specific North American contexts (e.g., pro-slavery ideology in the antebellum South or the Jim Crow claim of separate but equal), the concept has more recently been deployed precisely to deconstruct and historicize those older ways of thinking. Many U.S. scholars now see race as a mutable and historically contingent ideological construct, a flexible framework for apprehending ideas of difference in their particular contexts. In this sense, it seems to me, American efforts at demystifying race are eminently exportable. What they help us to see are the more localized ways of constructing difference—whether in relation to physical attributes, culture, nationality, or religion—that are never transparently "real" in the older modes of nineteenth-century racial science or Jim Crow, but which nonetheless continue to have historical efficacy, especially when they are unmarked, unnamed, and above all, undiscussed. Indeed, this is why so many U.S. black critics have rejected the notion of a postracial America, even after the election of Barack Obama as the president of the United States.[41]

In short, the refusal of many scholars and policymakers to take the key role of race in the Federal Republic seriously has come at a high cost. This stance has made it extremely difficult to grasp the myriad ways in which assumptions of essential difference naturalize the legal and social exclusion of Turks—from the basic expectations inscribed in the term "guest worker" to the reluctance to revise Germany's outdated citizenship law based on blood and ancestry; from the vociferous insistence by many contemporary critics that Turks are inassimilable to the continuing struggle to imagine any notion of a national culture that might encompass different traditions, customs, values, and religions. Thinking through "race" in the sense of racial *formation* or racial*ization*, then, is absolutely crucial for grasping the obvious and not-so-obvious ways in which difference has structured and continues to structure postwar German society.

The problem of difference in contemporary Germany ultimately connects back to Angela Merkel's bold pronouncement of multiculturalism as an obvious failure, a past experiment that must be recognized as unsuccessful. At a very basic level, this rhetorical move suggests the considerable stakes—ideological, cultural, and political—of the broader patterns this chapter has tried to explicate. To occlude "race" as a category of national discourse is not simply a matter of rhetorical preference or mere semantics. In this case, especially, it has also served to enable broader forms of social blindness, new modes of erasure. Without a more fluid conception of race, it is virtually impossible to describe and critique with any precision the complicated exchange between Ogungbure and Halle soccer fans, the assumptions about illegal immigrants that made the black architecture student a target for repeated ID checks, or the reflexive belief that Turkish girls are subjected to forced marriage. Without a more capacious conception of race, it's all too easy to pronounce the recent experiments with multiculturalism over, as if the ongoing patterns and complications of everyday coexistence don't continue irrespective of official declarations. By engaging more directly and seriously with the problems of race on the ground, we begin the hard work of imagining what a more vibrant, multiethnic democracy might look like in the future.

## Notes

1. "Integration: Merkel erklärt Multikulti für gescheitert," *Spiegel Online*, 16 October 2010, accessed 17 July 2013, http://www.spiegel.de/politik/deutschland/integration-merkel-erklaert-multikulti-fuer-gescheitert-a-723532.html.

2. On the web, for instance, Merkel's pronouncement produced immediate headlines: "Merkel says German Multicultural Society has Failed," BBC News, 17 October 2010, accessed 16 September 2013, http://www.bbc.co.uk/news/world-europe-11559451; "Chancellor Merkel says German Multiculturalism Has 'Utterly Failed'," Deutsche Welle, 17 October 2010, accessed 16 September 2013, http://www.dw.de/chancellor-merkel-says-german-multiculturalism-has-utterly-failed/a-6118859; "Merkel says German Multiculturalism Has Failed," Reuters News Service, 16 October 2010, accessed 16 September 2013, http://www.reuters.com/article/2010/10/16/us-germany-merkel-immigration-idUSTRE69F1K320101016.

3. Rita Chin, *The Guest Worker Question in Postwar Germany* (Cambridge: Cambridge University Press, 2007), 216.

4. All quotes from Merkel's speech are from a transcript I made from the YouTube video of Merkel's entire speech at the Deutschlandstag der Junge Union, 16 October 2010, accessed 19 July 2013, http://www.youtube.com/watch?v=WaEg8aM4fcc.

5. Angela Merkel, Deutschlandstag der Junge Union, 16 October 2010, YouTube video, accessed 19 July 2013, http://www.youtube.com/watch?v=WaEg8aM4fcc.

6. Alice Schwarzer, *Die große Verschleierung. Für Integration, gegen Islamismus* (Cologne: Kiepenheuer & Witsch, 2010); Thilo Sarrazin, *Deutschland schafft sich ab. Wie wir unser Land aufs Spiel setzen* (Munich: DVA, 2010).

7. Bachelard is primarily concerned with scientific thought and "objective knowledge." But his insight into the effect of epistemological obstacles to our understanding of the world is useful for me as well, especially his recognition that "obstacles arise in the act of cognition because the mind is not a tabula rasa" (p. 6). Bachelard explicitly discusses values, social feelings, and moral feelings as examples of epistemological obstacles. See Gaston Bachelard, *The Formation of the Scientific Mind*, trans. Mary McAllester Jones (Manchester: Clinamen Press, 2002), 24–32. I first became aware of Bachelard's

concept of the "epistemological obstacle" from a lecture given by Didier Fassin, "The Denial of Racial Discrimination," University of Michigan, Ann Arbor, 29 January 2013, unpublished manuscript. I thank Didier Fassin for sharing the text of his unpublished lecture with me.

8. Heide Fehrenbach, *Race after Hitler: Black Occupation Children in Postwar Germany and America* (Princeton: Princeton University Press, 2005), 4.

9. Heide Fehrenbach, "Black Occupation Children and the Devolution of the Nazi Racial State" in *After the Nazi Racial State: Difference and Democracy in Germany and Beyond*, eds. Rita Chin, Heide Fehrenbach, Geoff Eley, and Atina Grossmann (Ann Arbor: University of Michigan Press, 2009), 32.

10. Fehrenbach, "Black Occupation Children," 34.

11. For useful discussions on the efforts to deal with the Nazi past during the early Federal Republic, see Norbert Frei, *Adenauer's Germany and the Nazi Past*, trans. Joel Golb (New York: Columbia University Press, 2002); and Jeffrey Herf, *Divided Memory: The Nazi Past in the Two Germanys* (Cambridge, MA: Harvard University Press, 1999).

12. The increase in discussion was spurred by a number of events, big and small: a welter of anti-Semitic graffiti and especially the appearance of swastikas on the newly rebuilt Cologne synagogue on Christmas Eve 1959; the Adolph Eichmann trial in Jerusalem that began in 1961; the Auschwitz trials in Frankfurt between 1963 and 1965; and the mid-1960s parliamentary debate over extending the statute of limitations for Nazi war crimes. See Axel Schildt, *Ankunft im Westen: Ein Essay zur Erfolgsgeschichte der Bundesrepublik* (Frankfurt a.M.: Fischer, 1999); Detlef Siegfried, "Zwischen Aufarbeitung und Schlußstricht: Der Umgang mit der NS-Vergangenheit in den beiden deutschen Staaten," in Axel Schildt, Detlef Siegfried, and Karl Christian Lammers, eds., *Dynamische Zeiten: Die 60er Jahre in den beiden deutschen Gesellschaften* (Hamburg: Christians, 2000), 77–113; Michael Schmidtke, *Der Aufbruch der jungen Intelligenz: Die 68er-Jahre in der Bundesrepublik und den USA* (Frankfurt a.M.: Campus, 2003); Friso Wielenga, "An Inability to Mourn? The German Federal Republic and the Nazi Past," *European Review* 11, no. 4 (2003): 551–72; Jeremy Varon, *Bringing the War Home: The Weather Underground, the Red Army Faction, and Revolutionary Violence in the Sixties and Seventies* (Berkeley: University of California Press, 2004), 31–2; and Philipp Gassert and Alan E. Steinweis, eds., *Coping with the Nazi Past: West German Debates on Nazism and Generational Conflict, 1955–1975* (New York: Berghahn, 2006).

13. Varon, *Bringing the War Home*, 31.

14. To 1968ers, as Andy Markovits and Phil Gorski put it, "the Federal Republic's coming to terms with its past seemed shallow and false. Instead of really getting to the roots of … the origins of fascism, West Germany was busily constructing a self-serving ideology of rabid anti-communism. This credo … had blocked the process of democratic reform in West Germany. Just as anti-communism had replaced democracy in this 'feel good' Germany, so too did general prosperity mask the immense social costs of capitalism. It was necessary, the Left argued, to confront the brutal facts of the past head on …" Andrei S. Markovits and Philip S. Gorski, *The German Left: Red, Green and Beyond* (New York: Polity Press, 1993), 52.

15. John Abromeit, "The Limits of Praxis," in *Changing the World, Changing Oneself*, ed. Belinda Davis et al. (New York: Berghahn, 2010), 26.

16. Markovits and Gorski, *The German Left*, 52.

17. Hans Kundnani, *Utopia or Auschwitz: Germany's 1968 Generation and the Holocaust* (New York: Columbia University Press, 2009), 17–19. New Left intellectuals—and the more politically conservative West German historical profession—had not yet acknowledged

the uniqueness of National Socialist crimes or the single-mindedness with which the Nazi regime pursued its Jewish victims. The historical centrality of the Holocaust for understanding National Socialism only tentatively emerged in the 1970s and gained momentum in the 1980s and beyond. On this point, see Nicolas Berg, *Der Holocaust und die westdeutschen Historiker. Erforschung und Erinnerung* (Göttingen: Wallstein, 2003).

18. In fact, some New Left activists also condemned Israeli foreign policy as imperialistic and fascistic vis-à-vis the Palestinians, particularly following the Six-Day War. In protest, a handful of West German "urban guerillas" planted a bomb, which did not detonate, in a synagogue in Berlin on the anniversary of Kristallnacht, 9 November 1969. In his recent book, Wolfgang Kraushaar argues that manifest anti-Semitism was not limited to the radical right, but informed the actions of the radical left as well. Wolfgang Kraushaar, *Die Bombe im Jüdischen Gemeindehaus* (Hamburg: Hamburger Edition, 2005). See also the useful September 2007 book review by Karrin M. Hanshew for H-Net Book Review Project, in which she notes that "Members of both the liberal and radical Left seconded... the belief that 'there are no left-wing antisemites[sic]!' and remained stubbornly deaf to traditional anti-Jewish sentiments resurfacing in anti-imperialist critiques of Israel and calls for Palestinian liberation." Also Matthias Brosch, Michael Elm, Norman Geißler, Brigitta Elise Simbürger, and Oliver von Wrochem, eds., *Exklusive Solidarität. Linker Antisemitismus in Deutschland. Vom Idealismus zur Antiglobalisierungsbewegung* (Berlin: Metropol-Verlag, 2007). For a different analysis of the New Left's relationship with the Nazi past, see Dagmar Herzog, *Sex after Fascism* (Princeton: Princeton University Press, 2005).

19. The filmmaker Rainer Fassbinder, the social activist Günter Walraff, and the SPD's Young Socialists all questioned the treatment of guest workers in the Federal Republic. Fassbinder's 1969 film, *Katzelmacher*, depicted the miserable existence of a Greek guest worker. Walraff published a book in 1973 with a chapter on the living conditions of guest workers called, *"'Guestworkers' or Capitalism as Usual."* It is worth noting that recent scholarship has claimed that Walraff was a paid informant for the Stasi, the East German secret police. According to Hubertus Knabe, for example, Walraff received information for his books from the Stasi. See Knabe, *Die unterwanderte Republik: Stasi im Westen* (Berlin: Propyläen, 1999).

20. Didier Fassin, "The Denial of Racial Discrimination" (lecture, Center for European Studies, University of Michigan, Ann Arbor, 29 January 2013).

21. Sigmund Freud, *Three Essays on the Theory of Sexuality*, trans. and ed. James Strachey (New York: Avon, 1965). See especially the first case study.

22. See Freud's *Introductory Lectures on Psychoanalysis*, 1916–17, trans. and ed. James Strachey (New York: Norton, 1977), which is where he starts to use the term *"verleugnen"* regularly.

23. Merkel, Deutschlandstag der Junge Union, 16 October 2010, YouTube video, accessed 19 July 2013, http://www.youtube.com/watch?v=WaEg8aM4fcc.

24. Sigmund Freud, "Negation" in *The Standard Edition of the Complete Psychological Works of Sigmund Freud, Volume XIX (1923–1925): The Ego and the Id and Other Works*, trans. and ed. James Strachey (London: Hogarth Press, 1966–74), 234.

25. Freud elaborated on the usefulness of negation as a therapeutic tool later in his career. "Negation," he writes, "is a way of taking cognizance of what is repressed; indeed it is already a lifting of the repression, though not, of course, an acceptance of what is repressed." Sigmund Freud, "Negation," 234–5.

26. Patrice Poutrus has argued that the asylum law served as a loophole for immigration in the absence of an immigration law. See Patrice G. Poutrus, "Asylum Law in Postwar Germany: Refugee Admission Policies and Their Practical Implementation in

the Federal Republic and the GDR between the Late 1940s and the Mid-1970s," *Journal of Contemporary History* 49, no. 1 (2014): 115–33.

27. Helsinki Watch, *"Foreigners Out." Xenophobia and Right Wing Violence in Germany* (New York: Human Rights Watch, 1992), 33. Cited in Maryellen Fullerton, *Germany for Germans: Xenophobia and Racist Violence in Germany* (New York: Human Rights Watch, 1995), 5.

28. Triadafilos Triadafilopoulos, *Becoming Multicultural: Immigration and the Politics of Membership in Canada and Germany* (Vancouver: University of British Columbia Press, 2012), 148–51; Alice Holmes Cooper, "Party-Sponsored Protest and the Movement Society: The CDU/CSU Mobilises Against Citizenship Law Reform," *German Politics* 11.2 (2002): 88–104.

29. Charmaine Chua, et al., "'Something's Missing in Germany': An Exploration of Discriminatory Terminology in German Discourse," Humanity in Action, accessed 19 August 2013, http://www.humanityinaction.org/knowledgebase/158-somethings-missing.exploration-of-discriminatory-terminology-in-german-discourse.

30. Rita Chin and Heide Fehrenbach, "Introduction: What's Race Got to Do With It? Postwar German History in Context" in Chin, Fehrenbach, Eley, and Grossman, *After the Nazi Racial State: Difference and Democracy in Germany and Beyond* (Ann Arbor: University of Michigan, 2009), 1–3.

31. "Player Silences German Racists with Hitler Salute," *Spiegel Online*, 3 April 2006, accessed 7 September 2014, http://www.spiegel.de/international/racism-in-soccer-player-silences-german-racists-with-hitler-salute-a-409517.html.

32. The sign is illegal in Germany under paragraph 86a of the criminal code, which prohibits using the symbols of unconstitutional organizations, including and especially the Nazi party.

33. See, for instance, Christian Rath, "Deutliche Kritik am Urteil," taz.de, 28 March 2012, accessed 13 August 2013, http://www.taz.de/Kontrollen-nach-Hautfarbe/!90513/; and Daryl Lindsey, "Profiling 'Sows Seeds of Distrust and Racism," *Spiegel Online*, 29 March 2012.

34. In the case of racial profiling on certain train routes, a higher court ultimately overturned the Koblenz decision, forbidding ID checks based on the color of a person's skin. See Christian Rath, "Gericht verbietet Polizei-Rassismus," taz.de, 30 October 2012, accessed 7 September 2014, http://www.taz.de/!104549/.

35. See, for instance, Uta G. Poiger, *Jazz, Rock, and Rebels: Cold War Politics and American Culture in a Divided Germany* (Berkeley: University of California Press, 2000); Maria Höhn, *GIs and Fräuleins: The German-American Encounter in 1950s West Germany* (Chapel Hill: University of North Carolina Press, 2002); Heide Fehrenbach, *Race after Hitler*; and Timothy L. Schroer, *Recasting Race after World War II: Germans and African Americans in American-Occupied Germany* (Boulder: University of Colorado Press, 2007).

36. For discussions of race and German colonialism, see Sara L. Friedrichsmeyer, Sara Lennox, and Susanne M. Zantop, eds., *The Imperialist Imagination: German Colonialism and Ist Legacy* (Ann Arbor: University of Michigan Press, 1999); Pascal Grosse, *Kolonialismus, Eugenik und bürgerliche Gesellschaft in Deutschland 1850–1918* (Frankfurt a.M.: Campus, 2001); Lora Wildenthal, *German Women for Empire, 1884–1945* (Durham: Duke University Press, 2001); Jürgen Zimmerer and Joachim Zeller, eds., *Genocide in German South-West Africa: The Colonial War of 1904–1908 and Its Aftermath*, trans. E.J. Neather (London: Merlin Press, 2008); Sebastian Conrad, *German Colonialism: A Short History*, trans. Sorcha O'Hagan (Cambridge: Cambridge University Press, 2012); and Michelle R. Moyd, *Violent Intermediaries: African Soldiers, Conquest, and Everyday Colonialism in German East Africa*

(Columbus: Ohio State University Press, 2014). For discussions of race and the Rhineland occupation, see Fatima El-Tayeb, *Schwarze Deutsche: Der Diskurs um Rasse und nationale Identität, 1890–1933* (Frankfurt a.M.: Campus, 2001). For discussions of race and the Third Reich, see Michael Burleigh and Wolfgang Wippermann, *The Racial State: Germany 1933–1945* (Cambridge: Cambridge University Press, 1991); and Tina M. Campt, *Other Germans: Black Germans and the Politics of Race, Gender, and Memory in the Third Reich* (Ann Arbor: University of Michigan Press, 2005).

37. Wolfgang Benz, ed., *Islamfeindschaft und ihr Kontext. Dokumentation der Konferenz "Feinbild Muslim – Feinbild Jude"* (Berlin: Metropol-Verlag, 2009).
38. Michael Omi and Howard Winant, *Racial Formation in the United States from the 1960s to the 1980s* (New York: Routledge, 1986), 61.
39. Omi and Winant, 64.
40. See the recent critique of the French pattern by Didier Fassin and Eric Fassin, *De la question sociale à la question raciale?: Représenter la société française* (Paris: Edition La Découverte, 2006).
41. See, for instance, David Dante Troutt, "Stalking Points," *The Crisis*, Centennial Issue 2010, accessed 8 September 2014, http://mydigimag.rrd.com/article/Stalking_Points/608598/57893/article.html; and Ta-Nehisi Coates, "Fear of a Black President," *The Atlantic*, September 2012, accessed 8 September 2014, http://www.theatlantic.com/magazine/archive/2012/09/fear-of-a-black-president/309064/.

# Works Cited

Abromeit, John. "The Limits of Praxis." In *Changing the World, Changing Oneself*, edited by Belinda Davis, et al. New York: Berghahn, 2010.

Bachelard, Gaston. *The Formation of the Scientific Mind*. Translated by Mary McAllester Jones. Manchester: Clinamen Press, 2002.

BBC News. "Merkel says German Multicultural Society has Failed," 17 October 2010. Accessed 16 September 2013. http://www.bbc.co.uk/news/world-europe-11559451.

Benz, Wolfgang, ed. *Islamfeindschaft und ihr Kontext. Dokumentation der Konferenz "Feinbild Muslim—Feinbild Jude."* Berlin: Metropol-Verlag, 2009.

Berg, Nicolas. *Der Holocaust und die westdeutschen Historiker. Erforschung und Erinnerung.* Göttingen: Wallstein, 2003.

Brosch, Mattias, Michael Elm, Norman Geißler, Brigitta Elise Simbürger, and Oliver von Wrochem, eds. *Exklusive Solidarität. Linker Antisemitismus in Deutschland. Vom Idealismus zur Antiglobalisierungsbewegung.* Berlin: Metropol-Verlag, 2007.

Burleigh, Michael, and Wolfgang Wippermann. *The Racial State: Germany 1933–1945.* Cambridge: Cambridge University Press, 1991.

Campt, Tina M. *Other Germans: Black Germans and the Politics of Race, Gender, and Memory in the Third Reich.* Ann Arbor: University of Michigan Press, 2005.

Chin, Rita. *The Guest Worker Question in Postwar Germany.* Cambridge: Cambridge University Press, 2007.

Chin, Rita, and Heide Fehrenbach. "Introduction: What's Race Got to Do With It? Postwar German History in Context." In *After the Nazi Racial State: Difference and Democracy in Germany and Beyond*, edited by Rita Chin, Heide Fehrenbach, Geoff Eley, and Atina Grossmann. Ann Arbor: University of Michigan Press, 2009.

Chua, Charmaine, et al. "'Something's Missing in Germany': An Exploration of Discriminatory Terminology in German Discourse." Humanity in Action. Accessed 19 August 2013. http://www.humanityinaction.org/knowledgebase/158-something-s-missin.exploration-of-discriminatory-terminology-in-german-discourse.

Coates, Ta-Nehisi. "Fear of a Black President." *The Atlantic*, September 2012. Accessed 8 September 2014. http://www.theatlantic.com/magazine/archive/2012/09/fear-of-a-black-president/309064/.

Conrad, Sebastian. *German Colonialism: A Short History*. Translated by Sorcha O'Hagan. Cambridge: Cambridge University Press, 2012.

Deutsche Welle. "Chancellor Merkel says German Multiculturalism Has 'Utterly Failed'." 17 October 2010. Accessed 16 September 2013. http://www.dw.de/chancellor-merkel-says-german-multiculturalism-has-utterly-failed/a-6118859.

El-Tayeb, Fatima. *Schwarze Deutsche: Der Diskurs um Rasse und nationale Identität, 1890-1933*. Frankfurt a.M.: Campus, 2001.

Fassin, Didier. "The Denial of Racial Discrimination." Lecture, Center for European Studies. Ann Arbor: University of Michigan, 29 January 2013. Unpublished manuscript.

Fassin, Didier, and Eric Fassin. *De la question sociale à la question raciale? Représenter la société française*. Paris: Edition La Découverte, 2006.

Fehrenbach, Heide. "Black Occupation Children and the Devolution of the Nazi Racial State." In *After the Nazi Racial State: Difference and Democracy in Germany and Beyond*, eds. Rita Chin, Heide Fehrenbach, Geoff Eley, and Atina Grossmann. Ann Arbor: University of Michigan Press, 2009.

Fehrenbach, Heide. *Race after Hitler: Black Occupation Children in Postwar Germany and America*. Princeton: Princeton University Press, 2005.

Frei, Norbert. *Adenauer's Germany and the Nazi Past*. Translated by Joel Golb. New York: Columbia University Press, 2002.

Freud, Sigmund. *Three Essays on the Theory of Sexuality*. Translated and edited by James Strachey. New York: Avon, 1965.

Freud, Sigmund. *The Standard Edition of the Complete Psychological Works of Sigmund Freud. Volume XIX (1923–1925): The Ego and the Id and Other Works*. Translated and edited by James Strachey. London: Hogarth Press, 1966–74.

Freud, Sigmund. *Introductory Lectures on Psychoanalysis*. Translated and edited by James Strachey. New York: Norton, 1977.

Friedrichsmeyer, Sara L., Sara Lennox, and Susanne M. Zantop, eds. *The Imperialist Imagination: German Colonialism and Ist Legacy*. Ann Arbor: University of Michigan Press, 1999.

Fullerton, Maryellen. *Germany for Germans: Xenophobia and Racist Violence in Germany*. New York: Human Rights Watch, 1995.

Gassert, Philipp, and Alan E. Steinweis, eds. *Coping with the Nazi Past: West German Debates on Nazism and Generational Conflict, 1955–1975*. New York: Berghahn, 2006.

Grosse, Pascal. *Kolonialismus, Eugenik und bürgerliche Gesellschaft in Deutschland 1850–1918*. Frankfurt a.M.: Campus, 2001.

Helsinki Watch. *"Foreigners Out." Xenophobia and Right Wing Violence in Germany*. New York: Human Rights Watch, 1992.

Herf, Jeffrey. *Divided Memory: The Nazi Past in the Two Germanys*. Cambridge, MA: Harvard University Press, 1999.

Herzog, Dagmar. *Sex after Fascism*. Princeton: Princeton University Press, 2005.

Höhn, Maria. *GIs and Fräuleins: The German-American Encounter in 1950s West Germany*. Chapel Hill: University of North Carolina Press, 2002.

Holmes Cooper, Alice. "Party-Sponsored Protest and the Movement Society: The CDU/CSU Mobilises Against Citizenship Law Reform." *German Politics* 11.2 (2002): 88–104.

Knabe, Hubertus. *Die unterwanderte Republik: Stasi im Westen*. Berlin: Propyläen, 1999.

Kraushaar, Wolfgang. *Die Bombe im Jüdischen Gemeindehaus*. Hamburg: Hamburger Edition, 2005.

Kundnani, Hans. *Utopia or Auschwitz: Germany's 1968 Generation and the Holocaust*. New York: Columbia University Press, 2009.

Lindsey, Daryl. "Profiling 'Sows Seeds of Distrust and Racism'." *Spiegel Online*, 29 March 2012. Accessed 13 August 2013. http://www.spiegel.de/international/germany/german-press-review-on-court-ruling-allowing-police-checks-based-on-skin-color-a-824601.html.

Markovits, Andrei S., and Philip S. Gorski. *The German Left: Red, Green and Beyond*. New York: Polity Press, 1993.

Merkel, Angela. "Deutschlandstag der Junge Union." Speech, Deutschlandtag, Junge Union, Potsdam, Germany, 16 October 2010. YouTube video. Accessed 19 July 2013. http://www.youtube.com/watch?v=WaEg8aM4fcc.

Moyd, Michelle R. *Violent Intermediaries: African Soldiers, Conquest, and Everyday Colonialism in German East Africa*. Columbus: Ohio State University Press, 2014.

Omi, Michael, and Howard Winant. *Racial Formation in the United States from the 1960s to the 1980s*. New York, Routledge, 1986.

Poiger, Uta G. *Jazz, Rock, and Rebels: Cold War Politics and American Culture in a Divided Germany*. Berkeley: University of California Press, 2000.

Poutrus, Patrice G. "Asylum Law in Postwar Germany: Refugee Admission Policies and Their Practical Implementation in the Federal Republic and the GDR between the Late 1940s and the Mid-1970s." *Journal of Contemporary History* 49, no. 1 (2014): 115–33.

Rath, Christian. "Deutliche Kritik am Urteil." taz.de, 28 March 2012. Accessed 13 August 2013. http://www.taz.de/Kontrollen-nach-Hautfarbe/!90513/.

Rath, Christian. "Gericht verbietet Polizei-Rassismus." taz.de, 30 October 2012. Accessed 7 September 2014. http://www.taz.de/!104549/.

Reuters News Service. "Merkel says German Multiculturalism Has Failed." 16 October 2010. Accessed 16 September 2013. http://www.reuters.com/article/2010/10/16/us-germany-merkel-immigration-idUSTRE69F1K320101016.

Sarrazin, Thilo. *Deutschland schafft sich ab. Wie wir unser Land aufs Spiel setzen*. Munich: DVA, 2010.

Schildt, Axel. *Ankunft im Westen: Ein Essay zur Erfolgsgeschichte der Bundesrepublik*. Frankfurt a.M.: Fischer, 1999.

Schmidtke, Michael. *Der Aufbruch der jungen Intelligenz: Die 68er-Jahre in der Bundesrepublik und den USA*. Frankfurt a.M.: Campus, 2003.

Schroer, Timothy L. *Recasting Race after World War II: Germans and African Americans in American-Occupied Germany*. Boulder: University of Colorado Press, 2007.

Schwarzer, Alice. *Die große Verschleierung. Für Integration, gegen Islamismus*. Cologne: Kiepenheuer & Witsch, 2010.

Siegfried, Detlef. "Zwischen Aufarbeitung und Schlußstrich: Der Umgang mit der NS-Vergangenheit in den beiden deutschen Staaten." In *Dynamische Zeiten: Die 60er Jahre in den beiden deutschen Gesellschaften*, edited by Axel Schildt, Detlef Siegfried, and Karl Christian Lammers. Hamburg: Christians, 2000.

*Spiegel Online*. "Player Silences German Racists with Hitler Salute." 3 April 2006. Accessed 7 September 2014. http://www.spiegel.de/international/racism-in-soccer-player-silences-german-racists-with-hitler-salute-a-409517.html.

*Spiegel Online.* "Integration: Merkel erklärt Multikulti für gescheitert." 16 October 2010. Accessed 17 July 2013. http://www.spiegel.de/politik/deutschland/integration-merkel-erklaert-multikulti-fuer-gescheitert-a-723532.html.

Triadafilopoulos, Triadafilos. *Becoming Multicultural: Immigration and the Politics of Membership in Canada and Germany.* Vancouver: University of British Columbia Press, 2012.

Troutt, David Dante. "Stalking Points." *The Crisis.* Centennial Issue 2010. Accessed 8 September 2014. http://mydigimag.rrd.com/article/Stalking_Points/608598/57893/article.html.

Varon, Jeremy. *Bringing the War Home: The Weather Underground, the Red Army Faction, and Revolutionary Violence in the Sixties and Seventies.* Berkeley: University of California Press, 2004.

Wallraff, Günter. *Neue Reportagen, Untersuchungen und Lehrbeispiele.* Berlin: Aufbau-Verlag, 1974.

Wielenga, Friso. "An Inability to Mourn? The German Federal Republic and the Nazi Past." *European Review* 11, no. 4 (2003): 551–72.

Wildenthal, Lora. *German Women for Empire, 1884–1945.* Durham: Duke University Press, 2001.

Zimmerer, Jürgen, and Joachim Zeller, eds. *Genocide in German South-West Africa: The Colonial War of 1904–1908 and Its Aftermath.* Translated by E.J. Neather. London: Merlin Press, 2008.

**Rita Chin** is associate professor of history at the University of Michigan, Ann Arbor. She is the author of *The Guest Worker Question in Postwar Germany* (2007) and co-editor of *After the Nazi Racial State* (2009). She has received fellowships from SSRC, DAAD, the Woodrow Wilson International Center for Scholars, ACLS, and the Institute for Advanced Study. Her two current projects are *The Crisis of Multiculturalism in Europe: A History* (forthcoming 2017, Princeton University Press) and *The European Left and Postwar Immigration*.

# PART III
## Reconsidering History, Memory, and Identity in the Postunification Period

*Chapter 9*

# NATIONALISM AND CITIZENSHIP DURING THE PASSAGE FROM THE POSTWAR TO THE POST-POSTWAR

*Dietmar Schirmer*

Migration was a fixture of German history even before there was a German national state. People exited the German lands and entered them; they volunteered to do so and were coerced; they acted on their own or became subjects of government-orchestrated schemes. Since the eighteenth century, Germany has variously delivered migrants eastward along the Danube and to Czarist Russia, and westward to the Americas. It received migrants continuously: from French Huguenots seeking shelter in Protestant Prussia to Poles laboring on East Elbian estates or in the coal mines and steel mills of Silesia or the Ruhr Valley, from forced labor exploited in the war economy of the Third Reich to the largely Mediterranean labor migrants brought in to fuel the postwar economic miracle. While Germany had been a country of net emigration from the eighteenth to the early twentieth century, it objectively—though, it appears, not undeniably—became a country of immigration in the postwar period. Initially, postwar immigration to West Germany had been driven by ethnic Germans from the Soviet Union and Central and Eastern Europe, but as the economic boom of the 1950s and 1960s gained momentum, its texture changed toward labor migration from Italy, Spain, Greece, Turkey, and Yugoslavia, predicated on the "guest worker" model.

While the first wave of postwar immigration was construed as a homecoming rather than as immigration proper, and political and economic capital were expended on a massive scale to secure integration into West German society, the second wave fared less well. The "guest worker" model promised that migration would be temporary—an easy fix for shortages at the low-skill end of the labor market, to be brought in as

Notes for this chapter begin on page 249.

needed and expected to leave when it was not. This stance survived, against all empirical evidence. All the while, as the labor migrants of the first hour started families, and even as their children started families, the ideology of the "guest worker" secured that negative externalities could safely be filed away as an *Ausländerproblem*—a foreigners' problem—that concerned the majority of society only at its margins.

The mantra "Germany is not a country of immigration" remained until the 1980s, and even longer at the right of the political spectrum. The purpose of this chapter is to explore if and how this has changed as Germany has transitioned from the postwar to the post-postwar.

I use the term "post-postwar" to refer to the period ushered in by the fall of the Berlin Wall, German unification, and the Maastricht Treaty. Like with all "posts"—postmodernism, postindustrialism, etc.—the prefix betrays uncertainty about the signature of the time so signified. Having the "post-postwar" begin at that time logically implies fixing the "postwar" as the period bookended by the end of World War II and the fall of the wall, respectively. It should be noted that this is a fairly recent—and expansive—understanding that owes much to the late Tony Judt's book of the same title.[1] However, since the unification of the two German postwar states, conceiving of the postwar in this fashion is without alternative. The post-postwar period is hence in full swing and its character cannot yet be fully ascertained. This chapter's modest goal is to probe trends in something that is still very much becoming.

In the first section I shall reconstruct the historical foundations of nationalism and citizenship in Germany since the turn of the nineteenth century. Its premise is that the usual emphasis on ethnonationalism is incomplete; to properly understand the trajectory of inclusion and exclusion policies in Germany, one needs to attend to a second vector, i.e., a statist logic that is centered upon presumptions regarding loyalty or disloyalty to the state. In the second section, I will examine more closely how these two vectors have converged to determine stances toward nation, citizenship, and immigration in the postwar. The third section will turn to the post-postwar and evaluate two major policy initiatives, i.e., the citizenship and naturalization reform law of 2000 and the search for an immigration and integration policy. In the concluding section, I shall discuss continuity and change with special emphasis given to the distinction between incremental and out-of-type change.

Historical and sociological research on German nationalism typically emphasizes its groundedness in an ethnocultural conception of the nation.[2] As a political movement, German nationalism was the unlikely child of romanticism and Napoleon: romanticism fixed the nation as a zone of substantive cultural homogeneity; Napoleonic occupation spurned its politization. The flipside of the anti-French militancy of early German nationalists was the call for a unified German nation state, which by default made the movement an enemy of the authorities of the many existing German states. The semantics of *Kulturnation* (cultural nation), however, are much older.[3] Its roots are in fifteenth- and sixteenth-century humanism, which identified the nation as a cultural and linguistic community, and which derived the historical continuity between the Germanic tribes of antiquity and contemporary Germans from the rediscovery of the texts of the ancients. The idea of the nation as an endless chain of generations that binds the present to the hoariest of pasts, as well as to the yet unborn—so effectively put to use in the call to arms against French occupation in the last of Fichte's 1808 *Addresses*[4]—has its roots here.

Hence, the affirmation of the nation as a space of cultural homogeneity has a long tradition and, given the continuity between ethnocultural and *völkisch* nationalism, it is perhaps unsurprising that the discourse on German nationalism after Hitler should put it center stage. However, I contend that the idiosyncratic German version of nationalism has a second source, i.e., a mode of integration that foregrounds loyalty toward the state. I shall follow Gregg Kvistad's lead and call this source statism.[5] Its historical roots are Prussian rather than German. The period of its institutional emergence is bracketed by the Prussian General Code of 1794 and the constitutionalization of Prussia in the course of the arrested revolution of 1848, and hence includes the Prussian reform era of 1807–19.[6]

Thus, German nationalism and Prussian statism evolved roughly around the same time, yet they did so incongruously: whereas the former was oppositional to the political status quo, the latter defended it; whereas the former imagined the nation as a fellowship of co-equals, the latter managed inclusion and exclusion by degrees of loyalty; whereas nationalism offered a concrete, self-identical collectivity, the latter presented the state as an abstract idea, *objektiver Geist* (objective spirit) in Hegel's terms, impossible to be attained by any individual, social estate, or class. "Since the state is objective spirit, it is only through being a member of the state that the individual himself has objectivity, genuine individuality, and an ethical life."[7]

With the state as abstract idea and transcendental order, political integration becomes, as Gregg Kvistad has argued, a function of the relative distance or proximity of individuals or social classes to that unattainable center that is the spirit of the state.[8] That nobody can ever embody the spirit of the state proper, but only display a degree of loyalty that at best would be considered adequate, establishes the rationale for the permanent monitoring of state servants' convictions. This realm of definitional loyalty is, as the realm of the state, demarcated from the realm of civil society, where particularistic interests rule and threaten the state with anarchy.

The Reich of 1871 was truer to Prussian statism than to romantic nationalism. As a nation state, it fell woefully short. Neither did it include the whole nation as understood by romantic nationalists — "as far as the German tongue is spoken"[9] — nor did it come true on the egalitarian promise nationalism had originally made, contra the privileges of church and nobility. Universal male suffrage for Reichstag elections may count as a nod in this direction, but remained of little consequence, given the truncated rights of parliament. Instead, the Reich remained a *Fürstenstaat* (state of princes), and Prussian statism survived intact — witness that the Reich identified the Social Democrats and the Catholic Church as its enemies, groups, as it were, suspect of particularism of class and denomination, respectively, and hence by definition disloyal toward the state.

This is of course not to say that nationalism — rabid, aggressive nationalism, even — had no place in the Reich. It did in rhetoric and practice and was directed against the French, English, and Russian competitors for great power status externally, and against the Poles and Jews internally. Bismarck's Reich actively and successfully courted the liberal nationalists — a task made easy because after 1849 German liberalism had taken on an idiosyncratically "governmental character," as Rudolf Vierhaus called it, i.e., an orientation toward state rather than popular sovereignty, which reduced the liberal defense of individual rights against the state to the state-affirmative ideology of the *Rechtsstaat* (constitutional state).[10] Nationalism was hence resolutely reduced to a tool at the service of the Reich's statist logic. As a consequence, the Reich increasingly managed an asymmetric fusion of statist and nationalist principles.

The emerging composite turned out narrower and pettier than either of its components. From nationalism it retained the idea of ethnocultural homogeneity, but shed its emancipatory traditions. From statism it retained the suspicion toward political activity in the realm of civil society and the monitoring of state loyalty, but shed its relative inclusiveness toward long-term residents of non-German stock. From the late 1880s onward, the authorities turned to excessively restrictive immigration policies, and the obstacles to naturalization became practically insurmountable. The target of these policies were the Poles, particularly Polish Jews.

The terms of the citizenship law of 1913 suggest continuity rather than change between the old and new sets of rules. It retained the indirect nature of German citizenship: one was a citizen of the Reich by virtue of possessing citizenship of one of its composite states; it only added the institution of immediate Reich citizenship, but that remained an exception.[11] The law also retained the *jus sanguinis* tradition of acquiring citizenship, but made it purer: naturalization of ethnic non-Germans remained possible by law, but became almost impossible in practice, because of an increasingly *völkisch* consensus in government, administration, and the parties of the right, combined with the introduction of additional veto players who guaranteed that any liberal tendencies in individual states or among the lower levels of the administration would be effectively checked.

Perhaps the most significant change concerned the rules according to which citizenship could be revoked. Before the 1913 law, the German concept of citizenship had contained a negative element of *jus soli*, i.e., ten years of absence from the territory of the Reich and its federal states automatically led to the loss of citizenship.[12] The new law not only shed this provision, but even made citizenship transmittable from generation to generation, without any person in the chain of *Reichsbürger* (citizen of the [German] Reich) ever having to set foot on home territory.

German citizenship thus became an oddly deterritorialized institution. That the 1913 law seems to rely on *jus sanguinis* alone and uncontaminated explains why it has the reputation of being a document of pure and genuine ethnonationalism. But this interpretation is incomplete. On the one hand, the law continued to specify conditions under which citizenship could be revoked, although prolonged absence was no longer one of them. Desertion, draft evasion, the unauthorized entry into the services of a foreign government, or acquisition of the citizenship of another state continued to carry the threat of citizenship annulment. That these are all breaches of loyalty gives evidence as to how entrenched the logic of statism remained.

But why would prolonged absence from the Reich no longer be treated as proof of a lack of loyalty? Wolfgang Mommsen has pointed to the turn toward imperial expansion:

> The citizenship law was to take into consideration that the German Reich had by now acquired in many regions of the world formal and even more numerous informal outposts where Germans or persons of German descent played an important role as local agents of German economic and political interests.[13]

The absent *Reichsbürger* thus morphed from a lowly emigrant to a German patriot fulfilling his patriotic duty.

The 1913 law was hence two-pronged. On the one hand, it minimized access to citizenship for ethnic non-Germans within the Reich and rendered the many Polish, Ukrainian, Italian, and so forth labor immigrants permanent objects of restrictive foreigner laws. On the other hand, it maximized access to citizenship for ethnic Germans outside the Reich.

The "ethnonationalism cum statism" formula survived the transition to the Weimar Republic as well as from the republic to the national-socialist

*Führerstaat.* After 1918, the statist ethos of the corps of civil servants allowed most of its members to serve more or less loyally under the new republican government—not because they liked it, but because, as Baron v. Stein, a high-ranking civil servant mused, "There is something higher, above the constitutional form of the state: the State itself."[14] The civil service ethos worked again in 1933—although to less laudable effect. Like the Republican government in 1919, the Nazis, too, found the vast majority of the state's civil servants trustworthy. According to the Law on the Restitution of the Professional Civil Service of April 1933,[15] purges were limited to the comparatively small number of republican civil servants appointed during the Weimar years—derogated as "party book civil servants"—who amounted to a substantial group only in Prussia, where the continuity of Social Democratic governments had allowed for the creation of a largely republican body of civil servants. What highlights the exclusionary effects of the combination of statist and ethnic/racist principles is the fact that in paragraph 3, the law takes aim at "civil servants of non-Aryan decent": Jews were to be summarily dismissed, although at the insistence of President Hindenburg an exception was made, for the time being, for Jewish war veterans. The law fused the racist rationale of German purity with the statist rationale of the civil service as occupying a realm above self-interest and political particularism. *"Racially and ideologically* alien elements were eliminated from the civil service," as presiding judge of the Volksgerichtshof, Roland Freisler, summarized its intent.[16]

The two German states that emerged from Allied occupation in 1949 relied for citizenship matters on prewar laws, *sans* the Nazi additions since 1933.[17] The ethnonationalist concept of German citizenship thus carried over into the postwar, including the assumption that it could be transmitted in emigration indefinitely. And yet, despite continuity regarding the letter of the law, its function changed. Having originally been written to expand Germanness beyond Germany's territorial borders in a period of imperial expansion, it now became the vehicle for accommodation *within* the territory of the West German state of all Germans, i.e., German citizens, including those who found themselves outside Germany as a consequence of the territorial realignments after the war, as well as all *Volkszugehörige* (ethnic Germans) who came to West Germany as refugees and expellees from the Soviet Union and the communist states of Central and Eastern Europe.[18]

The second, statist pillar survived into the postwar as well—most visibly in the fierce and eventually successful struggle for restoration of the *Berufsbeamtentum* (professional civil service) against the expressed will of the Western Allies. Instead of moving to a civil service modeled on the

Anglo-Saxon tradition, where the relationship between state and civil servant is defined in contractual terms and resembles that between employer and employee in the private sector, the Federal Republic fully restored the German tradition of the state being run by a corps of *Beamte* (civil servants) divorced from and above the particularistic conflicts of civil society. This includes the obligation to political restraint, conformity with and active defense of the constitutional principles of the state, appointment for life, promotion based on seniority, state pensions, and the prohibition of strikes.

The special status of the *Berufsbeamte* may not immediately be related to those matters at the core of our concerns, but the statist logic that underwrites it is of constitutive importance for the treatment of immigrants as well. Statism implies that both groups, *Beamte* and foreigners, require special attention regarding the monitoring of their activities: the *Beamte* because their privileged access to the state warrants elevated expectations regarding loyalty and reliability, and foreigners because their position as non-citizens marks them by definition as disloyal to the state, thus necessitating specific institutions for their control and surveillance, i.e., *Ausländerbehörde* and *Ausländerrecht* (foreigner office and foreigner law).

Throughout the postwar the characteristic traits of German immigration policy and the official stance on immigration remained, respectively, absence and denial. This may appear to be no small feat, given that between the end of World War II and the fall of the wall some twenty million persons took up residence in West Germany. The first wave of immigration to the postwar Federal Republic was of *Übersiedler* (German refugees from the German Democratic Republic, or GDR), ethnic German *Aussiedler* (ethnic German resettlers), and *Heimatvertriebene* (ethnic German expellees) from the Soviet Union and its satellite states. Their numbers were enormous, particularly in the immediate postwar period. Nevertheless, immediate access to citizenship for ethnic Germans, combined with generous state support and favorable economic conditions during the miracle years from the early 1950s until the late 1960s, made the integration of this population remarkably successful.[19] The wall generated a lull from 1961, until the numbers swelled up again in the late 1970s and early 1980s—when many *Aussiedler* came from Poland and Romania—and soared in the late 1980s, when Gorbachev's reforms in the Soviet Union and the dusk of socialism in East Central Europe pushed the doors for prospective emigrants wide open. Like the earlier cohorts, these late *Aussiedler* could rely on generous aid from the state, but unlike them, their integration into German society proved difficult— not least because dispersion since the war had broken up the old German communities, and language capacity was generally low. Particularly, those coming from the Soviet Union were perceived as Russians, not Germans, by the host population, and they tended to cluster in close-knit diaspora Russian communities.

While ethnic German immigrants could enjoy unusually high levels of aid toward integration, the non-German immigrants had to make do with unusually low ones. Beginning in 1955, Germany actively recruited "guest workers" from Italy, Yugoslavia, Turkey, and other mostly Mediterranean countries to grease the machinery of the economic miracle. The economic expansion of the 1950s and 1960s generated severe shortages, foremost at the low-skill end of the labor market. "Guest workers" were considered an easy and—most importantly—temporary fix.

While the term "guest worker" has a less conspicuous ring than the older version "*Fremdarbeiter*" (alien worker), the postwar practice of using foreign labor while avoiding the costs of integration and withholding the prospect of full citizenship had its roots in nineteenth-century Prussia.[20] The GDR was truer to the Prussian model in its treatment of "contract workers" than West Germany. While the GDR strictly enforced the principle of rotation and painstakingly segregated the non-German workers from its own citizens, the government of the Federal Republic of Germany (FRG) did not. Shortly after the start of the recruitment program, the Treaty of Rome committed the West German government to the free movement of workers from other member states of the European Economic Community (EEC) anyway, and the principle eventually carried over to recruits from Greece and Turkey as these countries entered into association agreements with the EEC in 1961 and 1963, respectively.[21]

The differential legal positions of EEC and non-EEC foreigners vis-à-vis the German state is an early indication of the emergence of what may be properly called "complex citizenship." Before this, and echoing the United Nations (UN) Declaration of Universal Human Rights of 1948, the Basic Law of 1949 had already followed a broader trend toward cosmopolitan citizenship by expanding the guarantee of human rights to everybody regardless of citizenship, thus legitimizing specific rights and principles on the basis of "universal personhood rather than national belonging."[22] European integration added to these universal rights another set of rights that extended to the citizens of other European states: nationals from other EEC/EC countries were thus entitled to a residence permit valid for at least five years (while permits for non-EEC foreigners were issued for a year at a time, with the authorities reserving ample discretionary power for themselves) and did not require work permits. The practical effects remained limited—the rights thus granted were few, as were the "guest workers" from EEC countries—until the 1992 Maastricht Treaty formally introduced EU citizenship.

"Guest worker" recruitment ended in response to the 1973 oil crisis, which presented foreigners living in Germany with the stark choice between either leaving with no option of return or staying on permanently. During the recession, some opted for exit. From 1974 to 1976, the number of foreigners living in West Germany dropped by some 200,000, or five percent, before it started to climb again.[23] However, the great majority stayed and transformed from "guest workers" into residents. With circular migration impossible, and family reunification the only effective option for entry, those who remained did so permanently, and those who did not yet have a family established one in Germany.

For the rest of the postwar, West Germany's foreigner policy remained mired in contradiction. The official position that Germany was not a country of immigration remained in force, which precluded formulation of a comprehensive immigration policy. Instead, successive governments attempted simultaneously to halt further immigration, to incentivize past immigrants to repatriate, and to better integrate those unwilling to leave into German society. Thus, on the one hand, the government made the 1973 suspension of labor recruitment permanent in 1977 and repeatedly issued financial incentives for repatriation. On the other hand, introduction of a permanent residence permit in 1978 strengthened the legal status of long-term residents and reduced administrative discretion over their treatment.

For the emerging integration policy, the older "guest worker" frame and its labor market utilitarianism proved a heavy burden. Having been recruited for menial, low-skilled labor that offered little prospect for upward mobility, Germany's foreign workers were most vulnerable to the effects of recession and automation. Unsurprisingly, unemployment rates among foreign workers were significantly higher than among Germans, as were the rates of families depending on transfer payments of one or another kind. Since the late nineteenth century, the policies of imported labor had trained Germans to look at foreigners as a utility first and humans second. In an era of economic stagnation and elevated levels of unemployment, this tradition echoed in the perception of foreigners as a problem, not a resource; education of their children as a burden, not an opportunity; and the presence of other cultures and customs as a threat to national identity, not an enrichment of social and cultural life.

The policies of keeping newcomers out and offering limited integration to those already there survived the change in government from the center-left coalition under Chancellor Helmut Schmidt to Kohl's center-right coalition in 1982 more or less intact; what changed, however, was the rhetoric, particularly among national conservatives and populists in the Christian Democratic and Christian Social Unions (CDU/CSU), who had few qualms about stirring the fire among the more xenophobic parts of the electorate. But this never translated into consistent anti-foreigner policies, not only because the conservative wing met the resistance of liberals inside their own party and in the CDU's coalition partner, the Free Democratic Party (FDP), but also because their policy prescriptions, such as forced extraditions and the tightening of the eligibility requirements for family unification, ran afoul of the Protestant and Catholic Churches and the party's traditional emphasis on the sanctity of the family. Nothing demonstrates the policy paralysis on matters of immigration and integration better than the fact that passing a reformed Foreigners Law took from 1984 until 1991—and then "essentially ratified what constitutional court rules had long established."[24] The most tangible effect of the new law, which modestly liberalized the naturalization regime, was that naturalization numbers, which had hovered below 40,000 for two decades, increased to around 90,000 in the 1990s.

But overall, little happened one way or the other, policy-wise. The development of an actual immigration policy, or at least an integration policy that would promote citizenship as the goal of integration, remained foreclosed by the continued insistence that Germany was not an immigration country. Attempts to prevent further immigration faltered, because family unification, asylum, and refugee law took the place of "guest worker" recruitment as vehicles for entry. From 1984 forward, economic improvement and decreasing numbers of asylum seekers reduced the salience of the "foreigner problem" in public discourse. And toward the end of the postwar period, the public's attention switched from foreign immigration to the soaring numbers of ethnic Germans from Eastern Europe.[25]

Germany's post-postwar period began in November 1989, as people danced joyously atop the Berlin Wall. Exultation did not last, however. In the summer of 1990, currency conversion first wiped out the competitiveness of East German producers in their traditional East European markets, and then the producers themselves. As the *Treuhand* began its reign over the state property of the deceased GDR, closing down unprofitable businesses and privatizing the rest, it became evident that the "blooming landscapes" promised by Chancellor Kohl in the summer of 1990 would not materialize anytime soon. Eastern Germany deindustrialized in a hurry, and unemployment rates soon rose to upward of fifteen percent, and did not peak until 2005.

As economic prospects in eastern Germany dimmed into ever-darker shades of grey and the economic gap between east and west widened instead of closing, non-German immigrants had to bear the brunt—although their numbers in eastern Germany were miniscule. The early years after unification saw a string of xenophobic incidents, mostly, but not exclusively, in the east. The grim spectacle of rioting mobs, attacking hostels housing contract workers and asylum seekers with stones and firebombs in Hoyerswerda, Rostock, Cottbus, and other eastern German towns in 1991 and 1992, shocked the German public, but could still be explained away as the combination of the "foreigner problem" and the provincialism of eastern Germany. The government signaled understanding and responded not by cracking down on the perpetrators, but by tightening the Asylum Law. The tide turned only after an arson attack on the house of a long-term resident Turkish family in the West German town of Solingen in May 1993, which left five persons dead, three of them children, and injured fourteen more. Now the public responded with vigils and demonstrations, and President von Weizsäcker, in a speech at the memorial service, spoke of the decades-long failure of West German society to include its foreign residents, and suggested that long-term residency without access to full citizenship was unsustainable.[26]

By the mid-1990s, all major parties had come around in favor of citizenship reform; even the Christian Democrats accepted, however grudgingly, that a positive right to naturalization had become unavoidable. When the 1998 federal elections returned a parliamentary majority for the Social Democratic Party (SPD) and the Greens, the door opened wide for citizenship reform, which both parties had presented as a key project during the election campaign. The Red-Green coalition proposed to amend the traditional *jus sanguinis* to *jus soli*: children born in Germany would automatically receive German citizenship if at least one parent had acquired a residency permit prior to the birth of the child. Naturalization of resident foreigners was to be made easier, first by lowering the barriers toward eligibility, and second by generally accepting dual citizenship.

Before the legislation could pass, the CDU scored a surprise victory in the 1999 state elections in Hesse, based on a campaign that vigorously agitated against dual citizenship. As a result, the center-right parties regained a majority in the Bundesrat (Upper House of the Federal Republic of Germany), and the Red-Green coalition had to seek a compromise with the Christian Democrats to see the reform through parliament. As a consequence, the dual-citizenship provision was scrapped, and the children of immigrants who gained citizenship qua birth became *Optionsbürger*, i.e., they would have to decide between the ages of eighteen and twenty-three which citizenship they would retain permanently. The setback regarding dual citizenship notwithstanding, the law of 1999 marks a highly significant departure in the history of citizenship and belonging in Germany: for the first time since the age of feudalism the new citizenship law provided for the acquisition of German citizenship *jure soli*.

For the policy areas of immigration and integration, the post-postwar saw less progress. Shortly after citizenship and naturalization reform took effect in January 2000, Chancellor Schröder appeared set to jumpstart immigration reform when he proposed a "Green Card" as a vehicle to bring thirty thousand much-needed IT experts to Germany. This was the first time since the end of "guest worker" recruitment that immigration was framed as an economic opportunity rather than a burden. But the initiative greatly overestimated the attractiveness of Germany as a destination for foreign professionals: the German "Green Card" fell short of its American namesake insofar as it facilitated only temporary, not permanent, residence and required an exceptionally high minimum salary, which even well-paid young professionals were unlikely to meet. Its initiators also failed to take into account the obstacles presented by the language barrier (the U.S. and U.K. offered language-barrier-free labor market entry to the Indian IT experts that Schröder had had in mind), as well as Germany's well-deserved reputation for being less than welcoming to foreigners.[27]

Even before the Green Card surprise, the Independent Commission on Immigration (known as the Süssmuth Commission after its president Rita Süssmuth) had recommended a comprehensive approach to immigration and integration whose two main pillars were an immigration policy oriented toward a) the effects of demographic change and b) the labor market's needs at the high end of the skill scale, as well as one that aimed at compelling immigrants to become stakeholders in German society by increasing participation in social, economic, and political life. The commission's report attempted to present a third approach somewhere between multiculturalism and assimilation, and specifically included a chapter on the "Public Perception of Immigration" as an obstacle to integration.[28]

The Süssmuth Commission's report was intended to be the basis for the 2004 *Zuwanderungsgesetz* (immigration law), but little of it was left after legislation had been run through the mill of a parliament divided between a Bundestag (Lower House of the Federal Republic of Germany) dominated by the left and a Bundesrat dominated by the right. The law that eventually emerged was a disappointment. Regarding immigration, it did little more than remove some of the clutter that had made the laws it replaced a bureaucratic nightmare, implement the European Union (EU) free movement law with which Germany had to comply anyway, and offer non-German graduates of German universities a grace period in which to seek adequate employment. With regard to integration, it one-sidedly focused on those measures recommended in the report that stepped up the demands made on foreigners, specifically the mandatory language and civics courses.[29]

*

What should we make of this? More specifically, how relevant are the changes that have occurred in the post-postwar regarding nationalism and membership, citizenship, and immigration in Germany? And do they add up to out-of-type change, i.e., change that fundamentally departs from the German tradition of reserving citizenship for those who are part of a substantively homogenous national community, and treating foreigners as a temporary expedient to labor market imbalances?

The strongest piece of evidence that speaks for out-of-type change is the *jus soli* component that is at the core of the 1999 citizenship law and that has brought Germany broadly in line with other west European countries such as France or the Netherlands.[30] In July 2014, the Bundestag voted in favor of abandoning the provision that second generation immigrants who have acquired two citizenships by birth have to decide, at the brink of adulthood, which of them they would permanently retain. Dual citizenship was thus at last accepted. Social institutions are generally sticky and become stickier the older they are and the more they are embedded in social identities. Citizenship is certainly one of those institutions, which further emphasizes the magnitude of change.

With regard to the second major goal, i.e., to make naturalization more accessible, the 1999 law has had limited impact. Immediately after the law went into effect, naturalization numbers jumped from a 1990s average around 90,000 up to 178,000, but then quickly returned to pre-2000 levels. Germany continues to have one of the lowest naturalization rates among high-income OECD countries.[31] The reasons are not entirely clear. Naturalization fees are part of the explanation,[32] as are identity-related constraints and the perception of not being welcome in the host society. It should further be mentioned that social citizenship—i.e., participation in the welfare state—is dependent on labor market participation rather than legal citizenship, which removes what would otherwise be the strongest incentive for citizenship acquisition.[33] Another reason for Germany's low naturalization rate is that the legal status of long-term residents has significantly improved and the discretion of the authorities reduced over the last decades. In other words, a secure legal status no longer requires the acquisition of citizenship, as non-nationals have transformed from subjects of a paternalistic state authority to sovereign bearers of rights and privileges.

While developments regarding accessibility of citizenship and the vastly improved legal status of non-citizen long-term residents hence indeed point toward out-of-type change, changes regarding immigration and integration regimes are much more incremental. Channels for immigration other than family unification have recently broadened, mainly as an effect of the EU Blue Card program and the free movement provision for EU citizens.[34] In 2013, the job search period for non-German graduates from German universities was expanded from twelve to eighteen months. All of these changes work in favor of highly skilled labor. In 2011, some 54,000 work authorizations were issued to university-educated non-EU nationals.[35] German immigration policy seems to be gradually adapting to contemporary labor market requirements—but at a rate woefully inadequate to compensate for the changing demographics of a rapidly aging society.[36]

Frustratingly little has changed with regard to social and educational mobility among immigrants. Low social mobility has long been a characteristic trait of the German migration regime. Originally this outcome was intended: the host society expected "guest workers" to do the menial labor Germans did not desire, not to move up on the occupational ladder; and the "guest workers" were content as long as their income opportunities remained markedly better than in their countries of origin. But as "guest workers" turned into permanent residents, lacking social mobility became a problem because it threatened to create a permanent underclass locked in the low-wage end of the economy or in outright dependency— hence the strong focus on integration and education in the 2004 immigration law. It is too early to tell whether these policies will have any tangible effects on educational and social mobility. So far, non-German students continue to be dramatically less likely to enter the highest tier of the three-tiered secondary education system, which opens the path to university, and much more likely than Germans to remain stuck in the lowest tier, which severely limits students' educational and occupational prospects.[37] The hierarchical nature of Germany's secondary education system has long been identified as a major obstacle not only to educational mobility for immigrants, but for society at large. And while the borders between the different tracks have become more permeable over the last two decades, they are still difficult to overcome, and systemic change toward a one-track system is not in the cards—particularly not in Germany's cooperative federalism, where educational reform has to overcome an excessive number of veto players.

Public sector employment can be an efficient vehicle for generating better labor market outcomes for disadvantaged groups—see the role of the public sector in increasing female labor market participation and reducing the gender wage gap in Scandinavian countries. With integration as a major policy goal, one might expect that the state would avail itself of this instrument. Alas, it does not. While immigrants are underrepresented in public sector employment in all OECD countries save Sweden, Germany is among the countries where underrepresentation is most pronounced. Immigrant public sector employment hovers around seventy percent of that of the native population for naturalized immigrants, and forty percent for non-naturalized immigrants. These are the third lowest and the fifth lowest rates, respectively, among eleven high-income OECD countries.[38]

Changes at the level of society's perception of immigrants are notoriously difficult to gauge, and the available evidence is conflicting. The "ethnic penalties," which job applicants of Turkish or ex-Yugoslav background have to pay, are lower than those levied on North Africans in France or the Surinamese in the Netherlands, but they are statistically significant.[39] And even the increased probability that a person who does not look ethnically German may indeed be a German citizen has not yet changed the immediate perception: to too many Germans, a Turk remains a Turk, no matter the passport. There are, however, positive signs as well: in 2006, the ALLBUS survey included an item about relevant criteria for the acquisition of German citizenship. Among the choices were two that tap into ethnonational orientations: only one in five of the respondents opined that *deutsche Abstammung*—German descent—should be relevant, and fewer than one in ten named religious affiliation with a Christian denomination. In contrast, choices that tapped into statist orientations, where loyalty and reliability matter, triggered much higher positive response rates: more than eighty percent of the respondents agreed that acquisition of citizenship should require "commitment to the constitution" and "a clear criminal record."[40]

With out-of-type change regarding citizenship acquisition, advanced incremental change regarding the legal status of long-term residents, halting or beginning incremental change with regard to immigration, integration, and the host society's perception of immigrants, there can be little doubt that in the German post-postwar, matters of nationalism and citizenship are moving at a quicker pace than at any time at least since World War II, and probably much longer. The pace of change may be inadequate to compensate for the challenges presented by an aging society and a globalizing world, but this is unsurprising, given the inertia presented by well-embedded social institutions and a political system geared toward the prevention of sudden and radical change.

Older truisms regarding the inclusiveness of traditionally civic nations like France and the United States and the exclusiveness of ethnic nations like Germany can no longer be upheld. The immediate linkage between nationalism and citizenship originally suggested by Hans Kohn in his 1944 landmark work *The Idea of Nationalism* and still the dominant argument in Rogers Brubaker's influential *Citizenship and Nationhood in France and Germany* (1992) certainly has had its merits, but seems less and less capable of explaining empirical citizenship and immigration policies in the contemporary period. Rather, these policies appear to be converging across high-income countries, regardless of civic or ethnic traditions of national identity.[41]

It is not the case, however, that national governments arrive at similar policies independently simply because similar problems tend to trigger similar responses. Policy convergence is also facilitated by social learning and emulation, and by the standards set by international and supranational organizations. In this regard, the European Union is of exceptional importance—not only via intentionally created mechanisms of coordination such as the "best practices" approach of the Open Method of Coordination (OMC) or the effect of conditionality (which has had significant impact on citizenship policies in, for instance, the Baltic states and Slovakia during the EU accession phase), but also via spillover. Thus, the EU Council Directive 2003/109[42] concerning the status of long-term third-country residents, which has been implemented in paragraphs 9a and 38a of the German residency law, effectively extends rights and privileges attached to EU citizenship to non-EU nationals who are long-term residents of EU member states.[43] Deepening EU integration hence does not necessarily, nor in all respects, trend toward "Fortress Europe" and the exaggeration of differences between EU citizens and third-country nationals.

The changes we have observed are substantial. Their causes are multiple: domestically, postmaterialism and the rise of the Green Party induced changes in attitudes and political preferences that slowly rippled through the German party system and eventually helped produce a majority in favor of citizenship reform. The emergence of German entertainers and athletes of non-German ethnic backgrounds has greatly increased the visibility of the multicultural composition of German society.[44] Such cultural changes, however, would probably have amounted to little had it not been for socioeconomic challenges such as the threat of a permanent underclass of immigrants and their descendants, the needs of an increasingly high-skill labor market, and below-replacement fertility rates among ethnic Germans.

Transnational developments, too, have critically contributed to the transformation of nationalism and citizenship in Germany. Those include the shift from a national to a personal logic in the provision and protection of human rights, as well as processes of social learning that help citizenship and immigration policies converge among high-income societies facing similar cultural, demographic, and economic problems. A set of particularly important transnational mechanisms is clearly the result of European integration: the best practices approach of policy coordination helps successful policies travel from one EU member state to others and makes domestic policy production less parochial; EU citizenship and the right to free movement are important drivers of the denationalization of citizenship and the enculturation of EU citizens into models of complex citizenship; and the spillover of rights and privileges of EU citizens to EU residents who are third-country nationals aids the legal status and the mobility chances of the largest groups of immigrants in EU countries, such as ethnic North Africans in France or ethnic Turks and Kurds in Germany. It seems fair to say that national citizenship, immigration, and integration policies have by now been soundly embedded in a European frame, either directly by EU law or in the more mediated fashion of spillovers, social learning, and the diffusion of practices.

## Notes

1. See Tony Judt, *Postwar: A History of Europe since 1945* (New York: Penguin Books, 2006). For contemporaries of that period, the term had different and altogether less expansive connotations—if it was used at all. In practical usage, the postwar—whose beginning was of course uncontested—variously ended with the founding of the two German states in 1949, the closure of the "German Question" in 1961, or the policy of détente of the late 1960s and early 1970s.
2. See Rogers Brubaker, *Citizenship and Nationhood in France and Germany* (Cambridge, MA: Harvard University Press, 1992). Jürgen Habermas, "Citizenship and National Identity," in *Theorizing Citizenship*, ed. Ronald Beiner (Albany, NY: State University of New York Press, 1995). Claus Leggewie, "Ethnizität, Nationalismus und multikulturelle Gesellschaft," in *Nationales Bewußtsein und kollektive Identität: Studien zur Entwicklung des kollektiven Bewußtseins in der Neuzeit*, ed. Helmut Berding, vol. 2. (Frankfurt a.M.: Suhrkamp, 1994), 46–65. Henry Ashby Turner Jr., "Deutsches Staatsbürgerrecht und der Mythos der ethnischen Nation," in *Nation und Gesellschaft in Deutschland: Historische Essays*, eds. Manfred Hettling and Paul Nolte (Munich: C.H. Beck, 1996), 142–50, and many more.
3. For the conceptual history of *Volk* and nation in Germany, see Otto Brunner, Werner Conze, and Reinhart Koselleck, eds., *Geschichtliche Grundbegriffe: Historisches Lexikon zur politisch-sozialen Sprache in Deutschland*, vol. 7 (Stuttgart: Klett-Cotta, 1978), 171–431.
4. Johann G. Fichte, *Addresses to the German Nation*, ed. George Moore (Cambridge/New York: Cambridge University Press, 2009), 183–96.
5. Gregg O. Kvistad, "Segmented Politics: Xenophobia, Citizenship, and Political Loyalty in Germany," in *Identity and Intolerance*, eds. Norbert Finzsch and Dietmar Schirmer, (Cambridge/New York: Cambridge University Press, 1998), 43–70. Gregg O. Kvistad, *The Rise and Demise of German Statism: Loyalty and Political Membership* (New York/Oxford: Berghahn, 1999).
6. See Dietmar Schirmer, "Closing the Nation: Nationalism and Statism in Nineteenth- and Twentieth-Century Germany," in *The Shifting Foundations of Modern Nation-States*, eds. Sima Godfrey and Frank Unger (Toronto: Toronto University Press, 2004), 35–58.

7. Georg W.F. Hegel, *Elements of the Philosophy of Right*, ed. Allen W. Wood (Cambridge/ New York: Cambridge University Press, 1991), 276.

8. See Kvistad, *The Rise and Demise of German Statism*, 27–54.

9. This paraphrases the popular poem *Des Deutschen Vaterland* by the singer of German Romantic nationalism, E.M. Arndt: "… Soweit die deutsche Zunge klingt, Und Gott im Himmel Lieder singt, Das soll es seyn! Das, wackrer Deutscher, nenne Dein!" Ernst Moritz Arndt, *Gedichte von E.M Arndt* (Leipzig: Weidmann'sche Buchhandlung, 1840), 211.

10. Rudolf Vierhaus, "Liberalismus, Beamtenstand und konstitutionelles System," in *Liberalismus in der Gesellschaft des deutschen Vormärz*, ed. Wolfgang Schieder (Göttingen: Vandenhoeck und Ruprecht, 1983), 39–54.

11. "Unmittelbare Reichsangehörigkeit," "Reichs- und Staatsangehörigkeitsgesetz vom 22 July 1913," *Reichs-Gesetzblatt* (Berlin: Reichsamt des Inneren 1913), 583–93, paragraphs 33–5.

12. In 1871, the citizenship law of the Northern German League of 1870 became the law of the Reich, see "Gesetz über den Erwerb und den Verlust der Bundes- und Staatsangehörigkeit vom 1. Juni 1870," *Bundes-Gesetzblatt des Norddeutschen Bundes* (Berlin: Gesetz-Sammlungs-Komtior 1870), 355–60). Conditions for the loss of citizenship are detailed in paragraphs 13–23; for the prolonged absence rule, see paragraph 21.

13. Wolfgang Mommsen, "Nationalität im Zeichen offensiver Weltpolitik: Das Reichs- und Staatsangehörigkeitsgesetz des Deutschen Reiches vom 22 Januar 1913," in Hettling and Nolte, *Nation und Gesellschaft in Deutschland*, 128–41, 130 (author's translation).

14. Quoted in Hagen Schulze, *Weimar: Deutschland 1917–1933. Die Deutschen und ihre Nation*, vol. 4 (Berlin: Siedler Verlag, 1982), 107 (author's translation).

15. "Gesetz zur Wiederherstellung des Berufsbeamtentums vom 7. April 1933," *Reichsgesetzblatt I* (Berlin: Reichsruckerei, 1933), 175.

16. Quoted in George L. Mosse, *Nazi Culture: A Documentary History* (New York: Schocken Books 1966), 338 (emphasis added).

17. Further, the Basic Law of the Federal Republic reinstituted citizenship for all those who had been stripped of it during Nazi rule "for political, racial, or religious reasons," Basic Law article 116 (2), (author's translation).

18. The operational definition of ethnic Germanness and the rights and obligations of refugees and expellees were codified in the Federal Expellee Law of 1953 and the Law on the Clarification of Questions Regarding Citizenship of 1955. See "Gesetz über die Angelegenheiten der Vertriebenen und Flüchtlinge (Bundesvertriebenengesetz – BVFT)," *Bundesgesetzblatt I* (Bonn/Cologne: Bundesanzeiger-Verlags-GmbH), no. 22, 22 May 1953, 201–21 and "Gesetz zur Regelung von Fragen der Staatsangehörigkeit," *Bundesgesetzblatt I* (Bonn/Cologne: Bundesanzeiger-Verlags-GmbH), no. 6, 25 February 1955, 65–8.

19. The bulk of this migration occurred between 1945 and 1949, when around 12.5 million people arrived on the territories of what would become the FRG and the GDR. Between 1950 and the fortification of the inner-German border in 1961, 3.8 million *Übersiedler* moved from the GDR to West Germany. An additional 400,000 came from Eastern Europe and the Soviet Union.

20. Douglas B. Klusmeyer and Demetrios G. Papademetriou, *Immigration Policy in the Federal Republic of Germany: Negotiating Membership and Remaking the Nation* (New York/Oxford: Berghahn Books, 2009), 86–90.

21. Klusmeyer and Papademetriou, *Immigration Policy*, 91.

22. Yasemin N. Soysal, *Limits of Citizenship: Migrants and Post-National Membership in Europe* (Chicago and London: The University of Chicago Press, 1994), 1. See also Rainer

Bauböck, *Transnational Citizenship: Membership and Rights across International Borders* (Cheltenham: Edgar Elger Publishing Ltd., 2007) and David Weissbrodt, *The Human Rights of Non-Citizens* (Oxford/New York: Oxford University Press, 2007).

23. Stefan Rühl, *Grunddaten der Zuwandererbevölkerung in Deutschland*. Working Paper 27 of the Forschungsgruppe des Bundesamts für Migration und Flüchtlinge (Berlin: Bundesamt für Migration und Flüchtlinge, 2009), 49, accessed 22 July 2014, http://www.integrationskompass.de/global/show_document.asp?id=aaaaaaaaaaadfpa.

24. Christian Joppke, *Immigration and the Nation-State: A Comparison of the United States, Germany, and Great Britain* (Oxford: Oxford University Press, 1999), 84. See also Klusmeyer and Papademetriou, *Immigration Policy*, 113–18.

25. During the last three years of the postwar (from 1988 to 1990), almost one million ethnic Germans migrated to Germany from Central and Eastern Europe, mainly from Poland and the Soviet Union. Susanne Worbs et al., *(Spät-) Aussiedler in Deutschland: Eine Analyse aktueller Daten und Forschungsergebnisse*, Forschungsbericht 20 (Berlin: Bundesamt für Migration und Flüchtlinge, 2013), 31–2.

26. Klusmeyer and Papademetriou, *Immigration Policy*, 152. For the full text of Weizsäcker's speech, see Richard von Weizsäcker, *Demokratische Leidenschaft – Reden des Bundespräsidenten*, ed. Eberhard Jäckel (Stuttgart: Deutsche Verlagsanstalt, 1994).

27. How well deserved the CDU hastened to demonstrate with its embarrassingly parochial "Kinder statt Inder" (children instead of Indians) slogan in the 2003 electoral campaign in the state of North Rhine-Westphalia, with which it essentially suggested that the government, instead of courting Indian IT experts, should devise policies to increase fertility rates in Germany, thus breeding additional children, some of whom would be able to fill the vacant IT jobs a mere twenty-five years later. The numbers of highly qualified individuals who entered the German labor market via the Green Card program remained low. By the end of 2007, a mere 519 (including 53 scientists) had made use of the opportunity, "Qualifizierte Zuwanderer in Deutschland," *Frankfurter Allgemeine Zeitung*, 10 August 2014. In 2012, the German Green Card program was discontinued and replaced with the EU "Blue Card", which is less constraining with regard to eligibility and renewability.

28. Unabhängige Kommission "Zuwanderung," *Zuwanderung gestalten, Integration fördern. Bericht der Unabhängigen Kommission "Zuwanderung,"* 4 July 2001 (Berlin: Bundesministerium des Inneren), accessed 21 July 2014, http://www.bmi.bund.de/cae/servlet/contentblob/123148/publicationFile/9076/Zuwanderungsbericht_pdf.

29. See "Gesetz zur Steuerung und Begrenzung der Zuwanderung und zur Regelung des Aufenthalts und der Integration von Unionsbürgern und Ausländern," *Bundesgesetzblatt I* (Bonn: Bundesanzeiger-Verlags-GmbH 2004), no. 41, 5 August 2004, 1950–2011.

30. The German law is actually more inclusive than the French or Dutch nationality laws in so far as it gives citizenship automatically to second generation immigrants if at least one parent has been legally resident in Germany for at least eight years, while the French and Dutch laws only pertain to third generation immigrants.

31. OECD, *International Migration Outlook 2010* (Paris: OECD Publishing, 2010), 162, accessed 15 July 2014, http://www.oecd-ilibrary.org/social-issues-migration-health/international-migration-outlook-2010_migr_outlook-2010-en.

32. Fees for naturalization proper and the fees for language and naturalization tests add up to some four hundred euros per person. In addition, fees may apply to renunciation of original citizenship. The country of origin may further penalize citizenship renunciation, for instance by punitive inheritance taxes levied on ex-citizens.

33. This, however, is true for most welfare state provisions in most high-income countries, and can hence only help to explain why significant numbers of immigrants in all such countries choose not to naturalize despite meeting the eligibility requirements. It cannot explain why German naturalization rates are consistently at the low end of the distribution.

34. The EU Blue Card is a one-track scheme for the acquisition of an EU work permit for highly skilled third-country nationals. It is valid for two years and is renewable.

35. OECD, *International Migration Outlook 2013* (Paris: OECD Publishing, 2013), 254.

36. To put these numbers into perspective, it might be useful to add that from 2000 to 2010 the Bundesagentur für Arbeit used to issue some 300,000 work permits for seasonal labor in agriculture per year.

37. Petra Ahrens, *Soziale Integration von Migrantinnen und Migranten* (Berlin: Agentur für Gleichstellung im ESF, 2011), 12–14, accessed 22 July 2014, http://www.esf-gleichstellung.de/fileadmin/data/Downloads/Aktuelles/expertise_soziale_integration_migrant_innen.pdf.

38. OECD, *International Migration Outlook 2010*, 173. See also T. Alexander Aleinikoff and Douglas Klusmeyer, *Citizenship Policies for an Age of Migration* (Washington, DC: Carnegie Endowment for International Peace, 2002), 71–2.

39. OECD, *International Migration Outlook 2013*. Ethnic penalties in the job market are experimentally measured by sending otherwise identical job applications once under a German (French, Dutch, and so forth) sounding name and once under a name that suggests the ethnicity of a major immigrant group. The difference in positive replies, such as an invitation for an interview, constitutes the ethnic penalty (see Anthony F. Heath and Sin Yi Cheung, *Unequal Chances: Ethnic Minorities in Western Labour Markets* (Oxford/New York: Oxford University Press, 2007)).

40. The numbers refer to respondents who ranked the respective issues with 6 or 7 on a scale reaching from 1 (not at all important) to 7 (very important). The item was a repeat question from ALLBUS 1996; across-time comparison shows a clear trend away from ethnic decent and toward issues that measure either civic reliability or the capacity to blend into majority society.

41. See, for instance, Riva Kastoryano, *Negotiating Identities: States and Immigrants in France and Germany* (Princeton, NJ: Princeton University Press, 2002). Patrick Weil, "Access to Citizenship: A Comparison of Twenty-Five Nationality Laws," in *Citizenship Today: Global Perspectives and Practices*, eds. T. Alexander Aleinikoff and Douglas Klusmeyer (Washington, DC: Carnegie Endowment for International Peace, 2001), 17–35.

42. EU Council Directive 2003/109 has been implemented in all EU member states save Denmark and the Schengen opt-outs Ireland and the U.K.

43. Paragraph 9a specifies the acquisition of Long-Term Residency EU status for third-country nationals who are legal long-term residents in Germany; paragraph 38a deals with the reverse case, i.e., the right to residency in Germany for third-country nationals who have long-term residence rights in another EU country. The main difference between EU citizens and third-country long-term residents in the EU is that the right to free movement for the former is unconditional, while Long-Term Residency EU for third-country nationals is dependent on the applicant's demonstration of economic self-sustenance. See "Gesetz zur Steuerung und Begrenzung der Zuwanderung und zur Regelung des Aufenthalts und der Integration von Unionsbürgern und Ausländern," *Bundesgesetzblatt I*, no. 41, 5 August 2004, 1950–2011.

44. The national soccer team is the prime exhibit. However, the players of non-German or mixed ethnicities are afforded special scrutiny regarding their willingness to sing the

national anthem before international matches, which serves as a reminder that the traditional combination of ethnonationalism and statism still lingers.

# Works Cited

Ahrens, Petra. *Soziale Integration von Migrantinnen und Migranten*. Berlin: Agentur für Gleichstellung im ESF, 2011. Accessed 22 July 2014. http://www.esf-gleichstellung.de/fileadmin/data/Downloads/Daten_Fa.ten/expertise_soziale_integration_migrant_innen.pdf.

Aleinikoff, T. Alexander, and Douglas Klusmeyer. *Citizenship Policies for an Age of Migration*. Washington, DC: Carnegie Endowment for International Peace, 2002.

Arndt, Ernst Moritz. *Gedichte von E.M Arndt*. Leipzig: Weidmann'sche Buchhandlung, neue verbesserte verminderte und doch vermehrte Ausgabe, 1840.

Bauböck, Rainer. *Transnational Citizenship: Membership and Rights across International Borders*. Cheltenham: Edgar Elger Publishing Ltd., 2007.

Brubaker, Rogers. *Citizenship and Nationhood in France and Germany*. Cambridge, MA: Harvard University Press, 1992.

Brunner, Otto, Werner Conze, and Reinhart Koselleck, eds. *Geschichtliche Grundbegriffe: Historisches Lexikon zur politisch-sozialen Sprache in Deutschland*, 8 vols. Stuttgart: Klett-Cotta, 1972–97.

*Bundesgesetzblatt I*. "Gesetz über die Angelegenheiten der Vertriebenen und Flüchtlinge (Bundesvertriebenengesetz – BVFT)." Bonn/Cologne: Bundesanzeiger-Verlags-GmbH, 1953. No. 22, 22 May 1953, 201–21.

*Bundesgesetzblatt I*. "Gesetz zur Regelung von Fragen der Staatsangehörigkeit." Bonn/Cologne: Bundesanzeiger-Verlags-GmbH, 1955. No. 6, 25 February 1955, 65–8.

*Bundesgesetzblatt I*. "Gesetz zur Steuerung und Begrenzung der Zuwanderung und zur Regelung des Aufenthalts und der Integration von Unionsbürgern und Ausländern." Bonn: Bundesanzeiger-Verlags-GmbH, 2004. No. 41, 5 August 2004.

*Bundes-Gesetzblatt des Norddeutschen Bundes*. "Gesetz über den Erwerb und den Verlust der Bundes- und Staatsangehörigkeit vom 1. Juni 1870." Berlin: Gesetz-Sammlungs-Komtior, 1870, 355–60.

Fichte, Johann G. *Addresses to the German Nation*. Edited by George Moore. Cambridge/New York: Cambridge University Press, 2009.

*Frankfurter Allgemeine Zeitung*. "Qualifizierte Zuwanderer in Deutschland." 10 August 2014.

Habermas, Jürgen. "Citizenship and National Identity." In *Theorizing Citizenship*, edited by Ronald Beiner. Albany, NY: State University of New York Press, 1995.

Heath, Anthony F. and Sin Yi Cheung. *Unequal Chances: Ethnic Minorities in Western Labour Markets*. Oxford/New York: Oxford University Press, 2007.

Hegel, Georg W.F. *Elements of the Philosophy of Right*, edited by Allen W. Wood. Cambridge/New York: Cambridge University Press, 1991.

Judt, Tony. *Postwar: A History of Europe Since 1945*. New York: Penguin Books, 2006.

Joppke, Christian. *Immigration and the Nation-State: A Comparison of the United States, Germany, and Great Britain*. Oxford: Oxford University Press, 1999.

Kastoryano, Riva. *Negotiating Identities: States and Immigrants in France and Germany*. Princeton, NJ: Princeton University Press, 2002.

Klusmeyer, Douglas B. and Demetrios G. Papademetriou. *Immigration Policy in the Federal Republic of Germany: Negotiating Membership and Remaking the Nation*. New York/Oxford: Berghahn Books, 2009.

Kohn, Hans. *The Idea of Nationalism: A Study in Its Origins and Background*. New York: Macmillan, 1944.

Kvistad, Gregg O. "Segmented Politics: Xenophobia, Citizenship, and Political Loyalty in Germany." In *Identity and Intolerance*, edited by Norbert Finzsch and Dietmar Schirmer, 43–70. Cambridge/New York: Cambridge University Press, 1998.

Kvistad, Gregg O. *The Rise and Demise of German Statism: Loyalty and Political Membership*. New York/Oxford: Berghahn, 1999.

Leggewie, Claus. "Ethnizität, Nationalismus und multikulturelle Gesellschaft." In *Nationales Bewußtsein und kollektive Identität: Studien zur Entwicklung des kollektiven Bewußtseins in der Neuzeit*, edited by Helmut Berding, 46–65. Vol. 2. Frankfurt a.M.: Suhrkamp, 1994.

Mommsen, Wolfgang. "Nationalität im Zeichen offensiver Weltpolitik: Das Reichs- und Staatsangehörigkeitsgesetz des Deutschen Reiches vom 22 Januar 1913." In *Nation und Gesellschaft in Deutschland: Historische Essays*, edited by Manfred Hettling and Paul Nolte, 128–41. Munich: C.H. Beck, 1996.

Mosse, George L. *Nazi Culture: A Documentary History*. New York: Schocken Books, 1966.

OECD. *International Migration Outlook 2010*. Paris: OECD Publishing, 2010. Accessed 15 July 2014. http://www.oecd-ilibrary.org/social-issues-migration-health/international-migration-outlook-2010_migr_outlook-2010-en.

OECD. *International Migration Outlook 2013*. Paris: OECD Publishing, 2013. Accessed 15 July 2014. http://www.oecd-ilibrary.org/social-issues-migration-health/international-migration-outlook-2013_migr_outlook-2013-en;jsessionid=2mcap90q4mxpr.x-oecd-live-03.

*Reichs-Gesetzblatt*. "Unmittelbare Reichsangehörigkeit." "Reichs- und Staatsangehörigkeitsgesetz vom 22.7.1913." Berlin: Reichsamt des Inneren, 1913, 583–93.

*Reichsgesetzblatt I*. "Gesetz zur Wiederherstellung des Berufsbeamtentums vom 7. April 1933." Berlin: Reichsruckerei, 1933, 175.

Rühl, Stefan. *Grunddaten der Zuwandererbevölkerung in Deutschland*. Working Paper 27 of the Forschungsgruppe des Bundesamts für Migration und Flüchtlinge. Berlin: Bundesamt für Migration und Flüchtlinge, 2009. Accessed 22 July 2014. http://www.integrationskompass. de/global/show_document.asp?id=aaaaaaaaaaaadfpa.

Schirmer, Dietmar. "Closing the Nation: Nationalism and Statism in Nineteenth- and Twentieth-Century Germany." In *The Shifting Foundations of Modern Nation-States*, edited by Sima Godfrey and Frank Unger, 35–8. Toronto: Toronto University Press, 2004.

Schulze, Hagen. *Weimar: Deutschland 1917–1933. Die Deutschen und ihre Nation*. Vol. 4. Berlin: Siedler Verlag, 1982.

Soysal, Yasemin N. *Limits of Citizenship: Migrants and Post-National Membership in Europe*. Chicago and London: The University of Chicago Press, 1994.

Turner, Henry Ashby Jr. "Deutsches Staatsbürgerrecht und der Mythos der ethnischen Nation." In *Nation und Gesellschaft in Deutschland: Historische Essays*, edited by Manfred Hettling and Paul Nolte, 142–150. Munich: C.H. Beck, 1996.

Unabhängige Kommission "Zuwanderung." *Zuwanderung gestalten, Integration fördern. Bericht der Unabhängigen Kommission "Zuwanderung."* Bundesministerium des Inneren, 4 July 2001. Accessed 21 July 2014. http://www.bmi.bund.de/cae/servlet/contentblob/123148/ publicationFile/9076/Zuwanderungsbericht_pdf.

Vierhaus, Rudolf. "Liberalismus, Beamtenstand und konstitutionelles System. In *Liberalismus in der Gesellschaft des deutschen Vormärz*, edited by Wolfgang Schieder, 39–54. Göttingen: Vandenhoeck and Ruprecht, 1983.

Weil, Patrick. "Access to Citizenship: A Comparison of Twenty-Five Nationality Laws." In *Citizenship Today: Global Perspectives and Practices*, edited by T. Alexander Aleinikoff and Douglas Klusmeyer, 17–35. Washington, DC: Carnegie Endowment for International Peace, 2001.

Weissbrodt, David. *The Human Rights of Non-Citizens*. Oxford/New York: Oxford University Press, 2007.

Weizsäcker, Richard von. *Demokratische Leidenschaft – Reden des Bundespräsidenten*. Edited by Eberhard Jäckel. Stuttgart: Deutsche Verlagsanstalt, 1994.

Worbs, Susanne, et al. *(Spät-) Aussiedler in Deutschland: Eine Analyse aktueller Daten und Forschungsergebnisse*, Forschungsbericht 20. Berlin: Bundesamt für Migration und Flüchtlinge, 2013.

Wunder, Bernd. *Geschichte der Bürokratie in Deutschland*. Frankfurt a.M.: Suhrkamp, 1986.

**Dietmar Schirmer**, is currently professor in the Department of Political and Social Sciences, Zeppelin University, Friedrichshafen. He earned his PhD at the Freie Universität, Berlin and has held positions at Cornell University, the University of British Columbia, and University of Florida. His research interests include historical comparative politics, specifically nationalism, and state formation. Current research projects concern the relations between states and national minorities in the European Union, and state architecture in Europe since the Renaissance.

*Chapter 10*

# LEARNING TO LIVE WITH THE OTHER GERMANY IN THE POST-WALL FEDERAL REPUBLIC

*Kathrin Bower*

> The GDR could not be a foreign country; otherwise we would
> have run across it at some point. But it was definitely not
> domestic either. East Germany was so far away that it had
> disappeared from our map of the world. Not foreign. Not
> domestic.
>
> —Susanne Leinemann

The ambiguity of the relationship between the two Germanys as neither foreign nor familiar lies at the heart of Susanne Leinemann's 2002 memoir about her experiences coming of age in the Federal Republic during the 1970s and 1980s.[1] Born in 1968 in Hamburg, Leinemann belonged to the generation of Germans for whom the Berlin Wall was at once an unquestioned feature of the German landscape and a barrier that rendered the German Democratic Republic nearly invisible. It was not until Leinemann traveled to East Germany in 1985 to visit her pen pal in Dresden that she began to feel a sense of kinship with the other Germany. She mused over the fact that the encounter with the real people of East Germany, with whom she formed lasting friendships, did not inspire the wish for a unified country, but rather stimulated anger at the injustice of the travel restrictions imposed on East German citizens.[2] The wall was an impediment to freedom of movement, but the division itself went unquestioned. Although Leinemann's memoir represents only one account from the West German perspective, the general lack of curiosity and indifference she described until her visit to Dresden was characteristic of a majority of West Germans, who had largely made their peace with the division of the country by the

---

Notes for this chapter begin on page 271.

1980s.[3] The Federal Republic of the 1980s preferred to characterize itself as a postnational nation, loyal to the principles of the European Economic Community, an alliance that in turn would further help to assuage the nationalist blemishes of the past. East Germany for its part had at last achieved recognition as a sovereign nation on the world stage and continued to emphasize how its founding ideology of antifascist socialism distinguished it in body and spirit from the Federal Republic. While the West German government had modulated earlier rhetoric urging reunification in order to preserve prosperity and peace, the East German government insisted on the division as the basis for its self-definition and raison d'être.

## Forward into the Past

After forty years of separation, neither the West Germans nor the East Germans were prepared for the impact of reunification. But had the peoples of the two countries developed separate cultural identities to such an extent that the dissolution of the border represented merely the illusion of a return to sociocultural community? Since the collapse of the East German state in 1989 and the subsequent suturing of divided Germany in 1990, scores of books and articles have been published on the economic and political conditions that led inexorably, or less so, to the demise of the GDR, as well as myriad personal accounts by East German citizens describing their ideological and critical distance to the state, their blinkered view of the world, or their cheerful memories of childhood guided by compliant citizenship and populated with the products of *Ostalgie*.[4] Other accounts by East and West Germans offer perspectives on life after unification and the perceived, real or imagined, differences between *Ossis* and *Wessis* as well as speculation on how long such differences will persist.

It would certainly appear that in the early post-wall years *Ossis* and *Wessis* had become terms of cultural difference designating competing conceptions of "Germanness," ironically undermining the myth of reunification by revealing the otherness within the idealization of *ein Volk*. In the discussion to follow, I will first examine how the two Germanys managed and learned to live with their separation, and will then explore how the lingering effects of those lessons influenced responses to unification. How did the two Germanys define themselves during the years 1949 to 1989? Did the clash of political ideologies and social realities in the FRG and GDR outweigh any shared cultural history? How has the master narrative of the GDR state as an *Unrechtsstaat* (a state *not* based on the rule of law or the constitution) largely dictated by a West German imagination affected relationships between East Germans and West Germans? What steps are necessary to establish a collective sense of responsibility and engagement with the past in pursuit of a truly unified future in a post-wall, renationalized Federal Republic? To offer some preliminary answers to these questions, I have selected a range of published protocols, memoirs, and essays as a basis for analyzing a variety of perspectives across generational and geographic boundaries in response to unification: Helga Königsdorf's *Unterwegs nach Deutschland* (1995), Daniela Dahn's *Westwärts und nicht vergessen* (1997), Jana Hensel's *Zonenkinder* (2002), Susanne Leinemann's *Aufgewacht. Mauer weg* (2002), and Claudia Rusch's *Meine freie deutsche Jugend* (2003).[5] Although many more accounts could be considered, works by these five writers already serve to complicate overly simplistic views of East versus West Germans as *Jammerossis* and *Besserwessis*, while also shedding light on the complexity of the German-German relationship, past and present.

In order to evaluate the impact of 1989 and beyond on the perceptions of *Ossis* and *Wessis*, it is first necessary to look back over the forty years of division and the history of East and West German relations that preceded it. From its very beginnings, the Federal Republic viewed itself as a provisional, partial state that would one day become whole again. When the Soviets issued a note of support for unification in March 1952, however, the conditions were unacceptable to the West German government and its American ally. Without democratic elections in all of Germany, the Americans insisted, there could be no unification or peace agreement.[6] As the Cold War heated up, it became obvious that the Western Allies and the Soviets would not reconcile their differences on the terms of unification. In the first two decades of its existence, the Federal Republic arrogated to itself the right to speak for Germany as a whole (*Alleinvertretungsanspruch*), because it alone had a democratically elected government. In tandem with this assertion of voice, the Federal Republic sought to deter other countries from recognizing the sovereignty of the GDR by refusing to establish diplomatic relations with countries that did so (with the exception of the Soviet Union).[7] Although West Germany and East Germany signed a basic treaty in 1972 in which each recognized the other country's sovereignty, West Germany tacitly continued to regard itself as the only legitimate German government, evidenced by its policy of automatically granting citizenship to any East German who wished to live in the Federal Republic.

## Mirror, Mirror on the Wall

During four decades of division, each Germany developed images of the other that served as foils. West Germany contrasted its democratic political system and capitalist economy with the socialist dictatorship in East

Germany, while East Germany touted its own antifascist credentials and portrayed the Federal Republic's commitment to capitalist democracy as the continuity of fascism by other means. As a counter to the coupling of West Germany's acceptance into NATO and its rising economy, which could easily absorb reparations payments to the victims of the Holocaust, East Germany's antifascist origin story not only denied shared responsibility for World War II, but also firmly established its moral superiority as the "better" Germany. In this version of history, the line between the two Germanys had miraculously been drawn so as to divide the fascists from the communists, separating them into discrete geographic compartments. The construction of the Berlin Wall in 1961, with its SED label as an antifascist protective bulwark, only reinforced the idea of a demarcation line. The wall itself came to serve as a kind of projection screen for images of the other Germany and as an affirmation of each state's core values. In his 1982 story *Der Mauerspringer*, West German writer Peter Schneider described the wall as a mirror that reflected the Federal Republic's sense of superiority while also obscuring any real interest in what lay beyond it: "the wall became a mirror for the West Germans, telling them day after day who was the fairest in the land. Whether there was life beyond the death strip soon became a matter of interest only to pigeons and cats."[8] As a mirror for the West's narcissistic satisfaction with its political and economic system, the wall seemed to have only one side, oddly mimicking in reverse the official maps of the GDR capital issued by the East German government, which showed nothing but blank space where the streets of West Berlin should have been.[9]

At once a border and a threshold, the wall symbolized the confrontation between two different ideologies, as well as their mutual mission of repression and denial. In an analysis of the division and subsequent unification of the Federal Republic, political scientist Wolf Wagner noted that the projection of totalitarianism onto the GDR made it easier for the Federal Republic to repress or deny the fascist continuities in its own government, as well as its persecution of communists,[10] while the projection of fascism onto the FRG enabled the Democratic Republic to repress or ignore its own totalitarian tendencies.[11] For his part, anthropologist Dominic Boyer portrayed each Germany's projection of negative qualities onto the other as the basis for their symbiotic relationship, noting that for each "the 'truly' forward-looking Germany defined itself in opposition to the backward glance of the other Germany. For each Germany, the other represented the national-cultural past against which its ideal national-futurity could be measured. Neither Germany, in the end, made sense without the other."[12] While consumed with casting aspersions on each other's politics and morality, each Germany studiously disregarded the resistance to fascism in the other, with the exception of the politically neutral White Rose.[13] The willful blindness toward morally redemptive activities on both sides of the wall at the state level was offset by an exaggerated indulgence toward the GDR on the part of West German leftists. Whether due to blindness or indulgence, the foundation for such misperceptions resulted from a combination of indifference and ignorance regarding real existing conditions in the GDR.[14]

By the mid-1970s, the two Germanys had reached a level of wary coexistence and mutual recognition codified in the basic treaty of 1972, but remained at odds on the issue of unification. For the East German government, the treaty was a vehicle for cementing its identity as a separate state, distinct from the Federal Republic on ideological grounds that precluded any *Zusammengehörigkeitsgefühl* (shared sense of belonging).[15] In a report to the Central Committee of the SED in May 1973, Erich Honecker was adamant that no special relationship existed between the GDR and the FRG, and denied any unity between the two states: "The GDR is not part of the FRG and the FRG is not part of the GDR."[16] The West German government took a more ambivalent course. The Federal Republic continued to see itself as the legitimate representative of the German nation and in a judgment passed by the Federal Constitutional Court in July 1973 affirmed the two-states-one-nation concept, arguing that the "The German Democratic Republic belongs to Germany and cannot be seen as a foreign country in relation to the Federal Republic of Germany."[17]

Despite the FRG's official commitment to unification, the two countries increasingly drifted apart, divided by ideological differences, social values, and a deadly border. As time passed, West Germans became less and less interested in unification and had comfortably reconciled themselves to life on the more prosperous side of the wall. In his review of polling data from the mid-1980s, Hans-Georg Betz observed that over half of the West Germans polled between the ages of 14 and 29 regarded East Germans as a separate people and viewed East Germany as a foreign country.[18] Other studies showed that some two-thirds of West German youth had neither interest in nor knowledge of the GDR.[19] It was not until the latter half of the 1980s when reforms swept the eastern bloc countries and Mikhail Gorbachev became a household name that West Germans began to take notice of what was transpiring in the GDR.[20]

## Migration, Revolution, Unification

When Hungary opened its borders to Austria in the summer of 1989, thousands of East Germans took advantage of the opportunity and fled to the West in a wave of mass immigration that would continue unabated until the GDR officially opened its own borders in November 1989. In a 1997 article published in the now defunct journal *East European Quarterly*, political scientist Peter O'Brien suggested that "migration (or the threat of it) inspired the revolution and determined the collapse of the GDR" and also "set the pace and terms of unification."[21] While one could argue that the mass defection of East German citizens did not so much inspire the revolution as represent a symptom of the problems with the GDR system, the hemorrhaging of able-bodied and well-trained young citizens was something the state could neither afford nor effectively stop by a show of force. For Daniela Dahn, a GDR writer, intellectual, dissident, and SED party member, the late 1980s represented a moment in GDR history in which the citizens had finally found their voice and the solidarity and strength to express themselves: "Finally it seemed that futility had been vanquished and the age of meaning had dawned."[22] The many discussions and forums she attended at that time were inspired by ideas of reform and not by the desire to emulate West Germany. Yet as events unfolded, it became obvious that reform of the derelict East German state was neither politically possible nor economically feasible and unification was seen as the best solution to the crisis.

In August 1990, the GDR and the FRG signed a unification agreement determining that the GDR would be incorporated into the Federal Republic according to article 23 of the Basic Law. On 3 October 1990, the German Democratic Republic together with the majority of its laws and civil institutions ceased to exist. This absorption of the GDR into the Federal Republic gave rise to assertions of colonization and the creation of a subordinate East German class paradoxically transformed into subalterns simultaneous with their recognition as *de jure* citizens of the Federal Republic. Despite their equal citizenship on paper, however, they were not seen as fully committed to the democratic principles of the unified state. In O'Brien's analysis, West Germans viewed both foreigners and East Germans as in need of resocialization "to respect the liberal democratic values of West German political culture."[23] This perception of the East Germans' deficient democratic commitment was contradicted by their actual attitudes, reflected in the results of an Allensbach Institute survey in 1990 that showed East German and West German endorsements of democratic government to be virtually identical.[24]

The sudden and sweeping erasure of the state that was once their country, combined with widespread prejudices and negative perceptions of life in the GDR held by West Germans, generated a sense of culture shock among East Germans in the expanded Federal Republic. As Wolf Wagner reported in his 2005 *Kulturschock* study, what had previously been normality for East Germans was equated with poverty, while at the same time East

Germans were struggling with pressing, present concerns about their live-lihood in a new Germany where they felt humiliated and devalued.[25] For some East Germans, it was as if they had become migrants without ever leaving their home. The sense of anomie that followed unification was dif-ficult for many East Germans, while others welcomed the challenges of the transition. Regardless of how successful they were at negotiating life in the unified Federal Republic, almost half of East Germans responding to a 2003 survey reported that they still felt like second-class citizens in the FRG.[26]

## *Wende* Migrants and German *Ausländer*

Despite the Federal Republic's implicit recognition of one people, two states, the *Volk* had indeed evolved in different ways as a result of forty years of socialization under oppositional political systems, lending some truth to the popular retort regarding the unification slogan "'We are one people.' 'We are, too.'"[27] Building a sense of community to bridge the social and cul-tural differences that grew out of political division is a slow process and the designations East and West German as well as their more pejorative cous-ins *Ossi* and *Wessi* persist more than two decades after the so-called *Wende* or unification. As Peter Schneider prophetically predicted in 1982, the wall in people's heads would take much longer to dismantle than the physi-cal wall that had divided the country.[28] Public opinion surveys, historical analyses, and sociological studies provide insights into important facets of unification and its effects, but personal accounts offer a more fine-grained and multidimensional perspective that both individualizes and human-izes the lives of respective German others before and after the wall. In the following discussion, I will look at examples of personal accounts by East and West Germans describing their relationships to the GDR state, their sense of identity in postunification Germany, and their perspectives on *Ossis* and *Wessis*: Helga Königsdorf's collection *Unterwegs nach Deutschland* based on interviews with East and West Germans between 1990 and 1995; Daniela Dahn's *Westwärts und nicht vergessen* (1997); Susanne Leinemann's *Aufgewacht. Mauer weg* (2002); Jana Hensel's bestselling *Zonenkinder* of 2002; and Claudia Rusch's alternate version of a GDR childhood in *Meine freie deutsche Jugend* published in 2003.

Helga Königsdorf's collected interviews with East and West Germans provide insights into geographic differences as well as generational ones. As a former citizen of the GDR, Königsdorf enjoyed a success-ful career as a mathematician and writer. After unification, she made a name for herself as a critical voice on the GDR past and the complexi-ties of the German-German relationship in several collections of stories, an autobiography, and two volumes of *"Protokolle"* offering a range of personal impressions on unification: *Adieu DDR* (1990) and *Unterwegs nach Deutschland* (1995). In the foreword to *Adieu DDR*, Königsdorf wrote: "Without changing our location, we enter a foreign land."[29] Five years later, she assessed the situation somewhat differently: "Becoming one people was not difficult ... Being one people is more difficult than becoming one. ... Our relationship to history separates us more than it unites us."[30] The competing historical narratives constructed to identify and justify the GDR and the FRG continued to exert influence on attitudes and perceptions after unification, complicated by the nearly wholesale rejection of GDR institutions, rituals, and social structure along with its designation as an *Unrechtsstaat*. The undifferentiated dismissal of the GDR as an *Unrechtsstaat* only served to deepen the divide between East and West, described by Konrad Jarausch, Hinrich Seeba, and David Conradt as a binary opposition between the good, liberal, and democratic West Germany and the bad, repressive, and communist former East Germany.[31] Königsdorf acknowledged that East Germans were tempted to invent new biographies for themselves as an alternative to accepting the negative image of their past that dominated West German perceptions: "And so it happens that everyone has their own truth in the end. The other's truth is painful when it calls one's life into question."[32] In that atmosphere of insecurity and rapid change, Königsdorf envisioned her book as an invitation and inspiration to dialogue, especially to those uncomfortable with the pace and dimensions of unification.

*Unterwegs nach Deutschland* is an apt title for a collection of multiple viewpoints on identity and belonging, concepts of freedom and democracy, future possibilities, and missed opportunities in the transition from divided to united Germany. While Königsdorf's sampling was far from statistically significant, the diversity in responses among older and younger generation East Germans punctured any simplistic arguments about a clear age divide in attitudes toward the GDR and the new, post-wall Germany. One university student interviewed in 1993 claimed that she would always be a product of the GDR and saw no reason to be ashamed of that fact. Yet she also felt abandoned by her parents' generation, who were so absorbed in transforming themselves that they did not take time to address the confusion felt by their children.[33] A young man interviewed in 1990 insisted that the ideals of the revolution had been betrayed and he was concerned about a resurgence of fascism.[34] Such concerns are bolstered by views such as those expressed by a nineteen-year-old *Gymnasium* student that right-wing extremism was a strong influence on the young people in his town and that it would have been better to keep Germany divided into two sovereign states.[35]

Among the older generation of East Germans, there were also a range of views, from those who felt betrayed by the SED government because of the opportunities they missed to those who defended their service and allegiance to the GDR. In some cases, the defense of past actions blended with a supple mindset regarding the conditions for success in united Germany. The experiences of a former Stasi official interviewed for *Adieu DDR* illustrate the opalescence of attitudes not only across and within generations, but also within individuals. Whereas he still felt affinity with the East German state in 1990, by 1993 he claimed to have no identity, except perhaps for a continued sense of being different from West Germans. In a telling statement, he equated his neutral feelings toward West Germans with his attitude toward foreigners in general: "I have never held prejudices towards West Germans. Now I'm going to say something really terrible: just as I've never held prejudices against any other foreigners."[36] Despite a common language and a shared cultural heritage in which four decades of separation could be seen as a mere interlude, the sense of estrangement encouraged by division remained.

## Hierarchies of Belonging

In contrast to Königsdorf's postunification interviews with a diverse group of informants, Dahn, Leinemann, Hensel, and Rusch focused on their own experiences both before and after unification and used these as bases for more general assertions and assumptions about the state of *Ossi-Wessi* relations. Daniela Dahn's *Westwärts und nicht vergessen: Vom Unbehagen in der Einheit* (1997) combines her reckoning with the process of unification with a critique of the double standard the new Federal Republic applied when reviewing GDR history. Dahn is a journalist, intellectual, writer, and critical voice from the GDR whose discomfort with unification was fueled in part by her resentment towards the devaluation of her past. Spurred by the West German presumption that East Germans are resistant to confronting the effects of a socialist dictatorship on their lives as GDR citizens, Dahn set out to balance the scales by showcasing "the modest advantages of the GDR and the immodest disadvantages of the Federal Republic."[37] She rejected the view that critics of the GDR regime could only opt for exile or inner immigration, but acknowledged that dissidence and opposition came with a price:

> Not one of us succeeded in being a hero all of the time. We made compromises and paid for our courage to resist with phases of weakness. But the genuine books strengthened the need for civic courage, dignity, and truth. That our

product was a form of sustenance was evidenced by the long lines in front of bookstores and book bazaars. … Nobody can take that experience of being needed away from me.[38]

Despite the surveillance, state controls, and socialization practices, Dahn described a vibrant culture of protest and dialogue that nourished the civic courage that enabled the *Wende*.[39] Dahn is indignant about the *Doppelmoral* (double standards) she perceives in the Federal Republic's postunification master narrative of the GDR as an *Unrechtsstaat* and the implication that its citizens were complicit in their own oppression. As evidence of the hypocrisy and uncritical self-perception of the West German position, Dahn pointed to the FRG's indulgent treatment of former Nazis who were entitled to state pensions despite their service to a fascist dictatorship.[40] Dahn did not deny the injustices perpetrated by the GDR regime, but also refused to remain silent about injustices in the Federal Republic's political and social practices, specifically targeting the FRG's persecution of political opponents and dissidents under the auspices of emergency laws and the suppression of critique in the workplace.[41] For Dahn, the nearly exclusive focus on surveillance and the state security apparatus in the GDR actually shored up the status quo in the FRG and represented a kind of colonizing mentality, obstructing progress toward genuine unification.[42] Most galling for East Germans in this context, Dahn contended, was the West German blindness to the faults and failures of their democratic system, combined with the assumption that East Germans should be grateful for this gift of democracy.[43]

The West German expectation that East Germans were both unschooled in and uncommitted to democracy is a theme that comes up in other accounts of the *Wende*, and appears to be grounded in preconceptions and ignorance rather than actual experience. In a study on the political culture in united Germany published in 2010, Russell Dalton and Steven Weldon traced the results of surveys from the first two decades following unification and concluded that the majority of East Germans were strong supporters of democratic principles, but with differing expectations for democracy in practice than their West German peers, and on the whole far less satisfied with actually existing democracy in the Federal Republic.[44] In *Westwärts und nicht vergessen* Daniela Dahn portrayed East Germans as critical, self-aware, and discerning in their engagement with their past as well as the realities of life in the Federal Republic, implying that their views and perceptions were and are both valuable and largely untapped resources for the future of a truly democratic and unified Federal Republic.

As if in response to Dahn's depiction of the possibility and reality of political critique in the GDR and her call for a balanced confrontation

with the past in united Germany, Susanne Leinemann in *Aufgewacht.
Mauer weg* painted a negative picture of the official West German publications used for the political education of youth in the mid-1980s,
because of their dismissal of any oppositional movements in the GDR and
their failure to acknowledge the impact of reforms in the Soviet Union
under Gorbachev.[45] As a result of this one-sided portrayal of the GDR,
Leinemann claimed that she and her peers expected GDR citizens to be
brainwashed zombies, an expectation that could only be dispelled by
actually traveling to East Germany.[46] When Leinemann spent time with
her pen pal's family and friends in Dresden in 1985, she came to understand and appreciate the East Germans as people. Although she initially
romanticized the GDR social fabric as more textured, authentic, and direct
than that of the FRG,[47] she also came to recognize its roughness, deficiencies, and inhumanity, particularly evident in accounts of systemic abuse
in the Nationale Volksarmee (NVA, National People's Army) training she
heard about from her friend Andreas.[48]

In contrast to Leinemann's personal experience of kinship and affinity with her friends in Dresden, the FRG's official attempts to cultivate
cross-cultural understanding and a sense of shared national history
through youth group safaris into the wild East foundered on preconceptions and stereotypes held by both sides that prevented genuine connections with the realities of life in either Germany.[49] Leinemann, whose
generation of West Germans was considered apolitical, hedonistic, and
consumer-oriented, argued that the youth trips organized by the West
German government in the late 1980s were not so much attempts at cultural outreach as they were lessons in appreciation for the wealth and
opportunities offered by the Federal Republic.[50] In Leinemann's account,
the biggest obstacle for West German youth was not the perceived differences, but rather the striking similarities they observed in their East
German peers' desires and attitudes, including a focus on consumption as
an element of the good life and disaffection with politics.[51] The similarities were powerful enough for Leinemann to refer to her generation and
its counterpart in East Germany as twins,[52] a familial comparison that
ironically vanished once the division was lifted and the two groups had
unimpeded views of each other. The relationship with her East German
boyfriend Andreas, which Leinemann had cultivated and cherished
despite or because of their forced separation, could not survive unification
because of mutually disappointed expectations. Reminiscent of Dahn's
critique of West German democracy, Andreas channeled his dismay at
the rift between his vision of life in the FRG and the reality into relentless
criticisms of West German society, which Leinemann countered with petty
attacks on his limited cultural experience.[53]

Looking back at the events of 1989, Leinemann questioned the lack of solidarity and support in West Germany for the East German reform movement and its quest for democratic government. Recalling the human chain East German citizens formed spanning the north-south and east-west axis of the GDR, Leinemann asked herself and her readers why West Germans did not follow suit, not only to show their support with the reformers but also to demonstrate that they understood change was coming to both sides of Germany.[54] In retrospect, the absence of an echo in the West could be read as political apathy or complacency fed by the sense that the FRG had already achieved the favored state of democracy that East Germans could only aspire to. Leinemann noted that after unification West German politicians assumed the role of victors who looked down upon the East Germans as naïve or as incorrigible socialists.[55] In addition, East Germans were stigmatized because of their origins according to West German stereotypes: "For us West Germans there was no such thing as a half-GDR citizen. Whoever had been part of it, now had to answer for everything—false antifascism, surveillance state, deformation by socialist education, moral cowardice, bad fashion sense, absent food culture … "[56] While readers may take issue with Leinemann's appropriation of a collective voice for West Germans in general and for her generation in particular, her criticisms of official policies and individual practice in the interactions between West Germans and East Germans shed light on political and personal elements of unification affecting both sides.

Like Leinemann, Jana Hensel has a propensity to generalize from her individual experience to that of an entire generation. In her bestselling memoir *Zonenkinder*, published in 2002, Hensel's childhood became *"unsere Kindheit"* (our childhood) and her account is peppered with pronouncements of *"wir haben"* (we have), *"wir wollten"* (we wanted), and *"unsere Eltern"* (our parents) in an uncritical blend of first person singular and plural. Although Hensel has justly been criticized for fabricating a homogeneous generational collective of East German youth,[57] *Zonenkinder* in its own way attempts to counter the equally homogenized portrayal of life in the GDR as steeped in repression and misery. By recalling the moments of transition, as well as the before and after of unification, Hensel reconstructed a version of the GDR where ideology was subordinate to lived experience. The erasure of *Heimat* (represented by street names, school traditions and curricula, consumer products, and rites of passage) that accompanied unification impacted the lives of East German children and adults. Much of Hensel's book is about the difficulty of reconstructing memories in a landscape where everything that was once familiar has disappeared, causing her to compare her childhood to a museum without a name or address.[58] Yet, when the wall fell, Hensel insisted that she and members of her generation quickly adapted to the new conditions and were eager to forget their past.[59] From Hensel's perspective, the eagerness to adapt was a generational characteristic borne of the desire to be accepted and not be perceived as inferior: "We were the sons and daughters of the losers, made fun of by the victors as proletarians tainted by the odor of totalitarianism and reluctance to work. We did not intend to remain that way."[60] As a result, Hensel claimed that she and her East German peers became hybrid East-West children,[61] having more in common with their generational cohort in the West than with the generation that preceded them in the East.[62] Nevertheless, as the first generation whose childhood experiences straddled division and unification, "the first *Wessis* from East Germany,"[63] their acceptance as bona fide *Wessis* could only be partial because they did not share the same memories.[64] The children of the *Zone* referred to in Hensel's title are thus at once hybrids of East and West and products of a space in a state of becoming where they could take charge of their relationship to the past.[65]

Five years older than Jana Hensel, Claudia Rusch completed her secondary schooling in the GDR and characterized her peer group as the last genuine *Ossis*, as well as the first new *Wessis* in the ironically titled collection of tales from her childhood in the GDR, *Meine freie deutsche Jugend.*[66] Unlike Hensel, Rusch grew up in a household opposed to the SED regime and committed to reform (her mother was a close friend of dissident Robert Havemann), guided and guarded by parents who sought to inoculate her against the influence of the state. Although as a child she often wished that she could have fit in better with her peers, in retrospect, Rusch felt she had a privileged childhood because she was aware of the GDR's deficiencies from a young age.[67] While Hensel's *Zonenkinder* portrayed GDR childhood as one dominated by rituals and consumer products that generated a sense of belonging that went largely unquestioned, Rusch had no interest in contemplating a GDR revival of any kind and rejected the nostalgia for East German products as uncritical sentimentality.[68] For Rusch, the deprivations she was aware of as a child were countered by the desire to one day become French and live in France.[69] It was not until the collapse of the GDR that Rusch discovered her loyalty to what one could call the "other" GDR, the human potential to resist the repressive tendencies of the socialist dictatorship and thereby give lie to the stereotype that all East German citizens were conformists and fellow travelers: "*We* were also the GDR. Not only spies and careerists, but also our families and friends lived here. Not only were those who wanted to press us into their preconceived molds part of this country, but also those who woke us up."[70]

As the daughter of dissident parents who recognized that their child did not have a future in the country they were committed to reforming,

Rusch was torn by conflicting emotions when she learned after the *Wende* that her parents were determined to help her realize her dream of moving to France, even if it meant never seeing her again. Her anger at the state's power over human relationships prevented her from feeling any inclination to either forgive or downplay the crimes committed by the GDR regime, most insidiously its capacity to destroy family life.[71] Reflecting on how her East German biography continued to affect her, despite her sense of liberation after 1989, Rusch admitted that the GDR had not vanished from her consciousness just because the country had ceased to exist, but instead continued to exert its influence over her through what she called "the absence of self-evidence."[72] This reference to a lack of naturalness or self-evidence even after the fall of the wall represented a condition of alterity that was at once more subtle and more complex than the terms *Ossi* and *Wessi* imply. A sense of self-consciousness inexplicable to West Germans and western Europeans about her freedom of movement and international friendships imbued her psyche, setting her apart from those who had grown up taking mobility and a cosmopolitan worldview for granted.[73]

## Embracing the Inner *Ampelmännchen*?

Taken together, the selections from Helga Königsdorf, Daniela Dahn, Susanne Leinemann, Jana Hensel, and Claudia Rusch offer a far more differentiated picture of East Germany and *Ossi-Wessi* relations than what is conveyed in the equation GDR = *Unrechtsstaat* and the nearly myopic focus on the state security apparatus that predominates in the official stock-taking of the East German past. Although Dahn and Hensel's reminiscences are almost at opposite ends of the spectrum, a divergence that can only in part be explained by their difference in generation (Dahn was born in 1949 and Hensel in 1976), both resented the imbalance in expectations regarding the history of the GDR versus the FRG. For Dahn, it was the FRG's foregrounding of the GDR's injustices without accompanying attention to the flaws in its democratic system both past and present. For Hensel, it was the assumption that the memories and personal biographies of East German citizens were of no interest, and consequently that there was nothing more worth saying about the GDR past.[74] In both cases, the dominant discourse and perceptions discouraged accounts of normal life in East Germany, which in all of its complexity and banality also included moments of happiness and triumph. In her demand that "We must be allowed to remember the normal, pleasant, and upstanding moments of our earlier life,"[75] Daniela Dahn expressed the need and desire to balance criticism and self-affirmation, a balance that was perhaps most closely achieved by Claudia Rusch, whose indefatigable joie de vivre infused the pages of *Meine freie deutsche Jugend*.

Despite the diversity of voices represented in memoirs and essays about life in the GDR, more than two decades after unification the fascination with the East German state security apparatus shows little sign of abating. Films such as *Das Leben der Anderen* (2006) have fanned public interest, and the award-winning TV series *Weißensee* broadcast on ARD brought the experiences of a fictional Stasi family in episodes festooned with GDR clichés into German living rooms. The Stasi prisons and archive are tourist attractions and books such as Ruth Hoffmann's *Stasikinder. Aufwachsen im Überwachungsstaat* (2012) serve as companion pieces to stories about the lives of ordinary East German citizens. Historian Mary Fulbrook was an early voice among scholars to criticize the wholesale condemnation of the GDR state and has enjoined Germans of all stripes to embrace a more differentiated and pluralistic view of the divided past that unites them. For Fulbrook, it is "the plurality of debate on values and virtues—without necessarily a scapegoated other as the essential counterpoint" that will allow East and West Germans to establish a shared sense of identity.[76] The ubiquity of the *Ampelmännchen* at crosswalks or the cultivation of *Ostalgie* through niche markets and the tourist magnet DDR Museum in Berlin do little to offset the prevailing view that equates East Germany with the Stasi. Both representations of the GDR, as a surveillance state and a place of homey nostalgia, deny the multidimensionality of a past that is an integral part of the legacy and national identity of all citizens in today's Federal Republic.

To return to one of the questions raised at the beginning of this chapter, what steps are necessary to establish a collective sense of responsibility and engagement with the past in pursuit of a truly unified future? In other words, how can the "Germans" in all of their multiplicity come to recognize and accept their diversity as a core value, and in the particular case of East Germans and West Germans, learn to live with the complex and contradictory experiences and memories of the other Germany? One hopeful example is the initiative *Dritte Generation Ostdeutschland* and its network component *3te Generation Ostdeutschland*, which seeks to harness the experiences and insights of those whose biographies bridge East and West to shape a future that is more attentive to the relationship between personal and political history and more attuned to the responsibilities of the present. The emphasis on *Ostdeutschland* in the title is an intentional effort to recover and unpack the GDR legacy from multiple perspectives in dialogues spanning generations across the new and old *Bundesländer* (German federal states, the "*Länder*").[77] In many ways, *3te Generation Ostdeutschland* is a continuation and an expansion of the project that

Helga Königsdorf launched with *Adieu DDR* in 1990, motivated by the belief in the importance of individual stories. The book *Dritte Generation Ost*, published in 2012 with contributions from thirty-three individuals, demonstrated that there are still many stories left to tell, while the *3te Generation* network has created a forum for communication and dialogue. Although the *Dritte Generation Ostdeutschland* initiative is to be applauded for its efforts to celebrate the value of East German experiences and their potential for invigorating the Germany of today and tomorrow, with its backward glance at only one side of a divided country it neglects the work of memory that West Germans must engage in as well regarding the pre-unification FRG. It is the shared commitment to recognize and interrogate the merits, deficiencies, ideals, and hypocrisies of both Germanys that is needed to break through the lingering metaphorical wall between *Ossis* and *Wessis* and thereby bring Germans in all regions of the postunification Federal Republic closer to parity in citizenship even as economic disparities persist.

## Notes

1. This note refers to the epigraph that opens the essay. "Die DDR konnte kein Ausland sein, sonst hätten wir sie ja unterwegs mal getroffen. Inland war sie erst recht nicht. Sie lag so fern, daß sie von unserer Weltkarte verschwunden war. Kein Ausland. Kein Inland." All translations from German to English are mine (KB). Susanne Leinemann, *Aufgewacht. Mauer weg* (Stuttgart: Deutsche-Verlags-Anstalt, 2002), 23–4.
2. Leinemann, *Aufgewacht*, 35.
3. In fact, Leinemann's memoir is both unique and unusual as an account by a West German whose friendships with GDR citizens caused her to reflect on her own prejudices and preconceptions, as well as those of her West German cohort, the so-called Generation Golf, known for its political apathy and consumerist orientation.
4. Daniela Dahn and Claudia Rusch are two writers whose works reveal their critical distance to the GDR state, whereas Jana Hensel's bestseller *Zonenkinder* seeks to rehabilitate the mundane pleasures of GDR rituals and consumer products and offset the bleak image of the GDR as an unmitigated surveillance state.
5. The dominance of texts produced by East Germans in this list is at once an attempt to offset the West German master narrative on unification and the GDR state, and evidence of the paucity of memoirs by West Germans about their experiences and relationships in East Germany in the two decades preceding the fall of the wall.
6. Peter Longerich, ed., *"Was ist des Deutschen Vaterland?" Dokumente zur Frage der deutschen Einheit 1800–1990* (Munich: Piper, 1995), 193.
7. From 1955 to 1972, the Federal Republic refused to establish diplomatic relations with any country that recognized the sovereignty of the GDR, with the exception of the Soviet Union. Known as the Hallstein doctrine, this policy created political and economic difficulties for the FRG and was repudiated by the basic treaty between the two

Germanys in 1972. See also Konrad Jarausch, ed., *After Unity: Reconfiguring German Identities*, (Providence/Oxford: Berghahn Books, 1997), 45.

8. "Die Mauer wurde den Deutschen im Westen zum Spiegel, der ihnen Tag für Tag sagt, wer der Schönste im Lande ist. Ob es ein Leben gab jenseits des Todesstreifens, interessierte bald nur noch Tauben und Katzen." Peter Schneider, *Der Mauerspringer* (1982; Reinbek bei Hamburg: Rowohlt, 1995), 12.

9. Political science professor Wolf Wagner also characterized the wall as a projection screen for each country's perceived superiority in his 2005 study of unification and its aftermath, *Kulturschock Deutschland – revisited*, where West Germany emphasized its wealth and freedom and East Germany its moral and cultural supremacy. See Wolf Wagner, *Kulturschock Deutschland – revisited 2005*, online version made accessible by author, 2009, 18. http://www.erato.fh-erfurt.de/so/homepages/wagner/Zuindex/Kulturschock%20Deutschland%202005.pdf. Accessed 10 March 2014.

10. Cf. Daniela Dahn, *Westwärts und nicht vergessen. Vom Unbehagen in der Einheit* (Reinbek bei Hamburg: Rowohlt, 1997).

11. Wagner, *Kulturschock*, 50.

12. Dominic Boyer, "*Ostalgie* and the Politics of the Future in Eastern Germany," *Public Culture* 18, no. 2 (2006): 369–70.

13. See Jarausch, *After Unity*, 125.

14. Wagner, *Kulturschock*, 52–3.

15. Cf. Jarausch, *After Unity*, 43.

16. "Die DDR ist kein Inland der BRD und die BRD kein Inland der DDR." Longerich, "*Was ist des Deutschen Vaterland?*" 258.

17. "Die Deutsche Demokratische Republik gehört zu Deutschland und kann im Verhältnis zur Bundesrepublik Deutschland nicht als Ausland angesehen werden." Longerich, "*Was ist des Deutschen Vaterland?*" 255.

18. Hans-Georg Betz, "Perplexed Normalcy: German Identity after Unification" in *Rewriting the German Past*, eds. Reinhard Alter and Peter Monteath (Atlantic Highlands, NJ: Humanities Press International, 1997), 49.

19. Leinemann, *Aufgewacht*, 22.

20. Joyce Mushaben, *From Postwar to Post-Wall Generations: Changing Attitudes toward the National Question and NATO in the Federal Republic of Germany* (Boulder, CO: Westview Press, 1998), 100.

21. Peter O'Brien, "Germany's Newest Aliens: The East Germans," *East European Quarterly* 30, no. 4 (1997): 449.

22. "Endlich schien die Vergeblichkeit besiegt, das Zeitalter der Sinngebung angebrochen." Dahn, *Westwärts*, 11.

23. O'Brien, "Germany's Newest Aliens," 460.

24. See Russell Dalton and Steven Weldon, "Germans Divided? Political Culture in a United Germany," *German Politics* 19, no. 1 (2010): 13.

25. Wagner, *Kulturschock*, 31.

26. Wagner, *Kulturschock*, 8.

27. "'Wir sind ein Volk.' 'Wir auch.'" Quoted in Steve Crawshaw, *Easier Fatherland. Germany and the Twenty-First Century* (London: Continuum, 2004), 91.

28. Schneider, *Mauerspringer*, 110.

29. "Ohne den Ort zu verändern, gehen wir in die Fremde." Helga Königsdorf, *Adieu DDR. Protokolle eines Abschieds* (Reinbek bei Hamburg: Rowohlt, 1990), 9.

30. "Ein Volk zu werden war nicht schwer. ... Ein Volk zu sein ist schwieriger, als eins zu werden. ... Unser Umgang mit Geschichte teilt uns mehr, als daß er uns eint." Helga

Königsdorf, *Unterwegs nach Deutschland. Über die Schwierigkeit, ein Volk zu sein: Protokolle eines Aufbruchs* (Reinbek bei Hamburg: Rowohlt, 1995), 7.

31. Jarausch, *After Unity*, 54.
32. "So kommt es, daß jeder am Ende seine eigene Wahrheit hat. Die Wahrheit des anderen bereitet ihm Schmerzen, wenn sie sein Leben in Frage stellt." Königsdorf, *Unterwegs*, 8.
33. Königsdorf, *Unterwegs*, 29.
34. Königsdorf, *Unterwegs*, 45.
35. Königsdorf, *Unterwegs*, 52.
36. "Ich habe gegenüber Westdeutschen noch nie Vorbehalte gehabt. Jetzt sage ich mal was ganz Schlimmes: genauso, wie ich gegenüber anderen Ausländern noch nie Vorbehalte hatte." Königsdorf, *Unterwegs*, 162.
37. "Die bescheidenen Vorteile der DDR und die unbescheidenen Nachteile der Bundesrepublik." Dahn, *Westwärts*, 10.
38. "Niemandem von uns ist es gelungen, die ganze Zeit ein Held zu sein. Wir haben Kompromisse gemacht und für den Mut zur Auflehnung mit Phasen der Schwäche bezahlt. Aber die wahrhaftigen Bücher haben das Bedürfnis nach Zivilcourage, Würde und Wahrheit bestärkt. Daß unser Produkt ein *Lebensmittel* war, bezeugten die Schlangen vor den Buchhandlungen und bei Buchbasaren. … Die Erfahrung, gebraucht worden zu sein, kann mir niemand nehmen." Dahn, *Westwärts*, 23.
39. Dahn, *Westwärts*, 68. In an essay published in 1997, historian Mary Fulbrook confirmed that subversive activities and civil unrest were more pervasive than had been assumed, but noted that fascist symbols also persisted despite the GDR's official antifascist policy. See Mary Fulbrook, "Reckoning with the Past: Heroes, Victims, and Villains in the History of the German Democratic Republic," in *Rewriting the German Past* (Atlantic Highlands, NJ: Humanities Press International, 1997), 187.
40. Dahn, *Westwärts*, 40–1.
41. Dahn, *Westwärts*, 196.
42. Dahn, *Westwärts*, 148.
43. Dahn, *Westwärts*, 191–2.
44. Dalton and Weldon, "Germans Divided," 15.
45. Leinemann, *Aufgewacht*, 78.
46. Leinemann, *Aufgewacht*, 81.
47. Leinemann, *Aufgewacht*, 27.
48. Leinemann, *Aufgewacht*, 115–6.
49. Leinemann, *Aufgewacht*, 86–7.
50. Leinemann, *Aufgewacht*, 55.
51. Leinemann, *Aufgewacht*, 93.
52. Leinemann, *Aufgewacht*, 119.
53. Leinemann, *Aufgewacht*, 213–4.
54. Leinemann, *Aufgewacht*, 202.
55. Leinemann, *Aufgewacht*, 226.
56. "Für uns Westdeutsche gab es keine halben DDR-Bürger, wer einmal dabei war, mußte jetzt auch für alles Rede und Antwort stehen – falscher Antifaschismus, Stasi-Staat, Deformation durch sozialistische Erziehung, Duckmäusertum, schlechter Modesgeschmack, fehlende Eßkultur …" Leinemann, *Aufgewacht*, 238.
57. In *Geteilte Träume*, Robert Ide objects to Hensel's tendency to collectivize and generalize, arguing that there were significant differences in how individuals responded to life in the GDR depending on their social position, family background, religious and political

beliefs, and contacts with the West. See Robert Ide, *Geteilte Träume. Meine Eltern, die Wende und ich* (Munich: Luchterhand, 2007), 104–5.

58. Jana Hensel, *Zonenkinder* (Reinbek bei Hamburg: Rowohlt, 2002), 25.

59. Hensel, *Zonenkinder*, 14.

60. "Wir waren die Söhne und Töchter der Verlierer, von den Gewinnern als Proletarier bespöttelt, mit dem Geruch von Totalitarismus und Arbeitsscheu behaftet. Wir hatten nicht vor, das länger zu bleiben." Hensel, *Zonenkinder*, 73.

61. Hensel, *Zonenkinder*, 74.

62. Hensel, *Zonenkinder*, 158.

63. "Die ersten Wessis aus Ostdeutschland." Hensel, *Zonenkinder*, 166.

64. Hensel, *Zonenkinder*, 26.

65. Hensel, *Zonenkinder*, 159.

66. Claudia Rusch, *Meine freie deutsche Jugend* (Frankfurt: Fischer, 2003), 101.

67. Rusch, *Meine freie deutsche Jugend*, 35.

68. Rusch, *Meine freie deutsche Jugend*, 88.

69. Rusch, *Meine freie deutsche Jugend*, 68.

70. "Wir waren auch DDR. Nicht nur Spitzel und Karrieristen, auch unsere Familien und Freunde lebten hier. Nicht nur diejenigen, die uns in ihr Schema pressen wollten, waren ein Teil dieses Landes, sondern auch die, die aus uns wache Köpfe gemacht hatten." Rusch, *Meine freie deutsche Jugend*, 100.

71. Rusch, *Meine freie deutsche Jugend*, 134.

72. "Die Abwesenheit von Selbstverständlichkeit." Rusch, *Meine freie deutsche Jugend*, 135.

73. Rusch, *Meine freie deutsche Jugend*, 135.

74. Hensel, *Zonenkinder*, 133–4.

75. "Es muß einfach erlaubt sein, sich an die normalen, angenehmen und aufrechten Momente des früheren Lebens zu erinnern," Dahn, *Westwärts*, 26.

76. Fulbrook, "Reckoning with the Past," 194.

77. See network website: http://www.dritte-generation-ost.de/3te_generation/faq.html. Accessed 17 June 2014.

## Works Cited

Betz, Hans-Georg. "Perplexed Normalcy: German Identity after Unification." In *Rewriting the German Past*, edited by Reinhard Alter and Peter Monteath, 40–64. Atlantic Highlands, NJ: Humanities Press International, 1997.

Boyer, Dominic. "*Ostalgie* and the Politics of the Future in Eastern Germany." *Public Culture* 18, no. 2 (2006): 361–81.

Crawshaw, Steve. *Easier Fatherland. Germany and the Twenty-First Century.* London: Continuum, 2004.

Dahn, Daniela. *Westwärts und nicht vergessen. Vom Unbehagen in der Einheit.* Reinbek bei Hamburg: Rowohlt, 1997.

Dalton, Russell, and Steven Weldon. "Germans Divided? Political Culture in a United Germany." *German Politics* 19, no. 1 (2010): 9–23.

Fulbrook, Mary. "Reckoning with the Past: Heroes, Victims, and Villains in the History of the German Democratic Republic." In *Rewriting the German Past*, edited by Reinhard Alter and Peter Monteath, 175–96. Atlantic Highlands, NJ: Humanities Press International, 1997.

Hacker, Michael, et al., eds. *Dritte Generation Ost. Wer wir sind, was wir wollen.* Berlin: Ch. Links, 2012.

Hensel, Jana. *Zonenkinder.* Reinbek bei Hamburg: Rowohlt, 2002.

Hoffmann, Ruth. *Stasi-Kinder. Aufwachsen im Überwachungsstaat.* Berlin: Ullstein, 2012.

Ide, Robert. *Geteilte Träume. Meine Eltern, die Wende und ich.* Munich: Luchterhand, 2007.

Jarausch, Konrad, ed. *After Unity: Reconfiguring German Identities.* Providence/Oxford: Berghahn Books, 1997.

Königsdorf, Helga. *Adieu DDR. Protokolle eines Abschieds.* Reinbek bei Hamburg: Rowohlt, 1990.

Königsdorf, Helga. *Unterwegs nach Deutschland. Über die Schwierigkeit, ein Volk zu sein: Protokolle eines Aufbruchs.* Reinbek bei Hamburg: Rowohlt, 1995.

Leinemann, Susanne. *Aufgewacht. Mauer weg.* Stuttgart: Deutsche-Verlags-Anstalt, 2002.

Longerich, Peter, ed. *"Was ist des deutschen Vaterland?" Dokumente zur Frage der deutschen Einheit 1800–1990.* Munich: Piper, 1995.

Mushaben, Joyce. *From Postwar to Post-Wall Generations: Changing Attitudes toward the National Question and NATO in the Federal Republic of Germany.* Boulder, CO: Westview Press, 1998.

O'Brien, Peter. "Germany's Newest Aliens: The East Germans." *East European Quarterly* 30, no. 4 (1997): 449–70.

Rusch, Claudia. *Meine freie deutsche Jugend.* Frankfurt: Fischer, 2003.

Schneider, Peter. *Der Mauerspringer.* 1982; Reinbek bei Hamburg: Rowohlt, 1995.

Wagner, Wolf. *Kulturschock Deutschland – revisited 2005.* Online version made accessible by author, 2009. http://www.erato.fh-erfurt.de/so/homepages/wagner/Zuindex/Kulturschock%20Deutschland%202005.pdf. Accessed 10 March 2014.

**Kathrin Bower** is associate professor and coordinator of German studies at the University of Richmond in Richmond, Virginia, where she teaches courses in German language, literature, and culture, as well as in film and Holocaust studies. She has written and published on German-Jewish writers, Holocaust representation, German cinema, integration, and Turkish-German comedy and cabaret. Kathrin Bower is also the author of *Ethics and Remembrance in the Poetry of Nelly Sachs and Rose Ausländer* (2000).

# Chapter 11

# CONFLICTING MEMORIES, CONFLICTING IDENTITIES

Russian Jewish Immigration and the Image
of a New German Jewry

*Karen Körber*

The fall of the Berlin Wall in 1989 did not just usher in the final stage of the postwar history of the two German states, which ended with their reunification. These events also initiated a process that opened up a new chapter in German Jewish history: the immigration of Russian-speaking Jews to Germany. This migration was triggered by an initiative by members of civil rights movements in the GDR (German Democratic Republic) who, following media reports of anti-Semitic attacks in the USSR in January 1990, used their influence as members of the *Runder Tisch* (Round Table Forum) to pressure the GDR into taking in Soviet Jews.[1] In April, the final *Volkskammerregierung* (People's Parliament) acknowledged for the first time in the history of the GDR, "co-responsibility for the humiliation, deportation and murder of Jewish men, women and children," and declared to grant residence to "Jewish citizens of other nations threatened with persecution and discrimination, on humanitarian grounds."[2] The first such immigrants entered East Berlin on tourist visas and in doing so initiated a process that, in the light of recent historical events, no one would ever have predicted.

In 1948, the World Jewish Congress urged that after the mass murder of European Jews by the National Socialists, Germany should never again be a home to Jews. Yet this appeal was thwarted by the re-establishment early on—in both German states—of Jewish communities made up of German Jewish survivors, returnees from exile, and those who had survived the Holocaust in Eastern Europe, the so-called DPs (Displaced Persons). In 1950, the Central Council of Jews in Germany (Zentralrat der Juden in

Deutschland) was founded in West Germany to represent the religious Jewish communities. The state anti-Semitism of neighboring Eastern European countries ensured a relatively small but nevertheless steady flow of immigrants to West Germany. Even so, for decades this Jewish minority lived with packed suitcases. This self-image would change with the coming of age of the second generation of Jews in Germany, but it remains the case that by the end of the 1980s, the largely elderly Jewish communities in West Germany numbered no more than thirty thousand members; in the GDR the figure was roughly 380. Had it not been for the immigration of Russian-speaking Jews, the Jewish community would, over the following years, have struggled to survive.[3]

Today, Germany is home to Europe's second-largest Jewish community, after France. Since 1991, around 220,000 Jews and their non-Jewish family members have immigrated to Germany from the former Soviet Union as so-called quota refugees.[4] Over the course of the 1990s, this immigration resulted in an increase in the number of Jewish religious communities in Germany to 108. Of the approximately 120,000 individuals who belong to a Jewish religious community, approximately ninety-eight percent are Russian-speaking Jews.[5] According to estimates, another roughly 120,000 people do not belong to any religious community. If one adds to this the small but steady contingent of American and young Israeli Jews who have settled in Berlin in increasing numbers since the 2000s, then it is fair to say that the demographic makeup of the Jewish community in Germany has been fundamentally altered.

It is, however, not just the figures that document a change. Over the last two decades, the Jewish community has increased not just in size, but also in visibility. At the same time, it has become increasingly pluralistic in religious and cultural terms. Thus, while it may be possible to speak of a revival of Jewish life, this process is also bound up with numerous conflicts that are primarily concerned with the future identity of the Jewish community in Germany. In this context, the historian Dan Diner has predicted that the immigration of Russian-speaking Jews means the end of one phase in "the Jewish history of the federal republic."[6] In doing so he points to a caesura that, particularly in Jewish communities, has become a point of contention between old and new members, namely the different ways in which World War II and the Holocaust are remembered. These divergent memories of the Holocaust are not simply a point of reference for conflicts within the Jewish community; they also reveal a shift in its relationship with Germany that has considerable implications for German Jewish relations.

Yet, it is not just the Jewish community that has changed; so, too, has the host country Germany. In postwar West Germany, German Jewish relations were characterized above all by the politically symbolic function of the Jewish minority's presence, which served to prove the democratization of the German state.[7] After reunification, Germany faced a contested state of affairs, at the heart of which was the gradual political and legal recognition that Germany could handle diversity and immigration as a modern pluralistic society. Recently, the social experience of this ethnic, cultural, and religious pluralization has also raised questions regarding a national identity that grew out of a sense of historical responsibility for the Holocaust and whose memory politics has led to the formation of two groups: the Jews as victims and the Germans as perpetrators. As critics have argued, this construction of a community of memory not only follows a binary logic, it also ultimately has ethnicizing elements, because it excludes the experiences and memories of all those who have migrated to Germany and who have no place in the national culture of commemoration.[8] This binary logic, however, harbors a number of pitfalls for the understanding of the Jewish diaspora in Germany: for one, the symbolic image of a community of victims risks clashing with the actual heterogeneity of Jewish lives in present-day Germany. Further, it stands increasingly in conflict with the manifold narratives that, following the Russian Jewish migration, have gained in importance and have resulted in a shift in the identity of the Jewish community in Germany. Accordingly, I will place the focus on the host country and its migration regime by describing the admission procedure for Russian-speaking Jews in the first part of this chapter. The second section will demonstrate that the symbolic public role of the Jewish community has entered a crisis as a result of the immigration of Russian-speaking Jews by concentrating on the central conflicts and dilemmas faced by Jewish communities. Finally, through a consideration of the second generation of Jewish immigrants, the focus will turn to processes of pluralization and transnationalization that are definitive for the future of the Jewish diaspora in Germany.

## The Host Country of Germany: The Nation of Non-Immigration Takes in Jewish Migrants

In January 1991, in newly reunified Germany, the first conference of state premiers passed a resolution on the admission procedure for "Jewish quota refugees."[9] The negotiations over how the immigration of Russian-speaking Jews should be regulated laid bare two distinguishing features of German politics that would continue to clash with each other in the future. The first of these was the newly reunified Germany's insistence that it was not a country of immigration, despite the fact that since the 1950s labor migration saw people emigrating to both West and East Germany. The second feature was the continuation, even postunification, of what journalist Jörg Lau has coined as Germany's "commemorative phase." This phrase refers to the series of public and political events and displays—starting with Federal President Richard von Weizsäcker's famous speech on 8 May 1985 and ending with the unveiling of the Memorial to the Murdered Jews of Europe in 2005—that were shaped mainly by the debates over the correct way of remembering German crimes, the perpetrators, and their victims.[10]

In the specific debates about the Memorial to the Murdered Jews of Europe, the literary and media studies scholar Hanno Loewy has identified the irresolvable dilemma: a national identity that acknowledges the necessity of remembering the "unspeakable" while simultaneously being confronted with the "impossibility" of "founding a national identity on this event" without perpetuating "the project of an ethnic nation."[11] The conflict that Loewy described here, namely the shift from Germany's self-image as a community of memory toward the politics-driven present of a modern immigration society, revealed itself paradoxically through a glance back at those media images and political discourses related to Russian Jewish migration that dominated the public sphere during the 1990s.

The immigration of Soviet Jews laid bare a dilemma in German politics at the time of reunification that initially resulted in the admission policy of the final GDR government being abandoned. This dilemma was, on the one hand, a result of the fact that the new German state was keen to avoid the impression of having a historical axe to grind in the hour of its birth and was anxious to formulate an appropriate admission policy for Soviet Jews seeking entry into Germany. Yet, on the other hand, Germany was "by definition not a country of immigration," and feared that an opening of its borders would result in a poverty-driven flood of migrants from Eastern Europe.[12]

When finally, in the fall of 1990, a debate on the issue of the admission policy took place in the German Bundestag (Lower House of the FRG), opinions quickly converged to form an approach to the issue that from then on would define the discourse about Jewish immigration in the media and political sphere. Germany's conception of itself as a "community of memory,"[13] and thus as a nation responsible for the crimes of the country's past, formed the context for a symbolic interpretation of Russian-speaking Jews as part of a community of victims. During the Bundestag session, representatives of all parties emphasized the importance of demonstrating unity in relation to this "extremely sensitive topic."[14] The immigration of Jews to Germany was approved amid calls for particular "generosity

and magnanimity" to be shown toward Jews in the light of "our responsibility toward our own German history."[15] A member of the party Bündnis
90/Die Grünen (Alliance 90/The Greens)[16] referred to the numerous reactions from the population to the freeze on admissions and read out from
a public appeal: "The new German state should not, in the hour of its
birth, refuse help to those who were persecuted and exterminated by the
earlier state."[17] The particular historical moment of the debate—October
1990—lent the discussion further weight; in the context of German reunification, Jewish immigration became an issue against which the legitimacy
of the newly unified German state was to be measured. This indicates
how Jewish emigration from the Soviet Union was viewed more than
anything through the lens of German history. In turn, this had an impact
on the image that formed within German society of the Soviet Jews as
mainly representative of a community of victims created by the National
Socialists' policy of extermination. Symbolically, the difference between
the victims of the Holocaust, its survivors, and the Jewish emigrants of the
present seemed to have been eradicated.

The legal framework within which the intake would be regulated
appeared to do justice to this special group of immigrants. The Quota
Refugee Act, which was first applied in 1980 in connection with the
admission of Vietnamese "boat people," now served as the legal basis
for regulating this immigration movement.[18] The category of the "Jewish
quota refugee" provided the Russian-speaking Jews with refugee status
when they would have had little chance of being approved as political
refugees in a regular asylum application procedure. In effect, however,
this solution formed the basis for a rash and unbureaucratic admission
procedure that foreclosed the possibility of rejection.[19] Following the
resolution of the state premiers' conference of January 1991, a formal procedure in which the Jewish immigrants would need to provide evidence
according to specific criteria of Jewish identity was done away with. Still,
there was a need, as in any immigration procedure, for verifiable entry
regulations. Ethnic belonging thus became the determining criterion for
admission: whoever could prove his or her Jewish heritage was allowed
to immigrate to Germany.[20]

While the political decision in favor of a separate admission procedure
reflects the Germans' specific sense of responsibility with regard to persecuted Jews, it nevertheless obscures a structural dilemma that is crucial
for the self-declared non-immigration country of Germany. Since there
were no general guidelines for an immigration policy, the only recourse
for the government was the juridical step of categorizing the Soviet Jews
as quota refugees in order to facilitate their admission.[21] In comparison
with other migrant groups, this chosen admission policy was one that

privileged Jewish immigrants. They had the right to apply for German citizenship after eight years, at a time when citizenship—available only on the basis of *jus sanguinis*—was almost impossible to acquire, thus producing a third generation of German-born Turks in the 1990s. Furthermore, they were allowed to immigrate with their entire families, whereas in the case of labor migrants, for example, residency was only granted to the respective jobseeker. The historian Ulrich Herbert has pointed out that this procedure of breaking down migration processes into countless laws and procedures dovetails with Germany's decades-long political practice of negating the factuality of immigration movements.[22] It was not until the fiercely contested and hard-won immigration law of 2005 that a migration policy framework was established that acknowledged the reality of immigration processes.

Over the course of the 1990s, local and national media began to give voice to a certain disappointment upon the realization that the Jewish immigrants were failing to live up to both the image of victims and their role as pillars of Jewish culture, and cracks began to form in the figure of the persecuted refugee. Media coverage soon shifted from cultured "professors, artists, and doctors"[23] with their academic qualifications, forced as refugees to leave behind their "private libraries,"[24] to the image of the "difficult-to-employ engineer" who refused to conform to the role of supplicant. In government agencies, doubts grew about the "real" motives for immigrating, as officials found themselves dealing with "Frau Doktor" and "Herr Professor" fighting for the recognition of their status acquired back in their home country. The suspicion that economic reasons more than anything had played a role in the decision to leave intensified; the immigrants were accused of having been thrilled to discover the all-important "drop of Jewish blood" in their family.[25] Indignation began to stir, particularly in German government agencies, when it also emerged that the migrants were in possession not only of a permanent residence permit, but also of passports of their country of birth. The idea of the migrant traveling, indeed commuting, stands in sharp contrast to the definition of the refugee as a beneficiary of the welfare state. Refugees enjoy protection because they have been forced to leave their country. By contrast, the migrants' periodic return to their home countries was a sign of their transnational belonging.

What fueled people's mistrust more than anything else, however, was the fact that the immigrants had not affiliated themselves with Jewish communities to the extent that had been expected of them. With the growing realization that a considerable number of the Jewish immigrants were not very religious, nor had they sought membership in a Jewish community, there was an increasing tendency to reproach them for having an instrumental relationship with their own identity, that is, for having co-opted their Jewishness for the purpose of leaving without committing anything further to it. With this, the legality of Jewish immigration as a whole was thrown into doubt.

At the beginning of 1996, the magazine *Der Spiegel* did in fact publish a letter from the Foreign Office, under the heading "As quietly as possible," which revealed that a halt to the "too generous" admission policy was being deliberated. The letter reasoned that anti-Semitic discrimination in the former Soviet Union no longer constituted a real threat, and that the strengthening of the communities in Germany had not occurred to the extent that people had wished for.[26] Rather, it was argued, the Jewish migrants were using these institutions merely for material and social support at the beginning of their stay, only to drop out soon after. The then president of the Central Council of Jews in Germany, Ignatz Bubis, was able to prevent the stop on immigrant admissions.

Thus, the persecuted Soviet Jew had, in crossing the border, become an economic migrant. He was regarded as having an instrumental relationship with his Jewish identity: he did not avow himself to the Jewish faith, nor did he feel permanently obliged to the community. As such, the sociologist Zygmunt Bauman has analyzed, he evoked the distorted image of the disloyal, slippery Jew, who revealed his identity precisely in the way that he hid, denied, and mimicked it.[27] What was striking in these interpretations was not just the return of anti-Semitic stereotypes; they also revealed that Germany as a country of non-immigration primarily saw Jewish immigration as legitimized through its strengthening of Jewish communities. Other ways into the host society could only be regarded as being in conflict with this, rather than as alternative methods for Jewish immigrants to integrate independently following their migration.

## A New *German* Jewish Community?

These inflated expectations placed on Russian-speaking Jews and the renewal of Jewish life reveal the specific symbolic political role assigned to the Jewish community in West Germany in the decades following the war. In his "German-Jewish History of the Federal Republic," Anthony Kauders points out that both Jewish and non-Jewish functionaries had a shared interest in assigning to the Jewish community a function with public visibility.[28] The aim of this "exchange of gifts"[29] was the reciprocal recovery of legitimacy and, in connection with this, the growing international recognition of the German state and its small resident Jewish community, the presence of which stood as evidence of successful democratization. As early as the 1980s, authors such as Micha Brumlik and Y. Michael Bodemann voiced their criticism of the politics of these Jewish representatives and pointed to the precarious nature of such a privileged status, which was due in large part to its symbolic public role and had little bearing on the everyday reality of the small, rather reclusive community.[30]

The difference between the Jewish community's public role and the reality was exposed once again in the disputes that erupted in the wake of the immigration of Russian-speaking Jews after 1990. The readiness of the German state to strengthen the Jewish minority through the admission procedure went hand in hand with the expectation that it was the responsibility of the Jewish communities to integrate "their" immigrants. This approach was also in keeping with an institutional structure that has defined the organization of the Jewish community in Germany. In a departure from the racial constructs of the National Socialists, the Jews in postwar Germany are defined as a religious community. As such the Jewish community acquires the status of a "public corporation" in accordance with the German state-church law.[31] This status is otherwise reserved exclusively for Christian churches and small Christian communities while, for example, the approximately four million Muslims living in Germany are still fighting to be awarded the status of a religious community. In the wake of this immigration, local Jewish communities acquired a structural role in the model of the German welfare state.

The readiness of the Jewish communities to align with the expectations of the German state stemmed from their shared vision of what counted as successful immigration. In contrast to, for example, the United States, migrant-driven processes of self-integration, such as the formation of ethnic enclaves, were regarded as normative and therefore as problematic and undesirable. Instead of this, the predominant idea was that Jewish immigrants should both integrate into German society as well as identify with a specific Jewish identity forged within existing Jewish institutions. What such an identity was meant to look like can be illustrated by the following statement by a long-term leader from a Jewish community:

> I say to people, do you have any idea why you came to Germany? If they say, yes, life was not good in Russia, I tell them, the agreement between the Central Council and the Federal Republic states *expressis verbis* [explicitly]: you should help to rebuild the Jewish communities destroyed by the Nazis. And that means that you need to get involved in the community and the community is not a cultural association, but a religious one, an institution of faith.[32]

This statement gives voice to a twofold integration mission, which clearly defined the relationship between long-term residents and new immigrants. The purpose of this mission was the integration of Jewish immigrants into a German Jewish religious community. This was a task that took for granted two points that, for the majority of Jewish immigrants, were initially alien, namely the understanding, firstly, of Jewishness as a primarily a religious identity and, secondly, of Jewish history as the history of Jews in Germany.

It was particularly this need to redefine their collective identity once they had crossed the German border that was one of the central and most trying migration-related experiences for Russian-speaking Jewish immigrants. Whereas in the Soviet Union they had been members of a national minority, in Germany they were regarded as members of a religious community. For the mostly secular Jewish immigrants, this shift from a national to a religious minority constituted a controversial process that was a frequent source of conflict within the communities.[33]

In the early years of the immigration movement, an increasing sense of disappointment set in among the long-term community members. This disappointment was a result of the realization that although the communities had gained new members, this had not led to fewer empty seats in the synagogues. Instead, they saw the Russian Jews as being driven by a sense of entitlement aimed above all at turning the communities into benefit facilities that should also serve the preservation of Russian culture.[34] The demographic shift that occurred as a result of this immigration quickly placed doubt on the long-term community members' integration demands. In effect, the Jewish communities were transforming into immigration communities made up of a minority of long-term members and a large majority of new members. In the following years, the German media, in the light of continuing conflicts between the two groups, explained this as the consequence of a split community divided between "Jews" and "Russians."

What these accounts fail to bring to light is the way in which the Soviet Union's atheist and repressively anti-Semitic politics had generated among the Jews who lived there a specific group consciousness that the sociologist Zvi Gitelman has described as a "latent ethnicity."[35] Characteristic of this symbolic group affiliation was a growing distance from a religious-cultural understanding of Jewishness during the course of Sovietization that went hand in hand with a process of either forced or voluntary assimilation.[36] Yet the hoped-for outcome of their total adoption of Soviet norms and values came to nothing; their assimilation failed as a result of their collective experience of daily and institutional anti-Semitism. This structural racism found its most succinct expression in the notorious Section 5 of their identity cards, which specified nationality. In an unofficial but powerful ethnic quota system, the entry *Jevrej* (Jew) governed professional and other kinds of opportunities, in the same way as an outwardly perceived Jewish appearance or a Jewish-sounding name.[37]

Their specific experience of being integrated on the one hand, and being socially and institutionally stigmatized as Jews on the other, formed part of an ethnic Jewish identity that was also brought to light in the disputes over Jewish communities in Germany. In these disputes, the immigrants lay claim to a sense of belonging largely formed passively in relation to their origin as different from an understanding of a religious Jewish community.

However, since the 1990s there has also been another area of conflict that has frequently erupted in the day-to-day running of the community. This conflict can be described as the result of an encounter between competing narratives. For the Jewish communities in postwar Germany, the memory of the Holocaust formed the central point of reference in their identity that also fundamentally shaped their relationship to the Federal Republic. In this context, Dan Diner speaks of a "spell"[38] cast over Jews living in Germany in the first decades following the end of the war to describe the Jewish people's constitution of itself through its dissociation from everything the Holocaust represented. Even when the second generation's coming of age made it clear that the Jews would stay in Germany, the relationship with the "land of the perpetrators" remained ambivalent and problematic.[39]

A brief look at the increasingly state-coordinated memory culture underscores once again the symbolic role that the Jewish community acquired in postwar Germany. Whereas in the 1950s events commemorating the Holocaust were organized by Jews and other persecuted groups and took place either in private or away from the public sphere, as early as the 1960s we can observe a development toward public forms of commemoration, in which the Catholic and Protestant Churches and local and state politics were partly involved alongside Jewish communities.[40] This process of an increasingly nationalized commemoration of the Holocaust peaked in the 1980s and to this day is symbolically represented in the annual events commemorating the November pogroms of 9 November 1938. In the different forms of public commemoration, the Jewish communities occupy a self-evident position as representatives of the collective of victims.

The immigration of Russian-speaking Jews introduced a new collective memory that had at its center not the Holocaust but the "Great Patriotic War," and, connected with this, the victory over Germany. In many communities the rift between these different narratives has erupted in connection with the celebrations on 9 May, the day of the victory over fascism, which in the Soviet Union was regarded as the most important public holiday. In particular, the generation that had participated in the war regarded it as self-evident that this day should be publicly marked in the community. This included the chance for veterans to display their medals as well as the communal singing of old battle songs and the occasional request, as part of these celebrations, to hoist the Russian flag in front of the Jewish community.

It is not just in the stories of contemporary witnesses that the "Great Patriotic War" assumes a central role, but also of successive generations; after all, there is hardly a Soviet family that did not lose someone to the war. Nevertheless, the difficult history of Russian-speaking Jews also includes the fact that the Holocaust was not part of official Soviet memory. Jewish victims were counted as civilian war victims and in the wake of the anti-Zionist politics of the postwar years, commemoration of the Holocaust was forbidden.[41] After the Six-Day War of 1967, anti-Zionist propaganda intensified. It was only in the middle of the 1980s that the reform programs *Perestroika* and *Glasnost* introduced a shift in memory politics as a result of which, hesitant as it was, the commemoration of Jewish victims of the Holocaust became possible.

Thus, at first glance it seems that there are two opposing memory cultures in the Jewish communities that have the winners of the war on one side and the victims of the Holocaust on the other. However, looking more closely at the family stories of the Russian-speaking Jews, we can observe a process of revaluation, deferral or overlapping of different memories enabling both the war and the specific fate of the Jews to become visible. The cultural theorist Aleida Assmann describes personal memory as a "dynamic process, in which one constantly engages with the past anew in accordance with the conditions and needs of the present and in doing so only admits as much of the past as one needs or can tolerate."[42] In the case of the Jewish immigrants, the experience of the present includes the encounter with Germany's writing of history and the identity of the Jewish communities in which the Holocaust has become an elementary part of the collective memory. Reflecting the effects of Soviet ideology, which had no interest in emphasizing the specific fate of the Jewish minority in World War II, many of our interviewees point out how little they knew about the Shoah in the past. Their encounter with the memory culture of the Jewish communities now meant that the Holocaust was gradually becoming incorporated into their own post-Soviet consciousness. The different forms that this process can take are shown using the examples of the quotations below from contemporary witnesses and members of later generations, in which the influences of family stories, political commemoration, and traditions overlap. Nevertheless, it is striking that the memories of the specific fate of Jews remains, across generations, embedded in the context of World War II:[43]

The blockade [of Leningrad] had a strong impact on me as a child and as a person. It was the most difficult time of my life. … People were starving and dying. My mother was hit in an airstrike on 22 September 1942. She was badly injured and died the next day. … The city where my sister lived was occupied by the Germans. Years later, I received a letter which described in detail how they murdered all the Jews. They were rounded up, forced to undress and were shot in a mass grave.[44]

It is not a matter of one dictatorship conquering another. Thousands, hundreds of thousands of Jews fought in the Red Army because if Hitler had defeated the Soviet Union all Jews would have been killed. And everyone knew this. And the Jews had no other choice. They also fought for their own lives, for their families, against the National Socialist dictatorship. If the Soviet power had lost this war, what would have happened then? Who [*sic*] of us Jews would have survived? No one. And unfortunately, when we start to discuss this, the Jews who have been here for a long time don't understand this.[45]

The war makes up the *leitmotif* of these stories, yet its significance for the Russian-speaking Jews has changed since their migration. Soviet memory culture and the memory of the Holocaust do not simply stand unrelated in opposition to one another. Rather, as transnational actors, the Jewish immigrants refer to both forms of collective memory in order to cultivate their own forms of memory within these. This also has a bearing on how both these forms of collective memory are positioned in the present day. In this context, the witness's quotation about the Leningrad blockade and the mass shooting of Jews once again draws attention to the fact that the Holocaust is not one uniform narrative, but is composed of multifaceted layers of experience that only become visible through the (hi)stories of the Russian-speaking Jews. That the successive generations also pay tribute to the specific experiences of their relatives in the war years is shown in the example of the Russian Jewish author Lena Gorelik. In 2013 the successful writer wrote a moving preface to the diary of Lena Muchina, a young girl who survived and portrayed part of the Leningrad Blockade of 1941–42.[46] Gorelik's family come from Leningrad, which today is once again called St. Petersburg. The blockade was part of her history education and featured in Soviet propaganda, but it is also the history of her family, and the stories of hunger, death, and survival during those years are part of her family's shared memory. Her text makes clear that the Russian-speaking Jewish immigrants have contributed to the pluralization of the Jewish community's communicative memory with their own painful, different experiences that also demand a place around the central narrative of the Holocaust. This is not so much a countermemory as an extension of the collective Jewish memory that, in turn, will also cause the identity of Jewish communities in Germany to change.

# Jews in Contemporary Germany: An Outlook

The conflicts that have arisen since the early 1990s through the immigration of Russian-speaking Jews shed light on how a minority, whose public profile and self-image were essentially defined in relation to the Holocaust, is increasingly characterized by internal negotiations about its future form as a heterogeneous community that takes its presence in Germany as given. At the same time, the conflicts and problems outlined here document the ambivalent effects of an institutional and symbolic structure that up until now has been formative for the way in which the Jewish minority in Germany organizes itself. The definition of the Jewish community as a religious community that is organized through local Jewish organizations and is represented by the Central Council of Jews in Germany gives the Jewish minority a voice in the political arena. After all, the Jewish community enjoys a "corporative identity," that is, a group identity legitimized by the state and its institutions, and which acquires a special symbolic role against the background of German history. Particularly in Germany, a country whose jurisdiction for a long time did not allow for the political participation of immigrant minorities, it represented a precarious yet enduring exception, toward which—as the sociologists Michal Bodemann and Göcke Yurdakul have demonstrated with the example of the Muslim community—other minorities have also oriented themselves in their struggle for recognition.[47] Nevertheless, within the Jewish communities this has been a source of continuing conflict that has manifested itself in particular through the immigrants' move from a national to a religious minority. What is at stake here is a group identity that, although it promises public recognition, does so under the condition that this group formation take place within boundaries marked by both the host society and the Jewish community. As a result, the Jewish communities are at the center of symbolic struggles that essentially boil down to disputes over the shift in meaning of the category "Jewish."

These struggles gain in significance in light of the fact that, in the process of integrating Jewish immigrants, the communities have taken on a central role that, approximately twenty years on, has left them exposed to considerable problems. Similarly to 1989, they are struggling with high numbers of elderly members and declining membership figures. In short: they are lacking young members, or, more accurately, young members who have jobs.

A current study being run by the Jewish Museum in Berlin has produced initial insights into the everyday reality of those young adults aged between twenty and forty who immigrated as children with their families within the framework of the quota policy.[48] Preliminary results have indicated a trend similar to the latest results published by the PEW Research Center in 2013 on American Jews in the age group of those born after 1980.[49] These identify a trend toward a more secular understanding of Jewish identity that dovetails with a drop in figures as far as membership of a Jewish community is concerned. In an online survey we asked 268 women and men from our study group, among other things, how they would define Jewishness. In contrast to the official definition in Germany of a religious community, in first place, forty-four percent of the participants cited ethnic belonging, followed by nineteen percent who stated the idea of a cultural community, followed by an understanding of Jewishness as defined by a Jewish lifestyle. The definition of a religious community only came in at fourth place. When asked whether they belonged to a Jewish community, thirty-seven percent said they were not members of any community. Over fifty percent of those asked described their Jewishness as liberal and secular.[50]

These numbers tie in with a criticism frequently leveled at the perceived rigid, religious character of the communities, in particular where the exclusion of non-Halachic Jews is concerned. Further, membership is often based on strong local ties and the assumption that people will be part of the community for a long time—factors that are not in keeping with interviewees' own needs, interests, and mobile lifestyles that favor flexible, temporary forms of belonging. This criticism of established communities is paralleled by a trend that can also be observed elsewhere in Europe toward new kinds of religious and cultural community formation.

Thus, while we can observe a shift in the religious-cultural practices and forms of belonging within the Jewish religious sphere in Germany, there are also differences concerning the meaning and form of state and cultural belonging. While participants in previous Jewish migrations in the decades following the war felt only loose connections with their countries of origin, in this context we can identify, by contrast, multiple forms of belonging not only in the first but also in the second generation. One example of this is the German politician Marina Weißband, the former chief executive of the "Pirates" Party. Ms. Weißband emigrated to Germany in 1993 at the age of six, from Kiev, Ukraine with her Ukrainian Jewish family. Her accounts of her family's migration highlight the very circumstances that had brought Jewish immigration at the beginning of the 1990s into such disrepute. For instance, she reveals how difficult the departure from Ukraine had been for individual family members; how virtual and real contact with her country of origin is simply a fact of life. Marina Weißband is Jewish, a German citizen and a Russian-speaking Ukrainian citizen. She holds both passports and over the past few months has spent weeks at a time on Majdan Square in Kiev supporting the democratic movement during the current conflict. In doing so she is the epitome of those simultaneous or "mobile forms of belonging."[51] Her case not only demonstrates that in a globalized world belonging and biographies have been set in motion, but also that people inhabit different worlds at the same time and are able to position themselves quite comfortably within this perpetual being-in-motion.

The example of Marina Weißband highlights a further feature that distinguished Russian Jewish immigration and has by now been vocalized as a political issue by various figures. In 2012, the aforementioned author Lena Gorelik, during the debate around the xenophobic arguments of the German politician Thilo Sarrazin, published a book in which she describes her experiences as a migrant in a country that, twenty years and four successful German-language novels later, still registers with amazement that she really does speak German rather well.[52] In a similar way, but in another debate, the author Olga Grjasnowa, who also immigrated to Germany as part of the quota policy, has also raised her voice.[53] Both authors described experiences of exclusion and discrimination that have nothing to do with their Jewish origins, but rather with their status as migrants in Germany. They criticized the non-acceptance of educational qualifications and the disregard for educational success acquired outside of Germany, and characterized these exclusion mechanisms as the structural failure of a society that still responds to the challenges of immigration with strategies that isolate migrants. This is a political position that they shared with many other migrants, male and female, in Germany.

Thus, the new Jewish community in Germany represents less a "new German Jewish identity" and rather the fiercely contested outcome of a newly forming Jewish diasporic community, whose origins, frames of reference, and forms of organization do not—crucially—just lie in Germany. To put it more generally, the changes in the Jewish community in Germany document tensions and struggles that are typical of diaspora communities in general in today's world. These include the attempt to assert forms of cultural autonomy as an alternative to nationalist migration regimes and their institutional constraints. In addition, they highlight the challenge of being confronted with the heterogeneity of concepts of belonging that consider themselves to be sub- or transnational and are therefore constantly changing and challenging the boundaries of the community.

At the same time, these disputes around the Jewish community's new identity also highlight a dilemma in German politics, a consequence of the shift from Germany's self-image as a "community of memory" toward the politics-shaped present of a modern immigration society. This shift calls for the acknowledgement of diversity within one migrant group just as much as the realization that successful forms of immigration fundamentally depend on how the host society provides structural opportunities for participation. To put it differently: the legal construct of the Jewish quota refugee exposes the pitfalls of a German policy that took in persecuted Jews in an eager demonstration of its moral grounding as a community of responsibility, but that was doomed to disappointment when migrants with a Jewish background showed up instead.

## Notes

1. Irene Runge, *Vom Kommen und Bleiben. Osteuropäische jüdische Einwanderer in Berlin* (Berlin: Ausländerbeauftragte des Senats, 1992), 12.
2. Translated from German. "Gemeinsame Erklärung der Fraktionen der Volkskammer der DDR am 12.4. 1990", *Berliner Morgenpost*, 13 April 1990, 15.
3. Anthony Kauders, *Unmögliche Heimat* (Munich: Beck, 2007), 197.
4. "Gesetzliche Regelungen," Zentralrat der Juden in Deutschland, last modified 12 January 2013, accessed 14 April 2014, http://www.zentralratdjuden.de/de/topic/62.html.
5. "Mitglieder," Zentralrat der Juden in Deutschland, last modified 06 February 2014, accessed 11 June 2014, http://www.zentralratdjuden.de/de/topic/5.mitglieder.html.
6. Dan Diner, "Deutsch-jüdisch-russische Paradoxien oder Versuch eines Kommentars aus Sicht des Historikers," in *Ausgerechnet Deutschland! Jüdisch-russische Einwanderung in die Bundesrepublik*, eds. Dmitrij Belkin and Raphael Gross (Berlin/Frankfurt a.M.: Nicolaische Verlagsbuchhandlung, 2010), 18.
7. Kauders, *Unmögliche Heimat*, 126.
8. On this, see ViolaB. Georgi, *Entliehene Erinnerung. Geschichtsbilder junger Migranten in Deutschland* (Hamburg: Hamburger Edition, 2003), and Jürgen Motte and Rainer Ohliger, eds., *Geschichte und Gedächtnis in der Einwanderungsgesellschaft. Migration zwischen historischer Rekonstruktion und Erinnerungspolitik* (Essen: Klartext, 2004), passim.
9. Paul Harris, "Russischsprachige Juden in Deutschland," in *Enzyklopädie Migration in Europa. Vom 17. Jahrhundert bis zur Gegenwart*, ed. Klaus J. Bade (Paderborn: Schöningh, 2007), 37–8.
10. Jörg Lau, "Gründe für ein jüdisches Museum," *Jüdisches Museum Berlin Journal* (Berlin: Jüdisches Museum Berlin, 2011), 21.
11. Translated from German. Hanno Loewy, "Ein kurzer, verschämter, paradoxer Augenblick des Einverständnisses. Deutsche Identitäten vor und nach dem Holocaust," *Frankfurter Rundschau*, 7 October 2000, 21.
12. Interview with Wolfgang Schäuble on 8 July 2009 in Berlin, in *Ausgerechnet Deutschland! Jüdisch-russische Einwanderung in die Bundesrepublik*, eds. Dmitrij Belkin and Raphael Gross (Berlin/Frankfurt a.M.: Nicolaische Verlagsbuchhandlung, 2010), 53.
13. Loewy, "Ein kurzer, verschämter, paradoxer Augenblick," 21.
14. Translated from German. "Aktuelle Stunde des Bundestages zur Einwanderung von Juden aus Osteuropa," *Tagesspiegel*, 26 October 1990, 6.
15. Ibid.
16. Alliance 90/The Greens (Bündnis 90/Die Grünen) is a green political party in Germany, formed from the merger of the German Green Party (founded in West

Germany in 1980) and Alliance 90 (founded during the revolution of 1989–90 in East
Germany) in 1993.

17. Translated from German. "Auszüge aus der Bundestagsdebatte am 31. Oktober 1990 über
die Aufnahme sowjetischer Juden", *Allgemeine Jüdische Wochenzeitung*, 15 November
1990, 4.

18. The Quota Refugee Act of 1980 allows for the recognition of an applicant's refugee status,
in accordance with the Geneva Convention, when the applicant is still in his/her country
of origin or in a third country, without him/her having to go through an official asylum
procedure. On this, see Kai Hailbronner, *Ausländerrecht. Ein Handbuch* (Heidelberg:
Kohlhammer, 1989).

19. Paul A. Harris, "The Politics of Reparation and Return: Soviet Jewish and Ethnic German
Immigration to the New Germany" (PhD diss., Auburn University, 1997).

20. The distribution of the Jewish quota refugees was the responsibility of the Cologne-based
Federal Office of Administration. Distribution was decided in consultation with the
individual federal states on the basis of the asylum seeker allocation system, that is,
according to the population density of each of the federal states. This was followed by
the issue of an entry permit. Applicants received a letter entitling them to a permanent
residence and work permit, to social services such as integration support (e.g., language
courses), welfare benefits, housing benefit, child allowance, and study grants. Upon
completion of a recognized language course, immigrants could make use of services
provided by the employment office (further training, retraining, job-creation measures)
and after eight years they could apply for German citizenship. Most Jewish immigrants
came from Russia and Ukraine, followed by the Baltic states, Central Asia, Moldova,
and the Caucasus. In their countries of origin, most of the immigrants had lived in cities
and the proportion of marriages to a non-Jewish partner was over fifty percent. Overall,
the group of immigrants was highly qualified. See Julius H. Schoeps, Willi Jaspers, and
Bernhard Vogt, *Russische Juden in Deutschland. Integration und Selbstbehauptung in einem
fremden Land* (Weinheim: Beltz, 1996), 31–3.

21. The solution of the quota policy also helped to avoid diplomatic tensions. After all, it was
important for Germany to avoid the impression that it was accusing the CIS countries
of persecuting Jews. It was equally important, however, that Germany remain loyal to
Israel. See M. Tress, "Soviet Jews in the Federal Republic of Germany. The Rebuilding of
a Community," *Jewish Journal of Sociology*, 37, no. 1 (1995), 39–54.

22. Ulrich Herbert, *Geschichte der Ausländerpolitik in Deutschland – Saisonarbeiter, Zwangsarbeiter,
Gastarbeiter, Flüchtlinge* (Munich: Beck, 2001), 341.

23. "Von Moskau nach Berlin," *Der Tagesspiegel*, 12 January 1991, 8.

24. Ibid.

25. For more on this in greater detail, see Karen Körber, *Juden, Russen, Emigranten.
Identitätskonflikte jüdischer Einwanderer in einer ostdeutschen Stadt* (Frankfurt a.M./New
York: Campus, 2005), 67–9.

26. "So leise wie möglich", *Der Spiegel*, Nr. 22, 27 May 1996, accessed 05 March 2013, www.
spiegel.de/spiegel/print/d-8928367.html.

27. Zygmunt Bauman, *Moderne und Ambivalenz. Das Ende der Eindeutigkeit* (Hamburg:
Hamburger Edition, 1992).

28. Kauders, *Unmögliche Heimat*, 126.

29. Ibid., 129.

30. Micha Brumlik et al., eds., *Jüdisches Leben in Deutschland nach 1945* (Munich: Athenaeum,
1988), Y.Michal Bodemann, *Gedächtnistheater. Die jüdische Gemeinschaft und ihre deutsche
Erfindung* (Hamburg: Rotbuch, 1996), 11.

31. The corporative status has its origins in the German state-church law that was adopted in the Weimar constitution in 1919 and was incorporated, unchanged, into the German constitution in 1949 (art. 140 GG/art. 137 V). Although this guaranteed everyone a right to religious freedom, which religions could enjoy this status, and with it the public recognition of a legally endorsed equal religious community, was subject to a legal decision. The corporative status in fact represents a privileging of certain religious communities; it allows for example the right to tax collection and to own endowment property as well as a right to social benefits with state support.

32. Translated from German. Interview with the chairman of the Israelite Religious Community of Nuremberg, Transcript, 12.

33. Körber, *Juden, Russen, Emigranten*, passim.

34. "Jüdische Gemeinden streiten über echte Mitglieder," *Frankfurter Rundschau*, 5 December 1995, 7; "Ein Fall für den Mond," *Süddeutsche Zeitung*, 13 October 1997, 7.

35. Zvi Gitelman, "Becoming Jewish in Russia and Ukraine," in *New Jewish Identities. Contemporary Europe and Beyond*, eds. Zvi Gitelman, Barry Kosmin, and Andrew Kovács (Budapest/New York: Central European University Press, 2003), 108.

36. See Yuri Slezkine, *The Jewish Century* (Princeton: Princeton University Press, 2004), 105–14. Michael Stanislawski, "Russian Jewry, the Russian State, and the Dynamics of Jewish Emancipation," in *Paths of Emancipation. Jews, States and Citizenship*, eds. Pierre Birnbaum and Ira Katznelson (Princeton: Princeton University Press, 1995), 262–84.

37. Gitelman, "Becoming Jewish in Russia and Ukraine," 106.

38. Dan Diner, "Im Zeichen des Banns," in *Geschichte der Juden in Deutschland*, ed. Michael Brenner (Munich: Beck, 2012), 15–66.

39. Hendrik Broder et al., eds., *Fremd im eigenen Land. Juden in der Bundesrepublik* (Frankfurt a.M.: Fischer, 1979), Lea Fleischmann, *Dies ist nicht mein Land. Eine Jüdin verläßt die Bundesrepublik* (Munich: Heyne, 1980), passim.

40. Bodemann, *Gedächtnistheater*, 93–100.

41. Ilja Altman, "Shoah: Gedenken verboten! Der weite Weg vom Sowjettabu zur Erinnerung," *Osteuropa*, 55, no. 4 (2006), 149–64.

42. Aleida Assmann, *Der lange Schatten der Vergangenheit. Erinnerungskultur und Geschichtspolitik* (Bonn: Beck, 2007), 175.

43. The quotations are taken from interviews with Russian-speaking members of Jewish communities from a comparative study of communities which was undertaken from 2005–08 as a joint project between the University of Applied Science of Erfurt and the University of Erfurt.

44. Translated from German. Alexander P., b. 1924, Transcript, 2, male, 84, 3.

45. Translated from German. Nikolaj S., b. 1964, Transcript, 9.

46. Lena Gorelik, "Die Blockade war immer da," preface to *Lenas Tagebuch*, Lena Muchina (Munich: Graf, 2013), 7–13.

47. Y.Michal Bodemann and Gökce Yurdakul, "Geborgte Narrative: Wie sich türkische Einwanderer an den Juden in Deutschland orientieren," *Soziale Welt* 56, no. 4 (2005), 441–51.

48. Karen Körber, "Lebenswirklichkeiten – Jüdische Gegenwart in Deutschland. Eine Onlinebefragung unter jungen russischsprachigen Juden." Unpublished manuscript (Berlin, 2014), 1–48.

49. "A Portrait of Jewish Americans," Pew Research Center, 1 October 2013, 1–20, accessed 10 November 2013, http://www.pewforum.org/files/2013/10/jewish-american-full-report-for-web.pdf.

50. Körber, "Lebenswirklichkeiten – Jüdische Gegenwart in Deutschland," 9–12.

51. Sabine Strasser, *Bewegte Zugehörigkeiten. Nationale Spannungen, Transnationale Praktiken, Transversale Politik* (Vienna: Turia + Kant, 2009).
52. Lena Gorelik, *'Sie können aber gut Deutsch!' Warum ich nicht mehr dankbar sein will, dass ich hier leben darf, und Toleranz nicht weiterhilft* (Munich: Pantheon, 2012).
53. Olga Grjasnowa, "Deutschland Deine Dichter – bunter als behauptet," *DIE WELT*, 8 February 2014.

# Works Cited

Allgemeine Jüdische Wochenzeitung. "Auszüge aus der Bundestagsdebatte am 31. Oktober 1990 über die Aufnahme sowjetischer Juden," 15 November 1990, 4.

Altman, Ilja. "Shoah: Gedenken verboten! Der weite Weg vom Sowjettabu zur Erinnerung." *Osteuropa* 55, no. 4 (2006): 149–64.

Assmann, Aleida. *Der lange Schatten der Vergangenheit. Erinnerungskultur und Geschichtspolitik.* Bonn: Beck, 2007.

Aviv, Caryn and David Shneer. *New Jews. The End of the Jewish Diaspora.* New York: New York University Press, 2005.

Bauman, Zygmunt. *Moderne und Ambivalenz. Das Ende der Eindeutigkeit.* Hamburg: Hamburger Edition, 1992.

Benhabib, Sheila. *Kulturelle Vielfalt und demokratische Gleichheit. Politische Partizipation im Zeitalter der Globalisierung.* Frankfurt a.M.: Fischer, 1999.

Berliner Morgenpost. "Gemeinsame Erklärung der Fraktionen der Volkskammer der DDR am 12.4. 1990," 13 April 1990, 15.

Bodemann, Y.Michal. *Gedächtnistheater. Die jüdische Gemeinschaft und ihre deutsche Erfindung.* Hamburg: Rotbuch, 1996.

Bodemann, Y.Michal and Gökce Yurdakul. "Geborgte Narrative: Wie sich türkische Einwanderer an den Juden in Deutschland orientieren." *Soziale Welt* 56, no. 4 (2005): 441–51.

Broder, Hendrik et al., eds. *Fremd im eigenen Land. Juden in der Bundesrepublik.* Frankfurt a.M.: Fischer, 1979.

Brumlik, Micha et al., eds. *Jüdisches Leben in Deutschland nach 1945.* Munich: Athenaeum, 1988.

Der Spiegel. "So leise wie möglich," Nr. 22, 27.05.1996. Accessed 05 March 2013. www.spiegel.de/spiegel/print/d-8928367.html.

Der Tagesspiegel. "Von Moskau nach Berlin." 12 January 1991, 8.

Diner, Dan. "Deutsch-jüdisch-russische Paradoxien oder Versuch eines Kommentars aus Sicht des Historikers." In *Ausgerechnet Deutschland! Jüdisch-russische Einwanderung in die Bundesrepublik*, edited by Dmitrij Belkin and Raphael Gross. Berlin/Frankfurt a.M.: Nicolaische Verlagsbuchhandlung, 2010.

Diner, Dan "Im Zeichen des Banns." In *Geschichte der Juden in Deutschland*, edited by Michael Brenner. Munich: Beck, 2012.

Fleischmann, Lea. *Dies ist nicht mein Land. Eine Jüdin verläßt die Bundesrepublik.* Munich: Heyne, 1980.

Frankfurter Rundschau. "Jüdische Gemeinden streiten über echte Mitglieder," 5 December 1995, 7.

Georgi, ViolaB. *Entliehene Erinnerung. Geschichtsbilder junger Migranten in Deutschland.* Hamburg: Hamburger Edition, 2003.

Gitelman, Zvi. "Becoming Jewish in Russia and Ukraine." In *New Jewish Identities. Contemporary Europe and Beyond*, edited by Zvi Gitelman, Barry Kosmin, and Andrew Kovács. Budapest/New York: Central European University Press, 2003.

Gorelik, Lena. *'Sie können aber gut Deutsch!' Warum ich nicht mehr dankbar sein will, dass ich hier leben darf, und Toleranz nicht weiterhilft*. Munich: Pantheon, 2012.

Gorelik, Lena. "Die Blockade war immer da." Preface to *Lenas Tagebuch*, Lena Muchina. Munich: Graf, 2013.

Grjasnowa, Olga. "Deutschland Deine Dichter – bunter als behauptet." *DIE WELT*, 8 February 2014.

Gromova, Alina. *Generation Kosher Light*. Bielefeld: transcript, 2013.

Hailbronner, Kai. *Ausländerrecht. Ein Handbuch*. Heidelberg: Kohlhammer, 1989.

Harris, PaulA. "The Politics of Reparation and Return: Soviet Jewish and Ethnic German Immigration to the New Germany." PhD diss., Auburn University, 1997.

Harris, Paul. "Russischsprachige Juden in Deutschland." In *Enzyklopädie Migration in Europa. Vom 17. Jahrhundert bis zur Gegenwart*, edited by Klaus J. Bade. Paderborn: Schöningh, 2007: 37–8.

Herbert, Ulrich. *Geschichte der Ausländerpolitik in Deutschland – Saisonarbeiter, Zwangsarbeiter, Gastarbeiter, Flüchtlinge*. Munich: Beck, 2001.

Kauders, Anthony. *Unmögliche Heimat*. Munich: Beck, 2007.

Körber, Karen. *Juden, Russen, Emigranten. Identitätskonflikte jüdischer Einwanderer in einer ostdeutschen Stadt*. Frankfurt a.M./New York: Campus, 2005.

Körber, Karen. "Pushkin oder Thora? Der Wandel der jüdischen Gemeinden in Deutschland." In *Juden und Muslime in Deutschland. Recht, Religion, Identität. Tel Aviver Jahrbuch für deutsche Geschichte XXXVII*, edited by Jose Brunner and Shai Lavi. Göttingen: Wallstein, 2009.

Körber, Karen. "Lebenswirklichkeiten – Jüdische Gegenwart in Deutschland. Eine Onlinebefragung unter jungen russischsprachigen Juden." Unpublished manuscript. Berlin, 2014.

Lau, Jörg "Gründe für ein jüdisches Museum." *Jüdisches Museum Berlin Journal*. Berlin, Jüdisches Museum Berlin, 2011.

Loewy, Hanno. "Ein kurzer, verschämter, paradoxer Augenblick des Einverständnisses. Deutsche Identitäten vor und nach dem Holocaust." *Frankfurter Rundschau*, 7 October 2000, 21.

Motte, Jürgen and Rainer Ohliger, eds. *Geschichte und Gedächtnis in der Einwanderungsgesellschaft. Migration zwischen historischer Rekonstruktion und Erinnerungspolitik*. Essen: Klartext, 2004.

Offenberg, Ulrike. *Seid vorsichtig gegen die Machthaber. Die jüdischen Gemeinden in der SBZ und der DDR, 1945–1990*. Berlin: Aufbau, 1998.

Pew Research Center. "A Portrait of Jewish Americans," 1 October 2013, 1–20. Accessed 10 November 2013. http://www.pewforum.org/files/2013/10/jewish-american-full-report-for-web.pdf.

Runge, Irene. *Vom Kommen und Bleiben. Osteuropäische jüdische Einwanderer in Berlin*. Berlin: Ausländerbeauftragte des Senats, 1992.

Schäuble, Wolfgang. "Interview on 8 July 2009, Berlin." In *Ausgerechnet Deutschland! Jüdisch-russische Einwanderung in die Bundesrepublik*, edited by Dmitrij. Belkin and Raphael Gross. Berlin/Frankfurt a.M.: Nicolaische Verlagsbuchhandlung, 2010.

Schoeps, Julius H., Willi Jaspers, and Bernhard Vogt. *Russische Juden in Deutschland. Integration und Selbstbehauptung in einem fremden Land*. Weinheim: Beltz, 1996.

Slezkine, Yuri *The Jewish Century*. Princeton: Princeton University Press, 2004.

Stanislawski, Michael. "Russian Jewry, the Russian State, and the Dynamics of Jewish Emancipation." In *Paths of Emancipation. Jews, States and Citizenship*, edited by Pierre Birnbaum and Ira Katznelson. Princeton: Princeton University Press, 1995.

Strasser, Sabine *Bewegte Zugehörigkeiten. Nationale Spannungen, Transnationale Praktiken, Transversale Politik*. Vienna: Turia + Kant, 2009.

Süddeutsche Zeitung. "Ein Fall für den Mond," 13 October 1997, 7.

Tress, Madeleine "Soviet Jews in the Federal Republic of Germany. The Rebuilding of a Community." *Jewish Journal of Sociology* 37, no. 1 (1995): 39–54.

Zentralrat der Juden in Deutschland. "Gesetzliche Regelungen". Last modified 12 January 2013. Accessed 14 April 2014. http://www.zentralratdjuden.de/de/topic/62.html.

Zentralrat der Juden in Deutschland. "Mitglieder". Last modified 06 February 2014. Accessed 11 June 2014. http://www.zentralratdjuden.de/de/topic/5.mitglieder.html.

**Karen Körber** is currently visiting professor at the Institute for European Ethnology/Cultural Studies of the Philipps-Universität, Marburg, and fellow of the Jewish Museum, Berlin. Her research focuses on the contemporary Jewish diaspora in Germany, migration, transnationalism, and the politics of remembrance. Among her publications is her monograph *Juden, Russen, Emigranten* (2005). She is also co-editor of "Imagined Families in Mobile Worlds," a special issue of *Ethnologia Europea, Journal of European Ethnology* (2012), and editor of *Russisch-Jüdische Gegenwart in Deutschland* (2015).

# Chapter 12

# Swept Under the Rug

### Home-grown Anti-Semitism and Migrants as "Obstacles" in German Holocaust Remembrance

*Annette Seidel-Arpaci*

In one of the classes on cinematic representations of the Shoah that I taught recently at a British university, I asked students about their experience of Holocaust education at school. As with previous classes, the vast majority of students thought that they had not learned about the Holocaust during their school years. Moreover, the students, now in their final year at university, felt that they had not learned about the history of National Socialism and the Holocaust during their studies either. Not to mention that most have never been exposed to the histories of Jews and other minoritized groups in Europe, and even less so to the history of anti-Semitism,[1] including the expulsion of Jews from England and the long-standing history of blood libel against Jews. It is World War II that is taught in schools; World War II frames the approach in the United Kingdom with added emphasis for instance, on "the air war" and "the Blitz." Meanwhile, a National Holocaust Memorial Day has been held in the United Kingdom since 2001. The date 27 January — chosen for the liberation day of Auschwitz by Soviet troops — is also meant to commemorate genocides in Cambodia, Rwanda, Bosnia, and Darfur and thus postulates the main dictum of Holocaust education and remembrance, "Never again." "Never again" is a vague notion if we have little detailed knowledge and understanding, and if the Shoah as Jewish catastrophe is — at least from classroom experience over the years — met with resistance, a resistance toward the notion of Jewish suffering, both on the grounds of an equally vague idea about other groups victimized by the Nazis as well as by evoking the Israel-Palestine conflict without much knowledge about its history or current politics. In principle, resistance to given narratives is what education thrives on, and is a necessary ingredient for critical thinking. I believe that what becomes apparent in the classroom, however, are the widespread ideas that knowledge and discussion about the Holocaust are "everywhere," as well as a competitive view of atrocities and suffering—both sentiments that initially block open-minded inquiry. Thus we are dealing with competing claims over persecution and victimhood, with questions of empathy and positionality, and with ideological amalgamations across society. Such intersections can be observed similarly across Europe. Rosa Fava asks in this context. "Why should the students believe me that 'the Palestinians' are not being sent to the gas chambers?"[2]

In Germany, the country responsible for National Socialism and the Holocaust, there is a debate construing a special need for Holocaust education for immigrants and their descendants. Migrants are seen as disinterested and not invested in commemorating the victims of the Nazis. This approach only functions by ignoring the multidirectional[3] dimension of negotiating diverse histories and memories and by ethnoculturalizing individuals in discussions about Holocaust remembrance and education.

What then is at stake for Germany when migrants are considered as not relating to Holocaust remembrance and education? And what is more, who are those migrants lamented about in newspapers, talk shows, and politicians' speeches?[4] These debates need to be considered not only in the context of the wider discourse of *Vergangenheitsbewältigung* (mastering of the past), but also in view of the renewed discussions, as of the 1990s, of a "German victimhood." Countless examples from the past two decades show that anti-Semitism after the Shoah in Germany and the resistance to Holocaust remembrance are home-grown, rather than linked to an immigrated disinterest or hostility toward the commemoration of the Holocaust and toward Jews. I discuss first the connection made between remembrance culture and ethnicity and descent. The link is, on the one hand, taken as a given factor for identity formation along the narratives received through particular socializations for identity formations of "Jews," "Germans," or "Turks"; on the other hand, it is a concept that is suddenly being overlooked, or not consequently applied when it comes to so-called native Germans, as well as to descendants of migrants. This approach both results from and perpetuates the idea of "history-neutral" migrants. Second—and resulting from the ethnoculturalizing framework—there is a view of migrants as obstacles to Holocaust remembrance. Immigrants and their descendants are considered resistant to the remembrance of the Holocaust, not least because of "imported" anti-Semitism. This is interwoven with a construct of all migrants as Muslims and of all Muslims as extremists, but also with the desire to project current anti-Semitism only to an "outside." Third, there is a neglected history of migrant activism and cultural production relating to the memory of the

Holocaust and other Nazi atrocities—a negotiating of Nazi history and the Shoah that existed prior to the discovery of migrants as key figures for German remembrance culture. I interrogate linguistic and political discursive frameworks that lead to a relegating of both disinterest in the history and memory of the Holocaust, as well as current anti-Semitism to an "outside," an "other" purportedly importing anti-Jewish resentments from elsewhere. The notion of migrants as a major obstacle or key figure for German Holocaust remembrance has to be read in the contexts of the invention of history-neutral migrants, the ongoing neglect of the history of Nazi forced labor, and the German post-Holocaust discourse about Jews and "German suffering."

## Migratory "Hour Zero": A "Guest Worker" is a Turk, is a Muslim

It is a recent development that Germany has begun to acknowledge the fact that it is an immigration country, and even more recent is the discourse about the relationship of immigrants and their descendants to the history and memory of National Socialism and the Holocaust. The debates after German unification remain firmly within the parameters of Germany's mastering the past, and merely add another participant to the dialogue allegedly taking place between "Germans" and "Jews." (Non-Jewish) immigrants and their descendants are presumed to be detached from the history of Nazi Germany and the commemoration of its victims. Wider public debates about National Socialism and the Holocaust began in Germany during the 1980s. Yet the budding discussion about German responsibility for the murder of the Jews of Europe and about Germans as perpetrators was simultaneously contested during the *Historikerstreit* (historians' debate) in the mid-1980s. By now the German discourse about "the past," or rather "the mastering of the past" has arrived at a point that accepts both a "German victimhood" at the hands of the Allied forces at the end of the war, and a "new Germany" that prides itself on an exemplary working through of Nazism and the Holocaust and that has learned its lessons and is prone to teach them to others. And, in their own way, both of these narratives result in a *Schlußstrich* (literally, final stroke), an end to the debate about the specific conditions that led to the Holocaust. Parallel to this development, the Berlin Wall came down, and in the wake of the newly found nationalism a wave of violent and deadly racism swept the country. In 2006, at the occasion of Germany hosting the World Cup, the former government spokesman Uwe-Karsten Heye publicly cautioned visitors "with a different skin color" to avoid areas in East Germany as "it is possible [they] wouldn't get out alive."[5] While his unexpected statement caused some uproar, anyone considered non-German in Germany already knew to stay clear of those parts of the country also known since the early 1990s by the neo-Nazi term "nationally liberated zones."[6] At the time of Heye's comment, the core members of the National Socialist Underground (NSU) had been living clandestinely for about eight years and in that time had shot dead nine men of Turkish and Greek descent in several cities across Germany, set off nail bombs in Cologne, and perpetrated numerous bank robberies in order to finance their racist terror. Meanwhile, there was another World Cup, this time with the German team as winner, and a sea of flags displaying a new national pride was visible throughout Germany, the country where *en masse* waving of national flags had been considered inappropriate for some time. The sea of German flags gave way to Palestinian flags and—not unlike the 2006 World Cup, which was followed by the Israel-Lebanon war—a wave of protests against the Israel-Gaza war. In the wake of large demonstrations with anti-Semitic slogans clearly referencing National Socialism, including Hitler and the death camps, the debate about migrants as a problem for Holocaust education and remembrance has regained momentum.

In Munich, we are nearing the end of a spectacle that by now no longer sparks much public interest: the NSU trial. After weeks of rows over seat allocations for journalists, the trial against members of the NSU started on 6 May 2012. The NSU was officially uncovered in November 2011, when two of its members, Uwe Mundlos and Uwe Böhnhardt, killed themselves after a bank robbery in the town of Eisenach went awry. The main defendant, Beate Zschäpe, is accused of involvement in ten murders and of being a member of a group whose aim was to commit murder and criminal acts dangerous to public safety, for the purpose of intimidating the public and damaging the state. Also on trial are four other men, who are accused of having aided the group. All of them came up in the nationalist and racist climate of the 1990s and have been neo-Nazi activists for years. Moreover, disturbing facts about involvement of the secret services have been coming to light in the case. How the NSU core members were able to evade authorities for nearly thirteen years despite being on watch lists is one of the questions in the context of the investigative failures. The astonishment surrounding the group's living for over a decade in East German towns, being friendly with neighbors, and going on holidays while being wanted by authorities, can only be understood in the context of the denial regarding the deep roots that the beliefs and attitudes of this neo-Nazi group hold in society as a whole. While politicians expressed shock and spoke of a scandal and disgrace upon the so-called discovery of the NSU, there seems little willingness to look deeper. The problem of widespread racism in society is still denied. Germany, after all, considered itself as a country without racism after 1945. Accordingly, the misleading term for racism has been for the longest time "hostility towards foreigners." The idea that victims of racism had to be foreigners at once reveals the underlying dictum: a concept of nationality that considers the very existence of Black Germans, Turkish Germans, and many others an oxymoron. The envisioned norm is white, Christian, and elusively "German-German."[7]

It is not surprising, then, that investigations of the NSU murders focused on the victims and betrayed racist overtones. For a decade investigators had assumed that the men murdered by members of the NSU had been shot dead in the context of an unidentified mafia connection, likely involving drug trafficking. In every case, the families of the victims were interrogated for years in order to find the expected link to organized crime. To add insult to injury, the murder series was dubbed "Döner-Killings," named after a popular Turkish dish. Thus far, the existence of institutionalized racism has never been officially acknowledged in the country. As of the 1990s, in the face of increasing neo-Nazi hegemony in countless areas, especially in East Germany, local authorities gave preference to so-called "accepting youth work" as a preventative measure. This approach enabled neo-Nazis to flourish unchallenged and organize further, effectively sponsored by youth work programs. While Germany still grappled with acknowledging the fact and existence of racism, migrants and descendants of migrants have turned from "guest workers" into Turks, and in the context of the war on terror and an international discussion about Islam, into "Muslims." Or, in Eren Güvercin's words, "Within the 'Islam-debate' during the past years the Turk, Albanian, Kurd and Arab has mutated from the Kanak to a 'Muslim.'"[8] The debate following from Thilo Sarrazin's book *Deutschland schafft sich ab* (Germany does away with itself),[9] which proclaimed a clash of cultures in Germany, is ongoing and declares immigration, non-integration, and Muslims as the main social and political problems. In order to make sense of the debates on remembrance of the Holocaust and the integration of migrants in what is referred to as "our remembrance culture," we need to take account of the aforementioned context. A closer look at the ethnicized positions assigned to descendants of migrants within German Holocaust remembrance discourse shows that immigrants are considered as separate from the history of National Socialism and the Holocaust. Debates over the integration of immigrants, or rather "young migrants," into German remembrance culture only started in the early 2000s. The scholars putting the issue on the agenda at the time must be credited for acknowledging the general exclusion of those considered as migrants from major German debates, including the German remembrance of the Holocaust. At the same time, this acknowledgement perpetuates the ethnicized remembrance culture—without taking the consequential step of looking precisely at the existing intersections of immigrated history and memory with the history of National Socialism and the Holocaust.

Viola B. Georgi's *Entliehene Erinnerung* (Borrowed Memory) was among the early works taking note of and discussing in depth the exclusionary character of German remembrance culture. Georgi's interview-based research was conducted against the backdrop of the demographic development of German society, and was aimed at discovering empirical information concerning young migrants' historical reference patterns, as well as their relationship with the memory of the Holocaust and National Socialism.[10]

The title of Georgi's book implies that there could be a non-borrowed memory, a kind of memory that is properly one's own, an "authentic" one. Here, we may want to turn to Kaja Silverman's suggestion that "every human psyche is organized around memories which are both deeply fantasmatic, and which are riven through and through with 'otherness' and that 'memories' do not have to be authentic to work upon us."[11] If the past is less the accumulated events of a given life than the history of representation and the persistence of certain collective structures,[12] then all memory is in some sense borrowed; there is no authentic ownership. For instance, a young German-German person does not actually remember Stalingrad, yet this memory is part of a collectively referential framework transmitted through family conversations, and thus is part of what Welzer et al. call the "album."[13] As Georgi acknowledges, these questions about the shaping of individual and collective memories are interdependent with agency. She distinguishes four modes of identification with different foci: first, the identification with the victims of National Socialism; second, with the *Mitläufer* (fellow travelers) and perpetrators; third, with one's own ethnic community; and fourth with humanity. Georgi's interviews are based on the assumption that young migrants have to deal with National Socialism and the Holocaust as the historical legacy of the *Einwanderungsland* (immigration country). Although she questions the emergence of an exclusive German national remembrance community, and although she also interviews young people whose grandparents were victimized by the Nazis, Georgi, too, does not acknowledge these varied identifications and positions beyond the legacy of Germany as a (postwar) immigration country.

Moreover, many of the young people interviewed cannot be categorized within only one of the types developed, and their identifications clearly point to a multidirectional and self-positional dimension of remembrance culture. Georgi assigns to these young people a dominant memory type which she calls "post-ethnic" and "post-national."[14] This seems at first an apt description considering the interviews in the volume. And yet it becomes obvious in the interviews that the migrantized young people aim for a post-ethnic position but are confronted with being positioned as foreigners in Germany. A post-ethnic memory is, as Georgi herself says, much less developed among young German-German people,[15] a suggestion supported by studies by Birgit Rommelspacher, Harald Welzer, and others on intergenerational identification and the handing-down of narratives about National Socialism and the Holocaust in German families.[16] This side of the ethnicizing remembrance discourse is hardly discussed in the exclusionary terms found toward migrants, i.e., German-German youth are not considered disinterested in the Holocaust *because* of their familial descent. Indeed, one of the most compelling examples in Georgi's book of a desired yet impossible post-ethnic positioning is sixteen-year-old Bülent, who has a Turkish familial background and whose mother was born in Germany. He took part as the only pupil from his class, "voluntarily," Georgi stresses, in a memorial site trip to Terezin, and in the Czech Republic experiences what it is like to be considered German in another country. This positioning of Bülent as German, however, is challenged by his classmates, who deny him the capacity to empathize and mourn on the basis of belonging neither to the descendants of the victims nor to those of the perpetrators: "Ey, as a foreigner, you don't even have a clue."[17] While he is addressed abroad as a member of a German memory collective and is partaking in its responsibility, he is regarded by German-German members of this community as not belonging. What is more, Astrid Messerschmidt rightly criticizes the German remembrance discourse where the collective Nazi history and the Holocaust are supposed to provide the basis for a common, instead of an east/west-divided, national identity. She points to the exclusion of descendants of victims from the national discourse precisely on the grounds of their alleged inability to empathize with a "suffering of the descendants of the perpetrators," and to the fact that the descendants of victims are always regarded as a source for further suffering on part of "the Germans."[18]

Another early example is a conference held in the city of Bielefeld in June 2003,[19] with the rather unusual title "Young Migrants and 'Aussiedler': Key Figures of Remembrance Pedagogy? Impulses for the Further Development of our Remembrance Culture." The title is remarkable not only because of its linking of migrants, *Aussiedler* (ethnic Germans from Eastern Europe),[20] and the problem of commemoration, but because it pointedly expresses some perplexing manifestations in the discourse on remembrance. Particularly interesting is the term *Schlüsselkinder*, which was certainly intended to mean "key figures." However, the term additionally means "latch-key kids," and these are commonly viewed as neglected and forlorn. The notion of a "key" additionally implies the function of a device meant to open something and in a wider sense to remove a barrier, an obstacle. Two things become obvious: first, it is taken to be inconceivable that young people with a family background of migration could have as much interest or disinterest in the history of National Socialism and the Holocaust as any other young person whose family has not moved in over a century. Second—and striking in particular due to the inclusion of *Aussiedler*—is the neglect of the fact that many "guest workers", or labor migrants, came to West Germany from countries like Greece, Yugoslavia, and Italy, and may have familial memories of German camps or of atrocities committed against civilians and partisans alike. Many so-called *Fremdarbeiter* (foreign workers) came, mostly as forced laborers rather than of their own will, from the same countries as the first "guest workers" did later. And when Zafer Şenocak asks in relation to his own Turkish familial background, "What access does someone whose father experienced World War II on the radio, far from the battlefields, have to this event?,"[21] he, too, partakes in construing a migrant neutrality. Marc David Baer reminds us of the Turkish Jews living in Germany who perished in the Shoah, and concludes that the exclusion of Germans of Turkish descent is facilitated by two common beliefs: first, that Turks were not affected by National Socialism because "the experiences and atrocities of the war remained far away" from Turkey, and second, that it was nearly two decades after the Jews had been annihilated in the death camps that Turks first migrated to Germany as "guests."[22] The "guests" have come, however, as of the mid-1950s, from Italy, Morocco, Yugoslavia, Greece, Spain, Tunisia, and Portugal. While the majority came over time from Turkey, this cannot be seen as the only reason for turning Turks into *the* "guest worker." Turks are indeed considered far away from Nazi Germany and the Holocaust but if we extend "affected by National Socialism" to include the experience of occupation and war, the intertwined histories with other, and early, "guest workers" come into view.

One example negotiating such overlooked complexities is the essay film *Passing Drama* by Angela Melitopoulos. The filmmaker traces the history of her family from their deportation as part of the Greek minority from Turkey, her father's stay as a so-called *Fremdarbeiter* in Vienna, his imprisonment in an SS "re-education camp," to his later migration as a "guest worker" to Germany—the latter an experience many people from his village shared.[23] The non-recognition of such links, which are only present as hauntingly split and fragmented memories, results from the desire to forget the Nazi war crimes within and beyond what is considered Europe. Despite the ways in which these histories are significantly different, there are, nonetheless, ways in which they intersect. Certain treatments of "guest workers" in West Germany can be traced to National Socialism, such as the housing of "guest workers" often in the very buildings where forced laborers had had to live one or two decades earlier, as well as humiliating medical examinations carried out by German doctors before people were allowed to travel to West Germany to work.[24] The assumption of migrants' detachment from the memory of National Socialism has always been challenged in cultural production, such as in *Passing Drama* and *Die leere Mitte* (The Empty Center),[25] and by political and social activism. For decades, the migrantized have interrogated in political and cultural practice the experience of racism as well as the persistence of anti-Semitism against the background of German history. While there are works that are widely available, there is also a large amount of "grey literature" and little documented activism. Hence we are dealing with multiple marginal(ized) debates. Nonetheless, "guest workers" surely arrived with as little or as much interest in recent history as German-Germans, who might not pass a citizenship test today or know about the site of a former concentration camp relatively nearby. The assumption of a general neutrality of (only) migrants in relation to the history and aftermath of National Socialism and the Holocaust can only be upheld in an exclusionary and one-directional framework of thought.[26] In the years after unification the process of renationalization had been increasingly enacted through exclusionary violence, and has led also descendants of migrants to further engage with Germany's history and with the Holocaust. Thus Erdal Kaynar and Kimoko Suda write in a chapter about the history of migrant self-organization in Germany: "The experience of collective labelling, deprivation of rights, expulsion and annihilation of people who were defined as un-German during the Third Reich has structured the behavior of Germans toward the minoritized."[27] Aside from being part of wider organizations, migrants and self-organized migrant groups intervened in debates and against local anti-Semitic mobilizations in Babenhausen,[28] Gollwitz,[29] and other places after unification.

In 1994, the Bundesgerichtshof (Germany's highest court of civil and criminal jurisdiction) acquitted a soldier of the Wehrmacht, Lieutenant Lehnigk-Emden, who had murdered twenty-two people in the Italian village of Caiazzo near Naples in 1943. Some months later, migrants protested against this decision, against the silence about the crime, and against the support for the perpetrator in his home town of Ochtendung, near Koblenz. An Italian court had sentenced him in absentia to lifelong imprisonment as a war criminal.[30] Meanwhile, the man was not held responsible for his crime in Germany—until December 1993, when he was arrested for the first time, only to be acquitted one year later. Until

1993, Lehnigk-Emden had lived as a respectable citizen in the town of Ochtendung, where he worked as an architect, and was a Social Democratic politician with a seat on the local council. Additionally, he held the presidency of the Karnevalsgesellschaft (carnival society),[31] and was engaged in the Arbeiterwohlfahrt, which is a charitable Social Democratic organization.[32] A clear statement speaking against the construed zero hour for migration and the history-neutral migrant can be found in a speech held during a protest in front of Lehnigk-Emden's home. Not only can we read, "We could convince ourselves that history is in no other country as alive as here. But not the history as we have got to know it from our parents and grandparents," but moreover, "From them we know what you and your fathers and grandfathers have brought about in our countries during the time between 1940 and 1945. This knowledge haunts us."[33] The statement emphasizes that men and women migrated to work in Germany after 1945 with these memories and that they were communicated in the family. If we link this episode back to the assumption that all migrants have a neutral memory in relation to German history, the necessity of the construct becomes apparent: it is needed to block out multidirectional memories, and it is needed for construing the migrant as "Muslim."

Those who are principally addressed, or just spoken about, as it were, in pedagogic and political debates about migrants and remembrance culture themselves feed sometimes into the notion of the history-neutral migrant. After the anti-Semitic terror attacks on synagogues in Istanbul on 15 November 2003, the Migrantische Initiative gegen Antisemitismus (Migrant Initiative Against Antisemitism [sic]), which has now been renamed as Kreuzberger Initiative gegen Antisemitismus, was established in Berlin. In a leaflet, announcing a rally to commemorate the victims of the attacks in Istanbul, they state: "We, in the majority people with Turkish and Kurdish background, see ourselves as having the responsibility to publicly express our revulsion at the anti-Semitic terror." After a brief reference to the increasingly open articulation of anti-Semitism in Germany, it is noted, that "anti-Semitism grows, too, within sections of the non-German communities. It is a scandal that people who show themselves as Jews, have to be afraid in Kreuzberg or Neukölln."[34] Only the Berlin areas of Kreuzberg and Neukölln are mentioned—precisely the ones with the highest numbers of migrant populations—whereas verbal and physical assaults against Jews in other areas, such as at Kurfürstendamm, in Steglitz, Spandau, and elsewhere are not mentioned. The initiative was founded only after the attacks in Turkey, and it presented its members as Turkish and Kurdish. Turkey as a country without anti-Semitism is indeed a myth; a whole array of anti-Semitic conspiracy theories exists in Turkey that express themselves not least in suspicions against people assumed to be *Dönme* (converts), such as descendants of Sabbatai Zevi's followers.[35] Toward the end, the flyer reads:

> As non-German people in this country we know what it means to be subjected to discrimination, exclusion, and violence. Although it is not the reason for our solidarity with Jewish people, we want to recall something: when in Mölln, Rostock, Solingen, and elsewhere people were murdered, because they originated from Turkey, from Vietnam or from Angola, when *Volksparteien* [catch-all parties] collected signatures against foreigners, it was representatives of the Jewish community who, without reservation, offered resistance against racism. Until now, the migrant communities have left Jewish people in this country to stand alone in the fight against antisemitism [*sic*].[36]

The same motif is repeated in an interview with Yücel, one of the organizers, in the *Tageszeitung*. As one reason for the event he cites the need "to symbolically give back to the Jewish communities something of the solidarity which we experienced at the beginning of the 90s, for example when in Rostock the asylum seekers' homes were set on fire."[37] The various "we's" constructed throughout the call for the event as well as in this later interview deserve some attention: at first, it seems, the migrant initiative defines their "we," or "migrant we," mainly as Turkish and Kurdish. Later, the "we" turns into an all-embracing "migrant, refugee, asylum-seeker we," which is most amazing at the point when Yücel says that "we" want to give solidarity back, which "we" experienced at the time of the pogroms in Rostock. There it becomes obvious that this "we" includes apparently everyone who is "othered" (in the sense of racialized) in Germany; everyone but the Jews. The interviewer could then have asked him why he and others with Turkish and Kurdish backgrounds living in Berlin would be able to construct an empathic "we" that included people from Angola, Vietnamese refugees, and Sinti and Roma in Rostock-Lichtenhagen, but apparently not, for instance, Jews in Lübeck, Gollwitz, or Berlin, or in other places that saw anti-Semitic incidents and violence. It is also remarkable because the majority of Jews in Berlin are recent migrants from the former Soviet Union. Moreover, it becomes clear that in this case a structural "sameness" of experience of racism is projected onto those identified *as* migrants and refugees, whereas Jews are categorized as completely outside of these experiences as an otherwise homogenous entity. The title of the article quotes Yücel as saying, "It is absurd for migrants to exclude others."[38] This implies a desire for the disadvantaged subject, who *necessarily* transforms her/his own experience of discrimination into awareness and understanding of other oppressions. Daniel Boyarin has summarized the problem of this approach as there being no "politically privileged access to 'truth' that is the ordained inheritance of the disadvantaged subject—gay, female, colonized, black, Jewish—but rather a condition of the possibility of access to such a position of understanding."[39] If we also consider this desire in the context of exile and diaspora versus nation-statehood, it would appear that the above suggestion of absurdity also rests on the assumption that "diaspora communities were a priori more ethical than other types of 'imagined communities,' in particular the nation-state."[40] But neither the "non-German communities" nor the "we" includes Russian Jews and Israeli Jews.[41]

A fairly recent construction appears as well: a "Turkish-Arab community." This invention adopts the majority's stereotypes that function along ethnoculturalizing lines. The common denominator for "Turkish" and "Arab" is likely to be "Muslim." A thus-construed Turkish-Arab community feeds into a culturalizing imagination, which "muslimizes" people from Turkish and Arab familial backgrounds. Following this logic then, in exchange, Muslims are "Turkified" and "Arabified," with, for instance, Muslim "guest workers" from Yugoslavia and Greece disappearing. The intervention of the Berlin initiative, with its focus on Turkey, affirms the idea of history-neutral migrants to some extent.[42] It is thus, on the one hand, an important expression against diaspora communities' demands for united fronts and a gesture of solidarity in particular for the small number of Turkish Jews in Berlin. On the other hand, though, in its terminology it does fulfill mainstream society's desire to delegate responsibility for anti-Semitism elsewhere. Raed Saleh, a Social Democrat who was a candidate in the internal party elections for mayor of Berlin in 2014, also insists that successful integration is paramount for countering anti-Semitism among "young people with a migration background." However, he clearly situates the problem within German society, which was not providing perspectives for young people of any background in particular areas. Saleh vehemently criticizes anti-Semitism, while at the same time taking to task German Bundespräsident (President of the Federal Republic of Germany) Joachim Gauck for his recent comments in the context of the anti-Semitic demonstrations in the summer of 2014. Gauck located the rampant anti-Semitism as something prevalent in "foreign societies" and as "imported" to Germany. Saleh's positioning responds to the ethnoculturalizing discourse while simultaneously dismantling it with an emphasis on a concept of multiethnic nationality still not common in Germany.[43]

The issue at stake appears to be how migrants, construed as so homogenous, present challenges or obstacles to the desired German politics of remembrance. Ultimately, a paradoxical situation is created: young migrants are expected to adapt to the forms of commemoration of a history that is perceived as not being their own. This demand for authentic identification means that their multidirectional perspectives, including any "imported" histories and memories, are denied. All the same, they are expected to integrate into German society, and thereby, its history. The discourse is thus built on a migratory version of the much-cited myth of a *Stunde Null* (zero hour). The attempt to continuously represent postwar labor migration and the different minority communities as "neutral" in relation to Nazi Germany's war and the Holocaust serves manifold purposes for a narration of the past as well as for the present. These agendas relate to present politics against minorities, and, indeed, are connected to foreign policy and intra-European politics, too. The atrocities committed by Germans in occupied countries disappear—insofar as they have ever been a topic at all—from debates and thus from awareness. This has a decidedly current topical aspect: Germany is still confronted with moral and legal demands from governments, organizations, and individuals from, for instance, Italy and Greece, seeking restitution for destroyed villages and acknowledgement of responsibility for the murder of its inhabitants. Remembrance of the Holocaust and of National Socialist crimes is turned into a form of *German* memory work that asserts a monopoly on narration and access to remembrance culture. Thereby the denial of "other pasts," and the demand that the migrantized integrate into a German memory discourse becomes a precondition for integration into German *Leitkultur* (leading culture).[44] Not only does this suggest that German remembrance culture holds the only valid form of memory, it implies, too, that migrants and their descendants are themselves without history and memory, or at the very least, have none that is relevant. This shows a lack of understanding that, to borrow from Andreas Huyssen, a "migration into other pasts"[45] would have to be a mutual enterprise.

## Imported Anti-Semitism? German Postunification Debates on "Victimhood" and "the Jews"

According to Theodor Adorno, Jews came to represent, within the unconscious of German society, the *memory* of the suppressed crime, of the history of the Holocaust. Jews are disliked as a persistent reminder of the Holocaust, and this adds a new component to traditional anti-Semitism, as many critics have remarked during the past few decades. This form of anti-Semitism, after or because of the Shoah, is often referred to as "secondary anti-Semitism," and comes to the fore, for instance, in attitudes toward Israel. In recent times, contemporary German discourse has no longer silenced public debates about the Shoah, but, on the contrary, has built a new narrative of a "German nation" that utilizes the murder of the Jews as one of its central foundations, whether by actively including commemorative representations of the Holocaust in a new narrative of history and the present, or by simultaneously making aggressive demands for a *Schlußstrich* (clean break). In 1997, Hanno Loewy observed the shift towards a new German national sentiment "which does not exclude the Holocaust anymore, but rather mystifies its allegedly so cathartic, educational aftermath virtually as the foundation-myth, as the founding sacrifice of a new German sense of mission."[46] The simultaneity of rejecting responsibility while integrating or "incorporating" the crime became common only after reunification. After 1989, these intra-German (non-)debates about National Socialism and the Holocaust are essentially interwoven with the desire to break a taboo. The alleged taboo is that it was not possible to criticize Jews. The discourse of taboo breaking is here, as with the debates over German wartime suffering, based on the need to construe the alleged taboo in the first place, in order to claim its dismantling.

From the beginning of the historians' debate, we can recognize the move toward equating Jews with perpetrators and diverting the responsibility for the Shoah, and finally, reversing the roles of perpetrators and victims. It is essential to look at these developments in the context of a discussion about the view of migrants as a problem within remembrance culture. The debates about guilt, responsibility, and "the Jews" have developed simultaneously with public awareness and beginning debates about National Socialism and the Holocaust as well as with Germany's reluctant turn toward being an immigration country. National Socialism and the murder of the Jews has been discursively projected onto the Israel-Palestine conflict throughout, and not only by the most outspoken anti-Semites on the militant left and extreme right. In June 2002, the former Christian Democratic minister of the Kohl government, Norbert Blüm, spoke about the "actions of the Israeli military as 'nothing but extermination'."[47] Half a year later, in January 2003, Udo Steinbach from the German *Orientinstitut*, which is sponsored by the foreign ministry, said: "When we see how Israeli tanks drive through Palestinian villages and how the desperate people defend themselves with stones, then we must be allowed to ask with regard to Warsaw and the uprising of the Jews in the Warsaw Ghetto, was this not terror, too?"[48] Martin Hohmann, a member of the Bundestag at the time, took a step further in a speech on the German national holiday on 3 October 2003. He stated that nobody had the right to call the Germans a *Tätervolk* (a perpetrator people), since one could then describe the Jews just the same as *Tätervolk* in view of their high numbers in "the leading ranks of the murderous Bolsheviks."[49]

These are merely a few examples within a discourse that at the same time, in the early 2000s, decided on the need for more Holocaust education of migrants. These statements are by political and academic figures from the center of society. While it is common in part of the left and on the right to shift the history of Nazism and the Holocaust into the context of the Israeli/Palestinian conflict, this strategy became ever more pronounced in the German mainstream from the 1990s onward. Moreover, the political center merged the anti-Zionism from the radical left and the extreme right with the construction of Jews as responsible for Stalinist crimes. All these statements have in common the desire to construct Jews in general and Israelis in particular—in any case, all Jews are viewed as potential Israelis, Bartov notes[50]—as perpetrators, and highlight several discursive strategies that are interdependent. The strategies rest on linguistic shifts, i.e., the direct transfer of terminology connotatively tied to the Shoah into another context of meaning. Thus Blüm, similar for instance to Jörg Friedrich,[51] used the term *Vernichtung* (annihilation or extermination). However, unlike Friedrich, who shifts terms signifying German crimes to actions of the Allies, Blüm goes at once backward and forward with his linguistic taboo breaking: he links up with the old post-1968 radical left anti-Zionism, while at the same time moving from the German self-image as victim (of the Allies) toward shifting the role of the perpetrators of extermination onto Israelis. Following from there, Steinbach equates Israel directly with Nazi Germany, compares the Jewish resistance in the Warsaw Ghetto to terrorism, and construes the Jew as perpetrator, not even in the context of Jewish statehood. Hohmann, then, obviously adheres to the infamous contributions of Ernst Nolte that were at the center of the historians' debate during the mid and late 1980s.[52] Hohmann incorporated, in an as yet unheard of way, the anti-Zionist tropes from the political fringes as well as the victim constructions of the center-right. He significantly overtook Nolte, who had construed the Bolsheviks as the source of all evil in the twentieth century, yet had not ascribed anything other than an ideological group identity onto them.[53] Thus Hohmann closes the discursive cycle and arrives at the departure point of Nazi conspiracy myth: the Bolsheviks were made up in large numbers, and particularly in high ranks, of Jews. Therefore, in this new version of German unburdening, the Jews (as Bolsheviks) were responsible for the original politics of large-scale annihilation, which the Nazis were trying to prevent by copying. In Hohmann's line of reasoning, then, Jews were actually responsible for the Holocaust. Jews are discursively construed as Stalinist perpetrators, and therefore also as perpetrators—in the form of the liberating Soviet army—against Germans. Lars Rensmann argues that Martin Walser, in his infamous speech at Paulskirche in 1998, publicly expressed exactly this close correlation of defence-aggression and post–Holocaust anti-Semitism—without mentioning Jews *as* Jews—that results in a reversal of perpetrators into victims and vice versa.[54] While Walser, as Rensmann notes, had resorted to latently anti-Semitic notions in the above examples, the aggression and the desire for a reversed understanding of the factual roles of perpetrator and victim are openly directed against Jews. The anti-Zionism of the center, too, is essentially linked to the construction of a German victimhood: one is not only *also* a victim (of the war) but, moreover, by now—after half a century leaning over backwards—a victim of ongoing demands for atonement. The rationale following is "if the Jews behave like Nazis, they no longer have a special moral claim on us; if they are as bad as were our forefathers, we can un-shoulder our inherited burden of guilt."[55] To state the obvious, it is within this discursive climate that both migrantized young people as well as German-Germans are socialized and educated.

If we return to the aggressive anti-Semitism on the streets during successive anti-Israel protests over the years, the home-grown problem is obvious. During demonstrations in July and August 2014, slogans betray an ever more outspoken anti-Semitism, chants in German call for murdering the Jews, with reference to the camps. In a number of cities, Jews were physically attacked by crowds consisting of Palestine-solidarity groups, neo-Nazis, and a variety of people from far left to right. The large demonstrations during 2002, while the political center was debating "the Jews" and "perpetrators," had leftist, diasporic organizations and neo-Nazis marching together.

Claudia Dantschke describes such a rally with nationwide participation in September 2002, under the motto "Freedom for Palestine." Dantschke notes that most of the people present were "men, women and children with an 'Arab migration background.'"[56] After observing the scenario of crowds of youths attempting to storm the embassies of the United States and the United Kingdom, Dantschke notices an older German participant at the rally, who watches these crowds apparently with understanding, although he seems upset. "When he looked around and saw a well-known representative of the Berlin Jewish community, whom he knew from common engagement against German right-wing extremism, his anger broke free: for too long had the Jewish communities in Germany not distanced themselves from Israeli politics. And now, so he angrily asserted, we had this escalation."[57] From this overheard comment the author deduces that the man's implicit message is that: "The Jews are to blame if youth with an Arab migration background blare 'Sieg Heil' on Berlin's streets and shout antisemitic [*sic*] slogans."[58] Thus, if we follow Dantschke's observation, in addition to expressing a classical anti-Semitic motif, the man appears to operate along the discursive lines of the victimhood construction. Hence, it is not Jews who are threatened by the anti-Semitism; rather, the man is concerned about a "we" that is now confronted with such escalation. It is the German "we" that turns into a victim here—and at the sight of his Jewish acquaintance, the man's "we" collapses entirely into an exclusively German-German one. The question of how and whether aspects of German discourse after the Shoah are compatible with anti-Semitism, and whether the anti-Semitism of (descendants of) migrants does not necessarily have to be "other" or "imported" does not figure in this logic.

The problem is, therefore, a discourse about "imported" anti-Semitism as an apology for "home-grown" anti-Semitism. It is not surprising that such positions are compatible with a general understanding that regards (descendants of) migrants as the sole source of not only aggressive but also general anti-Semitism.[59] However, the aggressive anti-Semitism displayed on the streets is also an echo of wider German debates, intensified during the normalization process after unification, about National Socialism, the Shoah, and "the Jews." There is undoubtedly the problem of massive anti-Semitism in the ideology of what has been called "jihadism." The existing and pressing problem of young people subscribing to antihumanist and violent politics, whether as neo-Nazis or jihadists, is fundamentally not one of ethnicity but of political ideology. Beate Zschäpe, for instance, the main defendant in the NSU trial, reportedly has a Romanian father, a fact that rather obviously did not prevent her from becoming part of a neo-Nazi terror network. Neo-Nazism and jihadism partly converge, for example, in their hatred of the United States and in their anti-Semitism, or Occidentalism in general,[60] which are elements that can be found in all sectors across German society.[61] The jihadist movement is growing just like in the United Kingdom, France, Belgium, and other European countries. Within Germany, the movement features numerous German-German converts in leading positions, and yet, ironically, "Muslim" still resonates only as "migrant." The problem thus has little to do with integrating migrant youth into our remembrance culture, since any and all non-Jewish youth in question, whether German-German Muslims or Turkish-German Christians, would not reject Holocaust remembrance due to their ethnicity, but on the grounds of politics. The German discourse over the past two to three decades constitutes the public intellectual and political climate within which the majority of those still addressed as "migrants" grew up, and thus both their empathically relating to as well as their resistance toward Jewish experience and the commemoration of the Holocaust are just as homegrown as are the attitudes of young Germans.

# Notes

1. "Anti-Semitism" is spelled here for editorial reasons with a hyphen, but is meant to convey the sense better expressed in its spelling as "antisemitism": a modern ideology construing Jews as absolute other with particular characteristics and supposedly involved in powerful machinations. The term *Antisemitismus* was coined toward the end of the nineteenth century by Wilhelm Marr in Germany, as a "positive" notion for volkish political agitation. The term in its hyphenated version suggests that something called "Semitism" exists. This is a misnomer that diverts attention onto the target or victim of the ideology, unlike, for instance, the term "anti-racism," which clearly connotes a positioning against racism and thus against the aggressor. The term anti-Semitism, carries the danger of, on the one hand, reinforcing the anti-Semitic fantasy of a Jewish or "Semitic" conspiracy, and, on the other hand, reaffirming the shift of a linguistic concept into a "racial" one in the first place.

2. Rosa Fava's case study reflects upon her experience of discussing with a Hamburg tenth-grade class the language used in politicians' comments about Israel. Rosa Fava,"Antisemitismus ohne Herkunft: Betrachtungen zu einem 'proto antisemitischen' Vorfall in einer Hamburger Schulklasse," in *Neue Judenfeindschaft? Perspektiven für den pädagogischen Umgang mit dem globalisierten Antisemitismus*, ed. Fritz Bauer Institut and Jugendbegegnungsstätte Anne Frank, *Jahrbuch zur Geschichte und Wirkung des Holocaust 2006* (Frankfurt a.M.: Campus, 2006), 247.

3. I borrow the term 'multidirectional' from Michael Rothberg, *Multidirectional Memory: Remembering the Holocaust in the Age of Decolonization* (Stanford: Stanford University Press, 2009).

4. I mainly use the term "migrants" and "the migrantized" herein because they it affords some acknowledgement of self-naming by a wide spectrum of people who are still widely considered "foreigners" even in the third or fourth generation. The term is meant to encompass "guest workers" and their descendants as well as later immigrants and refugees.

5. "Is Eastern Germany Safe for Foreigners? Racism Warning Has German Hackles Raised," *Spiegel Online International*, 18 May 2006, accessed 24 August 2014, http://www.spiegel.de/international/is-eastern-germany-safe-for-foreigners-racism-warning-has-german-hackles-raised-a-416904.html.

6. Uta Döring, "'National befreite Zonen': Zur Entstehung und Karriere eines Kampfbegriffs," in *Moderner Rechtsextremismus in Deutschland*, eds. Andreas Klärner and Michael Kohlstruck (Hamburg: Hamburger Edition, 2006), 177–206.

7. Of course, the criteria for the definition of the term "migrants" or the most recent invention "humans with a migration background" (*Menschen mit Migrationshintergrund*) mirrors the German-German elusiveness: just how many immigrant grandparents or parents are needed to qualify for a special need in Holocaust education and generally a concern about integration?

8. Eren Güvercin, *Neo-Moslems: Porträt einer deutschen Generation* (Freiburg: Herder, 2012), 12. The derogatory term "Kanak(e)" has been and is used commonly. It is a racist insult directed at people of allegedly Turkish background, but also toward Mediterranean people in general. During the last two decades, the term Kanak has been reappropriated by the migrantizedmigrants as a countermove against the derogatory mainstream use. While it originated in the day to day, mostly used by young people, it has been popularized by Feridun Zaimoğlu's books *Kanak Sprak: 24 Mißtöne vom Rande der Gesellschaft*

(Hamburg: Rotbuch, 1995) and *Koppstoff: Kanaka Sprak vom Rande der Gesellschaft* (Hamburg: Rotbuch, 1998), followed by the film adaptation of Zaimoğlu's *Abschaum: Die wahre Geschichte von Ertan Ongun* (Hamburg: Rotbuch, 1997) and *Kanak Attack*, VHS, dir. Lars Becker (Munich: Concorde, 2000). In 1998 a Germany-wide network of activists founded the platform "Kanak Attak" as "a community of different people from diverse backgrounds who share a commitment to eradicate racism from German society." They declared "Kanak Attak is not interested in questions about your passport or heritage; in fact it challenges such questions in the first place." "Kanak Attak," http://www.kanak-attak.de/ka/about/manif_eng.html.

9. Thilo Sarrazin, *Deutschland schafft sich ab: Wie wir unser Land aufs Spiel setzen* (Berlin: DVA, 2010).

10. Viola B. Georgi, *Entliehene Erinnerung: Geschichtsbilder junger Migranten in Deutschland* (Hamburg: HIS-Verlag, 2003).

11. Kaja Silverman, "Back to the Future," *Camera Obscura* 27 (1991): 119–22.

12. Silverman, "Back to the Future," 129.

13. Harald Welzer, Sabine Moller, and Karoline Tschugnall, *"Opa war kein Nazi": Nationalsozialismus und Holocaust im Familiengedächtnis* (Frankfurt a.M.: Fischer, 2002).

14. Stefan Reinecke, "Deutschland braucht neue Erzählungen des Holocausts, sagt Viola B. Georgi: Die deutsche Gesellschaft muss die Erinnerungsformen und die NS-Geschichte für die Kinder der Migranten öffnen," *die tageszeitung*, 13 February 2004, 12.

15. Reinecke, "Deutschland braucht neue Erzählungen des Holocausts," 12.

16. See Birgit Rommelspacher, *Schuldlos — Schuldig? Wie sich junge Frauen mit Antisemitismus auseinandersetzen* (Hamburg: Konkret Literatur Verlag, 1995) and Welzer, Moller, and Tschugnall, *"Opa war kein Nazi."*

17. In German "Eh, du als Ausländer, du hast doch keine Ahnung!" For this interview, see Viola B. Georgi, *Entliehene Erinnerung*, 149–53.

18. Astrid Messerschmidt, "Erinnerung jenseits nationaler Identitätsstiftungen: Perspektiven für den Umgang mit dem Holocaust Gedächtnis in der Bildungsarbeit," in *Erinnerungskulturen im Dialog*, ed. by Claudia Lenz et al. (Münster: Unrast-Verlag, 2002), 103.

19. The title in German read "Junge Migranten und Aussiedler: Schlüsselkinder der Erinnerungspädagogik? Impulse für die Weiterentwicklung unserer Erinnerungskultur," Humanities Net Online, H-Net online archive, conference announcement 12 June 2003, accessed 29 September 2014, http://h-net.msu.edu/cgi-bin/logbrowse.pl?trx=vx&list=h-museum&month=0306&week=b&msg=TbaMUsWD2s82xgXKWxxDzA&user=&pw=.

20. The so-called *Volksdeutschen* (ethnic Germans) from Eastern Europe gained easy access to German citizenship, based on the legal obligations of West Germany after World War II toward ethnic Germans in formerly German or German-occupied territories in Eastern Europe. See Rainer Ohliger and Rainer Münz, "Minorities into Migrants: Making and Unmaking Eastern and Central Europe's Ethnic German Diasporas," *DIASPORA* 11 (2002): 45–83.

21. Zafer Şenocak, *Atlas of a Tropical Germany: Essays on Politics and Culture, 1990–1998*, trans. and ed. by Leslie A. Adelson (Lincoln/London: University of Nebraska Press, 2000), 58.

22. Marc David Baer, "Turk and Jew in Berlin: The First Turkish Migration to Germany and the Shoah," *Comparative Studies in Society and History* 55 (2013): 353.

23. *Passing Drama*, VHS, dir. Angela Melitopoulos (Germany: Arsenal – Institute for Film and Video Art e.V. Berlin, 1999).

24. See Mark Terkessidis, *Migranten* (Hamburg: Rotbuch, 2000), 16–20.

25. *Die leere Mitte*, DVD, dir. Hito Steyerl, (Germany: Sixpack Film, 1998).

26. This critique of the construed "history-neutral" migrant relates equally to the histories of fascist organizations, countries in collaboration with the Nazis across Europe and far beyond, and nations who left their Jewish citizens to their fate. However, while these intersections would allow Germany to point to other nations' responsibility as well, if spoken about they would also bring the neglected history of occupation and war crimes against non-Jewish civilians into view. Thus the "Turks" as "Muslims" from a non-occupied country are the guarantor for upholding the disinterested, history-neutral migrant arriving at migratory "hour zero."

27. Erdal Kaynar and Kimiko Suda, "Aspekte migrantischer Selbstorganisation in Deutschland," in *Landschaften der Tat*, ed. Ljubomier Bratić (St. Pölten: Sozaktiv, 2002), 167–85. In the original: "Die Erfahrung der kollektiven Brandmarkung, Entrechtung, Vertreibung und Vernichtung von Menschen, die im Dritten Reich als 'undeutsch'definiert wurden, hat das Verhalten der Deutschen gegenüber Minorisierten geprägt." Author's translation.

28. In the town of Babenhausen, groups of locals repeatedly gathered in front of the property of its sole Jewish inhabitant, threatened his life and committed arson attacks, until he announced his emigration to the United States in 1993. See *Babenhausen*, VHS, dir. Hito Steyerl (Germany: Sixpack Film, 1997).

29. In 1997, inhabitants of Gollwitz (Brandenburg) threatened to follow the example of another former East German town, Dolgenbrodt, and hire someone to carry out an arson attack, if the politicians responsible failed to withdraw their plan to settle sixty Jewish immigrants from the former USSR in the so-called Herrenhaus (lord's manor) of their village. The threat was to destroy the very option of housing the immigrants. Together with the inhabitants, representatives from the local council demanded that the regional government change its decision. The then Social Democratic Ministerpräsident of Brandenburg, Manfred Stolpe, also called for a withdrawal of the settlement plans, and the villagers of Gollwitz finally succeeded in their demand. Shortly after the decision by the regional government to cancel the settlement, a protest organized largely by migrant groups took place in the village on the remembrance day of the November pogrom of 1938. Constanze von Bullion, "'Die sollen nach Israel:' 50 jüdische Aussiedler bringen das Dorf Gollwitz in Rage," *die tageszeitung*, 27 September 1997.

30. See Andrea Dernbach, "Demonstration gegen Kriegsverbrecher," *die tageszeitung*, 9 May 1995, and Michael Grabenströer, "Exoten Protest in dörflicher Idylle," *Frankfurter Rundschau*, 9 May 1995.

31. Dernbach, "Demonstration gegen Kriegsverbrecher."

32. Grabenströer, "Exoten Protest."

33. Café Morgenland, *Deutschland Verrecke - Texte des Zorns* (Leipzig: Selbstverlag, 1997), 91. In the original: "Von ihnen wissen wir, was ihr oder eure Väter und Großväter in der Zeit zwischen 1940 und 1945 in unseren Ländern angerichtet habt. Dieses Wissen lässt uns nicht mehr los." See also "Auf nach Ochtendung" Café Morgenland, accessed 29 September 2014, http://www.cafemorgenland.net/archiv/1995/1995.04_Auf%20nach%20 Ochtendung.htm.

34. Migrantische Initiative gegen Antisemitismus, "Gedenkkundgebung an die Opfer der Anschläge von İstanbul," Online Sinistra Forum: Antisemitismus, accessed 23 August 2014, www.copyriot.com/sinistra/discus/messages/211/148.htm.

35. Mustafa Kemal "Atatürk," who grew up in the Sabbatian center Salonika is regularly accused of a Dönme background, and thus the founding of the Turkish Republic and its politics are construed as originating from "outside," or from "inauthentic" Turks. For

discussions of anti-Semitic stereotypes as well as the attacks on synagogues in Turkey, see Corry Görgü, "Türkei nutzt OSZE Konferenz zur Selbstdarstellung – Die Türkei ist frei von Antisemitismus oder: Der Mond ist eine Scheibe," *HaGalil*, 18 May 2004, accessed 24 August 2014, http://www.hagalil.com/antisemitismus/europa/tuerkei.htm; and Corry Görgü, "'Hoffentlich war es keiner unserer Leute': Die Anschläge auf die Synagogen in Istanbul und die Rolle von Staat und Hizbullah," *HaGalil*, 19 May 2004, accessed 24 August 2014, http://www.hagalil.com/antisemitismus/europa/istanbul.htm.

36. Migrantische Initiative gegen Antisemitismus, "Gedenkkundgebung."

37. Susanne Amann "Absurd, dass Migranten andere ausgrenzen." Interview with Deniz Yücel, *die tageszeitung*, 22 November 2003, accessed 24 August 2014, www.taz.de/1/archiv/?dig=2003/11/22/a0204.

38. Ibid.; Deniz Yücel meanwhile is one of the most critical and prolific journalists in the new Germany, especially when it comes to the prevalent ethnoculturalizing "we's" and the politics toward "migrants." See, for instance, his "Meine Mudda gehört zu Deutschland," in his column, "Kolumne Besser" in the daily *tageszeitung*. Deniz Yücel, "Meine Mudda gehört zu Deutschland," *die tageszeitung*, 3 February 2015, accessed 4 February 2015, http://www.taz.de/Kolumne-Besser/!153965/.

39. Daniel Boyarin, "Homophobia and the Postcoloniality of the 'Jewish Science'," in *Queer Theory and the Jewish Question*, ed. Daniel Boyarin, et al. (New York: Columbia University Press, 2003), 178.

40. Michael Galchinsky, "Scattered Seeds: A Dialogue of Diasporas," in *Insider/Outsider*, ed. David Biale, et al. (Berkeley: University of California Press, 1998), 192.

41. See Fania Oz-Salzberger, *Israelis in Berlin* (Frankfurt a.M.: Jüdischer Verlag im Suhrkamp Verlag, 2001). Oz-Salzberger's travels through the "Israeli Berlin" and her conversations with Israeli migrants about their lives in the city reveal ambivalent and complex relationships, not least within "migrant spaces."

42. The "neutrality" of Turks in relation to Nazism and the Holocaust is misleading. Vamik Volkan, for instance, gives an account about his youth. A Turkish Cypriot during World War II, he encountered German Jews who escaped the Nazis; Vamik D. Volkan, "What the Holocaust Means to a Non-Jewish Psychoanalyst," in *Persistent Shadows of the Holocaust*, ed. by Rafael Moses (Madison, CT: International Universities Press, 1993), 81–105. However, narratives like this are perpetuated by Turkey in order to avoid discussions about anti-Semitism, the notion of who is a Turk—which still excludes Jews—and denial of help to Turkish Jews in Germany during the Holocaust. Baer notes, "Turkey has no interest in admitting to the discrimination and violence its own population of Jews has been subjected to in the Turkish Republic, or the tragedy of the Turkish Jews left to their fate in Europe during the Shoah by their own government. Such revelations would puncture the myth of tolerance of Jews that Turkey relies on and draw attention to the 'Turkish' and not foreign nature of 'Turkish Jews.'" Marc David Baer, "Turk and Jew in Berlin: The First Turkish Migration to Germany and the Shoah," *Comparative Studies in Society and History* 55 (2013): 352.

43. Raed Saleh, "Hausaufgaben statt Hass," *Der Spiegel*, 28 July 2014. Meanwhile, Saleh's suitability as mayor of Berlin was questioned by media outlets for allegedly not speaking sufficient German. This grotesque debate has led Sebastian Heiser from the daily *tageszeitung* to transcribe, analyze and publish Saleh's and other discussants' speeches during an entire TV talk show. Heiser shows that Saleh speaks grammatically more correctly than the German-German participants and attests that German journalists suffer from a racist "grammar-tinnitus." Sebastian Heiser, "Ein

dubioses Hörproblem," *die tageszeitung*, Accessed 28 August 2014, www.taz.de/
Berlins-Buergermeisterkandidat-Saleh/!145007/.

44. The integration minister of North-Rhine Westphalia, Armin Laschet stated that
    "thirty-eight percent of children under six years old have a migration history" and
    connected this issue with a demand for more integration into the German leading cul-
    ture. Armin Laschet, "Gedenken an Holocaust ist Teil unserer gemeinsamen Leitkultur,"
    *MiGAZIN*, 28 January 2010, accessed 23 August 2014, http://www.migazin.de/2010/01/28/
    gedenken-an-holocaust-teil-unserer-gemeinsamen-leitkultur/.

45. See Andreas Huyssen, "Diaspora and Nation: Migration into Other Pasts," *New German
    Critique* 88 (2003): 147–64.

46. Hanno Loewy, "Auschwitz als Metapher," *die tageszeitung*, 25 January 1997.

47. Quoted from the German (and translated by the author) in Tjark Kunstreich,
    "Spätzünder. Antizionismus: Was 1968 am linken Rand gepredigt wurde, ist inzwischen
    Allgemeingut geworden," *Jüdische Allgemeine*, no. 28, 14 July 2005. Joffe cites Blüm
    with having spoken about a *"Vernichtungsfeldzug"* (war of annihilation), Joseph Joffe,
    "Nations We Love to Hate: Israel, America and the New Antisemitism," *Posen Papers
    in Contemporary Antisemitism* 1, The Vidal Sassoon International Center for the Study of
    Antisemitism (SICSA), 8, accessed 29 September 2014, http://sicsa.huji.ac.il/ppjoffe.pdf.

48. Cited in Omer Bartov, "Der alte und der neue Antisemitismus," in *Neuer Antisemitismus?*
    ed. Doron Rabinovici et al. (Frankfurt a.M.: Suhrkamp 2004), 29. In the original: "Wenn
    wir sehen, wie israelische Panzer durch palästinensische Dörfer fahren und sich die ver-
    zweifelten Menschen mit Steinen wehren, dann müssen wir im Blick auf Warschau und
    im Blick auf den Aufstand der Juden im Warschauer Ghetto auch fragen dürfen, war das
    dann nicht auch Terror?"

49. Ibid., 30–31.

50. Ibid., 28.

51 Jörg Friedrich, *Der Brand: Deutschland im Bombenkrieg 1940–45* (Berlin: Propyläen, 2002).

52. Regarding Nolte's strategy of "unburdening" from responsibility, Saul Friedlander has
    noted: "In Ernst Nolte's texts we move from symmetry to the fringes of a reversed
    representation of historical responsibility. The central actor within the global historical
    context is now the Bolshevik. The Bolshevik is the original perpetrator of global annihila-
    tion in modern history, the historical agent who puts into practice the visions of social
    therapy through annihilation born with the rise of modernity. The Nazi—whose own
    exterminations are, again, certainly not denied, but who are said to have merely copied
    the Bolsheviks—become, in Nolte's presentation, perpetrators who may have acted out
    of anguish at the idea of being themselves potential victims of the Red Terror." Saul
    Friedlander, *Memory, History, and the Extermination of the Jews of Europe* (Bloomington:
    Indiana University Press, 1993), 34.

53. Nevertheless, in public opinion, in "the album," so to speak, there will likely be a strong
    resonance of "Bolsheviks" with a racialized "otherness", that is with "Slavs"/"Russians."

54. Lars Rensmann, "Entschädigungspolitik, Erinnerungsabwehr und Motive des
    sekundären Antisemitismus," in *Das Finkelstein-Alibi*, ed. by Rolf Surmann (Cologne:
    PapyRossa Verlag 2001), 129.

55. Joseph Joffe, "Nations We Love to Hate," 7.

56. Claudia Dantschke, "Antisemitismus in der Palästinasolidarität: Das islamistische
    Milieu," in *Trotz und wegen Auschwitz*, ed. AG Antifa/Antira im StuRa der Uni Halle
    (Münster: Unrast-Verlag 2004), 114.

57. Ibid., 116–17.

58. Ibid., 117.

59. This general shifting of contemporary anti-Semitism solely onto "others" and of Germans as those who safeguard the Jews, is apparent, for instance, in contributions like Gerda-Marie Schönfeld, "Interview mit Deidre Berger: Antisemitismus gibt es rechs-wie links," *Stern*, 18 May 2008, accessed 23 February 2015, http://www.stern.de/politik/ausland/juden-in-deutschland-antisemitismus-gibt-es-rechts-wie-links-620555.html.

60. I use Ian Buruma and Avishai Margalit's notion of "Occidentalism," which emphasizes that the prevalent anti-Westernism is "of" the West—not alien to the West, but first conceived in European literature, art, and philosophy.

61. See Andrei S. Markovits, *Amerika, dich haßt sich's besser: Antiamerikanismus und Antisemitimus in Europa* (Hamburg: KKV, 2004).

# Works Cited

Amann, Susanne. "Absurd, dass Migranten andere ausgrenzen." Interview with Deniz Yücel. *die tageszeitung*, 22 November 2003. Accessed 24 August 2014. http://www.taz.de/1/archiv/?dig=2003/11/22/a0204.

"Auf nach Ochtendung." Café Morgenland. Accessed 29 September 2014. http://www.cafemorgenland.net/archiv/1995/1995.04_Auf%20nach%20Ochtendung.htm.

Baer, Marc David. "Turk and Jew in Berlin: The First Turkish Migration to Germany and the Shoah." *Comparative Studies in Society and History* 55, no. 2 (2013): 330–55.

Bartov, Omer. "Der alte und der neue Antisemitismus." In *Neuer Antisemitismus?* edited by Doron Rabinovici et al., 19–43. Frankfurt a.M.: Suhrkamp, 2004.

Becker, Lars. dir. *Kanak Attack*. VHS. Germany: Concorde, 2000.

Boyarin, Daniel. "Homophobia and the Postcoloniality of the 'Jewish Science'." In *Queer Theory and the Jewish Question*, edited by Daniel Boyarin et al., 166–98. New York: Columbia University Press, 2003.

Bullion, Constanze von. "'Die sollen nach Israel': 50 jüdische Aussiedler bringen das Dorf Gollwitz in Rage." *die tageszeitung*, 27 September 1997.

Buruma, Ian, and Avishai Margalit. *Occidentalism: A Short History of Anti-Westernism*. London: Atlantic Books, 2004.

Café Morgenland. *Deutschland Verrecke – Texte des Zorns*. Leipzig: Selbstverlag, 1997.

Café Morgenland. "Auf nach Ochtendung." Accessed 29 September 2014, http://www.cafemorgenland.net/archiv/1995/1995.04_Auf%20nach%20Ochtendung.htm.

Dantschke, Claudia. "Antisemitismus in der Palästinasolidarität: Das islamistische Milieu." In *Trotz und wegen Auschwitz*, edited by AG Antifa/Antira im StuRa der Uni Halle, 114–36. Münster: Unrast-Verlag, 2004.

Dernbach, Andrea. "Demonstration gegen Kriegsverbrecher." *die tageszeitung*, 9 May 1995.

Döring, Uta. "'National befreite Zonen': Zur Entstehung und Karriere eines Kampfbegriffs." In *Moderner Rechtsextremismus in Deutschland*, edited by Andreas Klärner and Michael Kohlstruck, 177–206. Hamburg: Hamburger Edition, 2006.

Friedlander, Saul. *Memory, History, and the Extermination of the Jews of Europe*. Bloomington: Indiana University Press, 1993.

Friedrich, Jörg. *Der Brand: Deutschland im Bombenkrieg 1940–45*. Berlin: Propyläen, 2002.

Fava, Rosa. "Antisemitismus ohne Herkunft: Betrachtungen zu einem 'proto-antisemitischen' Vorfall in einer Hamburger Schulklasse." In *Neue Judenfeindschaft? Perspektiven für den pädagogischen Umgang mit dem globalisierten Antisemitismus. Jahrbuch zur Geschichte und Wirkung des Holocaust 2006*, edited by Fritz Bauer Institut and Jugendbegegnungsstätte Anne Frank, 245–61. Frankfurt a.M.: Campus, 2006.

Galchinsky, Michael. "Scattered Seeds: A Dialogue of Diasporas." In *Insider/Outsider*, edited by David Biale et al., 185–211. Berkeley: University of California Press, 1998.

Georgi, Viola B. *Entliehene Erinnerung: Geschichtsbilder junger Migranten in Deutschland.* Hamburg: HIS-Verlag, 2003.

Görgü, Corry. "Türkei nutzt OSZE-Konferenz zur Selbstdarstellung – Die Türkei ist frei von Antisemitismus oder: Der Mond ist eine Scheibe." *HaGalil*, 18 May 2004. Accessed 24 August 2014. http://www.hagalil.com/antisemitismus/europa/tuerkei.htm.

Görgü, Corry. "'Hoffentlich war es keiner unserer Leute': Die Anschläge auf die Synagogen in Istanbul und die Rolle von Staat und Hizbullah." *HaGalil*, 19 May 2004. Accessed 24 August 2014. http://www.hagalil.com/antisemitismus/europa/istanbul.htm.

Grabenströer, Michael. "Exoten Protest in dörflicher Idylle." *Frankfurter Rundschau*, 9 May 1995.

Güvercin, Eren. *Neo-Moslems: Porträt einer deutschen Generation.* Freiburg: Herder, 2012.

Heiser, Sebastian. "Ein dubioses Hörproblem." *die tageszeitung*, 28 August 2014. www.taz.de/Berlins-Buergermeisterkandidat-Saleh/!145007/.

Humanities Net Online. "Junge Migranten und Aussiedler: Schlüsselkinder der Erinnerungspädagogik? Impulse für die Weiterentwicklung unserer Erinnerungskultur." H-Net online archive, conference announcement, 12 June 2003. Accessed 29 September 2014. http://h-net.msu.edu/cgi-bin/logbrowse.pl?trx=vx&list=H-Museum&month=0306&week=b&msg=TbaMUsWD2s82xgXKWxxDzA&user=&pw.

Huyssen, Andreas. "Diaspora and Nation: Migration into Other Pasts." *New German Critique* 88 (2003): 147–64.

Joffe, Joseph. "Nations We Love to Hate: Israel, America and the New Antisemitism." *Posen Papers in Contemporary Antisemitism* 1. The Vidal Sassoon International Center for the Study of Antisemitism (SICSA). Accessed 29 September 2014. http://sicsa.huji.ac.il/ppjoffe.pdf.

Kanak Attak. Accessed 29 September 2014. http://www.kanak-attak.de/ka/about/manif_eng.html.

Kaynar, Erdal, and Kimiko Suda. "Aspekte migrantischer Selbstorganisation in Deutschland." In *Landschaften der Tat*, edited by Ljubomier Bratić, 167–85. St. Pölten: Sozaktiv, 2002.

Kunstreich, Tjark. "Spätzünder. Antizionismus: Was 1968 am linken Rand gepredigt wurde, ist inzwischen Allgemeingut geworden." *Jüdische Allgemeine*, no. 28, 14 July 2005.

Laschet, Armin. "Gedenken an Holocaust ist Teil unserer gemeinsamen Leitkultur." *MiGAZIN—Migration in Germany*, 28 January 2010. Accessed 23 August 2014. http://www.migazin.de/index.php?s=Gedenken+an+Holocaust+ist+Teil+unserer+gemeinsamen+Leitkultur.

Loewy, Hanno. "Auschwitz als Metapher." *die tageszeitung*, 23 January 1997.

Markovits, Andrei S. *Amerika, dich haßt sich's besser: Antiamerikanismus und Antisemitimus in Europa.* Hamburg: KKV, 2004.

Marshall, Christoph von. "Zugewanderter Antisemitismus." *Deutschlandradio Berlin*, 31 March 2004.

Melitopoulos, Angela, dir. *Passing Drama.* VHS. Germany: Arsenal – Institute for Film and Video Art e.V. Berlin, 1999.

Messerschmidt, Astrid. "Erinnerung jenseits nationaler Identitätsstiftungen: Perspektiven für den Umgang mit dem Holocaust-Gedächtnis in der Bildungsarbeit." In *Erinnerungskulturen im Dialog*, edited by Claudia Lenz et al., 103–14. Münster: Unrast-Verlag, 2002.

"Migrantische Initiative gegen Antisemitismus, Gedenkkundgebung an die Opfer der Anschläge von İstanbul." Online Sinistra Forum: Antisemitismus. Accessed 23 August 2014. www.copyriot.com/sinistra/discus/messages/211/148.htm.

Ohliger, Rainer, and Rainer Münz. "Minorities into Migrants: Making and Unmaking Eastern and Central Europe's Ethnic German Diasporas." *DIASPORA* 11 (2002): 45–83.

Oz-Salzberger, Fania. *Israelis in Berlin*. Frankfurt a.M.: Jüdischer Verlag im Suhrkamp Verlag, 2001.

Reinecke, Stefan. "Deutschland braucht neue Erzählungen des Holocausts, sagt Viola B. Georgi: Die deutsche Gesellschaft muss die Erinnerungsformen and die NS-Geschichte für die Kinder der Migranten öffnen." *die tageszeitung*, 13 February 2004.

Rensmann, Lars. "Entschädigungspolitik, Erinnerungsabwehr und Motive des sekundären Antisemitismus." In *Das Finkelstein-Alibi*, edited by Rolf Surmann, 126–53. Cologne: Papy Rossa Verlag, 2001.

Rommelspacher, Birgit. *Schuldlos—Schuldig? Wie sich junge Frauen mit Antisemitismus auseinandersetzen*. Hamburg: Konkret Literatur Verlag, 1995.

Rothberg, Michael. *Multidirectional Memory: Remembering the Holocaust in the Age of Decolonization*. Stanford: Stanford University Press, 2009.

Saleh, Raed. "Hausaufgaben statt Hass." *Der Spiegel*, 28 July 2014.

Sarrazin, Thilo. *Deutschland schafft sich ab: Wie wir unser Land aufs Spiel setzen*. Berlin: DVA, 2010.

Schönfeld, Gerda-Marie. "Interview mit Deidre Berger: Antisemitismus gibt es rechs wie links." *Stern*, 18 May 2008. Accessed 23 February 2015. http://www.stern.de/politik/ausland/juden-in-deutschland-antisemitismus-gibt-es-rechts-wie-links-620555.html.

Şenocak, Zafer. *Atlas of a Tropical Germany: Essays on Politics and Culture, 1990–1998*. Translated and edited by Leslie A. Adelson. Lincoln/London: University of Nebraska Press, 2000.

Silverman, Kaja. "Back to the Future." *Camera Obscura* 27 (1991): 108–33.

*Spiegel Online International*. "Is Eastern Germany Safe for Foreigners? Racism Warning Has German Hackles Raised." 18 May 2006. http://www.spiegel.de/international/is-eastern-germany-safe-for-foreigners-racism-warning-has-german-hackles-raised-a-416904.html.

Steyerl, Hito, dir. *Babenhausen*. VHS. Germany: Sixpack Film, 1997.

Steyerl, Hito, dir. *Die leere Mitte*. DVD. Germany: Sixpack Film, 1998.

Terkessidis, Mark. *Migranten*. Hamburg: Rotbuch, 2000.

Volkan, Vamik D. "What the Holocaust Means to a Non-Jewish Psychoanalyst." In *Persistent Shadows of the Holocaust*, edited by Rafael Moses, 81–105. Madison, CT: International Universities Press, 1993.

Welzer, Harald, Sabine Moller, and Karoline Tschugnall. *"Opa war kein Nazi": Nationalsozialismus und Holocaust im Familiengedächtnis*. Frankfurt a.M.: Fischer, 2002.

Yücel, Deniz. "Meine Mudda gehört zu Deutschland." *die tageszeitung*, 3 February 2015. Accessed 4 February 2015. http://www.taz.de/Kolumne-Besser/!153965/.

Zaimoğlu, Feridun. *Kanak Sprak: 24 Mißtöne vom Rande der Gesellschaft*. Hamburg: Rotbuch, 1995.

Zaimoğlu, Feridun. *Abschaum: Die wahre Geschichte von Ertan Ongun*. Hamburg: Rotbuch, 1997.

Zaimoğlu, Feridun. *Koppstoff: Kanaka Sprak vom Rande der Gesellschaft*. Hamburg: Rotbuch, 1998.

**Annette Seidel-Arpaci** holds a doctorate in Jewish studies and cultural studies and has held academic appointments at Leeds, Manchester, and

Yale. Among other publications, she co-edited the volume *Narratives of Trauma: Discourses of German Wartime Suffering in National and International Perspective* (2011). Her monograph *Between Holocaust Memory and Racism: The Politics of Belonging and Culture in Germany* is forthcoming with I.B. Tauris. Annette Seidel-Arpaci is currently working on a second monograph examining migratory archives, gender, and the "religious" in popular music culture.

*Afterword*

# STRUCTURES AND LARGER CONTEXT OF POLITICAL CHANGE IN MIGRATION AND INTEGRATION POLICY

Germany between Normalization and Europeanization

*Holger Kolb*

Analyzing changes in Germany's migration and integration policy has become a key subject in social science research on migration in recent years. Contrary to public perception, Germany— which had once been an outsider, marked by its distance and deviation from the political practices of other immigration countries—has become an average European nation. This at least is reflected in the Migration Integration Policy Index (MIPEX), in the book by Koopmans, Michalowski, and Waibel,[1] or in the annual report of the Council of Experts of German Foundations for Integration and Migration (SVR).[2] This chapter focuses on the structural factors behind this shift, and in the process it will discuss two structural conditions separately, even if they cannot always be very sharply delineated. What is relevant here, particularly with respect to the past, is a process of normalizing migration and integration policy. This normalization was related to the unification of Germany and the concomitant completion of the German nation-building process that provided its structural foundation. This in turn facilitated numerous forms of liberalization and the opening of restrictive institutional immigration and integration arrangements that had been introduced in light of the special situation resulting from the division of Germany. That situation has to be differentiated from processes of adaptation and convergence that can be observed right now and that will probably also persist in the future, though they, too, are subject to further internal differentiation. Thus we can observe, on the one hand, a Europeanization that is successful, albeit precariously. It is 'top-down' and is tied to communitarized policy efforts of migration and integration from EU institutions and the European Commission in particular. On the other hand, there is a variant of convergence 'from the bottom up'. It produces public responses that can be interpreted as "mimetic" processes of learning and adaptation. Both variants generate responses within all (European) immigration countries to the challenges posed by migration and integration.

## Policies of Migration and Integration after the Completion of the Process of Nation-Building: German Unification and the Normalization of Migration Policy

The structural conditions that were created for migration and integration policies by the specific history of the formation of the German nation state have been discussed comprehensively and convincingly in the ground-breaking study by Joppke.[3] German research on migration has not infrequently been cast as a critique, asserting that German migration policies had for decades been marked by a denial of immigration. It was a criticism that tended to be couched in terms of accusation and indignation. But, unlike other scholars, Joppke does not reduce these past conditions to an intellectual failure of the responsible political actors; rather he situates it in a German conception of citizenship with strong ethno-cultural roots that, in turn, are a legacy of the Second World War. The division of Germany into the Federal Republic and the German Democratic Republic resulted from the liberation of the country from National Socialism. There was also the separation of formerly German territories that led to the creation of a German diaspora in Eastern Europe. This supported the notion, current for a long time in the Federal Republic, that Germany was an incomplete, 'provisional' nation-state.[4] This notion was enshrined as an appeal in what was once the preamble of the Basic Law: "The entire German people are called upon to achieve in free self-determination the unity and freedom of Germany." This meant that for a long time Germany defined itself as the homeland (*Heimat*) of all Germans, including those who belonged to the diaspora in the East and were considered "as part of the national – if spatially separate—'community of fate' with respect to the burdens stemming from the Second World War".[5]

The logical consequence of this self-perception was the immigration and settlement of diasporic Germans via Article 116 of the Basic Law, which was given priority, but was semantically covered up as a "return". Joppke saw in this the structural foundations of a denial of immigration that could no longer be empirically justified but that at the same time could not be adequately explained by political ignorance. If the immigration situation had been officially recognized, it would inevitably have implied a questioning of the national identity of all Germans and thus would have weakened the historic obligation towards Germans living in the East.[6]

The collapse of the Soviet Bloc, the fall of the Berlin Wall in 1989 and the unification of Germany in 1990 fundamentally changed the foundations of migration and integration policy in Germany. The completion of the nation-building process enabled politicians to choose – or even forced them to adopt – what was, on the whole, a different approach with respect to problems of migration and integration. While the Federal Republic was still a "provisional" entity, it was still possible to comprehend why foreign laborers who were defined as "guest workers" were largely excluded politically. Joppke[7] called this a dual strategy that no longer made sense, since, next to their exclusion, diasporic Germans who were understood to be "German immigrants from Eastern Europe" were swiftly included.[8] After all, the German national state was now again complete. There was no need to rely on a special notion of migration and integration that at first glance was as strange as its critics had noted. It was an idea that was comprehensible only against the backdrop of earlier German history. It was only logical that thenceforth a process of normalization could be observed, beginning in 1990 and evolving through several stages.[9] In view of the fact that this process has been comprehensively covered by recent scholarship, only the most important stages shall be mentioned here briefly and with reference to the relevant further literature.[10]

The ratification of the law relating to foreigners in 1990 was no doubt the starting point of this process. The decisive innovation of this new Law was the – at first very cautious – replacement of the principle of citizenship acquisition that was not based on an administrative assessment (*Ermessen*) but on a claim to it (*Anspruch*). Before the implementation of this Law in 1991 the decision to grant citizenship depended on how much discretionary room for maneuver the responsible bureaucracy had. The new Law now conceded to foreigners a legal claim to citizenship if they fulfilled certain conditions, such as a minimum stay, no criminal record, and a regular income. This signified not least that it was no longer necessary, in view of the completion of the nation-building process, to give a special status to foreigners who had been recruited as "guest workers". Instead these immigrants were encouraged to seek citizenship by means of the simplified procedure so that they could become in-landers in the medium term.[11]

Another stage on the path toward normalization soon followed the ratification of the new Law. This was the basic revision of German asylum policy that has also become known as the "Asylum Compromise". During the period when the Federal Republic had remained an incomplete nation-state, Article 16 of the Basic Law had fixed an individual, subjective legal claim to political asylum. This Article was a kind of "moral declaration of intent"[12] that fulfilled an important role of legitimation and identity formation.[13] It was directly related to the claim of a special position of the country. However—and unlike other aspects of immigration policy—this did not mean that German asylum regulations were particularly restrictive in comparison to other European neighbors. In fact the reverse was true. Before the reform of its asylum laws Germany differed from its European neighbors by provisions that were uniquely liberal and deliberately generous in international comparison. In this context, Joppke dubbed Germany a country that conceded "literally the whole world a right of entry".[14] But in light of the new international situation after the opening of the Iron Curtain, and the slowly accelerating pace of European harmonization of national refugee and asylum policies, this special path proved increasingly impracticable. Consequently, Germany decided – after long hesitation and paralyzing political debates – to adjust its ultra-liberal asylum rights to European standards and thus to restrict them.[15] The hypothesis that is being advanced here as the leitmotif of German immigration policy appears therefore in various guises and dependent on the respective object of regulation: The step that had been taken in 1991 with the implementation of the foreigners law towards normalization meant a liberalization, while the revision of asylum law implied a normalization and adaptation to European standards that represented in fact a restriction.

The rules that had been established in the context of the so-called Asylum Compromise also introduced new regulations for another group of immigrants that in terms of its numbers was also significant at this point.[16] These related to a group of return migrants who for many years had been given a special option to enter as part of the "German Diaspora in the East" as long as the process of postwar nation-state building was still underway. However, with the reunification of Germany (and the political recognition of the Oder Neisse Line) that concluded the nation-building process, this special option lost its historic foundation. In 1992 yet another law was ratified that was to clear up the legal fall-out from the war. This law now required all migrants from outside the successor states of the former Soviet Union to supply documentation of a "pressure for expulsion" under which they had been living. This resulted in a restriction of immigration for persons who had been born before 1 January 1993. The law also introduced an annual quota. The introduction of this quota, which was again halved in 1999 within the framework of a budget reform law, reinforced the changed status of the return migrants. They were now part of a group that could be controlled with the standard instruments of migration politics.[17] The 1992 law was followed by further regulations, such as the obligation to offer proof of a rudimentary knowledge of German. These rules helped further to reduce the number of entries. Thus, in 2007, a mere 5,792 persons came to Germany as an "inevitably late consequence of Germany's state formation history".[18] By 2013 this number had once again been cut to 2,400 newcomers. Germany thus shed its status as a country that defined the right to migration in terms of the ethnic and cultural background of the migrant. This automatically resulted in another stage of the "normalization" of immigration policy, since the criteria for immigration that were recognized had also been re-evaluated. As criteria such as ethnicity, religion, or national origin became increasingly irrelevant and were no longer deemed legitimate features of control, other criteria of admission emerged. Increasingly, these involved the qualifications of the applicant and how far there was a demand for them in the country they wanted to go to.[19] This point will have to be examined in more detail later on in this chapter concerning persons who had specific qualifications that were explicitly sought in the labor market.

When the citizenship law was ratified at the turn of the millennium, it acquired greater prominence than the 1991 foreigners law and the 1993 law to clear up the consequences of the war. The key innovation of this law was an expansion of the criteria according to which German citizenship could be granted. The new principle was that citizenship could no longer merely be acquired on the basis of *ius sanguinis* (the blood tie) but also on the basis is *ius soli* (territorial principle). This changed a state of affairs that had increasingly been deemed untenable, i.e., that the children and grandchildren of families who had been hired as "guest workers" in the 1960s and 1970s had legally remained foreigners. However, up to 2014 this law contained a controversial stipulation: children born in Germany who had gained the citizenship of their parents were obliged to choose between German and their foreign citizenship after the completion of their 23rd birthday. This obligation was generally thought not to be particularly practicable.[20] When the Grand Coalition of Christian Democrats and Social Democrats was formed after the 2013 national elections, the decision was made to abolish this obligation for children and adolescents who were born in Germany and had been raised there. When the *ius sanguinis* was expanded by the *ius soli* in the citizenship law of 2000 this resulted in the virtual disappearance in the previously dominant ethnic-cultural tilt in German citizenship law that for a long time had been related to the incomplete process of nation-state formation. This development was independent of the 2014 law that required that children and grandchildren of "guest workers" opt for one citizenship. The problems that this gave rise to that have now been resolved.[21]

This concluded the development between liberalization and restriction in this field that ran in parallel to the migration law of 2005, which has been described here as a process of normalization of the political moderation of migration and integration. Core elements of the 2005 law were, first of all, the constitution of a large administration for migration and integration attached to the Federal Office for Migration and Refugees (BAMF). Secondly, there were programs of integration that were initiated at a national level. They were based on the maxim that had been made the guideline of a social policy of "Promote and Demand" that was put forward under the umbrella of the "Agenda 2010" and is closely interconnected with the BAMF's efforts.[22] Thirdly, Germany created opportunities for immigration for highly qualified persons that, by international standards, were initially being handled more restrictively, but were soon comprehensively liberalized. The 2005 law is therefore to be seen as the terminal point of a legal-institutional process of adaptation that took a quarter of a century. In comparison to other countries, German immigration policy no longer is marked by any serious legal-institutional peculiarities.

## The EU's Efforts to Communitarize and Mimetic Isomorphy: Two Variants of the Europeanization of Migration and Integration Policy

There is another development that clearly transcends Germany's borders and that creates structural conditions for action in migration and integration politics that has probably not even reached its climax. It is different from the development that has been described as "normalization" and as being largely completed. It is in its simplified version labeled the "European dimension" of German migration and integration policy and involved two processes: There is, first of all, the shift of authority "to Brussels". It is a "top-down" process and related to the EU-wide coordination of policies that automatically follows it. There is, secondly, not only the process of adjustment between individual EU members, but also the process of "institutional imitation" among many immigration countries as a result of mutual orientation and political interaction. This is a process that did not originate at the level of the EU to be imposed on individual member states.

Policies of migration and integration are essential for a European Union that is geared to expanding its competence and that views itself as being on a path towards becoming a supra-national organization. This touches upon and mediates Jellinek's doctrine of the three elements, i.e., a state territory, a permanent population, and a state authority, and does so more tangibly and directly than in other fields of politics. To be sure, the member states have some room for maneuver within the larger guidelines of the EU when it comes to their implementation in the fields of migration and integration. But it is above all the field of secondary law, i.e. regulations and directives, that simultaneously moves the member states automatically towards a common political framework. Thus the EU has used its powers intensively with respect to asylum seekers, refugees and migrants since 1997. Accordingly, there exist common conditions throughout the EU, especially in the former two areas and in terms of border protection.[23] Considerable progress was made in the summer of 2013 to build a "Common European Asylum System" (CEAS) that had long been identified as a goal of a EU policy. However, considerable deficits in the implementation of CEAS rules became evident. These called into question the established division of labor between the norm-setting EU institutions and the norm-implementing national states. This is why the options under discussion for full harmonization include an EU asylum administration that would confirm the implementation of these norms.[24]

Within the narrow limits that are legally fixed in the Basic Law and the European Human Rights Convention, there have resulted the successful creation of common rules for the unification of families. This applies in particular to the later immigration of family members that has for a long time been the channel of migration most relevant for Germany. It has been European prerequisites that have considerably restricted the room for shaping national policy. In fact the remaining spaces for maneuver have been quite limited,[25] but – as will be shown in a moment – they are nevertheless being utilized.

As far as the intensity of Europeanization is concerned, there is a distinct contrast between the policies of asylum and family migration, on the one hand, and the regulation of labor migration, on the other. Here we should remember that there continue to exist enormous differences in the structure of the labor markets that were being used as a key argument by those who opposed the shift to Brussels.[26] The EU promulgated a guideline relating to this issue in 2009 that was transferred into German law in 2012. It contained little that was new in material-legal terms in comparison to regulations that were not prescribed by EU law. However, it provided a "window of possibilities" for the Federal government with regard to the adoption (or obligation to adopt) these regulations. Following the installation of the 2005 immigration law, with its opportunity to liberalize further its repeatedly liberalized rules (and in the wake of the new Paragraph 18 of the Residence Law), there arose the possibility to add a new form of immigration regulation. This rule was not prescribed by EU law and also drew upon a heretofore unknown managerial philosophy.[27]

Apart from a European adaptation that the member states have triggered, the field of migration and integration policy experienced another
development that could not exclusively be observed in EU but also in the
other OECD countries. This was a development that was influential for
describing the transformation of Germany from an outsider with regard
to migration and integration policy to a country that held an average or
standard position in this field. Here the explanatory power is to be found
in phenomena that are described in the literature of neo-institutionalism
as mimetic isomorphy.[28] This refers to a progressive process of "institutional imitation"[29] caused by uncertainty and vacillation, as a result of
which problems in the shaping and legitimizing of migration and integration policy can be resolved by taking over the institutional design that
other countries have already established. This is illustrated, for example,
by the integration courses for new immigrants that have been introduced throughout Europe. These courses were established first in The
Netherlands in response to what the Dutch writer Paul Scheffer defined in
2000 as a "multicultural drama".[30] What he was referring to was his observation of the consequences of a specific minority policy that had led to an
ethnic underclass that was largely decoupled from the labor market. This
policy was subsequently introduced by other major immigration countries
in Europe, such as Germany and France.[31] The Dutch program must hence
be seen as "a blueprint for the construction of indigenous migration and
integration regimes that can be fitted in as variants" and can hence be
viewed as the point of departure of a "model copying"[32] that is observable
throughout Europe and even throughout the OECD. The immediate consequence of this are processes of convergence in the political sphere that help
to explain why Germany has seen in recent years an accelerated change
in its migration and integration policies. However, these transformations
have not been triggered by the EU within the framework of a successful
expansion of its own authority, but by the member countries themselves.
They seized the initiative in order to cope with existing uncertainties and to
tackle problems that were similar and transcended their borders.

A similar process of adaptation emerged in the sphere of family migration that could be described as a "Europeanization from below". It was
again triggered by The Netherlands and related to the obligation to demonstrate a knowledge of the local language prior to family reunion. It
was subsequently also introduced in France, Denmark, Austria, Britain,
and Germany. Given the danger of long-term reproduction of educational
deficits among the immigrant populations due to the persistence of (ethnically) endogamous marriages (as it was perceived at least by policymakers), this became a politically attractive option. These solutions came to be
practiced by other countries irrespective of their actual success. After all,

by invoking the already established political solutions of other countries it was possible to secure and even increase the legitimacy of the managerial measures that one had adopted inside one's own country.

In conclusion, we want to refer to yet another process of adaptation as part of the "model copying" that has been described above. It concerns also immigration countries outside the EU and falls into the sphere of labor migration. We are thinking here of the diversification of the methods of recruitment in the international competition for highly qualified experts with regard to numerous countries. A particularly good illustration of this is provided by comparing Germany and Canada. These two countries are assumed to represent an extreme difference. However, because of reforms introduced on both sides of the Atlantic, the two have become increasingly similar in terms of their recruitment and selection procedures.[33]

## Conclusion: Germany on the Road towards a Modern Immigration Country and Multicultural *Leistungsgesellschaft*?

Germany has become institutionally normalized in recent years due to an assimilation of its migration and integration control instruments to those of its European neighbors and other significant immigration countries. The 2015 annual report of the Council of Foundations for Integration and Migration (SVR) has stated that "Germany has rapidly improved its migration management schemes in a political and conceptual sense and introduced a much greater range of measures aimed at easing migrant integration and social participation in the course of the last few years. With these reforms, the country has caught up with the group of immigration countries widely regarded as having progressive migration and integration schemes."[34] What must be left open, however, is the question of how far this change in policy at the legal-institutional level was merely a project of elites without any support from among the population—or whether "Germany's Transformation to a Modern Immigration Country"[35] transcends policy and is also reflected in the relevant positions and attitudes of the public. Without being able to investigate the question in greater detail, reference shall be made here to one result of the Integration Barometer. This is a representative survey that is undertaken every other year of individuals living in Germany with or without a migration background that may be taken as a cautious indication that the changes described above have not been limited to the political-institutional level.

In this connection it is illuminating to look at the question, raised in the Barometer, concerning a sense of belonging. Persons with or without a migration background were asked to judge what in their view should be the characteristics that migrants had to bring with them in order to be part of German society. As a preliminary of belonging they were given the choice of replying if they had been born in Germany, had German ancestors, or professed the Christian faith. There were also questions on features that could be acquired such as German citizenship or whether the person concerned participated in the labor market.[36] The actual results were extensively evaluated in the SVR annual report of 2016. They showed that overall the link between belonging to German society and having been born on German soil was very tenuous. This also applied to the question of whether one had German ancestors or adhered to the Christian faith. These criteria had the force of conviction only for a minority. Instead the question of whether someone was working came to far ahead among the criteria of belonging to German society.[37] This may be taken, however, cautiously, as an indication that the question of change that stood at the center of this contribution is not restricted to the institutional and regulatory level; what has rather taken place is a shift in the mental dispositions of the population from the notion of an ethnically exclusive non-immigration country to a "multicultural *Leistungsgesellschaft*".

# Notes

1. Ruud Koopmans, Ines Michalowski, Stine Waibel, "Citizenship Rights for Immigrants: National Political Processes and Cross-National Convergence in Western Europe, 1980–2008," in *American Journal of Sociology*, 117(2012), 1202–45.
2. Council of Experts of German Foundations for Integration and Migration (SVR), *Immigration Countries: Germany in an International Comparison*, Berlin 2015.
3. Christian Joppke, *Immigration and the Nation State: The United States, Germany, and Great Britain*, Oxford 1999.
4. Ibid., 63.
5. Klaus J. Bade and Michael Bommes, "Migration und politische Kultur im 'Nicht-Einwanderungsland'", in Idem and Rainer Münz, eds., *Migrationsreport 2000. Fakten, Analysen, Perspektiven*, Frankfurt 2000, 183.
6. Joppke (note 3), 63, referring to Kay Hailbronner, "Ausländerrecht und Verfassung", in *Neue Juristische Wochenschrift*, 36(1983), 2105–13.
7. Ibid., 261.
8. Klaus J. Bade and Jochen Oltmer, eds., *Aussiedler: Deutsche Einwanderer aus Osteuropa*, Göttingen 2003.
9. In this context it will also become clear that the use of the concept of normalization does not imply a normative valuation. Rather it signifies a turning away from the notion that institutions and practices and the assimilation to European standards were unique and

diametrically different when compared internationally or at least to most European and extra-European immigration countries.

10. For further details on this process, see Holger Kolb, "Migrationsverhältnisse, nationale Souveränität und europäische Integration: Deutschland zwischen Normalisierung und Europäisierung", in Jochen Oltmer, ed., *Handbuch Staat und Migration in Deutschland seit dem 17. Jahrhundert*, Berlin-Boston 2016, 1021–40.

11. Of fundamental importance: Hellmuth Rittstieg, "Das neue Ausländergesetz: Verbesserungen und neue Probleme," in Klaus Barwig et al., eds., *Das neue Ausländerrecht*, Baden-Baden 1991, 25.

12. Michael Bommes, "Die Planung der Migration," in *Zeitschrift für Ausländer und Ausländerpolitik*, 29(2009), 377.

13. Bernhard Santel and Albrecht Weber, "Zwischen Ausländerpolitik und Einwanderungspolitik," in Bade/Münz (note 5), 116.

14. Joppke (note 3), 85.

15. On the technical translation of this turn in the sphere of asylum policy, see Günter Renner, "Aktuelle und ungelöste Probleme des Asyl- und Flüchtlingsrechts," in Bade/Münz (note 10), 185.

16. See the detailed analysis in: Barbara Dietz, "Die Bundesrepublik Deutschland im Fokus neuer Ost-West-Wanderungen," in Oltmer (note 10), 999–1019.

17. Joppke (note 3), 96.

18. Bommes (note 12), 377.

19. See the comprehensive analysis by Christian Joppke, *Selecting by Origin. Ethnic Migration in the Liberal State*, Cambridge, MA, 2005.

20. See, e.g., Ralph Göbel-Zimmermann, "Das neue Staatsangehörigkeitsrecht—Erfahrungen und Reformvorschläge," in Klaus Barwig and Ulrike Davy, eds., *Auf dem Wege zur Rechtsgleichheit. Konzepte und Grenzen einer Politik der Integration von Einwanderern*, Baden-Baden 2004, 153.

21. The compromise that the government coalition found was half-hearted in the sense that it granted double citizenship when gained by birth. However, when it comes to the granting of citizenship, Germany continues to adhere to the principle that having several passports is to be avoided. What also remains untouched is the problem of the permanent passing on of citizenship by the original migrants and the problems resulting from this with regard to jurisprudence and democratic theory. See Christine Langenfeld, "Der Spinnen-Fliegen-Kompromiss", in *Süddeutsche Zeitung*, 2 April 2014, 2.

22. Michael Bommes, "Integration durch Sprache als politisches Konzept," in Ulrike Davy and Albrecht Weber, eds., *Paradigmenwechsel in Einwandererfragen? Überlegungen zum neuen Zuwanderungsgesetz*, Baden-Baden 2006, 63; Ines Michalowski, *Integration als Staatsprogramm: Deutschland, Frankreich und die Niederlande im Vergleich*, Münster 2007.

23. Sandra Lavenex, *The Europeanisation of Refugee Politics. Between Human Rights and Internal Security*, Farnham 2001.

24. See, e.g. Christine Langenfeld and Harald Dörig, "Vollharmonisierung des Flüchtlingsrechts in Europa: Masszustrom erfordert EU-Zuständigkeit für Asylverfahren," in *Neue Juristische Wochenschrift*, 2016, 1–5.

25. Christine Langenfeld and Sarah Mohsen, "Die ED-Richtlinie zum Familiennachzug und ihre Einordnung in das Völkerrecht," in *Zeitschrift für Ausländerrecht und Ausländerpolitik*, 23(2003), 398–404.

26. See Bommes (note 12), 380.

27. Holger Kolb, "When Extremes Converge: German and Canadian Labor Migration Policy Compared", in *Comparative Migration Studies*, 1(2014), 229–47; Barbara Laubenthal,

"Europeanization and the Negotiation of a New Labor Migration in Germany. The Goodness of Fit Approach Revisited", in *Comparative Migration Studies*, 2(2014), 469–92.

28. Isomorphy is generally understood to refer to institutional adaptations within an organizational field. With respect to "forced", "mimetic", and "normative" isomorphy there are assumed to be three "drivers" of rapprochement resp. convergence. In the case of "forced isomorphy" it is a superior institution that demands and exerts pressures to adapt. The anti-discrimination laws that have meanwhile been introduced in the whole of Europe and often against the will of individual governments, represent an example. Normative isomorphic phenomena are in evidence above all when certain professional groups try to strengthen their professionalization efforts.

29. See the foundational article by Paul DiMaggio and Walter W. Powell, "The Iron Cage Revisited: Institutional Isomorphism and Collective Rationality in Organizational Fields." in *American Sociological Review*, 48(1983), 147–60.

30. Paul Scheffer "Het multiculturele drama," in *NRC Handelsblad*, 29 January 2000.

31. See, e.g., Michalowski (note 22).

32. Bommes (note 22), 70.

33. For details see Kolb (note 27); idem and Claudia Finotelli, "'The Good, the Bad and the Ugly' Reconsidered: A Comparison of German, Canadian and Spanish Labour Migration Policies," in *Journal of Comparative Policy Analysis*, accessed 3 May 2016, DOI: 10.1080/13876988.2015. 1095429.

34. SVR (note2), 13.

35. SVR, *Deutschlands Wandel zum modernen Einwanderungsland*, Berlin 2014.

36. The introductory text asked the following question: "Different things are important in order to belong to society. What are your views on this?" There followed a list of categories, beginning with the sentence: "In your opinion, how important is this …?" The results presented therefore show the significance of individual criteria in the personal view of the person surveyed.

37. SVR, *Viele Götter, ein Staat. Religiöse Viefalt und Teilhabe im Einwanderungsland*, Berlin 2016, 33-40.

# Works Cited

Bade, Klaus J. and Oltmer, Jochen, eds. *Aussiedler: deutsche Einwanderer aus Osteuropa.* Göttingen: vr unipress, 2003.

Bommes, Michael. „Die Planung der Migration." *Zeitschrift für Ausländerrecht und Ausländerpolitik* 29 (2009): 376–81.

Bommes, Michael. „Integration durch Sprache als politisches Konzept." In *Paradigmenwechsel in Einwanderungsfragen? Überlegungen zum neuen Zuwanderungsgesetz*, edited by Ulrike Davy and Albrecht Weber, 59–86. Baden-Baden: Nomis, 2006.

Dietz, Barbara. „Die Bundesrepublik Deutschland im Fokus neuer Ost-West-Wanderungen." In *Handbuch Staat und Migration in Deutschland seit dem 17. Jahrhundert*, edited by Jochen Oltmer, 999–1019. Berlin/Boston: De Gruyter, 2016.

DiMaggio, Paul J. and Powell, Walter W. "The Iron Cage Revisited: Institutional Isomorphism and Collective Rationality in Organizational Fields." *American Sociological Review* 48 (1983), 147–60.

Finotelli, Claudia and Kolb, Holger. „'The Good, the Bad and the Ugly' Reconsidered: A Comparison of German, Canadian and Spanish Labour Migration Policies." *Journal of Comparative Policy Analysis*, 2015, accessed May 3, 2016, DOI: 10.1080/13876988.2015.109 5429.

Göbel-Zimmermann, Ralph. „Das neue Staatsangehörigkeitsrecht – Erfahrungen und Reformvorschläge." In *Auf dem Weg zur Rechtsgleichheit: Konzepte und Grenzen einer Politik der Integration von Einwanderern*, edited by Klaus Barwig and Ulrike Davy, 148–68. Baden-Baden: Nomos, 2004.

Hailbronner, Kay. „Ausländerrecht und Verfassung." *Neue Juristische Wochenschrift* 36 (1983), 2105–13.

Joppke, Christian. *Immigration and the Nation State: The United States, Germany, and Great Britain*. Oxford: Oxford University Press, 1999.

Joppke, Christian. *Selecting by Origin: Ethnic Migration in the Liberal State*. Cambridge: Harvard University Press, 2005.

Kolb, Holger. „Migrationsverhältnisse, nationale Souveränität und europäische Integration: Deutschland zwischen Normalisierung und Europäisierung." In *Handbuch Staat und Migration in Deutschland seit dem 17. Jahrhundert*, edited by Jochen Oltmer, 1021–40. Berlin/Boston: De Gruyter, 2016.

Langenfeld, Christine. „Der Spinnen-Fliegen-Kompromiss." *Süddeutsche Zeitung*, April 2, 2014.

Langenfeld, Christine and Mohsen, Sarah. „Die neue EG-Richtlinie zum Familiennachzug und ihre Einordnung in das Völkerrecht." *Zeitschrift für Ausländerrecht und Ausländerpolitik* 23 (2003), 398–404.

Langenfeld, Christine and Dörig, Harald. „Vollharmonisierung des Flüchtlingsrechts in Europa: Massenzustrom erfordert EU-Zuständigkeit für Asylverfahren." *Neue Juristische Wochenschrift*, (2016), 1–5.

Lavenex, Sandra. *The Europeanisation of Refugee Politics. Between Human Rights and Internal Security*. Farnham: Ashgate, 2001.

Michalowski, Ines. *Integration als Staatsprogramm. Deutschland, Frankreich und die Niederlande im Vergleich*. Münster: LIT, 2007.

Renner, Günter. „Aktuelle und ungelöste Probleme des Asyl- und Flüchtlingsrechts." In *Migrationsreport 2002. Fakten – Analysen – Perspektiven*, edited by Klaus J. Bade and Rainer Münz (Hg.), 179–206. Frankfurt a.M./New York: Campus 2002.

Rittstieg, Hellmuth. „Das neue Ausländergesetz: Verbesserungen und neue Probleme." In *Das neue Ausländerrecht*, edited by Klaus Barwig, Bertold Huber, Klaus Lörcher, Christoph Schumacher and Klaus Sieveking, 23–32. Baden-Baden: Nomos, 1991.

Sachverständigenrat deutscher Stiftungen für Integration und Migration (SVR): *Deutschlands Wandel zum modernen Einwanderungsland*. Berlin, 2014.

Sachverständigenrat deutscher Stiftungen für Integration und Migration (SVR). *Unter Einwanderungsländern: Deutschland im internationalen Vergleich*. Berlin, 2015.

Sachverständigenrat deutscher Stiftungen für Integration und Migration (SVR): *Viele Götter, ein Staat: Religiöse Vielfalt und Teilhabe im Einwanderungsland*. Berlin, 2016.

Santel, Bernhard and Weber, Albrecht. „Zwischen Ausländerpolitik und Einwanderungspolitik: Migrations- und Ausländerrecht in Deutschland." In *Migrationsreport 2000. Fakten – Analysen – Perspektiven*, edited by Klaus J. Bade and Rainer Münz, 109–40. Frankfurt a.M./New York: Campus, 2000.

Scheffer, Paul, "Het multiculturele drama." *NRC Handelsblad*, January 29, 2000.

**Holger Kolb** is senior researcher and deputy director of the Expert Council of German Foundations on Integration and Migration, an independent and privately-funded think tank providing research-based policy advice in the field of migration and integration policy. His research interests are labor migration policies, comparative migration research as well as migration theory. His most recent work was published in *Comparative Migration Studies*, *Journal for Comparative Policy Analysis* and *Zeitschrift für Ausländerrecht*.

# INDEX

## Studies in Contemporary European History

Editors:

**Konrad Jarausch,** Lurcy Professor of European Civilization, University of North Carolina, Chapel Hill, and a Director of the Zentrum für Zeithistorische Studien, Potsdam, Germany

**Henry Rousso,** Senior Research Fellow at the Institut d'histoire du temps présent (Centre national de la recherche scientifique, Paris)

CPSIA information can be obtained
at www.ICGtesting.com
Printed in the USA
LVHW081415080219
606901LV00015B/236/P